Tom Brooking is Professor of History at the University of Otago, New Zealand. He is co-editor (with Eric Pawson) of *Environmental Histories of New Zealand* (2002) and is a member of the Council of the Agricultural History Society.

Eric Pawson is Professor of Geography at the University of Canterbury, New Zealand. He chaired the Advisory Committee for the *New Zealand Historical Atlas*. In 2007 he received the Distinguished New Zealand Geographer Medal.

ENVIRONMENTAL HISTORY AND GLOBAL CHANGE SERIES

Series Editor: Professor Ian Whyte, University of Lancaster

Editorial Board
Kevin Edwards, University of Aberdeen
Eric Pawson, University of Canterbury, New Zealand
Christian Pfister, University of Berne
I. Simmons, University of Durham
T.C. Smout, University of St Andrews
Harriet Ritvo, Massachusetts Institute of Technology

This important new series provides a much-needed forum for understanding just how and why our environment changes. It shows how environmental history – with its unique blend of geography, history, archaeology, landscape, environment and science – is helping to make informed decisions on pressing environmental concerns and providing crucial insights into the mechanisms that influence environmental change today. The focus of the series will be on contemporary problems but will also include work that addresses major techniques, key periods and important regions. At a time when the scale and importance of environmental change has led to a widespread feeling that we have entered a period of crisis, the *Environmental History and Global Change Series* provides a timely, informed and important contribution to a key global issue.

1. *Documentary Records of Climate Change*, Astrid Ogilvie
2. *A Dictionary of Environmental History*, Ian Whyte
3. *The Mediterranean World: an Environmental History*, Neil Roberts
4. *Seeds of Empire: the Environmental Transformation of New Zealand*, Tom Brooking and Eric Pawson
5. *Cities: an Environmental History*, Ian Douglas
6. *Japan: an Environmental History*, Conrad Totman

Seeds of Empire

The Environmental Transformation of New Zealand

Tom Brooking and Eric Pawson

with
Paul Star, Vaughan Wood, Peter Holland,
Jim McAloon, Robert Peden and Jim Williams

I.B. TAURIS
LONDON · NEW YORK

Published in 2011 by I.B.Tauris & Co Ltd
6 Salem Road, London W2 4BU
175 Fifth Avenue, New York NY 10010
www.ibtauris.com

Distributed in the United States and Canada Exclusively by Palgrave Macmillan
175 Fifth Avenue, New York NY 10010

Environmental History and Global Change: 4

ISBN: 978 1 84511 797 9

A full CIP record for this book is available from the British Library
A full CIP record is available from the Library of Congress

Library of Congress Catalog Card Number: available

Printed and bound in Great Britain by CPI Antony Rowe, Chippenham

Contents

Figures and Tables

FIGURES

FIGURES, TABLES AND BOXES

TABLES

Terminology, Māori Language Conventions, Place Names and Measurements

The Treaty of Waitangi was signed in 1840 between the British Crown and Māori tribes (or iwi). It established British sovereignty at the same time as guaranteeing a range of Māori rights. The Crown's representative was the Governor. The British Parliament passed the Constitution Act in 1852. This made provision for an elected General Assembly as well as a number of elected provincial councils. The colony became effectively self-governing in 1856; the provincial councils lasted until 1876. Central government was generally referred to as the 'colonial government' or the 'general government'. In 1907, New Zealand was styled a dominion rather than a colony. In 1917, the Governor was restyled the 'Governor General'.

Under the Māori Language Act, 1986, te reo Māori (the Māori language) has equal status with English. For that reason, it is not customary to highlight Māori words in print and we have not done so. The macron signifies a long vowel. Macrons are used on Māori words except when not used in the source being quoted or in the title being referenced. In written Māori, the singular and plural forms of most nouns have the same spelling. Some of the sources used, notably in chapter 3, however, used 'Maoris', 'the Maories', 'kiwis' and the like, and this spelling has been retained.

The map that follows on p. xvi shows broad topographical features, as well as regional and urban place names. Other place names are generally shown on maps in particular chapters. The scientific names of plants are given in Appendix 1; Appendix 2 consists of a series of entries about the pasture plants most commonly used or referenced in New Zealand between 1850 and 1930. We use metric measurements throughout except where imperial measures appear in quotations or in original sources.

Notes on Contributors

TOM BROOKING, MA (Massey) PhD (Otago) is Professor of History at the University of Otago. He trained as a political and agricultural historian at the Universities of Otago and Kent, England. He has published in a wide range of journals on environmental and agricultural history and produced eight books including *Environmental Histories of New Zealand* (2002) co-edited with Eric Pawson. Between 2005 and 2007 he served on a Cabinet advisory panel on walking access in New Zealand and is a member of the Council of the Agricultural History Society (USA). He is writing a biography of New Zealand's longest serving Prime Minister Richard John Seddon and is working in a collaborative project on Scottish migration to New Zealand.

PETER HOLLAND, BSc (University of New Zealand) MSc (Canterbury) PhD (Australian National University) is Emeritus Professor of Geography at the University of Otago. He trained as a biogeographer, and after graduation worked in Montreal, Nairobi, Cape Town and Christchurch before his appointment in 1982 as Chair of the Department of Geography at Otago. He was Associate Editor of the *Journal of Biogeography* for 25 years, and has published articles in biogeography, ecology and geography journals as well as several book chapters. He was elected President of the New Zealand Geographic Society in 2002, and served for four years. For the past 15 years he has worked with three academic audit agencies, and in 2008 he was awarded the Distinguished New Zealand Geographer Medal.

JIM McALOON, MA (Canterbury) PhD (Otago) is Associate Professor in History, Victoria University of Wellington. Previously he lectured in history at Lincoln University, in his home province of Canterbury. Originally trained in labour and social history, he has strong interests in the economic history of settler societies. As well as many articles and chapters in academic journals and edited collections, he has published two books, both of which won awards. The first is *Nelson: A Regional History* (1997) and the second, *No Idle Rich: The Wealthy in Canterbury and Otago 1840–1914* (2002), which discussed the making of a colonial ruling class and its agricultural, pastoral and mercantile bases. Current research includes a study of economic policymaking in New Zealand 1945–84 and a collaborative project on Scottish migration and New Zealand.

ERIC PAWSON, MA DPhil (Oxford) is Professor of Geography, University of Canterbury. He trained as an historical geographer in Britain and has lived in the South Island of New Zealand since 1976. He chaired the Advisory Committee of the *New Zealand Historical Atlas* from 1990 to 1997, and has been a member of the Advisory Committee for *Te Ara*, the New Zealand online encyclopedia, since its inception. He co-edited *Environmental Histories of New Zealand* (2002) with Tom Brooking, and has published a number of other books, a large number of book chapters, and articles in a wide range of journals in geography and environmental history. He received the Distinguished New Zealand Geographer Medal in 2007 and a national tertiary teaching excellence award in 2009.

ROBERT PEDEN, MA (Canterbury), PhD (Otago) spent 25 years working on high country stations in the South Island of New Zealand, including 18 years as a station manager. He specialises in agricultural and rural history, and has published his work in *Agricultural History*, and contributed to *Te Ara*, the electronic New Zealand encyclopedia. Robert was awarded a Claude McCarthy Fellowship in 2009 and has recently completed a book on pastoralism and the transformation of the tussock grasslands of the South Island during the pastoral era.

PAUL STAR, MA (Cantab) MA PhD (Otago) was brought up England. He moved to New Zealand in 1972 and worked for many years as a bookseller, returning to academic study in the 1990s. He lives rurally on the Otago Peninsula, near Dunedin. He was a postdoctoral fellow with the University of Otago's history department in 2004–7 and is now an independent scholar specialising in New Zealand environmental history. He contributed the chapter on this topic to *The New Oxford History of New Zealand* (2009) and has published widely on related themes in local and international journals.

JIM WILLIAMS, PhD (Otago), of Kai Tahu descent, is a Senior Lecturer in Te Tumu, The School of Māori, Pacific and Indigenous Studies, at the University of Otago, where he teaches a stream of Kai Tahu and environmental management papers. His area of research includes traditional Māori ways and Māori environmental management, with particular emphasis on his own iwi, Kai Tahu. He has published various book chapters and articles with a pre-European Māori focus, including a suggested research methodology for pre-contact topics.

VAUGHAN WOOD, BSc (Hons) MA (Canterbury) PhD (Otago) is a former research fellow of the Geography Department, University of Canterbury. He is also a contracted report writer to the Waitangi Tribunal in the hearing of indigenous land claims. His main area of research is agricultural history and environmental modification in nineteenth-century New Zealand. Previously he has published articles in the *Journal of Historical Geography*, *Agricultural History* and *Environment and History*, and he is writing a history of the Akaroa cocksfoot seed industry.

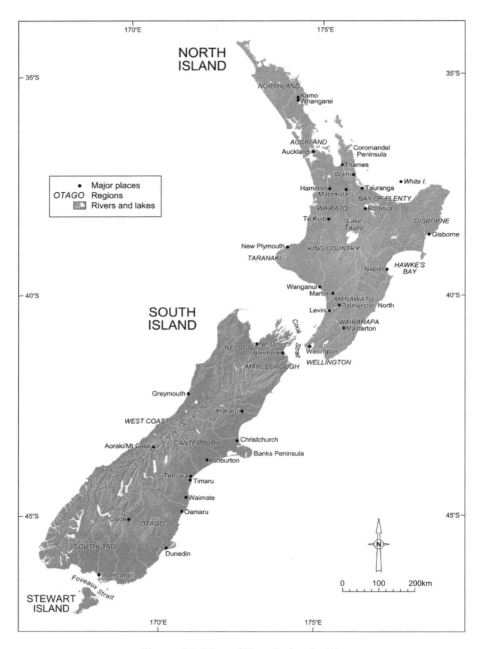

Figure 0.1: Map of New Zealand with
landscape features, regions and place names.

Preface

This book is the culmination of a team-based research project, supported by the Marsden Fund of the Royal Society of New Zealand. The award enabled us to assemble a multi-disciplinary group of scholars, at the three South Island universities, and to provide significant research support for the three funded years of the project from 2004 to 2007. The title of the research was 'Empires of grass'. This reflected our original purpose of applying and developing the insights of environmental history to better understand how and why New Zealand came to be clothed in introduced grasses between the 1850s and 1930s, a question that developed from an earlier joint undertaking, *Environmental Histories of New Zealand.*[1]

In writing the present book, we have expanded this question into three main themes. First, our concern with landscape change in New Zealand remains central, although we have sought to ask not only what changed and how, but also where, and on whose initiative? Second, we have tried to provide a more coherent analysis than previously of the wider global context within which this change occurred, and to which in turn it contributed. Here we are drawing on current ideas in imperial history and historical geography, and seeking to contribute to ongoing debates about the extent to which colonial change was driven by an imperial centre, or was relatively independent of it, or indeed contributed to bringing about change in the metropole itself. In this sense, we see the New Zealand story as having much wider purchase. Third, we wish to emphasise the significance of pasture plants, primarily grasses, in both making the new landscapes of empire and laying the foundations of world trade in products such as wool, meat, butter and cheese.

It is with these second and third themes that our concern with 'Empires of grass' has translated into understanding grass and grassland economies as 'Seeds of empire'. In recent years, a number of popular accounts have appeared about plants that are said to have changed the world, such as the potato, cotton, rubber and sugar. Like the others, a recent example, evocatively entitled *The Roots of Civilisation: Plants that Changed the World*,[2] passes over grass and pasture plants, although it does mention ryegrass, one of the most important, but only as a weed that colonises wheat fields. Elsewhere, we have referred to this as the 'silences of grass': a silence that is reflected in the ways in which grass was for long taken for granted, and its improvement largely ignored. In fact, as we have uncovered, by 1900 there was considerable experimentation with grass mixtures and pasture plant development, which was formalised in the early twentieth century through new forms of state intervention, including science.

Exploration of these issues has required a wide range of competencies and the use of a considerable array of historical sources. The development of New Zealand's grasslands began in the mid-nineteenth century when the infrastructure and apparatus of a modern state was becoming increasingly prominent. However, a great deal of this development was not state driven or even state supported before 1900. For many purposes, official records and parliamentary papers are not therefore as valuable as material in local newspapers, local histories, personal papers and photographic archives. In this regard, there is every possibility of being overwhelmed by quantity. Inevitably this means that some places, and some parts of the country, have been explored in more depth than others, although an initial focus on the South Island reflects the fact that it was here, before the 1890s, that the country's pastoral development was focused. In trying to trace change at the local and farm level, however, we run into the opposite problem. Useful farm diaries and journals do not survive in any numbers.

The size of our team of researchers reflects the generosity of the Marsden Fund and its recognition of the need for a project of this nature to draw upon a range of disciplinary skills. Although the team is rooted in the subjects of history and geography, and all members identify broadly as environmental historians, their range of backgrounds includes science, social science and humanities, as well as particular archival expertise, Māori ancestry and knowledge, and farming experience. As co-principal investigators, we each worked with a part-time postdoctoral fellow: Tom Brooking with Paul Star in the History Department at the University of Otago, and Eric Pawson with Vaughan Wood in the Geography Department at the University of Canterbury. There were two associate investigators: Peter Holland, of the Geography Department at the University of Otago, who also worked with both postdoctoral fellows and with Jim Williams of Te Tumu, School of Māori, Pacific and Indigenous Studies, University of Otago; and Jim McAloon, then of the Department of Social Sciences,

Parks, Recreation, Tourism and Sport, Lincoln University. Robert Peden was supported for the second year of his PhD.

The authorship of the chapters in the book reflects the working alliances in the team, although it is very much a collective effort within an overall conceptual and thematic agenda framed by the two principal investigators. We are grateful to many others for their contributions, interest or support over the period of the project, including John Acland, Paul Bealing, James Beattie, Hugh Campbell, Henry Connor, Geoff Cunfer, William Cronon, Philippa Dixon, Don Garden, Tom Griffiths, Tom Isern, Richard Le Heron, John MacKenzie, Henrik Moller, David Moon, Libby Robin, Michael Roche, Michael Vance, Richard White and Graeme Wynn. We have benefited from interactions with seminar or conference audiences in a number of places, including Dunedin, Christchurch, Auckland, Canberra, Sydney, Little Rock, Fargo, Madison, Saskatoon, Halifax (Nova Scotia), Dundee, Exeter, Plymouth, Amsterdam and Copenhagen.

We have depended on the good services of many archivists and librarians, notably those in the Hocken Collections, University of Otago, and the Otago Settlers Museum, Dunedin; Waimate Museum; South Canterbury Museum, Timaru; the Macmillan Brown Library, University of Canterbury, Christchurch City Libraries and the Canterbury Museum, Christchurch; Lincoln University Library; the Alexander Turnbull Library, the National Library, and National Archives, Wellington; Massey University Collections, Palmerston North; the Taranaki Research Centre, Puke Ariki, New Plymouth; Hamilton City Archives; Auckland City Libraries and the Auckland War Memorial Museum Library. Overseas, they include National Archives, Kew, and the Library of the Royal Botanic Gardens, Kew, London; the Museum of English Rural Life, Reading; the Library, Rothamsted Research, Harpenden; the West Yorkshire Archives Service, Bradford; and the Borders Regional Archive, Selkirk. Opportunities for a project such as this have also been opened up by the comprehensive online archival services now available such as the Papers Past website of the National Library of New Zealand, the Timeframes pictorial archive of the Alexander Turnbull Library, and *Te Ara*, the electronic New Zealand encyclopedia.[3]

The figures have been drawn by Tim Nolan, with those in chapters 3 and 4 drafted initially by Tracy Connolly. We are grateful to our respective departments for their backing, to the Research Cluster on Sustainable Agriculture at the University of Otago for both financial and academic support, to Professor Ian Town, Deputy Vice-Chancellor, University of Canterbury, for financial assistance towards completion of the book, and to the Marsden Fund for a subvention towards publication costs. Our publisher,

David Stonestreet, has been encouraging, patient and understanding of the dimensions of a team project. We hope that the end product not only meets its specific academic purpose but has something to say to those interested in environmental history, imperial history and historical geography, as well as to those involved in the history, science and practice of agriculture.

An American sage, quoted in New Zealand's *Poverty Bay Herald* on 23 November 1901, observed that grass 'yields no fruit in earth or air, and yet should its harvest fail for a single year famine would depopulate the world'. A century on, the state of our pastures remains crucial to our prosperity, and the way to a fuller understanding of them lies in their, and our, history.

Tom Brooking and Eric Pawson
September 2010

1   *Introduction*

Eric Pawson and Tom Brooking

SEEDS OF EMPIRE

In 1926–7 George (later Sir George) Stapledon, regarded as the foremost British grassland scientist of his day, took a voyage to Australia and New Zealand. He had established the Welsh Plant Breeding Station, outside Aberystwyth, in 1919, to develop new strains of ley grasses. Although Stapledon's journey was for purposes of convalescence, undertaken at the urging of his doctor, he wasted little time before observing and discussing the state of the grasslands that he saw. There were at least two specific outcomes. One was an agreement to share grassland expertise under the auspices of the Empire Marketing Board, which resulted in a trusted lieutenant, William Davies, spending time in these dominions between 1928 and 1930. The other was the publication by Oxford University Press in 1928 of Stapledon's observations made on the tour.

In the book's introduction, he wrote: '[P]robably grass land, equally with the sea, is to be regarded as one of the corner-stones on which the greatness of the British Empire has been built.'[1] This was a striking statement given that it was sea power, in the form of the navy and the merchant marine, that was usually credited for Britain's pre-eminence. In the preface, Sir Walter Elliot, Unionist politician, Secretary of State for Scotland, future Minister of Agriculture and ardent supporter of the Empire Marketing Board,[2] expressed Stapledon's sentiment more analytically. 'Of every five-pound note that Great Britain expends on overseas products of any and every kind, twenty-five shillings goes in purchasing what is, in essence, worked-up grass.'[3] By this he meant the principal pastoral products of wool, meat, butter, cheese and hides. Meat imports had risen from 10 to 40 per cent of consumption between 1870 and 1914; in the 30 years leading up to the First World War, per capita meat consumption had risen by half.[4]

The trade was also hugely significant from settler society perspectives. The surplus of pastoral products available from the United States declined after the first decade of the twentieth century, as its growing real incomes, population and industry absorbed much of its pastoral output. Consequently, Britain was increasingly reliant on lands in its formal and informal empires, including Ireland, for supplies of food and raw materials. New Zealand earned 93 per cent of its export income from grass-related products in 1921 (Table 1.1). For Australia the equivalent figure at its peak was 88 per cent in 1926.[5] Uruguay and Argentina, the key South American parts of Britain's overseas empire of investment, were as dependent on grassland farming (notably for beef) until after the Second World War.[6] Even Canada, despite its wheat growing, timber milling, mineral extraction and manufacturing, earned more than a quarter of its foreign exchange from grassland products until the 1920s.[7]

Table 1.1: New Zealand exports by value (per cent), 1853–1921.

	1853	1861	1871	1881	1891	1901	1911	1921
Wool	22	38	31	46	43	32	37	10
Meat					7	15	15	22
Butter					3	6	10	26
Cheese					2	2	6	18
Skins, tallow			1	2	3	3	14	17
Grain	6		3	10	6	10	2	1
Timber	36	2	3	5	4	5	4	2
Gold		55	53	12	9	14	10	1
Other	36	5	9	25	33	19	12	3

Source: New Zealand Official Yearbook, various dates.

Elliot pointed to the irony behind such figures: 'how small, relatively, is the proportion of investigation devoted to grass and grass lands out of the sum total of such activities'.[8] Grassland was one of the last components of the imperial agro-commodity chain to gain the attention of improvers, despite being central to the process of improvement that underlay the realisation of the trade potential of colonised landscapes.[9] All over the settler colonies indigenous plants, be they of grassland, forest or wetland, were being replaced with what were usually termed, not always accurately, 'English grasses'. These seeds of empire were in the vanguard of colonial development, although little overt recognition was given to them at the time, nor, in many respects, since. It is to address this story that we have written this book.

Our focus is on New Zealand: it was here that the process of grassland transformation was carried to an extreme. In the early nineteenth century, these mountainous islands in the South Pacific lacked such extensive areas of indigenous grasslands as those found in North and South America. Their ecosystems, long isolated from other landmasses and only occupied by Māori people from Polynesia within the previous millennium, are not specifically adapted to fire.[10] The native vegetation was therefore particularly vulnerable to European technologies such as the match and plough. From the middle of the nineteenth century on, hundreds of thousands of hectares of thick temperate rainforest, known to European settlers as 'bush', and mosaics of subalpine tussock and woody vegetation, were burnt and reseeded with imported grasses. About 35 per cent of New Zealand's landmass is now given over to improved pasture, compared to about 7.5 per cent in Australia.[11] At the peak of stock numbers in the 1980s, there were around 20 sheep for every person in New Zealand. The country had been remade, paddock by paddock,[12] farm by farm and district by district, into a patchwork of 'empires of grass'. To a lesser extent, the same could be said for much of the wider pre-1914 European settler world of which pastoral New Zealand was a far-flung but integral part.

MOBILITIES AND NETWORKS

The central question that we as environmental historians pose in this book is how, why and with what consequences did the transformation of New Zealand into these empires of grass occur? It is 70 years since the newly arrived British geographer Kenneth Cumberland claimed that the transformation had been 'profound. What in Europe took twenty centuries, and in North America four', he said, 'has been accomplished in New Zealand within a single century – in little more than one full lifetime.'[13] He was interested primarily in its historical geography, or in what was happening and where. Although these elements are of central importance to any environmental history, we need also to consider the wider political economy of the process, the cultural precepts of 'improvement' that framed it, and the environmental and economic outcomes. Figure 1.1 conceptualises these issues.

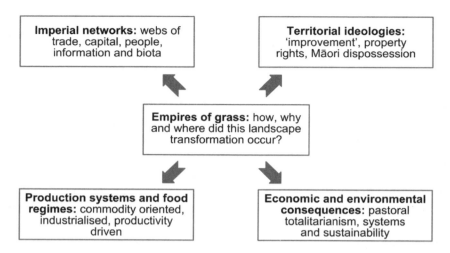

Figure 1.1: Key question and themes.

In order to explore them, it is useful to draw on the insights of the 'mobility turn' that has in recent years become prominent in social science.[14] Those who study societies are moving on from conceptualising them as bounded entities, to considering instead the mobilities that lie at the heart of social life.[15] An example of these is the great long-distance migrations of people out from Europe in the years up to 1914, of which the relatively small trickle of settlers to New Zealand constituted but a fraction. In parallel, geographers have developed dynamic theories of place, in which they seek to understand places, such as European colonies of settlement, in terms of their connections with other places (and times).[16] Similarly, there has been an upsurge of interest in mobility in historical work, particularly in imperial and environmental history where the metaphors of network and 'web' have gained prominence.[17] These are now used to analyse everything from the movement of ideas and information, to capital, technologies and, of particular relevance here, plant and animal materials.[18] Such networks were complex, dynamic, responsive, ever reformulating, and cast particular places in different relations to each other, depending on the connection being described. Any one point could thus be simultaneously both nodal and on the edge in relation to multiple other points.

This is not how the mobile nineteenth-century world has usually been understood. The concept of core and periphery has served since Marx to explain the nature of relationships between a metropolitan European hub (and later a north Atlantic world) and the rest of the globe. The 'capitalist imperialism' school of Hobson and Lenin emphasised economic drivers of imperial expansion, barely acknowledging environmental variability or transformation, including grasslands.[19] The hub was seen as the source of power, be this political or financial, and the place where low-cost raw materials from the peripheral edge were transformed into high-value manufactured goods for worldwide consumption. Much historiography has consciously or unconsciously echoed this view of the world. A notable example for present purposes is Alfred Crosby's book *Ecological Imperialism: The Biological Expansion of Europe 900–1900*, which argues that there was an imbalance in plant flows, outwards from Europe, with colonisation of the 'new world'. In other words, he suggested that plant mobilities exhibited a particular power geometry. This was asymmetrical, with a sharp contrast between 'the tiny number' of New World plants and weeds that naturalised in the Old World, compared to the success of what he called the European 'portmanteau biota' in the 'neo-Europes' of new colonial settlement.[20]

Crosby summarised the pattern that he read from the evidence with the memorable phrase 'the sun never sets on the empire of the dandelion'.[21] The dandelion was an inevitable fellow traveller with the grassland seeds of empire. His volume includes a lengthy case study of New Zealand, which dovetails with generations of quasi-Darwinian thinking there about the inevitability of the 'success' of European against indigenous species.[22] Such success has, however, been won only at the expense of continuous inputs of energy to maintain productive empires of grass. Without this, in many districts native bush and woody vegetation would soon regenerate. Furthermore, in framing his analysis in terms of core and periphery, Crosby underplayed the many other patterns of place-to-place plant transfer that characterised the post-Columbian world, such as the movement of the potato, the tomato, coffee and sugar.[23] And, as this book will demonstrate, apparently peripheral places like New Zealand could become central in the development and dispersal of their own seeds of empire.

The core-periphery framework remains central in recent writing in imperial history, where a metropolitan-focused, gentlemanly capitalism is still seen as the energising force of colonial development.[24] But as is the case with the complexity of biotic exchanges, the flows of information, capital and commodities involved in imperial grasslands development were also by no means all one way. Rather they were articulated as linkages that bound the Empire together in a multiplicity of networks, in resilient as well as transitory ways. These networks carried people, organisms, money, ideas and goods in many directions. They were dynamic in form and could easily be broken and just as easily rebuilt.[25] For example, although British farming practice informed the transfer of English grasses to New Zealand, flows of information sourced from continental Europe and the United States also shaped the creation of colonial pasturelands.[26] A great deal of the knowledge required was built up locally, and often subsequently exchanged in a two-way fashion, to help remake the pastures of Britain and other parts of the world.

GRASSLAND SILENCES

There were at least two reasons why much of the expertise for New Zealand's grasslands transformation was developed within its own shores. It was, as will become apparent in the second chapter, a country with a very specific set of environments. Notwithstanding the popular moniker of 'Britain of the South Seas',[27] New Zealand is a very particular place. Its soils are rarely as fertile as those in much of Britain, but nor is it prone to Australian-type droughts or North American snows. The climate is generally temperate, permitting year-round grass growth in many districts with the option of leaving stock to winter over outside. By the 1920s, this characteristic was increasingly seen as 'naturalising', or validating, an intensive grasslands future for the country. But before this there had been, at least in Britain, no tradition of grassland research and experimentation.[28] 'Grass is of all the crops the most generally neglected', said one observer there in 1900.[29] This is the second reason why New Zealanders experimented with and systematised much of their own grasslands knowledge.

Despite the lack of British grasslands research, there had long been some recognition there of the significance of grass. Two centuries earlier, Jonathan Swift, writing in *Gulliver's Travels*, opined 'that whoever could make two ears of corn, or two blades of grass, to grow upon a spot of ground where only one grew before, would deserve better of mankind, and do more essential service to the country, than the whole race of politicians put together'.[30] Swift was an Irishman, and he keenly felt England's blocking of Ireland's agricultural potential by the imposition of tariffs to discourage exports of beef, butter and wool based upon a steady expansion of pastoral farming.[31] But this was written in 1726, and despite some interest from early nineteenth-century improvers like William Marshall and Arthur Young, little had been done nearly 200 years later to attend to grassland productivity. Isolated clover trials were run at Rothamsted research station north of London in the 1850s, but the Royal Agricultural College at Cirencester in the Cotswolds focused on agricultural chemistry, soils and fertilisers, not grasses. Cockle Park station in Northumberland was set up to encourage pasture improvement, but this was not until the 1890s, a century after the proposal was first made.[32]

In 1914, the American Henry Seidel Canby adapted Swift's maxim when he wrote that 'To make two blades of grass grow where one grew before is surely no achievement unless the grass is good grass.'[33] Such views became more common after the First World War, when the threat posed by insufficient levels of grassland productivity had become very real, in that Britain would have starved without assistance from the farmers of its empire.[34] In an article entitled 'Better grass farming' published in 1920, *The Times* argued that 'The prevalent neglect of grass admits of no defence.' A little later, a writer in *Nature* averred that 'It is too often the case that grassland is left to take care of itself, and that no steps are taken for its improvement.'[35] A similar situation held sway in New Zealand where the *laissez-faire* British attitude had been inherited. There was but one agricultural college, founded at Lincoln, near Christchurch in the South Island, in 1878. When Frederick Hilgendorf, who became one of the country's foremost agronomists, was appointed in 1899 to lecture there, he 'didn't know a single grass or weed, although I could distinguish wheat from oats'.[36]

This relative neglect of grasses and pasture has been echoed subsequently in the historiography of imperial and environmental history.[37] As *The Oxford History of the British Empire* observes, the practice of the latter has had little influence on the former.[38] A companion volume has addressed one aspect of grasslands history, the expansion of Australia's artificial grasslands.[39] But this development only accelerated after the Second World War. It is also the case that despite the prominent place of environmental history within American historiography, not much has been written about American sown grasslands. For example, James Malin, described by some as a founder of environmental history[40] and author of the classic *The Grassland of North America*, showed initial interest in pasture formation, but soon turned his attention to social relations on the prairies. Even William Cronon's work on the ways in which Chicago and its industries remade the West and Donald Worster's study of the Dust Bowl discuss grass only as a backdrop to cattle raising and soil loss.[41]

More recently, Geoff Cunfer's revisionist study of the Dust Bowl helps to fill this gap by discussing the impact of both cropping and stock farming on the grasslands of the Great Plains. His reassessment analyses the search for ongoing accommodations between human imperatives and variable environmental conditions, as was also the case in the drought-prone agricultural areas of southern Australia.[42] Canadians have written about the prairies at length, stressing the importance of staple monocultures, economic manipulation by elites and heroic struggles with the elements, but none have focused on the reconstruction of indigenous grasslands through sowing of artificial pasture. This may reflect the fact that grasslands played a less crucial role in Canada's economic development than in New Zealand.[43] In New Zealand itself there was ample celebration by grasslands scientists of the 'grasslands revolution' of the mid-twentieth century, but little critical analysis of historical context, causes or environmental and broader consequences of the grasslands transformation that we discuss in this book.[44]

'IMPROVEMENT' AND PRODUCTIVITY

This transformation was the product of a preoccupation evidenced all over the European settler world: the drive to construct new landscape out of 'unimproved' territories. Landscape was a product of culturally specific ways of seeing. The 'pictorial colonisation' of unfamiliar colonial scenes resorted to recurring motifs, one of which was to envisage open territory as parkland. This motif was often accentuated by the use of panoptical viewpoints, the imagination of great vistas, and the boundlessness of distant horizons.[45] For example, William Fox's two paintings of the Wairau plains in the northern part of New Zealand's South Island replace a picturesquely located group of three Māori in the first (dated 1845 – and reproduced in chapter 3) with a surveying party in the second (dated 1848). But both are dwarfed by the grassy expanses beyond, implying the possibilities of improvement through demarcation, enclosure and stocking.[46]

Writers concurred with artists. John Nicholas in his narrative *A Voyage to New Zealand*, published in London in 1817, wrote that 'the lands of this country ... might be brought to produce grasses of every description; were the experiment tried, I doubt not it would prove invariably successful, and that the islands in general would afford as fine a pasturage for sheep and cattle as any part of the known world'.[47] 'Improvement' was thus an ideological, material and technical project.[48] It constituted a way of looking at the world, of imagining the possibilities for wealth creation, as well as the means by which these possibilities were brought to fruition. It has been described as 'an act of geographical violence through which space was explored, reconstructed, renamed and controlled'.[49] This is not how it was understood at the time. Many settlers thought that they were completing God's creation, redeeming what had been 'unproductive' land, in which barrenness was a sign of the absence of Christian people.[50]

Interwoven with such religious readings was the effect of the more secular interpretation constructed by John Locke in the seventeenth century. He saw improvement as an imperial territoriality, the aim of which was 'the recovery of the Earth's edenic fruitfulness'.[51] Locke derived this perspective from his theory of property, and it in turn informed the eighteenth-century presumption in international law that the addition of labour improved colonial 'wastelands'. From the perspective of hindsight there were a number of unstated social, economic and environmental results. The first was the displacement of indigenous peoples, who were considered to be living in 'unimproved' and therefore 'unused' environments: 'the people without history' as they have been called.[52] New Zealand, unlike Australia or much of the Americas, had a recognised treaty (the Treaty of Waitangi, 1840) that purported to protect indigenous rights, but the wastelands thesis nevertheless informed the widespread appropriation of land from Māori by financial, technical and military means.[53]

This set of transformational practices also had economic and environmental consequences. It was the assumption of many twentieth-century grassland improvers that a productivist model of intensive grassland farming was the end-point of improvement. Bruce Levy, perhaps New Zealand's most prominent grasslands improver, who from 1936 headed the Grasslands Division of the Department of Scientific and Industrial Research, wrote in retirement about how 'The glorious truth is now written fairly and squarely across the countryside. But we still need more and better grass, more and more stock ... surely the country's surest and soundest economic goal.'[54] Levy however was writing in 1970 towards the end of the period of expansion in sown grassland area and stock unit numbers (Figure 1.2).

In areal terms, continuous improvement was not possible, as witnessed by the fate of some of the returned soldier settlements planted on marginal lands in the 1920s and 1930s.[55] In environmental terms, the assumption that grass alone could hold higher stock numbers was undermined by the soil erosion episodes of the 1930s, which prompted Cumberland to produce his pioneering field-based text, *Soil Erosion in New Zealand: A Geographic Reconnaissance*, in 1944.[56] In economic terms, only after 1970 did it become apparent that a pastoral 'totalitarianism', focused on producing low value-added pastoral commodities such as wool, bulk dairy products and frozen meat, could no longer sustain high standards of living. Those grassland utopias that have moved on to exploit a much wider range of income-earning strategies (the United States, Canada, Australia) have fared rather better than those (Uruguay, Argentina, New Zealand) that on the whole have not.[57]

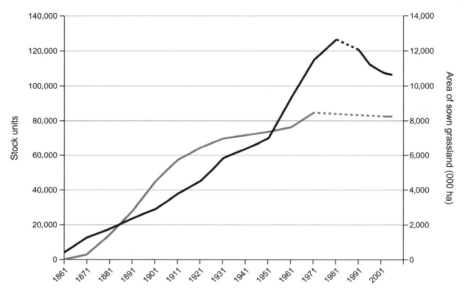

Figure 1.2: Changes in the area of sown grassland (grey line) and the numbers of stock units, 1861–2005. *Source*: *New Zealand Agriculture Statistics*.

STRUCTURE OF THE BOOK

The issues raised in this introduction are explored in a series of chapters that are broadly both thematic and sequential. The second chapter meshes with the first. It seeks to outline the contours of the grasslands transformation in New Zealand across time and space, and critically examines how grassland improvement was naturalised in a country in which there were initially other ideals for the future. It discusses the process of environmental change in a range of indigenous environments – wetland, tussock grassland, and bush – and the ways in which a remarkable uniformity of commodified landscape was produced. Apparent simplicity of outcome should not however be confused with the struggles of environmental learning, which is the focus of chapters 3 and 4.

Chapter 3 considers how three previously little-known generations of settlers came to terms with new places that were greatly different to what settler propaganda had suggested. Their environmental expectations were also very different to those of Māori, who could provide insights into weather conditions and routeways, but who had no experience to impart of cropping or stock. Colonial farmers therefore built up their working knowledge slowly, on the job. As they began to understand the colony's widely varying environmental conditions, experimentation and innovation was widespread, as is explored in chapter 4. This was exemplified by the approaches taken to matching pasture plants with conditions, and early approaches to fertilising.

The next two chapters focus on the relationship between pasture development, stock management and market specialisation. Chapter 5 reassesses one of the long-running controversies in New Zealand environmental history: the use and abuse of the South Island tussock grasslands. These were the early focus of pastoralism, and the evidence assembled shows their management to have been more considered, of both local conditions and markets, than has often been argued. The early dominance of Merinos imported from Australia gave way as market adjustments required coarser wool for the Bradford worsted industry and carcasses for the frozen meat trade. The economic drivers of the environmental changes induced by these shifts in practice are analysed in chapter 6, which highlights the creativeness of farmers to market opportunities. This depended on networks of relationships involving stock and station agencies, purchasers and suppliers of credit. This chapter consequently challenges notions of 'gentlemanly capitalism' centred in the City of London and highlights the important linkages between economic and environmental history.

Chapters 7 and 8 focus on two equally important but often-ignored aspects of these relationships: the trade in grass seed and networks of information. 'English grasses' were most highly valued, and use of native grasses was minimal. By the 1880s, however, New Zealand was not only producing much of its own seed, but exporting it to Australia, the United States, Britain and continental Europe. 'Akaroa cocksfoot' even formed the basis of improved strains developed at the Welsh Plant Breeding Station for wider use in Britain and elsewhere, another demonstration that imperial relationships were more complex than a core-periphery model allows. Chapter 8 discusses the means by which farming knowledge was exchanged and transferred through shows, farmers' clubs, newspapers and agricultural periodicals, and formal educational channels. New Zealanders were very well informed about issues such as the British ryegrass/cocksfoot controversy of the 1880s, but information was accessed and contributed through complex networks.

Chapters 9 and 10 explore the emergence of state initiatives in pasture development. This coincided with the development of bush burn pastures in the North Island and the emergence of the dairying industry. Greater productivity was sought through pasture improvement and refinement of stock breeds. Before and after the First World War, state institutions began to ally science to farming, through the activities of the early grassland specialists. Visits from influential Britons encouraged the establishment of a Department of Scientific and Industrial Research in 1926, and the fostering of cooperation on pasture plant development under the auspices of the Empire Marketing Board, but in turn New Zealand agricultural scientists persuaded British agrostologists to change their approach to grassland management in favour of a simple duoculture of perennial ryegrass and clover, dependent on heavy chemical inputs. Thereafter, a 'one model fits all' regime came to dominate New Zealand farming. It is argued that the achievements of this 'grasslands revolution' were exaggerated by some of the more nationalistic grasslands scientists, who overlooked the attainments of those early farmers, pastoralists and seed companies explored in earlier chapters.

In chapter 11, the significance of New Zealand's grassland transformation is assessed at several levels. The reports of the Royal Commission on Sheep Farming, which reported in 1949, shows the extent to which environmental problems could not be glossed over by the grasslands revolution. Despite ongoing gains in pasture productivity since, persistent issues remain. We question whether continued intensification within the unidirectional framework that was constructed for New Zealand farming a century ago remains feasible. New understandings of the New Zealand present are thereby illuminated by these insights from the past. In turn the wider significance of an informed analysis of the New Zealand grasslands experience lies in its contribution towards sharper readings of both imperial histories and global environmental histories. Of equal significance for these histories is a retrieval of the importance of pasture plants and the making of new pastoral landscapes.

2 The Contours of Transformation

Tom Brooking and Eric Pawson

INTRODUCTION

By 1896, the year in which the Māori population reached its nadir of 42,000, European settlers, known collectively as Pākehā, outnumbered Māori by more than sixteen to one. It was a very different New Zealand from that in which organized European settlement had begun around 1840 when there were barely 2,000 immigrants. Māori then numbered around 80,000, most of whom were concentrated in the northern half of the North Island, as its warmer climate was better suited to their Polynesian horticultural heritage. The dry eastern sides of the central ranges of the North Island, and of the Southern Alps in the South Island, were dominated by scrub and tussock grassland. These were culturally produced landscapes, the result of burning for purposes of hunting and forest clearance in the several centuries since the arrival of Māori. In contrast, on the wet western side of both islands, and across the North Island ranges, temperate rainforest remained almost ubiquitous. Wetlands, although collectively of much smaller extent, were typically found in low-lying coastal regions. These were of considerable significance to Māori as food-gathering sites.[1]

It was into this world that Pākehā settlers transported their suite of agricultural fauna and flora from farms that were half a world away. The sum result of the burning of bush, ploughing of tussock, draining of wetland and consequential sowing of grass seed was that New Zealand's modest 1.40 million hectares of formed grassland of 1880 doubled to 2.82 million hectares by 1890. This occurred despite the ongoing economic depression of that decade. By the dawn of the new century, and assisted by the return of improved economic conditions in the mid-1890s, it had risen to 4 million. With good times continuing, 5.9 million hectares had been sown by the start of the First World War. Farmers established a further 0.5 million hectares during the war years, despite the shortage of artificial fertiliser before the acquisition of Nauru and Ocean Islands with their huge deposits of phosphate.[2]

George Stapledon described this process of grassland transformation during his visit in 1926 using the familiar tropes of colonial improvement. 'The present merges rapidly into the future in new countries', he wrote. '[W]hat was begun at least over a thousand years ago in Europe has ... been begun and finished in little more than eighty years in New Zealand.'[3] In the North Island's 'transplanted sward' he observed ryegrass and clover growing in greater abundance than in England's prime stock-fattening county of Leicestershire.[4] New Zealand's improved grasslands relied on this narrow suite of seeds of empire, with the notable addition of cocksfoot, even if by this point most of the grass and pasture plants used, though exotic in origin, were domestically produced.

Was the grassland hegemony that came to dominance in late nineteenth-century New Zealand an inevitable outcome? As a way forward then, or now, it is certainly still rarely questioned. For much of the nineteenth century, however, there was no sense of inevitability that the future lay in grass; there was also some debate over the price of this style of landscape reconstruction once it began to emerge. So why and how did this pathway develop? Where and when did the remaking of pre-colonial landscapes proceed, and what sort of work was necessary to build new carpets of grass on farms, and in whole districts and regions? This chapter explores these themes, in order to provide a context of time and place for those that follow.

GRASSLAND ALTERNATIVES

In fact, a number of alternatives for New Zealand's farming development had been expressed from the time of Cook's landing in 1769. Joseph Banks, who accompanied Cook on the *Endeavour*, is perhaps the originator of a reverberating ideal: that of the fertility of the land. Referring to the forested wetlands of what became the Firth of Thames, he claimed that 'the great size of the plants' and especially 'the timber trees which were the streightest, cleanest, and may I say the largest I have ever seen ... sufficiently evincd the richness of their soil'. Referring to his father's draining of fenland on the family estate at Revesby Abbey in Lincolnshire, he predicted that these swamps 'might doubtless Easily be draind',[5] adding that the 'Woodland' (which was kahikatea) 'promisd great returns to the people who would take the trouble of Clearing it'. The populariser John Hawkesworth, in a book published in 1773 and often reprinted, pushed this optimistic reading of New Zealand's farming potential further. His exotically illustrated volumes promoted the idea that it was a largely empty and abundant land waiting to be developed by enterprising British settlers.

Hawkesworth assured his readers that Cook, Banks and others on the *Endeavour* such as Solander had concluded that 'if this country should be settled by people from Europe every kind of European grain, plant, and fruit would flourish here in the utmost luxuriance'.[6] This was the view of Charles Darwin when he visited the missionary gardens at Waimate in Northland in 1835. He expressed delight at finding 'fine crops of barley and wheat in full ear' and 'large gardens with every fruit and vegetable that England produces'. It seemed to him that 'this undulating country with its trees, might have well have been mistaken for our fatherland'. Waimate represented an oasis of peace, order and prosperity in a land Darwin generally dismissed as gloomy, unattractive and frightening. Taking a typical improver's perspective, he considered that the missionaries had waved an 'enchanter's wand' and shown how the islands might 'progress'.[7]

In 1834, the timber merchant Thomas McDonnell told the Royal Geographical Society that the soils everywhere in the North Island were 'uncommonly rich' and 'easy of culture'.[8] The young artist Augustus Earle concurred, noting that 'the soil appeared to me to be fat and rich' and 'every vegetable (yet planted) thrives, the introduction of European grasses, fruit, etc., etc., would be a great desideratum'.[9] Edward Gibbon Wakefield, architect of the 'systematic colonisation' of what became Britain's newest and most remote colony with the signing of the Treaty of Waitangi, and founder of the New Zealand Association (later Company), imagined that wheat growing would enable settlers to transplant in the Antipodes an economic and social system like that of southeastern England. When the Company's 'puffers' wrote the influential promotional pamphlet, *The British Colonization of New Zealand*, published in 1837, they referred to New Zealand's future as the 'granary of the Southern Hemisphere'.[10]

It early became apparent however that arable farming was not viable, despite the yields produced from the first flush of fertility in newly cropped soils. Rather it was wool that was to produce a good living for men of capital, especially when Australia suffered severe drought in the early 1840s.[11] Yet, despite the success of wool-growing from the late 1840s (Table 1.1), New Zealand's third and most powerful Governor, Captain George Grey, held out a different vision of colonial development. He despised sheep and

15

distrusted sheep squatters as representative of monopoly and incivility, even though he provided them with favourable leasehold tenures in the tussock grassland districts in return for accepting limits on the areas they could graze. He hoped that New Zealand would become a land of vigorous communities based around intensively cultivated small farms rather than degenerating into a giant underpopulated sheep walk.

Grey was an adherent of a recurrent vision that New Zealand would fare best if it developed Mediterranean-style industries, especially in the warmer northern districts. These included citrus and olive growing, viticulture and even sericulture. He recommended that a special agricultural school be established in North Auckland to train colonists in such endeavour.[12] But he did not go as far as William Cochran, who produced an abortive plan for tea and silk farming in the early 1880s. Cochran had examined the tea industry in China in 1864 before looking for a suitable new location for it. Because Grey and others advocated sericulture and silk production in a different season from that in which tea was harvested, Cochran proposed that the two industries be combined in New Zealand as 'chasericulture', perhaps utilising a workforce of female emigrants from depressed areas of Scotland.[13]

Whatever kind of agricultural development was to be pursued, however, was dependent on the acquisition of large tracts of land owned and controlled by Māori. John Weaver has described European expansion into indigenous territories throughout the new world as the 'great land rush'.[14] In New Zealand, it occurred through a range of strategies put into effect from the mid-1840s onwards. This was despite the apparent guarantees of territorial protection provided to Māori in the Treaty of Waitangi, and the success of northern tribes in particular in incorporating European agricultural methods.[15] Huge swathes of the less populated South Island were purchased at very low prices by the Crown between 1848 and 1853. After the fighting of the 1860s in the North Island regions of Waikato, Taranaki and Bay of Plenty, where Māori contested settler land incursions, confiscation and individualisation of title were widely enforced.[16] Subsequent land sales were rarely enough to generate ongoing income, and remnant tribal lands were often of poor quality. Many Māori thereby moved from being initial participants in improvement to a proletariat dispossessed by it.[17]

VISIONS OF GRASSLAND 'IMPROVEMENT'

The advocacy of multiple-use improvement strategies by people such as Grey began to lose out to a more narrowly focused British-style stock farming, based on grass, in the 1880s. The signal event was the first shipment of refrigerated meat, butter and cheese to London in 1882. This was dispatched through the port of Dunedin from one of the east coast South Island estates of the New Zealand and Australian Land Company (NZALC). The success of this shipment on the London market set meat and butter production in New Zealand onto a viable path. Refrigeration was not quite the magic bullet of received wisdom because it involved trial and error and initially benefited only large estate owners with capital.[18] By the early 1890s, however, farmers operating middling sized units of a few hundred acres also began to take up specialist fat lamb farming. Later that decade dairy farmers, often running small herds of 30 or so cows on modest holdings of about 20 hectares, 'with a few pigs, together with poultry and bees', began to flourish.[19] They produced cheese and butter largely for export. By 1911 there were over 20,000 of these specialist dairy farmers.[20] Many of them were on farms carved out of burned-over bush in the North Island regions of the Manawatu and Taranaki. The figures account for the increase in grassland formation, and for a renewed wave of Crown purchase of Māori lands, in the years up to the First World War.

The temperate farming model was familiar and had ready appeal to New Zealand's predominantly British migrants. They had no experience of viticulture or olive growing and did not use Mediterranean ingredients in their cooking. There were, anyway, limited opportunities when Mediterranean producers jealously guarded their monopoly of olive production, whilst New Zealand's beer-drinking habits greatly limited the market for locally produced wine. By 1909 the Department of Agriculture closed down its viticultural station at Te Kauwhata, south of Auckland, while the powerful temperance movement forced several promising vineyards in Hawke's Bay to cease operations. Experiments with apple growing and citrus production struggled as well. Horticulture survived and continued to receive some state assistance, but many years passed before it flourished. Similarly, market gardening did not expand significantly until cities grew larger.[21]

In 1879, Walter Pearson, Commissioner of Crown Lands for Southland, caught the Anglo-Celtic longing to create an idyll for yeoman farmers based on stock farming, supplemented by small amounts of cropping to provide winter feed. In a fanciful piece included in his annual report, he imagined himself looking across the plains from a hill above the Mataura River in 1871, observing how 'solitude brooded over the landscape'. In contrast, the scene in 1879 was one of biblically infused improvement:

the sunbeam dances over well tilled fields ripe with cultivated abundance ... resting for a moment, the farmer surveys the bright landscape, and proudly realises the great gift of 'the master' ... 'the earth and the abundance thereof' is being turned to its legitimate use – the blessing of many – while the grey smoke wreaths itself aloft from many a smiling homestead.

Pearson concluded that 'the Australian Colonies are doubtless better fields for the wealthy pastoral lords, but they will never compete with New Zealand in raising a substantial Yeomanry'.[22]

Visitors to New Zealand in the late nineteenth century could not help but notice the rapid transformation described by Pearson. Mark Twain arrived at Bluff in 1895, and went north through the most developed regions of the country, the regions of Southland, Otago and Canterbury. These were the places that had first prospered on sheep in the 1850s, raised on the dry plains, and downlands to the east of the Southern Alps, and on reclaimed wetland margins along the coast. He likened the fields outside the window to a 'junior England' as he travelled at fully 'twenty and half miles an hour' on 'a train that can't overtake its own shadow'.[23] The Irish land radical Michael Davitt, who came on the same ship as Twain, compared the green paddocks of Southland to those of Southern Ireland. He expressed pleasure at seeing 'such old friends as the hawthorn bush, the blackbird, thrush and sparrow', and judged the countryside to be 'neat and comfortable' with enough trees to be 'fairly sheltered'.[24] Both condemned the treatment of Māori, who had defended their lands and waterways with the same tenacity as the Irish, but they thoroughly approved of the colony's environmental transformation.

It was for this reason – as well as for progressive social, political and economic changes, such as female suffrage, industrial arbitration, and old age pensions – that commentators from the United States, Britain and Europe were attracted to the 'social laboratory' of New Zealand in the 20 years before the First World War. Visiting in 1899, the Chicago-based progressive journalist Henry Demarest Lloyd saw North Island settlers busily replacing forests and swamps with modern farms and improved pasture. Inevitably this involved the displacement of native plants and people.[25] Like the Liberal Government then in power, he equated 'progress' with advances in material comfort and increased prosperity for the majority of 'deserving' citizens, that is, those who were hard working, sober and thrifty. The title of fellow Californian Henry George's critique of capitalism, *Poverty and Progress*, encapsulated the belief that social engineering could overcome age-old problems such as poverty.[26] In this context, creating new pastures out of the bush, or by draining swamps, represented the best kind of improvement.[27]

Colonists themselves generally basked in such compliments. A better life was after all the driving force behind emigration to settler colonies like New Zealand, and belief in the possibilities of succeeding was deeply rooted in Pākehā society. Richard John Seddon (Liberal premier from 1893 to 1906) captured a widespread view of the meaning of progress in the 'experiment station' of New Zealand when he claimed in 1894 that 'every tree felled meant the improvement of the public estate of the country'.[28] In the 1890s and 1900s, there was widespread cutting and burning of the North Island bush, as the giant kauri of Northland and Coromandel, and much of the thick podocarp (southern hemisphere conifer) forests of Taranaki, Wanganui, Manawatu, Wairarapa, and then the interior King Country, were replaced by grass (Figure 2.1). Residual swamps were drained, notably in the Waikato, and the labyrinths of tall kahikatea that had so impressed Joseph Banks in the Thames wetlands were removed.

Figure 2.1: A bush farm near Stratford, with Mount Taranaki in the background, c. 1890–1900. *Source*: glass negative, photographer Alexander Walker Reid (PHO2006–329). Collection of Puke Ariki, New Plymouth.

Something like 85 per cent of New Zealand's original wetlands (probably a world record) disappeared in this drive to improve.[29] Few mourned the swamps, given their association in the European mind with poverty and disease. There was, however, some concern for the wholesale loss of native trees. Sir John Gorst had served as a magistrate in the Waikato in the 1860s. He returned as British delegate to the New Zealand International Exhibition held in Christchurch in 1906–07, and condemned burnt-over bush as an 'eyesore'. He missed the kahikatea groves that had grown along the rivers of the Waikato in his early adulthood and lamented that 'beauty was disfigured by the stumps of blackened trees, which stood up as memorials of the great forest which the dairy farms had displaced'. He expressed more pleasure when his party travelled through remnant bush in Taranaki and called for the 'preservation' of some forest.[30]

There were other questioning voices, such as the politician naturalist Thomas Potts, and the artist Alfred Sharpe.[31] J.P. Grossman condemned deforestation as 'evil', while his fellow historian Guy Scholefield complained that the landscape had been 'ravaged' by the 'feverish haste' of settlers who had caused 'wanton and profligate' waste in their 'pitiful and wicked war' on the bush.[32] W.P. Reeves expressed concern in a well-known poem (reproduced in many anthologies used in schools) 'The passing of the forest: a lament for the children of Tane'. First published in 1898 as an appendix to his best-selling history *The Long White Cloud*, he reworked the last lines in 1906 to read:

Ah bitter price to pay
For Man's dominion – beauty swept away.[33]

Perhaps the most famous lament came later from the farmer and naturalist Herbert Guthrie-Smith. After a lifetime of working his property in northern Hawke's Bay and observing in detail the effects on soils, plant life and birds, he wrote *Tutira: The Story of a New Zealand Sheep Station* (first published in 1921). His conclusion in the third edition of 1951 was: 'Have I for sixty years desecrated God's earth and dubbed it improvement?'[34]

Yet it was often implied that the ugliness would pass and temporary scarring of the landscape should be tolerated in the wider interest. In 1880, as the bush around Palmerston North was burned to make way for grass, the editor of the *Manawatu Times* declared that 'although the smoke may inconvenience us and the charred avenues offend the eye, we must accept all thankfully as a mark of local progress'.[35] By the turn of the century, grass could be found in many more places than wheat fields, with over 4 million hectares of pasture having been sown across the country, as against less than 0.4 million hectares of cereals concentrated in Otago,

Canterbury and the Manawatu.[36] A discourse of grassland improvement was widely established. Reeves himself exclaimed in *The Long White Cloud* that the 'cocks-foot, timothy, rye-grass, and white clover' growing amongst the vigorous 'furze' [gorse] hedges 'made New Zealand fields "green pictures set in frames of gold"'.[37] The 1905 *Official Yearbook* declared on its first page that: 'New Zealand is first a pastoral and secondly an agricultural country. Some grasses are grown almost everywhere. The soil is admirably adapted to receive these grasses, and, after the bush has been burnt off, is mostly sown over without previous ploughing.' The article added that 'the large extent of good grazing lands has made the colony a great wool, meat and dairy-produce country'. Later, in the 'Agriculture' section, this government publication boasted about the country's 'humid climate and fertile soil'.[38]

In 1911 a change of tone was apparent, with officialdom conceding that perhaps soils were not so rich after all. But the 'Agriculture' section still claimed that 'New Zealand is essentially suited for grazing purposes.' The 1913 edition added that 'The best grasses and fodder plants flourish in the congenial environment, and the country has already gained a world wide reputation for the quality of its pastures.'[39] Farmers, agricultural scientists and visitors repeated this mantra much more frequently in the 1920s. By the end of that decade descriptions of New Zealand as being covered in 'sward' were commonplace.[40] Posters devised by the London-based Empire Marketing Board in the late 1920s and early 1930s[41] portrayed settler New Zealand as a manicured if frontier land (Figure 2.2).

Figure 2.2: 'Wool' by Frank Newbould. Empire Marketing Board poster, early 1930s. The artist represents an orderly landscape of grass extending to the settler frontier. *Source*: CO 956/303, National Archives, Kew, London.

FARM AND DISTRICT

The hard work of improvement occurred on the farm and station,[42] and often in quite patchy ways in the districts of which they were a part. The celebration of new landscapes, or the wistfulness at the loss of what they replaced, disguised the extent of the work needed to bring about transformation on the ground. 'I have come to hate the very name of improvements', wrote Annie Wilson, of her family's station in the Manawatu district of the North Island, to her father-in-law George in Scotland.[43] An appreciation of the sheer labour involved is hard to assess, given the erratic survival of farm diaries and correspondence. Where these do exist, the information provided is usually illustrative rather than systematic, and often terse:[44] much is assumed, not least that the work was more important than writing about it. That said, there is enough, when combined with letters, memoirs, maps and newspapers, to draw out some key themes, not least of which was the 'immense capital ... invested in the creation of the rural landscapes of lowland New Zealand'.[45]

When Annie and her husband James Wilson arrived at Ngaio Station (near Bulls) in 1874, it had no fences, not even boundary fences, only one eighth was in grass, and that was native danthonia. The rest was native manuka scrub, fern and toetoe. Some parts of the station needed draining. Annie described the process of improvement as taking the land 'from a state of nature to a state of grace'.[46] The scrub was burned in late summer, with ploughing in the spring to take a crop of turnips, followed by oats, before planting in English grasses. The Wilsons began in 1875 with less than 4,000 sheep of mixed lineage. By 1886, in the midst of the depression, they had raised this to 9,000 Lincoln-Merino half-breeds, with 700 head of cattle and 60 horses. Stock was housed in 28 paddocks contained by 65 kilometres of fencing, mostly ditch and bank with gorse or seven wire with one barbed wire. In 1891, half the station was in English grasses or crops, and most of the balance had been burnt and surface sown (Figure 2.3).

Herbert Guthrie-Smith's sheep station, Tutira, was in even rougher country than Ngaio. He described his book about it as 'a record of minute alterations noted on one patch of land'.[47] He had come to Tutira in 1882, after a decade in which Pākehā leaseholders had supported several thousand Merino sheep by burning the bush and fern, section by section, each autumn, before surface sowing with grass and clover. But the application of hundreds of bags of cocksfoot and ryegrass had been in vain, as New Zealand flax, bracken and fern grew back. Slowly, Guthrie-Smith fenced new and smaller paddocks, reclaiming bracken for pasture, improving and building stock numbers with Lincoln rams, only to see much of his effort undermined as the land fertility declined. His book recorded not just these changes, but also the arrival and spread of introduced species. Nearly 50 were naturalised before 1882; about 240 by the 1930s. They included weedy grasses, foxglove and vetch that arrived in the cheap grass seed used to develop the first paddocks after 1882.[48]

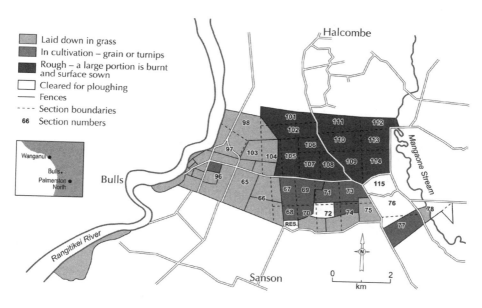

Figure 2.3: Map of Ngaio Station, as sent by James Wilson to his father in 1891. *Source*: Wild, L.J., *The Life and Times of Sir James Wilson of Bulls* (Christchurch, 1953), facing p. 64.

At a regional scale, Canterbury provides a South Island example of environmental variability and patchy development.[49] From the east coast to the front ranges of the Southern Alps there were extensive areas of dry, tussock grassland.[50] These were well suited to sheep, and after purchase from Māori in the late 1840s, were largely leased out by the Crown in the 1850s as pastoral runs. Timber licences were granted for wetter bush districts, such as Banks Peninsula and Waimate in Canterbury, with land being freeholded by small farmers as the sawmills moved on. The damp soils along the coastline and in the vicinity of the main settlements were freeholded relatively early, although the cost of draining swamplands meant that these fertile areas were not initially favoured for farming. By the late 1870s, however, an agricultural frontier had also incorporated many of the swamps as well as swathes of the tussock plains in freehold, as wheat and then permanent pasture became more profitable.[51] The only leasehold areas remaining were on the drier plains and in the high country districts of the alpine ranges, valleys and basins.

Within a year of the establishment of the Canterbury Association settlement in 1850–1, over 800 hectares of land had been fenced in the vicinity of Christchurch, the central town, with about 200 planted in pasture and crops. Freeholders initially favoured the margins of the swamps as they took up land further away. The example of the Lincoln-Tai Tapu district is illustrated in Figure 2.4, comparing surveyors' maps drawn at the time of the indigenous vegetation with the location of freehold. New Zealand flax and niggerhead dominated the swamp margins, which were easier to cultivate with the ploughs of the day than the tussock grasslands, and cheaper to 'improve' than the deep-water raupo swamps.[52] Canterbury University College established what it called the 'model farm', New Zealand's first school of agriculture, on these good soils at Lincoln in 1880. An early student wrote that 'When I entered the College the place was bare and open. The gorse hadn't been planted and the subdivision was by wire fence only.' Its first head, W.E. Ivey, experimented with all types of English grasses and clovers, using ryegrass on all classes of soil, and timothy on the heavier and cocksfoot on the lighter land.[53]

Another Canterbury property for which evidence survives is The Point, a sheep run about 100 kilometres west of Christchurch. The Point was a 4,000-hectare block on the north bank of the Rakaia River, encompassing both gently sloping land and steeper ranges fronting the Southern Alps. The Point Journal, kept by Thomas Phillips, allows analysis of work patterns for a five-year period from August 1866 to May 1871.[54] The run was first taken up in 1852, when much of it was open country covered by tussock grassland and low shrubs. Analysis of the journal has shown that The Point was effectively operated by Thomas and his brother, with a hired man and 'a string of other hired help'.[55] Work with stock accounted for a considerable proportion of the man-hours that they expended. These peaked in the summer when sheep were mustered from unfenced rough hill country, and the family relied on itinerant, often Māori, shearing gangs.

But activities relating to fencing, hedging and the provision of shelter absorbed as much as 40 per cent of man-days, in the spring, autumn and winter months in particular. There was a clear regularity to the work. In early spring, parts of the run were burned to promote fresh growth of the native tussocks for stock, as well as to control the unwanted spread of native shrubby plants, and of gorse. Gorse was used, as it was throughout Canterbury, for hedging. A typical gorse hedge was sown as seed on a clay wall about 0.75 metres high and 0.5 metres wide, the wall being made of layers of sod.[56] Hedges and fences were used initially to keep stock out (of valuable plantings) as much as in. By 1868, The Point had 'a sizeable area of arable land on which English grasses, hay, barley, oats for the draught horses, and root crops were grown'.[57] Fence lines also served more symbolic roles, imposing 'narrative landmarks' in such extensive country, enabling blocks and paddocks to be named, and the history of place to be constructed.[58]

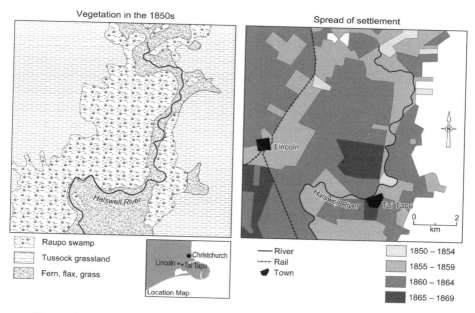

Figure 2.4: Comparison of vegetation and the spread of settlement in the Lincoln-Tai Tapu area, to the south of Christchurch. *Source*: redrawn from Cant, R.G., 'The agricultural frontier in miniature: a microstudy on the Canterbury Plains, 1850–75', *New Zealand Geographer* 24/2 (1968), p. 161.

In the 1860s, a rapid increase in New Zealand's fenced area occurred, notably in the east coast areas of the South Island used for extensive sheep grazing and (in the 1870s and 1880s) for wheat growing. As at The Point, the major live fence was gorse. By 1871, nearly 85 per cent of the fenced area was in the South Island, with much of the North Island fenced land concentrated in the pastoral southern Wairarapa and Hawke's Bay districts. The South Island percentage share fell slightly in the next decade as the farming frontier moved into the swamp and bush districts of the North Island. In the Waikato, hawthorn was used, and in Taranaki, barberry was popular, although wooden post and rail fences were the initial choice on bush farms. Wire was making an impact by the 1860s, and by the late 1870s, barbed wire, first used to fence the rangelands of the western United States, was being imported.[59]

TUSSOCK, WETLAND, BUSH

Samuel Butler, later famous as the author of *Erewhon* and *The Way of All Flesh*, lived the life of a sheep farmer for four years in the 1860s in the Rangitata Valley in central Canterbury. He once remarked that 'a mountain here is only beautiful if it has good grass on it. Scenery is not scenery – it is "country", subaudita voce "sheep"'.[60] He was lampooning the tendency of colonists to see only the productive possibilities in landscape. Consequently, as the Pākehā population swelled, whole districts and regions were being converted from indigenous vegetation into 'paddocks' of English grasses. By 1900, the tussock lands of the eastern districts of both islands, the thick forest or bush, which had clothed the interior of the North Island and many hill districts elsewhere, as well as small and large areas of wetland around the country, had been or were being improved.

A good example of this process on a large scale is provided by the Edendale estate in Southland, which was owned by the NZALC. As Walter Pearson had observed of the Mataura valley, Edendale (to the west of the river) seemed better suited to yeoman husbandry, rather than to the pastoral farming for which the NZALC had been established. The company used steam ploughs to convert hectares of red tussock, New Zealand flax and speargrass, ploughing them over twice, followed by a crop of turnips, rape or oats, and repeating the whole process before English grasses could be sown. It opened a new dairy factory in 1882 as part of its programme to subdivide Edendale for sale to private purchasers. This factory was the first to attempt cheese making on a large scale for export to the British market, winning a government bonus for producing a consignment of butter or cheese produced in a factory and sold overseas at a price indicating fair quality. It is often credited with being the birthplace of commercial dairying in New Zealand.[61]

The Edendale estate was enormous, its 50,000 hectares stretching from Gore in the north almost to Invercargill in the south. Most parts of it were too far from the factory, or too poorly improved before liming became widespread, to be of use for dairying. And before the 1890s export dairying was slow to take off, in part because frozen meat provided sufficient demand for the available supply of refrigerated shipping. Some farmers did purchase land in the subdivision, including John Hall, who took up 250 acres (about 100 hectares) at Edendale in 1882. He brought dairy cows south from his previous farm at Taieri Beach near Dunedin. The family found that their paddocks reverted from grass, and by the 1890s, they were spending a lot of time liming to counter the problem.[62] Other farmers acquired land from the company on deferred payment, in return for which the NZALC required that 'between the first two crops and the third the land must have lain in English grass, and been depastured for not less than two years, being sown the third year with green crops'.[63]

Despite the Company's attempts to dispose of this estate (it held many more in Southland, Otago and Canterbury), the holding never fell below about 19,000 hectares until it was sold to the Liberal Government in 1904 as part of a political programme of closer settlement. In 1904, about 53 per cent of the land purchased by the government (i.e. that which had not been sold to farmers, or which had reverted to NZALC ownership) was in English grasses. This was a high proportion compared to that on the estates of other land companies purchased by the government in western Southland: 18 per cent for Merrivale, 8.7 per cent for Otahu and 9.0 per cent for Beaumont. Improvement was therefore inconsistent, but it was widespread. As in the kinder climate of Canterbury, but with less success, grain was often sown as an interim crop to pay interest costs and deferred payment instalments.[64]

The growing of grain was not usually an option in bush clearance districts, where cutting and burning of the trees usually left their tangled roots untouched in the soil. This rendered ploughing impossible. A good example is the hilly volcanic district of Banks Peninsula, which protrudes into the sea south of Christchurch. The central and eastern parts of the Peninsula were thickly forested, but much of the bush was cut, or lost to fire, between 1860 and 1880. A report to the newly appointed Conservator of State Forests in 1876 noted that 'the main object of the landowners' was to 'get the ground cleared of timber and bush, and converted into pasture as rapidly as possible'. This conversion was revolutionised by what became known, after the Peninsula's main settlement, as 'Akaroa cocksfoot'.[65] Cocksfoot had reached the Peninsula from Europe via a Christchurch nurseryman in the 1850s; farmers soon found that it prospered in the conditions left by a bush-burn, to the point where other grasses were more or less excluded.

Akaroa cocksfoot was of a particularly long-lasting type that gave up seed year after year without any form of cultivation, so long as livestock were kept away from the maturing plants. It became an important export crop for Peninsula farmers in the 1880s, partly in response to a British debate, of which New Zealand farmers were well aware. This centred on whether perennial ryegrass (the usual mainstay in both British and Australasian introduced pastures) persisted long enough to justify its inclusion in seed mixtures intended for renewing or re-establishing permanent pasture (see chapter 7). Those farmers who began burning their way through the North Island bush in the 1870s and 1880s favoured cocksfoot-dominant pastures because of its more proven persistence. Some of their demand was met by local production, but they also provided an important market for Akaroa cocksfoot. In fact many of the thousand or more casual labourers who took part in the summer cocksfoot harvest on the Peninsula were from North Island bush farms. They collected, as part of their pay, the seed they would need when they burnt the bush on their land on returning.[66]

Districts that were being 'improved' in this way included the Forty Mile Bush in the northern Wairarapa, inland Manawatu, the Wanganui district, and Taranaki.[67] Much of Taranaki was confiscated from its Māori owners following the wars of the 1860s, and subsequently allocated or on-sold to Pākehā settlers.[68] Crown sales were heavily promoted in the early 1880s, not always accurately with respect to the labour investment required. The *New Zealand Gazette* said misleadingly of the Waimate Plains in south Taranaki: 'With the exception of a few rata, the bush consists mainly of soft woods and other light timber, and can easily be cleared. The country is well-watered, and is admirably adapted for conversion into grass lands.' Such land was available on various terms, including deferred payment, in which case 'improvement conditions' applied, i.e. sections inspected for the first time by the Crown Lands Ranger should have 10 per cent in grass; at the second inspection, this should be 15 per cent. Overall, farmers in south Taranaki in the mid-1880s exceeded these figures.[69]

The means by which such improvement was achieved is revealed in the diary of a bush farmer granted two 50-acre sections (about 20 hectares in total) in return for military service.[70] He farmed near Huirangi, inland from Waitara in north Taranaki, and began its development in 1874. Figure 2.5 shows the number of half-days of all those labouring on his farm for four selected years. Bush undergrowth was cut in late winter or spring, then

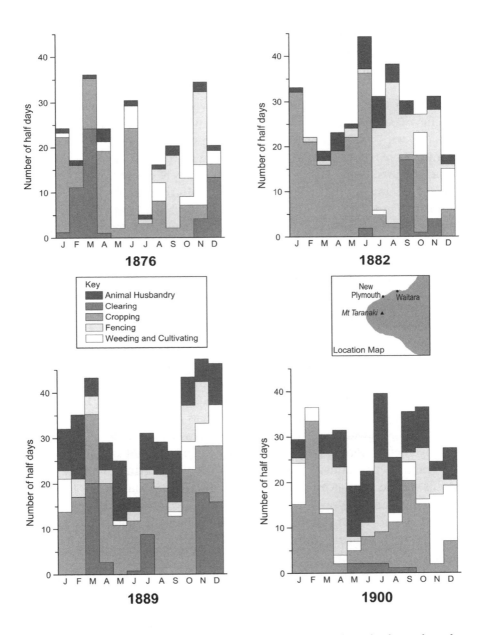

Figure 2.5: The annual round of work on a Taranaki bush farm for four selected years. *Source*: redrawn from Johnston, W.B., 'Pioneering the bushland of lowland Taranaki', *New Zealand Geographer* 17/1 (1961), p. 7.

allowed to dry to form a good fire bed, so that the bush when set alight in late summer burned cleanly. This can be seen for the year 1876, and again in 1889, after another bush section had been acquired. The removal of tree stumps took place in winter or spring, as illustrated in the years 1882, 1889 and 1900.

The first fences erected were to keep cows and horses off valuable new patches of oats, potatoes and young grass. Fence and rail posts were favoured initially, with wire not becoming common until the late 1880s. Early on, animals were free to roam in the bush, often getting lost or causing damage to neighbours' crops. Hence boundary fences were erected next. The third stage of fencing was that of systematic subdivision of the farm into paddocks, hand in hand with the final clearance of the bush, and the increase in livestock as the land was grassed. The seed mix for early temporary pasture was cocksfoot with ryegrass, with the addition by 1900 of timothy and clover. Over the 25 years of the diary, 'the common sequence was to fell the bush, burn, surface-sow grasses, cut and thresh grass seed for sale or for resowing, take a crop of wheat or barley, stump, plough, crop potatoes or carrots or turnips and grain, plough and finally sow down in long-term pasture'.[71]

In the north, Auckland, which was the colonial capital until 1865 (when that function was transferred to Wellington), had been for much of its existence closed off from land with native grass cover or land that could be easily converted.[72] As early as 1853, the suburbs of Epsom and Tamaki were reported to possess 'grass and clover paddocks as large, as rich, as well laid down, and as substantially fenced, as any grass land in England'.[73] But such improvements were expensive, as was the replacement of Merino sheep – prone to fleece damage and footrot in the wet northern climate – with breeds such as the Leicester. There were substantial populations of Māori in the vicinity and the early Crown land purchases to the north of Auckland turned out to be unsuited to the establishment of grass, coinciding as they did with infertile 'gumland' soils, from which kauri forests had been cleared.

In the 1850s, those within government who favoured a policy of assimilation of Māori into Pākehā ways sought to encourage Māori to the south of Auckland, in the Waikato, to take up sheep rearing. But Crown loans for the purchase of grass seed and plans to supply sheep were stopped when Te Wherowhero, the pre-eminent Waikato chief, objected. As his spokesman saw it, 'the name of the Queen would stick to all the land covered with grass'.[74] By the 1860s, however, powerful Auckland politicians and business interests were intent on occupying land that could be used to emulate the wealth generation of the southern regions. This was one factor leading to the military invasion of the Waikato in 1863 and the confiscation of 500,000 hectares of Māori land by the Crown in December 1864. Auckland speculators quickly moved to lease large areas even beyond the confiscation line, utilising the Auckland-sponsored Native Land Act of 1865, which set up the Native Land Court to individualise tribal title. By such means, the drier parts of the Waikato were acquired by Auckland businessmen as sheep and cereal farms. Josiah Firth, for example, chief partner in the town's largest flour mills, accumulated 21,000 hectares to form the Matamata Estate.[75]

From the 1880s, the rise of dairying began to have as dramatic an effect on the territories south of Auckland as in Taranaki. By the turn of the century, Matamata and many other such estates had been subdivided by the government for dairying. At the same time, the biologically diverse wetlands of the Waikato and Hauraki Plains were being drained. These supported the vast stands of kahikatea trees that had captivated Banks in 1769. Reaching up to 50 metres in height, kahikatea was valued for its timber: given its white colour and lack of odour or taste, particularly for butter boxes.[76] The 1913 Royal Commission on Forestry said of it that 'the soil of the white-pine swamps, when drained and the trees removed, forms the richest of agricultural land, which when grassed is of extreme value for dairy farms'.[77] Given the investment in these lands, Auckland became increasingly prominent as a business centre. By the First World War, the earlier dominance of the southern provinces was being undermined and the economic geography of New Zealand's development was increasingly weighted towards the north.[78]

CONCLUSION

By 1900, bordered paddocks of English grasses had become the normalised landscape of New Zealand. 'Landscapes are culture before they are nature', wrote Simon Schama in another context, or 'constructs of the imagination projected onto wood and water and rock'.[79] This imagination fuelled a powerful urge to improve, in the process largely destroying pre-existing indigenous environments and social territories. It was not only the economic imperative of entering into the trade of empire that underlay this, but also the cultural imperative that John Locke had captured in his theory of improvement. In an examination of early European writing about New Zealand, Paul Shepard found that the association of 'improved pastoral scenery with virtue and Godliness was the most persistent theme in the written record by the New Zealand pioneer'.[80]

In the second half of the nineteenth century, the cultural-economic basis to the seeding of empire was reinforced by a growing scientific legitimation drawn from a locally specific reading of Darwinism. In 1846, the missionary explorer William Colenso commented on the rapid spread of introduced species in parts of the North Island: 'The new comers appear to vegetate so fast, as quite to exterminate and supersede the original possessors of the soil.'[81] The politician and plant collector W.T.L. Travers, who was to be one of the founders of the New Zealand Institute, wrote from Canterbury to Joseph Hooker at Kew that the native plants 'appear to shrink from competition with these more vigorous intruders'.[82] Darwin himself, in *The Origin of Species*, considered that 'if all the animals and plants of Great Britain were set free in New Zealand, a multitude of British forms would in the course of time become thoroughly naturalised there, and would exterminate many of the natives'.[83]

Writing about New Zealand and the American South at this time, David Livingstone has argued that science was read and used in different ways in different places: 'For racial reasons, Darwin's theory enjoyed markedly different fortunes in Auckland and Charleston. In these two places Darwinism meant something vastly different. In one place it supported racial ideology; in another it imperilled it.' In New Zealand it was co-opted to justify the pathway of settler colonialism and embraced with fervour.[84] J.F. Armstrong, the Government Gardener in Christchurch, voiced this in 1871 in a not uncommon way:

> The indigenous Flora seems to have arrived at a period of its existence, when it no longer has strength to maintain its own against the invading races; indeed, every person who has attempted the cultivation of native plants knows how difficult it is … on account of their weakness of constitution.[85]

In retrospect, weakness of constitution had nothing to do with it, any more than the impoverishment, social and political dislocation, and territorial destruction of Māori iwi can be attributed to a supposed innate inferiority. Rather, both indigenous people and indigenous flora were subject to the increasing might of imperial improvement, being overwritten more and more vigorously on the ground as the numbers of Pākehā and their ambitions soared. It was not always this way. In the early years of European colonisation, Pākehā were necessarily more tentative, their survival often dependent on Māori hospitality and environmental awareness. The next two chapters explore the ways in which the grassing of New Zealand was built on these initial interactions, and the experimentation that followed.

3 Learning about the Environment in Early Colonial New Zealand

Peter Holland, Jim Williams and Vaughan Wood

INTRODUCTION

Takata pai, takata mohio
Knowledge makes a person good

Since the Enlightenment, European science has viewed the world as a web of interconnected and functionally related components. What has already happened in a place is believed to be a good guide to what lies ahead, and procedures as well as technical terms have been developed to record, store, interpret and report experiences and observations in readily understood words, numbers or symbols. In Māori society, whakataukī, such as the words at the head of each part of this chapter, were important ways to communicate knowledge. These widely known, commonly used and orally transmitted sayings were part of the collective wisdom of the people, and compare with the proverbs and wise sayings of literate societies; their origins might have been forgotten by users, but their meanings were understood.

This chapter discusses what European visitors, explorers and pioneers learned about the diverse landscapes of New Zealand that settlers wanted to transform into tracts of productive pasture for sheep and cattle. Pākehā and Māori observed, investigated and used the open country – that is, the lowland grass and shrub lands of eastern New Zealand – in distinctive ways: one framed by the modalities of European science, the other drawing on local environmental learning. Until the 1860s, Pākehā supplemented and extended their own discoveries with information from Māori about weather and climate, hydrology, living things, topography and mountain passes. They later became less reliant on such information, following their own procedures to observe, record, analyse and communicate important details about environmental processes, and how these could affect their lives and livelihoods.

Particular terms and procedures are needed whenever people from one culture seek access to information held by another, and inquirers must have special skills if they are to understand what has been said and how to interpret silences. Traditionally amongst Māori, some environmental knowledge was privy to the observer, some to immediate or extended family members, and some to the tribe. Its maintenance, communication and use were governed by protocols. While there were few restrictions to telling strangers about trails, landmarks and topography, information about valued native plants, animals and food-gathering places was normally tapu and not disclosed to people who lacked the right to know such things.[1]

Māori learned about their environment through close observation of proxies. They remembered the timing of extreme events primarily by reference to genealogies, they understood how weather and other environmental occurrences could restrict travel, affect food gathering, and limit gardening activities,[2] but they lacked concepts akin to maxima, minima and means. In the mid-nineteenth century, ordinary Europeans were used to metaphor and aphorism in political commentary and religious ceremonies, yet few Pākehā recognised the tension between traditional Māori and prevailing European modes of acquiring, storing and communicating environmental knowledge. The first were oral and ritualised, with metaphor and aphorism conveying complex meanings; the second literal and direct, where measurement, scientifically informed observation and the written word were valued.

WEBS AND MEMORIES

Kotahi te kohao o te ngira, he mea mā, he mea pango, he mea whero
The needle has but one hole, but through it pass many coloured
    threads, which, together, enhance each other

One means to frame the years between 1790 and 1870 metaphorically is as a strip of cloth woven from two hanks of coloured threads – shades of brown for Māori, and shades of cream for Europeans and other newcomers – on a loom strung with green threads to represent the land.[3] As affiliations within and between the two peoples changed, so did the textures and colours woven into the cloth. Before 1840, Europeans were few, transient and living in dispersed coastal settlements. Thereafter they became more numerous, bringing with them new goods, words, information, contacts, modes of employment and ways of life. What had been a mostly brown length of cloth gave way to one in which cream threads dominated the weave. Both threads were dependent upon knowledge about how to work, or work with, the green threads of the land.

This knowledge was learned very much 'on the job'. Educational psychologists describe the ways in which people use experience to create structures that frame their thinking as the operation of 'working memory'.[4] Working memory helps explain why humans are innovative, strategic thinkers given to long-term planning, and goal- as opposed to task-oriented. This perspective on environmental learning is captured by a statement in a handbook published in 1849 for the information of intending settlers:

The best interests of the farmer in a virgin soil are comprised in one word – 'experimentalise'. Never mind any man's opinions, for no one has had sufficient experience to form one worth listening to. The greatest talkers on agricultural subjects in a new Colony are invariably the most ignorant. The native [Māori] who pokes a hole in the ground with a stick and drops a potato therein, treading it down with his foot, will produce a better crop, in quality certainly, than the farmer who proceeds, *secundum artem*, to improve a soil which from its over-fertility needs disimproving. The question is how to improve on the native method, rather than how to improve on known [then current European] systems. The native is generally very free with his advice upon his own methods of agriculture, and this is worth listening to.[5]

The ways in which the products of working memory might pass between Māori and Pākehā, as well as amongst Māori and amongst Pākehā, are illustrated in Figure 3.1. Traditionally in Māori society, certain individuals were selected and trained to preserve and transmit vital knowledge: the diagram summarises pathways for the acquisition, retention, maintenance and communication of protected as well as accessible environmental information. Protected information could be reclassified by those responsible for it, then freely communicated. By contrast, within settler society access to potentially useful information was chiefly limited by language, economics and impediments to communication. From the mid-1850s onwards, itinerant shearing gangs, many of them Māori, travelled

36

widely from their home bases. There were also steady streams of visitors to rural homesteads. All dispersed information in written and spoken form around the countryside.[6] In such ways, banks of potentially accessible environmental knowledge expanded and grew more comprehensive.

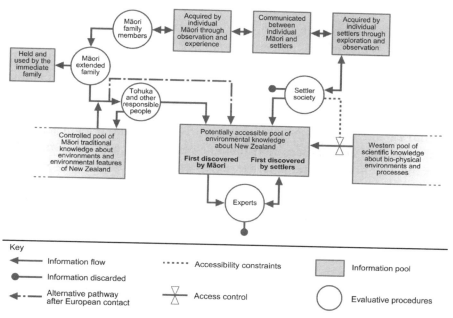

Figure 3.1: Environmental learning in early colonial New Zealand. A systems model of environmental learning by Māori and Pākehā, singly and together, in the open grasslands of New Zealand during the mid-nineteenth century.

Soon after organised settlement began in 1840, networks for compiling and disseminating news, environmental information and good practice were instituted. Newspapers had local reporters as well as correspondents in outlying areas.[7] By the mid-1860s, when provincial and larger rural centres had been linked by telegraph, the circulation of information was more rapid. With this came a greater degree of formalisation of working knowledge. This chapter chooses, however, to represent environmental learning through the eyes and ears of ordinary people. The principal sources for this are oral history, letter books and diaries, contemporary newspapers and magazines. These provide insight into the social interactions of three little-known generations of European settlers. They are also often the only sources of information about otherwise silent people and the changes they memorialised with trees and shrubs, fences and farm buildings on their properties in the New Zealand open grasslands.

LEARNING FROM EACH OTHER

Kei tētahi kakano, he kāhere
Each seed contains the potential for a forest

New Zealand's diverse climate and topography presented its first inhabitants with significant challenges. The Polynesian way of life was geared to the environmental conditions of tropical oceanic islands in the western and central Pacific. Māori arrived from Eastern Polynesia about eight hundred years ago, and close observation of their new home and development of effective technologies and practices were essential if they were to survive, let alone thrive.[8] That they recognised novel environmental opportunities and constraints is evident in their discrimination between varieties of New Zealand flax according to their uses.[9] Māori geographic skills were equally remarkable in an oral culture. When asked to sketch a map of the South Island in 1793, Chief Tuki-Tahua, after his abduction from Northland to Norfolk Island, was able to show the location of places hundreds of kilometres from his New Zealand home.[10]

During the late eighteenth and early nineteenth centuries many different food plants were brought into New Zealand by European visitors and settlers, and Māori skills in observation, adaptation and innovation ensured the successful adoption of many.[11] In 1820, a visiting mariner, Captain Cruise, wrote that Māori 'eagerly adopted the improvements we pointed out to them in their system of agriculture; and they were very grateful for the European seeds distributed among them'.[12] Some introduced food plants allowed Māori to practice horticulture in areas seasonally too cold for kūmara.[13] Soon after European and American sealers and whalers had set up camp on the south coast of the South Island, local Māori were harvesting potatoes and raising pigs for sale to them.[14] A telling measure of their success as cultivators of introduced food plants is that European settlers in towns like Auckland and Nelson were initially dependent on local Māori for potatoes, cabbages, turnips, Indian corn, melons and pumpkins.[15] As late as 1868 Chief Tareha gifted 15 tons (about 15 metric tonnes) of potatoes to hungry Pākehā settlers in Napier.[16]

Māori were acutely aware of place and usually scrupulous about not infringing another's property rights, as the Reverend Frederick Wilkinson found when told by his guide not to take a peach from a certain tree. A 'little way further he allowed me to take [one] from a tree belonging to a relation of his' because he could take that liberty.[17] Those scruples extended to not divulging details about important elements of the cultural landscape, as Walter Mantell became aware while surveying part of South Canterbury for Māori reserves and European agricultural settlement. Without his guides knowing it, he was reasonably fluent in te reo Māori and overheard them agreeing amongst themselves to give him false names of occupants.[18] But few Pākehā recognised that Māori knowledge was orally communicated and ritually maintained.

Māori appreciated use of their language by Pākehā. The surveyor and explorer Thomas Brunner, the ethnographer Herries Beattie, Governor George Grey and the government officer Edward Shortland, to name four of many, understood te reo Māori, learned from tāngata whenua (Māori people native to an area), and frequently acknowledged their sources by name. The instance of Shortland is informative. In the evenings, while traversing the eastern coast of the South Island during the 1840s, his guide Huruhuru told him about the grassy interior of the southern South Island and depicted its prime features on a sketch map.[19] The Englishman found that his Māori guides had names for large and small topographic features, so his knowledge of te reo Māori and protocol enabled him to ask about the environmental conditions and food resources of the South Island open grasslands, which had not then been formally surveyed.[20]

For the most part acknowledgement was generalised – 'as local Māori believe', or 'Māori legend has it' – with entries in Joseph Greenwood's diary indicating the opportunistic nature of many Pākehā contacts with Māori, and how Māori were perceived by European settlers in the 1840s.[21] Boatmen and carriers accounted for almost a third of the 176 entries that explicitly mentioned Māori, with conflict and litigation running a close second. Visits by Greenwood to Māori homes and villages were noted in 12 per cent of the entries, Māori labourers in 10 per cent, visits by Māori to Greenwood's home in 7 per cent, Māori guides in 5 per cent, and translation from English to te reo Māori in 2 per cent. There were also references to gifts of nails and dressed wood, purchased foods and visits by Māori travellers. Greenwood used the term 'native(s)' in 6 per cent of all entries in his diary and the words 'Maorie' and 'Maories' in 1 per cent. The Greenwood brothers had squatted on Māori land in the southern North Island, Banks Peninsula and North Canterbury, and were surprised when this was vigorously contested by its owners. There is nothing in his diary to suggest that Joseph learned from local Māori about the environments, weather systems and climate of those parts of New Zealand where he lived during the 1840s.

Greenwood was perhaps unusual; others valued Māori knowledge of these issues. Over much of the southern and eastern South Island, where grassland farming was concentrated between 1840 and 1870, Māori had little direct experience of horticulture and even less of agriculture and animal husbandry. But they did possess environmental knowledge that could be of much value to Europeans seeking to lessen risk in the conduct of pastoralism and agriculture. For these pursuits, awareness of warning signs about erratic weather changes and floods, and how to deal with these phenomena, was critical. Otherwise, the job would be made much harder, or stock might be lost and crops and gardens destroyed. In addition, in the first quarter-century of organised settlement, mountain passes and other routes over which livestock could be driven were of great interest to Pākehā.

For Māori, a good host was obliged to provide safe passage across tribal land, and Māori knowledge of hill and mountain country proved invaluable to settlers. During the 1840s, Europeans in South Canterbury used Māori tracks that ran inland from Caroline Bay on the South Pacific coast, several of which were later surveyed for roads and streets in the port settlement of Timaru.[22] Further north, the pastoralist T.S. Mannering had cut a track along an established Māori trail to drove sheep between Snowdale and Birch Hill Stations in mid-Canterbury.[23] In the Nelson settlement, local Māori told a New Zealand Company official about a track through the Wairau Gorge that had allowed members of the Rangitane tribe to escape during a raid by Te Rauparaha:[24] it was later used by settlers when they moved sheep and cattle southwards into the tussock grasslands of North Canterbury. An early depiction of the lower Wairau valley is shown in Figure 3.2. The surveyor Arthur Dobson was reported in *The Press* on 2 March 1864 as believing that Māori knew three routes from the Canterbury Plains across the Southern Alps to the West Coast. Mountain passes were of great interest to farmers in the grasslands as possible routes for droving stock west for sale in the goldfields.

Local weather and climate were of considerable interest to Pākehā. While visiting South Westland, Johannes Andersen was told by Māori that if Aoraki (Mount Cook) appeared red at dawn then bad weather would follow and canoes should not put out to sea. Another tradition, recorded by James Cowan, related to the development of an arch of clear sky above the Rangitata Gorge in central Canterbury: if ill-formed, then northwest winds would not persist and stormy weather would move in from the southwest.[25] Ngāi Tahu, the tribe whose territory covered much of the South Island, also realised that for storms which track up the east coast towards Banks Peninsula, the colour of the cloud bank and its apparent rate of approach indicated if the Peninsula would deflect the weather system eastwards into the South Pacific.

Figure 3.2: William Fox, *The Wairau Plain*, 1845. This watercolour shows a group of Māori in the foreground with the grassy, open plains of the Wairau Valley in Marlborough behind. Significantly, he painted the scene again in 1848, replacing the Māori with a Pākehā surveying party. *Source*: Hocken Collections, University of Otago, Dunedin.

For settlers as well as visitors, anticipation of weather events was essential if they were to ensure their comfort and safety and that of their livestock. One evening, while travelling up the east coast of the South Island, Edward Shortland was surprised to find that his overnight shelter had been erected by his Māori guides with the opening facing northeast, even though a stiff breeze was blowing from that direction. His principal guide and companion, Huruhuru, explained that a northeast wind normally dies down in the evening and gives way to a westerly. Shortland was also advised to raft across broad rivers in the eastern grasslands of the South Island during the early morning before the wind picked up and made the craft difficult to steer.

Māori recognised that diverse natural phenomena can indicate seasonal weather. During winter hunts for weka in the back country of the South Island, Māori had observed that these birds would 'go to ground' when the sky had a continuous cover of light grey cloud and air temperatures were warmer than the seasonal norm, both signs of impending snowfall.[26] Lady Barker described Māori as 'strong in weather traditions, and though they prophesied this one [the July–August 1868 storm], it is said that they have no legend of anything like it ever having happened'.[27] As she later wrote about her years at Steventon, a sheep station in the mountains of mid-Canterbury, 'we had nothing to go by except the Māori traditions, which held no record of anything the least like that snowstorm'.[28] During the 1860s there were frequent torrential rainstorms in the West Coast goldfields, and

European residents sought information from local Māori about episodes of foul weather. An article in the 6 January 1868 issue of the *West Coast Times* reported: 'There are Māori traditions which tell us, that at certain intervals, there come and go years without a West Coast summer. We can believe the truth of the legend.' Māori may also have recognised longer-term periodicity in New Zealand's weather and climate, and there is a hint of that in the editorial for the 15 February 1868 edition of the *Otago Witness*: 'From remote Māori tradition, the record of periodical heavy storms, about one in ten years, we believe, has been handed down.'

Rivers ruled the lives of Māori and Pākehā alike, and variations in discharge rate were of particular concern to travellers and stock drovers in the open grasslands. Edward Shortland reported that local Māori referred to the milky water of the Waitaki River as 'he wai-para-hoanga, or water of grinding stone dirt', and his guide Tarawhata assured him that during summer there were marked differences in the depth of water in the Rangitata River between early evening and morning, the latter being the shallower.[29] The guide believed that this was due to snow melt during the day, with discharge surging downriver, peaking by evening and ebbing overnight. That interpretation was not correct, but for many years the well-known owner of Longbeach Station, John Grigg, forbade his men from droving sheep across the Rangitata River between mid-afternoon and early the following morning because of the presumed risk of drowning.[30]

Rivers concerned both rural and town people. In the early 1850s, Henry Sewell described the Rakaia as 'the worst of our Rivers, [and] the terror of travellers'.[31] He also recognised the impediments to communications, including movements of people and livestock, posed by the eight larger and smaller rivers between Christchurch and Timaru, and referred to flooding as 'one of the Colonial questions' because of the often heavy losses incurred while crossing flocks of sheep.[32] Even Charles Hursthouse, ever the enthusiastic publicist for settlement opportunities in New Zealand, described the weather of eastern South Island as 'unquestionably boisterous' and the 'profusion of rivers' as having a 'vicious character'.[33] In his diary on 7 July 1857, the runholder, F.W. Teschemaker wrote that his party could have safely crossed the Rangitata River the previous afternoon but delayed doing so until the following morning: 'Alas for human judgement – the river has risen during the night very much. I suppose there must have been some N[orth] W[est] weather among the hills. What fools we were not to cross last night.'[34] Such anxieties persisted until ferries and bridges made river crossings safe.

Early European visitors found that Māori had an intimate knowledge of plants and animals, including their often complex natural histories. One of them, the Austrian botanist Baron Hugel, declared that 'there is not, in the northern island at least, a single tree, vegetable, or even weed, a fish, or a bird, for which the natives have not a name; and that those names are universally known'.[35] Māori knowledge extended to vegetation change in the tussock grasslands. As E.C. Chudleigh wrote in his journal on 28 May 1862: 'you find a good deal of burned wood all over the hill [in the East Otago goldfields]. The [Māori] have two traditions, one is that the northern tribes burned it when at war with them, the other is that they [themselves] burned the country ... [t]he whole country was wooded once ...'.[36] Edward Studholme, the son of a pioneering sheep and cattle raising family in South Canterbury, also inferred from the abundance of burned logs and root plates of forest trees that Māori had transformed forested areas into tussock grassland by their use of fire as an aid to hunting several centuries earlier, an interpretation that is now widely accepted.[37]

PĀKEHĀ LEARNING FOR THEMSELVES

He tītī huatahi
Muttonbird of one chick, *or* All the eggs are in the one basket

To promoters of British colonisation, the evergreen forests of the North Island suggested a temperate climate and fertile soils, snow-capped mountains implied ample precipitation and large rivers, and the geographical coordinates invited northern hemisphere comparisons: North Auckland with northern Morocco, southern New Zealand with the Bay of Biscay and southwestern France, and everything in between with the Iberian Peninsula. During their early years of residence rural settlers found that local climates were more complex, and required good understanding if pastoralism and agriculture were to thrive.

The climate of the open grasslands reflected the dynamic interplay of easterly and westerly weather systems. The former brought cool to mild air temperatures, low cloud, high relative humidity, occasionally stiff breezes, and episodes of drizzle or heavy rain, while the latter were marked by less settled, often drier, weather with occasional gales and extremes of temperature and precipitation. Most years, especially near the east coast, westerlies predominated in winter and spring, with easterly winds more frequent in summer and autumn. Through the operations of working memory, settlers learned that each weather system posed unique problems requiring strategic thinking if they were to protect, manage and foster valued plants, animals and soils: for example, by establishing a network of hedges and belts of tall trees to shelter livestock and crop plants, as well as to mark field boundaries. Their diaries and letter books describe life in what Henry Sewell termed 'the howling wilderness',[38] and their accounts run the gamut from unrestrained optimism to bitter disappointment.

In October 1842 Robert Stokes, a recent arrival from England who had settled north of Wellington, wrote that 'a flood in New Zealand seems to produce an opposite effect to what it does in England, or a colder climate to ours; it produces a fertilising effect in the deposit which it leaves, and, as it would appear, a salutary effect in destroying the [grass] grub'.[39] At about the same time a more sober observer, Constantine Dillon – the Civil and Military Secretary to Governor Grey – described the climate of Nelson in a letter to family in England as 'not so fine as Tuscany, but it is good. The summer is not hot enough, indeed at Wellington not enough so as to ripen grapes out of doors, but perhaps that is because of the violent gales which are always blowing here.'[40] The windiness of the New Zealand environment impressed other recent settlers, like T. Bremner of Nelson who observed 'the principal, if not the only wind blowing south-east or north-west, and the rapidity with which it changes from the one to the other [in Nelson] would astonish you'.[41]

One early commentator captured the sense of surprise amongst settlers:

Their expectations had been unduly raised by the representation of interested persons in England, who poured into not unwilling ears the most exaggerated stories of the beauty of the scenery, the more than Italian brilliancy of the sky, the delicious mildness of the climate, and the ease with which fortunes were sure to be made. They landed and found the vaunted Canterbury Plains ... little better than a howling wilderness ... Their welcome was sung perhaps by the terrible south-west wind, with its driving rain or sleet.[42]

Henry Sewell frequently described seasonal winds in Canterbury, and in his diary entry on 28 January 1855 wrote: 'The North East wind is the fine weather. It lasts for weeks and weeks together, varied for a day or two at a time with those dreadful Northwesters. The sun is hot, but from 10 o'clock till six there is a fresh breeze.'[43] In the southeast of the South Island, F.C. Pillans noted in his diary on 12 October 1851: 'It is generally observed here that bad weather seldom lasts over three days and as far as my experience goes I have found it to be pretty much the case.'[44] Contrary to expectations, settlers discovered that dry spells were common in the open grasslands of both main islands and that prolonged drought was usually broken by heavy rain. In the words of a columnist in the *Otago Witness*, 'the weather never fails to pay its own debts'.[45]

That European settlers progressively learned about the New Zealand environment is evident from entries in Joseph Greenwood's diary. The vertical axis of Figure 3.3 gives monthly averages for the number of informative weather words he used each day: for example, 'NE wind' counts as one word but 'SW gale' counts as two words because direction was noted and 'gale' implies high velocity. Before 1850 there were few Europeans in Canterbury and no local newspapers, so Greenwood can be regarded as a naive observer. The upwards trajectory in monthly averages over a run of more than two years hints at his growing skill in discerning and recording key elements of the weather where he lived, presumably because they affected his livelihood. Fifteen years later, another young settler in Christchurch, Joseph Munnings, recorded aspects of the daily weather in his diary and it provides a remarkably full account of weather and climate over a run of seven years.[46]

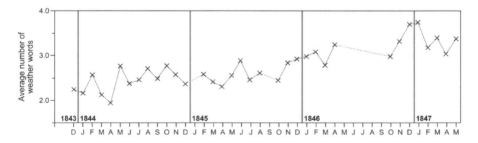

Figure 3.3: Learning about the weather.
In his diary, Joseph Greenwood, an early Pākehā settler on Banks Peninsula and in North Canterbury, used progressively more words to describe each day's weather, indicating his growing ability to discern informative features of the day's weather and his recognition of underlying seasonal patterns. *Source*: compiled from information in Greenwood's diary, Alexander Turnbull Library, Wellington.

Early residents were soon reporting large harvests of grain and potatoes, fruit and vegetables, prompting one correspondent in the 29 February 1848 issue of the *Nelson Examiner* to describe fruit exhibited at a horticultural show in that town as 'quite equal, we believe, to anything which could be produced with the most assiduous attention in any gardens in England'. Settlers were sensitive to the land's productivity and through daily work and observation learned that soil quality reflected environmental conditions. Francis Jollie, a settler in Nelson, noted 'one may observe over the place, as a pretty general rule, that the finer the crop the higher had been the fern which previously grew [there]'.[47] In the late 1840s the surveyor, Charles Torlesse, reported other correlations to the Canterbury Association: an abundance of New Zealand flax in low-lying areas near the coast indicated good soil water retention and a higher water table, whereas flax in combination with toetoe indicated a good moist fertile soil with considerable agricultural potential.[48] As Henry Sewell had seen in the early 1850s, tracts of manuka[49] coincided with thin, dry gravelly soils on the Canterbury Plains.

In his advice to intending settlers, Frederick Weld wrote:

> the first consideration will be the nature of the soil and pasturage, and natural features of the country. A cattle-holder will of course look to rich, succulent pasture, and will probably prefer low-lying land. The sheep-farmer, on the contrary, seeks bold, hilly land, or if it be low, [then] stony, and dry land, with short fine pasture, and shelter from wind and weather as afforded by the natural features of the country.[50]

Whilst little detailed information about New Zealand's diverse environments reached intending settlers before they set sail from Britain, the colonising agencies' assurances of a widespread benign climate were often corroborated by first-hand experience. Unlike those raised in northern Britain, farm animals in the New Zealand lowlands and hill country generally thrived outside year round, and pasture plants could put on some growth in winter. Entries in farm and personal diaries from the 1860s onwards highlight another difference:[51] the cultivation of virgin ground was often delayed until heavier and stronger ploughs manufactured locally replaced imported metal implements broken by the dense roots of perennial tussock grasses and low shrubs. Furthermore, the often-vaunted fertility of New Zealand soils had struck some observers as too good to be true.[52] The myth of virtually unlimited soil nutrients was exposed in the 1860s, when grassland farmers began to observe progressive decline in yields of grain and root crops.

Growing awareness of environmental conditions greatly increased interest in weather prediction. Stock comfort, safety, growth and reproduction were affected by the weather. As Edward Ward, an early Christchurch resident, noted in his diary: 'This outbreak of the weather coincides strongly with Mr Deans's prediction that winter would begin on May 15th, as it did last year.'[53] The often highly variable weather during the 1860s was a frequent topic for newspaper articles, and details were commonly reprinted by newspapers across the country. As the author of an article in the 15 February 1862 issue of the *Otago Witness* put it:

> What the new arrivals must think of the climate of New Zealand I can scarcely say, but I may safely predict that the opinion is not likely to be favourable. A quiet sunny morning will be succeeded by a blustery rainy mid-day, to be again followed by a thick misty evening.

On 8 March, the editor followed with a call for longer-term residents to share their experiences so that gold miners would not leave the Otago diggings for Australia over the winter. Reports from the goldfields, where sheep farming was well established, spurred the nascent interest in scientific weather forecasting. On 17 May 1862 the *Otago Witness* reprinted a long article from a British newspaper on the benefits that would accrue if people had two or three days' warning of an impending storm.

Experience, a continuous record of reliable observations, and sound scientific theories facilitate prediction, and by the mid-1860s settlers had access to almost two decades of informal and formal weather records. Overseas, efforts were underway to place weather forecasting on a scientific footing. One such attempt was the work of a retired naval engineering instructor, Stephen Saxby, who predicted weather events on the basis of the moon's orbit.[54] His book *Foretelling Weather* was published in London in 1861, with a second edition, entitled *Saxby's Weather System*, three years later. Both were known to and debated by colonial New Zealanders. On 8 April 1865, the *Southland News* noted that the previous day was 'one of Saxby's predicted stormy days … but the weather instead of being of a stormy character was remarkably fine and calm'. A few days later, however, it reported that Saxby had written 'if the day marked prove fine and still, distrust the following day and particularly the day after', which was remarkably prescient because the weather across Southland on the ninth and tenth of April was exceptionally bad. Three years later, on 5 December 1868, the *Otago Witness* carried a report from its correspondent in Waitahuna in the tussock grasslands of East Otago about the recent run of bad weather experienced throughout the district. 'Certes, this is a variable clime; and however much Mr Saxby's weather-wise reputation may suffer in other countries, here he can never fail of being regarded as the greatest prophet of atmospheric disturbance.'

By the 1860s, grasslands settlers as well as those in towns were becoming aware of the 'lessons taught' by adverse environmental events. On Christmas Day 1865 Joseph Munnings wrote in his diary:

> Our little peaceable, quick, clear Avon, [was] a torrent of muddy water, rushing along in hot haste to the sea, and [I] heard of much damage done by the over-flowing of the Waimakariri River, a portion of the overflow coming down into the Avon, hence the cause of the alteration. This was the highest fresh that has been for a long time, the highest ever known by many of the settlers, [and] a foretaste of a probable future?[55]

Two days later, the Editor of *The Press* wrote: 'It is idle to shut our eyes to the lessons taught by the floods in the Waimakariri on the last few days. Are we to treat this as a wholly exceptional circumstance or is there a probability of a frequent occurrence of such disasters?' This is one of the earliest references to such environmental hazards.

The year 1868 began badly and grew steadily worse for settlers across the eastern South Island and the southern North Island. During the first week of February, after a short spell of warm humid weather, a sub-tropical storm swept down the east side of the country. On 15 February, under the headline 'Lessons of the Storm', the *Otago Witness* reprinted a long article from the 10 February issue of the *Otago Daily Times* that called for buried telegraph lines to ensure against a repeat of the disruption caused. Flooding in the lower Wairau valley in Marlborough damaged farms and left much of Blenheim submerged. There had been a breakdown in telegraphic communications between the West Coast and Christchurch. Water from the Waimakariri River again seeped into the headwaters of the Avon River thence into Christchurch.[56] Rural homesteads in the Orari Gorge and on the banks of the ordinarily placid Selwyn River were damaged by flood waters, and flocks of sheep washed away. Heavy rain began falling in South Canterbury during the afternoon of 2 February and peaked the following day, when the Waihi River stood 17 feet (approximately five metres) above its normal height. The banks of the Rangitata and Orari Rivers were extensively undercut by flood waters, and residents were driven from the town of Temuka. At daylight on 6 February 'the whole of the [South Canterbury] plains had become a lake from the hills to the sea, with a few islands left here and there ... [and in] the hills the rain was a continuous cascade, every gully being the bed of a roaring torrent'.[57]

Mid-June saw the return of unsettled weather in South Canterbury, where floods as severe as those the previous February were experienced, but without loss of life. Across the tussock grasslands of rural East Otago and in Dunedin, the June flood was described as worse than the flood in February. An article in the *Oamaru Times*, reprinted in the 20 June 1868 issue of the *Otago Witness*, described conditions in North Otago as 'perfectly fearful' with gales from the south and southeast, the barometer falling to 28 inches of mercury, and all rivers in flood. Even worse was to come. Heavy rain began on 29 July and turned to snow over inland Canterbury. Snowdrifts in the mountains did not melt until mid-August, and few back-country properties were spared. Lady Barker's sheep station, Steventon in the upper Rakaia Valley, lost 4,000 sheep out of a flock of 7,000, and the Province of Canterbury lost 500,000 mature sheep and new-born lambs.[58] It was widely described as the worst snowstorm on record throughout Canterbury, and was almost as severe across Otago.

The next three years were wetter than average, and daily weather records in farm diaries show a progressive shift from strong westerly winds inland and northeasterly breezes along the South Island east coast, to easterly weather extending from the Pacific to the foothills of the Alps.[59] The area was experiencing the effects of the Southern Oscillation, although that term was not known then, and it had an adverse effect on agricultural and pastoral farming in the eastern low shrub and grasslands. Cool cloudy weather with rain from the easterly quarter persisted until 1871, when westerlies again began to prevail.[60]

CONCLUSION

Ka mahi te tutuā
People without knowledge must work harder

Well before Pākehā began to settle in New Zealand, Māori had learned to operate within the constraints of their physical environments using the tools and materials at their disposal. Despite being cushioned by relatively sophisticated technological, material and economic resources, the first European settlers still had to acquire local environmental information to survive, let alone thrive, in the open grasslands. They brought much with them, and through their extensive national and international networks had access to more, but those ideas and materials required testing and modification before they could be reliably used in the development of extensive artificial pastures in a new land. As communications within New Zealand and with Australia and the northern hemisphere improved, so the dependency of Pākehā on Māori for environmental information declined, and the newcomers assigned greater authority to the environmental information that they had learned through experience or acquired from the publications of scientists in Britain, Europe and North America. Traditional environmental learning was disregarded, and Māori were progressively marginalised and mythologised.

Even in the 1850s and 1860s, when the country's main pastoral export was wool (Table 1.1), landowners were burning and cultivating shrub and tussock grassland, and establishing improved pastures with imported species of palatable, fast-growing and nutritious grasses and broad-leaved herbs. With the exception of invasive introduced plants like sheep sorrel, Californian thistle and Scotch thistle[61] there are relatively few references in farm diaries and newspapers from the 1850s and early 1860s to pest animals and plants, or to the suite of severe physical environmental problems that later generations of grassland farmers had to resolve.[62] Land instability and river-bank erosion were locally severe in the Otago goldfields, but apparently less so elsewhere. Rabbits were released during the 1860s. Although they quickly spread through the tussock grasslands of both main islands, in 1870 they had still not attained the densities that were to threaten the economic survival of hill and mountain country pastoral properties in the 1880s and 1890s (see chapter 5).

In the lowland shrub and grasslands of the eastern South Island, the years between 1790 and 1870 were a time of adoption and adaptation, innovation and experimentation, when landholders were encouraged to trial imported pasture species and observe different breeds of sheep to discover which were best suited to the particular environmental conditions of their properties. In doing so they could call on what they had learned for themselves about the New Zealand environment, as well as information from importers of livestock, seeds and rooted plants, local newspapers, their neighbours, visitors, and correspondence with business associates and family members. These themes are picked up in the next chapter. In urban areas, interested individuals were keeping daily records of meteorological information and publishing statistical summaries in local newspapers, but timely warnings of adverse environmental events only became possible when telegraphic connections and a network of meteorological observatories were in place.

4 Pioneer Grassland Farming: Pragmatism, Innovation and Experimentation

Peter Holland, Paul Star and Vaughan Wood

INTRODUCTION

Within ten years of the start of organised settlement, British colonists had recognised that the carrying capacity of New Zealand's extensive low shrub and tussock grasslands was too low for economic well-being. It was apparent that these and other native ecosystems would have to be ecologically transformed before their properties could support viable numbers of sheep and cattle. Their response, as outlined in chapter 2, was to fell and fire forests, clear shrub lands, drain wetlands, periodically burn tracts of tussock to encourage growth of palatable and nutritious new shoots, cultivate flat to rolling ground in preparation for sown pasture, and broadcast seeds of pasture plants on steeper and higher land. The international and national models that grassland farmers followed, the expert and informal advice they received, and the mostly introduced plants they used to ensure nutritious grazing for livestock, are the subjects of this chapter.

The vision of the first two generations of European settlers in the open country of New Zealand accords with the general model proposed by the mid-twentieth-century French Canadian ecologist, Pierre Dansereau. Their goal was an ecological system with a persistent, simplified and closely managed food web comprising palatable and nutritious herbage grazed by sheep and cattle. They aimed for the suppression of ecological succession and biodiversity, whilst keeping primary and secondary productivity artificially high. Nutrients unavailable in locally grown herbage would come from mineral supplements, with control of pests and diseases, and management regimes favouring young female animals.[1]

In striving to achieve this goal settlers could draw on local and overseas experience, the published findings of agronomic investigations in Britain, Europe and North America, and commercial sources of plants and animals from across the world. The imperative of economic survival forced them to strike the balance between short-term pragmatic and longer-term experimental approaches to environmental transformation and good farming practice. Newspapers and magazines, like farmer groups and organisations, promoted a particular view of farming: each farmer a scientist, each field an experiment, and each farm a laboratory. Strong advocacy for this model was evident until the mid-1880s, when grassland farming began to change into an industrial activity geared to producing a narrow range of standardised food products for sale in bulk to distant markets.

By 1890, little remained of the once extensive native grass, shrubby and wetland ecosystems of lowland New Zealand, while forest clearance for grassland farming was well underway through much of the North Island. Recurrent economic and environmental difficulties checked progress, but throughout the country environmental transformation, expansion of grassland farming, and intensification of primary production were enhanced by technological developments in the processing and storage of meat and dairy products, and refrigerated transport of them to distant markets (as considered in chapter 6).

RISKS AND UNCERTAINTIES

It can be argued that farmers identify four main types of risk: production risk, price or market risk, institutional risk, and human or personal risk.[2] How a farmer perceives such risks – defined as 'uncertainty that can be approximated by subjective probabilities and the magnitude of the consequences' – is socially conditioned, psychologically subjective, and affected by personal circumstances.[3] In colonial New Zealand, most of the risks faced by European settlers were rooted in their scant understanding of local environmental conditions, the country's embryonic political arrangements, primitive transport and communication systems, conflict with Māori over access to productive land, persistent shortages of investment finance, and uncertain market demand for a narrow range of agricultural and pastoral exports.[4] In the difficult economic conditions of the late 1870s and 1880s (known as 'the Long Depression') the owners or tenants of small farms often worked as contract labour on large properties, learning on the job at no expense to themselves. Larger landowners were better able to carry the costs associated with innovation, experimentation, deploying new machinery, irrigating and making the land-use and management changes needed for agriculture and pastoralism to benefit from refrigerated shipping. Refrigeration enhanced the productive options for New Zealand grassland farmers, but they still faced diverse economic and environmental risks. Their responses included adopting good practice from across the country and overseas, innovating as much as their creditors would allow.[5]

The number and magnitude of risks faced by pioneer grassland farmers declined as their knowledge of the new land deepened through learning on the job, and they became more strategic in their management and planning. As grassland farming expanded, however, unanticipated environmental problems arose: seasonal soil moisture deficits in the inland basins of the South Island and on the arable plains and downlands of Marlborough, Canterbury and North Otago; impeded drainage in the soils of former kauri forest in Northland; and deficient supplies of plant macro-nutrients in the acidic soils of former fernland, and trace elements in the volcanic ash soils of the central North Island and the Bay of Plenty. Poor quality control, allied with considerable environmental variability, meant that grassland farmers lacked certainty that imported pasture plants would thrive on their properties. Differences in expert opinion about the best livestock breeds for the particular environmental conditions of a property further confounded grassland farmers' decision-making. As genetic material flowed into New Zealand, grassland farmers had to become alert to the risks posed by new microbes, new plants and new animals. Furthermore, generally mild weather during the 1840s and 1850s provided little warning of the stormy 1860s and 1870s.[6]

Of the many risks faced, insecure tenure was possibly the most serious. During the New Zealand Wars of the 1860s, Pākehā and Māori farmers alike in Waikato, Bay of Plenty, Taranaki and Hawke's Bay could find their land had become part of the theatre of war. Māori farming operations were further undermined by the state apparatus of land confiscation and individualisation of title through the Native Land Court, which expedited the transfer of Māori land to Pākehā (chapter 2). Where Crown land was held under short-term lease, as was common for pastoral properties in hill and mountain country, Pākehā farmers could also have land sold from under them to freeholders. Without secure tenure, grassland farmers were reluctant to undertake costly but necessary improvements.

Erratic export markets were another influential factor. By the mid-1850s the market for wheat in the Australian goldfields had collapsed, but wool prices were to increase for another decade. During the 1860s, the Otago and West Coast gold rushes had buoyed the South Island's pastoral farming sector by creating strong local demand for meat and dairy produce, but in 1869 farming throughout the country was adversely affected by slumping international prices for wool, the South Island gold rushes were almost over, local markets for primary produce had declined, most pastoral properties were fully stocked, and the Australasian demand for wheat had reached satiety. The early 1870s saw the end of the New Zealand Wars and the start of economic recovery. Until halted following the failure of the City of Glasgow Bank at the end of 1878, a decade of rising international wheat prices had driven up the price of arable land in the South Island, but the New Zealand grassland farming sector as a whole did not recover until well after the advent of refrigerated shipping in 1882.

FARMERS AS EXPERIMENTERS

In his historical account of the settlement of the semi-arid agricultural fringe of South Australia, the American geographer Donald Meinig described the pioneer farmer as 'experimenting with the northern wheat lands [where] water vanished into thin air, and a spark was a fearful agent of destruction in the brittle-dry countryside ... many dismissed the whole region as suitable only for grazing; but others set to work to test the soil and seasons'.[7] In facing their own challenges and risks, New Zealand grassland farmers were also urged to make observation, measurement, comparison and record keeping part of their daily routine. James Hector – soon to become Director of the New Zealand Geological Survey, the New Zealand Meteorological Service, and the Colonial Museum and Laboratory – called in 1862 for the close observation of the effects of local environmental conditions on wool quality:

[it] may lead to very practical results, by showing the correct way by which the natural pasturage should be nurtured and husbanded, and so enabled to carry a much larger proportion of stock than could be at present imagined possible. The kind of observation is simple, the qualified observers [are] many, and the results [are] very important. Let them set to work, therefore, and gather facts respecting this from year to year and experimenting, if they can, and in time they will reap a harvest at profit from this true scientific method.

Later in the decade the Governor, Sir George Bowen, echoed those words in his speech to the inaugural meeting of the New Zealand Institute: 'it might almost be said that every colonist is, unconsciously, more or less a scientific observer'.[8]

Rural experimentation was a contentious topic. An unattributed piece in the first issue of the *New Zealand Country Journal* (a periodical discussed in detail in chapter 8) reported the 'shrewd suspicion' amongst farmers that scientific farming was little more than 'a deception or an amusement'.[9] Some Canterbury farmers declared that they knew enough about farming to teach their sons all they needed to know,[10] but at the same time other farmers and their advisors perceived farming based on scientific principles as useful, interesting, economically beneficial and a valuable way to learn. As one commentator put it, colonial farmers had to conduct experiments if New Zealand agriculture was to advance:

The experiments that may legitimately be expected to be tried by colonial farmers should be limited in extent, but they should be varied in their character, and, to be of any value, they should be continuous. The record of them should also be made in the nearest agricultural papers, so that the lessons may be diffused over the adjoining district.[11]

Newspapers and magazines similarly urged farmers to ascertain through experimentation if a planned activity worked on their properties because any knowledge they personally acquired was more valuable than what they might obtain from others. As the writer of a letter published in the *Daily Southern Cross* on 27 April 1867 asserted with respect to trialling manures, 'although few New Zealand farmers can effect an experiment on so large a scale as Mr Lawes [at Rothamsted, the agricultural research farm outside London], still each, though ignorant of chemistry, may perform an experiment on the subject at a trifling expense of either time or trouble'. Most such experiments were rudimentary – little more than uncontrolled observations, even naive – but several were rigorous in design and implementation, and the findings supported the rational development of grassland farming across the country.

Leonard Wild, an eminent mid-twentieth-century scientist and administrator, argued that New Zealand farmers in the late nineteenth and early twentieth centuries had recognised the worth of agricultural science.[12] Several decades earlier, newspapers were reporting international and local examples of scientific research relevant to grassland farming. On 13 April

1867 the *Otago Daily Times* reprinted a long article from the *Australasian*, under the headline 'Experimental farm', that included these words: 'It is worthwhile now and again taking a trip to Mr Mitchell's Experimental Farm at Flemington [in the Australian State of Victoria] to see what a thoroughly experienced and intelligent farmer and gardener is attempting to do in the teeth of very considerable obstacles.' In a similar vein, some Auckland newspaper reporters wrote in August 1876 about experiments conducted locally by Mr Bollard, a graduate of Glasnevin Agricultural College in Ireland, to deodorise farm manure. They were 'highly gratified at the methodical and scientific manner in which he carries on his agricultural operations'.[13]

Education was seen as critical to allowing well-informed farmers to make the most of their situation. A sequence of newspaper articles available to Otago and Canterbury readers in 1867–8, a time when wool and wheat prices were simultaneously falling, illustrates this point. On 6 November 1867, the editor of the *Bruce Herald* called for agricultural education rooted in scientific knowledge, while on 4 January 1868, *The Press* reprinted an account of 'Science and farming' in Germany, particularly noting the improvements brought about by livestock breeding and reduction in areas of fallow land. The writer urged technical education for farmers akin to that available to trainee engineers and manufacturers. Three weeks later, the *Otago Witness* published an informative piece based on a British textbook, *Coleman's Agriculture*, under the headline 'Agricultural education'. It acknowledged that some topics are 'the province of science to examine and, if possible, determine [so] why should not the intelligent farmer seek to avail himself of this aid and gratefully accept it?'[14] Significantly, the editor of the *Otago Witness* on 22 February 1868 declared that success as a carpenter or a merchant was no guarantee of success as a farmer. For that, a training farm and associated school were needed.

The *Bruce Herald* returned to the educational theme on 1 April 1868, when it reported Sir David Brewster's speech to the Royal Society of Edinburgh, published in the *North British Agriculturalist*, in which he called for recognition of the key role played by science in education and daily life. But a cautionary note was sounded by Professor Wrightson in his speech to the Cirencester Chamber of Agriculture, reprinted in the *Bruce Herald* on 3 June 1868: 'While we decidedly give precedence to experimental knowledge, let us not rashly consign the experience of others to limbo.' In its 19 September 1868 issue, the *Otago Daily Times* published a perceptive, albeit condescending, piece about technical education for intending farm workers: 'To leave the labourer in a state of utter ignorance, as he is too often left, [is] to compel him with his darkened and unaided intellect either to acquire knowledge of scientific husbandry as best he may, or to remain ignorant of its principles through life.'

During this period, James Wilson was a powerful advocate for experimentation in grassland farming. His Ngaio Station has been described in chapter 2. Wilson was deeply interested in the application of science to agriculture and its role in rural education, and his close involvement with Agricultural and Pastoral Societies across New Zealand provided him with abundant opportunities to advance those interests. He also published articles on practical farming in the local newspaper, the *Rangitikei Advocate*. His Scottish father was a member of the Highland and Agricultural Society, read the current agricultural literature, followed developments in British farming, and during the final three decades of the nineteenth century sent to his son in the colony 'a constant stream of letters containing information and advice, exhortation and admonition'.[15]

INNOVATORS AND INVENTORS

The first half-century of grassland farming in New Zealand was the era of the practical farmer, and the still-admired qualities of flexibility and innovation were evident to the visiting French economist, André Siegfried, in 1904. He commented approvingly on the 'empiricism' of New Zealanders.[16] These qualities are also apparent in settlers' unpublished letters and diaries, and show in the questions that new arrivals asked members of the pioneer Deans family in North Canterbury (Table 4.1).

Table 4.1: Questions asked of members of the pioneering Deans family by recent arrivals in Canterbury.

• What is the weather like, and how does it compare with such-and-such a place in Great Britain?
• Is the farm accessible?
• Is there a nearby source of wood for fuel, fencing and construction?
• Will natural features stop livestock from roaming, and keep others' animals out, until I can erect boundary fences?
• How do the different soils on the property compare for fertility, drainage and friability?

Table 4.1 (continued)

• Is there sufficient well-watered flat land for crops of oats (to feed the horses), potatoes (to feed pigs, and for sale), and improved pastures / root crops for winter and supplementary feeding?
• Which livestock and crops are most likely to thrive?
• What implements will I need?
• Are other building materials (for example, rock and limestone) available locally?
• Where can I obtain supplies of flour, sugar, tea, salt and other basic provisions?
• To whom can I sell wool and other produce?

Sources: Association for Founding the Settlement of Canterbury in New Zealand, *Canterbury Papers*, New Series 1–2 (London, 1859), and Deans, J., *Pioneers on the Port Cooper Plains: The Deans Family of Riccarton and Homebush* (Christchurch, 1964).

Until the general advent of steamships, and connection to international telegraph networks, both of which took place in the 1870s, equipment, news and ideas could take several months to make the sea journey between Britain and New Zealand. The delay fostered indigenous solutions to common problems, details of which were diffused across the country by visitors, tinkers, itinerant farm workers, newspapers, magazines and commercial organisations. Joseph Munnings, a young Englishman who took up residence in Christchurch in 1859, exemplifies the wide interests of recent settlers and their diverse sources of information about environment and society (Figure 4.1).

Figure 4.1: (facing page) Where and how Joseph Munnings learned about the environments of Christchurch. Joseph Munnings left southern England aged 18 and emigrated to Canterbury. He arrived in mid-November 1859 and immediately found employment as a farm worker in Governor's Bay on Banks Peninsula, remaining there for 18 months before setting up on his own account in Christchurch as a carter and roading contractor. In December 1863 he entered into a business partnership and from then on ran a general store in central Christchurch. In his diary, he briefly described each day's weather, summarised his commercial and recreational activities, named people whom he had →

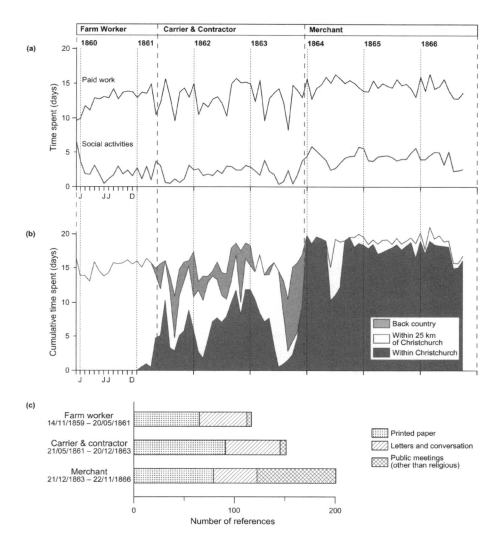

→ met, and commented on the social, commercial and political life of the young settlement. It was assumed that he spent 12 to 14 hours daily on social and business activities in and around Christchurch, and details were extracted from his diary to show (a) the time spent in three types of paid employment, (b) where he was employed (within central Christchurch, within 25 km of central Christchurch, or in outlying rural areas) and (c) his sources of information (books, newspapers and magazines, correspondence and conversations, or public meetings).*Source*: compiled with permission from a typed transcript of the diary (14 November 1859 to 22 November 1866), ARC 1990.50, held by the Canterbury Museum, Christchurch.

By the 1860s, grassland farmers could read about recent developments in science and engineering, agronomy and animal husbandry in locally published or imported newspapers and magazines. In the sniffy words of the editor of *The Press* of Christchurch on 17 March 1865, 'We read our *Times* and *Athenaeum*, and derive the same information from our *Builder* and *Illustrated News* as the inhabitants of any other part of the Empire.' By 1872 the larger towns and regional centres had been linked by telegraph line,[17] and daily newspapers – which regularly reprinted informative articles from local and foreign newspapers, books, magazines and official reports – were widely distributed by coastal shipping, mail rider, coach and, later, the railway. There were also national magazines for a rural readership, chiefly the *New Zealand Country Journal* from 1877 and the *New Zealand Farmer* from 1885. As Annie Wilson of Bulls wrote on 21 July 1887 to her formidable father-in-law in Scotland, 'All colonists are great readers of newspapers and one's papers pass from hand to hand after we have read them.'[18] Information and advice that helped grassland farmers match their operations with local environmental conditions were particularly valued.

Nonetheless, the economic historian Ian Hunter intimates that grassland farming in New Zealand remained exploratory until the 1880s, by which time farmers had developed sufficient practical responses to the risks of weather and climate (as outlined in chapter 3) to be able to rise to the challenge of producing meat and dairy products in bulk for export to Britain. The 'rudimentary landscape' of the new colony was, as he describes it, 'a seedbed for innovation'. His analysis suggests that 'a period of sustained and dramatic innovation was almost inevitable, as the society constructed itself to satisfy the expectations of those who lived within it'. Structural change created cascading effects because 'whole systems for production, transportation, supply, storage, and distribution needed to be created'. Individual entrepreneurs, many of them provincially based, 'forged collaborative links with other individuals and firms to create networks along the commodity chain', in marked contrast to the less flexible Latin American meat industry with its greater dependence on foreign capital and ownership.[19]

English gentry do not seem to have played a key role in the early development of grassland farming. Investors were as likely to be Highland Scots or British whalers.[20] In the words of Simon Ville, 'While US economic expansion was driven by large manufacturing corporations, with evolving internal capabilities, and manned by hierarchies of experienced executives, Australasian development was associated with a predominance of small family farming units of limited resources and experience.'[21] Of key importance in the commodity chain that connected New Zealand farmers and British consumers were the stock and station agents employed by pastoral finance companies, notably the Australian firm Dalgety (founded in 1858), Wright Stephenson (Dunedin, 1861) and the New Zealand Loan and Mercantile Agency (London, 1865). Nurserymen and seed merchants also played a major role in the development of the new grasslands.

On the ground, however, the transformation of New Zealand lowland landscapes for grassland farming was labour-intensive. In its 19 April 1867 issue, the *Otago Daily Times* summarised responses to questions in the recent census about the cost and skills of farm labourers and concluded that the problem was not so much a shortage of manpower as a dearth of skilled and affordable labour. Between 1871 and 1879 one large sheep and cattle station, Te Waimate in South Canterbury, employed in excess of 200 men per annum for periods of days to weeks. Most were itinerant workers, but at least a tenth had their own properties. Typically 50 to 60 young men were on the station payroll for the winter ploughing, and for shearing in December.[22] Entries in a journal kept by residents of The Point, a pastoral property on the high plains and foothills of mid-Canterbury, between 1867 and 1871 showed the total workforce varying between a winter low of five or six men to about 20 during shearing in January.[23] The people living on large nineteenth-century rural properties included owners or managers and their families, labourers, dairy maids, shepherds and stockmen. Seasonal tasks like ploughing, harvesting, shearing and carting were often done under contract. Internal fences were usually erected in winter by resident workers, but contract labour was also employed.

The cost of agricultural labour was high relative to Britain, if it could be found at all during the gold rushes; this gave a further incentive for farmers to embrace and invent new technologies. Despite the dominance of imported farm machinery, particularly from North America,[24] local tinkerers and inventors strove to improve standard agricultural machinery. In Southland, Robert Cockerell's mole plough allowed farmers to economically drain persistently damp areas in preparation for pasture establishment.[25] The *Otago Witness* on 5 September 1889 reported that Dobbie's patent broadcast seed sower had recently been demonstrated at Maheno near Oamaru. Described as 'splendid' for wheat and oats, it worked less well with lighter grass seed, an engineering problem that was resolved locally as more land was cleared and sown for pasture. In a few localities, environmental challenges were to prompt investment in grander capital works too. Duncan Cameron, for example, had constructed over 60 kilometres of water races on his land at Springfield in mid-Canterbury by 1880. About the same time, Murray,

Roberts and Co. drained about 600 hectares of their Henley estate on the Taieri Plain outside Dunedin. Henley was then subdivided into 15 farms of 40 hectares.[26]

MATCHING PLANTS TO PASTURES

Landscape transformation in the low shrub and grasslands was large scale and intensive during the nineteenth century.[27] For some writers on agriculture, the 'gold standard' was farming as practised in Northern Europe, particularly Prussia, where the 'miracle of the multiplication of food has been worked by knowledge of physical and economic laws'.[28] In general, only managed swards of introduced pasture plants were thought to ensure profitability. In the lowlands, typically in winter, landholders harrowed and ploughed the ground after tussock grasses and low shrubby plants had been flattened and burned. Seeds of selected pasture plants were usually sowed after three or four months' fallow, by which time frost had broken clods and produced a finer tilth. In former wetlands seeds were broadcast soon after drainage and cultivation, and in forest country seeds were usually scattered on the cool ashes after axe, saw and fire had reduced the above-ground cover. In forested areas, cultivation and levelling followed as tree stumps and charred logs were progressively removed and traces of the former forest cover were erased (Figure 2.1).[29]

The object was to create a functional, structured and self-sustaining mixture of pasture plants that would resist invasion by weeds, provide almost year-round grazing for sheep and cattle, and require minimal maintenance. It was widely assumed that the soil would continue to provide essential nutrients. To maximise their chances of creating such a sward, farmers were urged to devote considerable effort to matching grasses to environmental conditions.[30] In the words of the English industrialist turned capitalist farmer Joseph Mechi, reprinted in the *Bruce Herald* of 12 June 1867, 'one of the most important causes of success in agriculture is to adapt your crops and animals to the climate and soil. An infringement of this natural law is sure to be attended with loss.' The *Weekly Press* on 8 July 1865 promoted a safety-first policy for farmers sowing introduced grasses, observing that 'different soils require different mixtures of seed, and the more the varieties of the grasses the greater is the certainty of each adapting itself to its own particular soil and situation'. Two decades later, the words of farmer and agriculturalist, William Morgan, in the March 1883 issue of the *New Zealand Country Journal*, echoed Mechi's more ambitious goals:

'adaptability, that is, having grasses adapted to certain soils and situations' was as much a 'matter of intrinsic importance' as variety when attempting to establish a permanent pasture.[31]

The manager of Taipo Hill in North Otago exemplifies the innovative and inquiring spirit of these early grassland farmers. In the mid-1870s, a half-century before the quality of commercial grass and clover seed was officially certified, he established quarter-acre (0.1 hectare) plots, planted seeds of the 13 most common pasture grasses, checked germination, and measured seedling growth.[32] A decade later, another agricultural correspondent commended this practice to grassland farmers in formerly forested country in the North Island.[33] As the Taipo Hill letter book of December 1875 shows, the manager employed a similar experimental approach when sowing imported larch seeds in various situations to ascertain which favoured germination. In the following May he also scarified then harrowed several acres of arable land to determine if that would eliminate weeds before the crop was sown.

In a similar vein, the Dixon family at Eyrewell and the Moores at Glenmark in North Canterbury sowed seeds of native tussock grasses in recently burned manuka shrub land in an experiment to determine if the mature plants would provide shelter for finer and more palatable native species.[34] In 1879, a farmer at Dromore in mid-Canterbury identified one highly productive individual of perennial ryegrass and another of Italian ryegrass on his property, collected seeds from each, planted them, and later harvested the new crop of seeds. Within several generations he had achieved fairly pure lines of two important pasture grasses.[35] A decade later, after he had failed to establish a permanent sward dominated by perennial ryegrass, George Steel of Wairuna Bush in Southland ordered seeds of 16 different pasture grasses from a supplier in London. All but one germinated, and each summer thereafter he collected seeds from the most vigorous plants, sowed them, and in time achieved a productive, multi-species, permanent pasture. One widely read commentator called on grassland farmers across New Zealand to conduct experiments such as these because the findings of agronomic research done elsewhere could not be expected to apply with equal force in this country.[36]

In the early decades of organised settlement, provincial settler institutions also had a hand in this experimental work. Robert Wilkin, writing in 1879, recalled how the Christchurch Acclimatisation Society had taken an active interest in trialling new grasses 20 years earlier. The Auckland Acclimatisation Society, under the direction of J.C. Firth, went even further, conducting trials on pasture grasses in the Auckland Domain in the late 1870s. Curators of municipal botanical gardens, like the Armstrongs in

Christchurch and Thomas Waugh in Invercargill, monitored the growth of promising pasture grasses in experimental plots.[37]

While most of this effort went towards introduced grasses, indigenous plants were not entirely overlooked. Some farmers, amongst them knowledgeable owners of large pastoral holdings, were interested in tracing native New Zealand grasses and broad-leaved herbs that were fast growing and perennial, palatable and nutritious to livestock, tolerant of intensive grazing and able to produce economic yields of good-quality seed. A further desired trait was the capacity to re-establish spontaneously when the death of a mature plant created an opening in the sward. As W.T.L. Travers put it:

Of meadow and pasture plants, I believe we possess many valuable species . . . All stockmen agree in praising the feeding qualities of the native grasses, and I have seen sufficient to satisfy me that many of them could most advantageously be mixed with imported grasses in forming artificial pastures. The secret of the value for feeding purposes of old pastures lies in the fact that they contain a great variety of grasses of varying times of maturing, and we have but to take the hint in laying down new pastures in order to ensure equal feeding value.[38]

In the 1870s, the Canterbury Philosophical Institute established a committee to collect information about the growth features and requirements of more than 30 native pasture plants, but this move received little support from local farmers.[39] The eminent Otago botanist, John Buchanan, a firm believer in the superior fattening qualities of native grasses, felt that education had failed to promote this, and hoped that his *Manual of the Indigenous Grasses of New Zealand*, published in 1880, would bring redress. Within a decade, however, widespread cultivation of root crops rendered irrelevant the winter-feeding qualities that Buchanan had praised.

Travers was one of the first New Zealand commentators to argue that grassland farmers should mimic nature by selecting mixtures of grasses and broad-leaved herbs which had growth peaks at different times.[40] The functional structure of such a pasture would conform to the model advocated by British agronomists like Faunce de Laune: an emergent layer of tall, perennial, fairly coarse grasses; an intermediate layer of shorter, fine-leaf grasses; and a ground layer or 'sole' of red or white clover, with other broad-leaved herbs in small quantities to provide 'bite' for sheep. Figure 4.2 shows growth periodicity in important pasture plants of the 1860s and 1890s, arranged by layers: tall often coarse grasses, shorter fine grasses, and spreading legumes. A few species were widely used, but others were more localised.

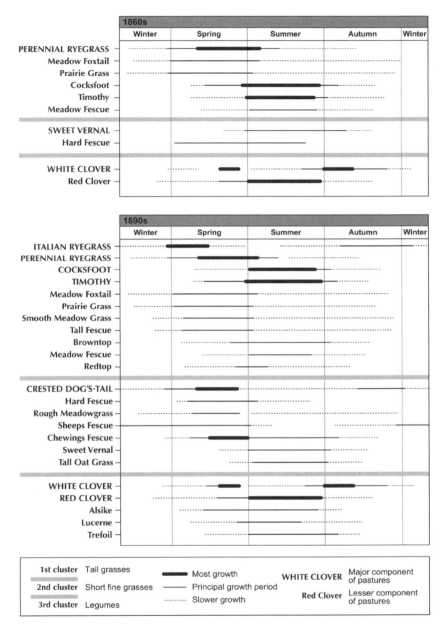

Figure 4.2: Plants for sown pastures in the 1860s and 1890s: an emergent layer of coarse grasses (first cluster), an intermediate layer of fine grasses (second cluster), and a ground cover mostly of clovers (third cluster). *Sources*: Levy, E.B., *Grasslands of New Zealand* (Wellington, 1951), pp. 123–24, supplemented by information in Appendix 2.

A farmer might not have sown all the listed species, but would have sown richer mixtures in well-watered sites where the pasture could be expected to last at least five years before resowing was required. Ideally, the mixture of species would quickly cover the top soil, persist and offer few ecological opportunities for weedy plants to become established. As one commentator stated:

If permanent pasture-land were brought by the plough and harrow to a proper tilth, and sown with a selection of grasses and clovers of various habits of growth that would be in equilibrium with each other, and so associated as to severally attain their times of blossoming at different periods, and thus afford a succession of succulent herbage from early spring to the end of autumn, it would – having regard to being allowed due rest at times by the shifting of the stock to other paddocks similarly cultivated, and the absence also of overstocking – carry more stock relatively, and fatten them more quickly ...[41]

Several broad-leaved herbs in recommended seed mixtures later became adventives on roadsides, in waste ground and domestic gardens, notably birdsfoot trefoil, chicory, parsley, plantain, yarrow and vetch.

Newspapers kept farmers informed of overseas innovations in pasture management (see chapter 8). One such innovation was the use of prairie grass. On 2 November 1864, *The Press* (Christchurch) reprinted a long article about Californian prairie grass sourced from the *Mark-Lane Express* (London) via a Melbourne newspaper, and originally published by the Imperial and Central Society of Agriculture of France. It had recently been introduced to France and Britain, where its nutritional qualities and its persistence for six to eight years were valued. The *Bruce Herald* on 22 February 1866 described it as a 'superior summer grass' for southern New Zealand pastures.

Pioneer farmers had access to many imported pasture plant species, and seed quality was the most pressing instance of *caveat emptor* they faced until compulsory seed certification in the 1920s and 1930s brought some certainty. Farm advisors and authors of newspaper and magazine articles warned grassland farmers about the critical importance of sowing only good-quality seed, but very often – as seen in chapter 1 – this advice was not heeded. Yet by 1890 grassland farmers could choose from more than 50 species of commercially available pasture plants and seek advice from seed merchants, periodicals and experienced farmers on the composition and application rate appropriate to the environmental conditions of their properties. Figure 4.3(a) shows changing numbers of commercial pasture

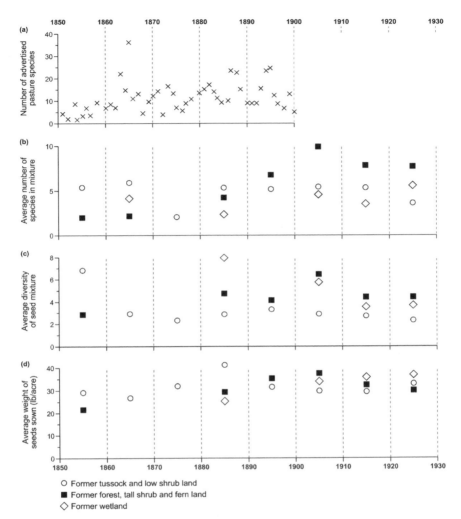

Figure 4.3: Changing mixtures of pasture plants: (a) numbers of pasture plant species advertised annually in the *Otago Witness* between 1851 and 1900; (b) recommended numbers of pasture plant species in seed mixtures, 1851 to 1929; (c) diversity of recommended seed mixtures for sown pasture, 1851 to 1929; and (d) application rates, in pounds of seed per acre (about 1.12 kilograms per hectare), of recommended mixtures of pasture plant seeds, 1851 to 1929. The graphed values of species richness, diversity and application rate are decadal averages for grassland farms in (1) former tussock and scattered low shrub land (open circles), (2) former forested, tall shrub and fernland (solid squares) and (3) former wetland (asterisks). *Source*: a wide range of contemporary newspaper articles, agricultural magazines, scientific serials and farm diaries.

plants advertised in the *Otago Witness* annually between 1851 and 1900. The peaks coincide with periods of economic boom for grassland farmers, and the troughs are when farm labour was too costly because of depressed economic conditions or competition from gold mining for manpower.

By tracing almost 1,000 recommended seed mixtures in newspapers, magazines and official reports published between 1850 and 1929, it was possible to portray decadal averages of pasture species (Figure 4.3(b)), the diversity of the mixture (Figure 4.3(c)), and the application rate in pounds per acre (Figure 4.3(d)). These are given for the three macro-environments of grassland farming in New Zealand: that is, the lowland shrub and grasslands, wetlands, and bush. Absence of an average simply signifies lack of information.

The average number of pasture species in recommended mixtures increased during the second half of the nineteenth century, peaked during the first decade of the twentieth century, and later declined. The graph uses the Modified Simpson's Index from plant ecology. A value close to 1.0 indicates dominance by one species. Larger values indicate two or more species dominating the mixture pasture – for example, either cocksfoot or perennial ryegrass alone or mixed with red clover or white clover – and values equal to or a little less than the total number of species sown indicate approximately equal weights of all recommended species in the seed mixture. In contrast to the diverse mixtures recommended for permanent pasture on well-watered sites, less diverse mixtures in keeping with temporary pastures (which made a break from cropping) were usually preferred for thin dry soils. Grassland farmers in New Zealand were not alone in testing ways to ensure species-rich ensembles for pastures, but Alfred (A.H.) Cockayne, the eminent agricultural scientist and administrator, considered that they probably sowed more species per hectare than farmers in other countries. As one commentator put it, 'no single grass will ever make a good pasture … [because] in this Colony all pastures have a tendency to run out; that is, the best grasses disappear, and their places are taken by inferior plants in a few years – [the pace] varying with the quality of the soil'.[42]

In line with British practice, perennial ryegrass was most frequently the dominant grass in sown pastures. It was palatable and nutritious for sheep and cattle, one of the first of the sown grasses to put on a surge of growth in spring, and a prolific seeder, but its acknowledged disadvantages were slow growth in summer, shallow roots, and commercial varieties that were not long-lived perennials (further details are given in the biographies of leading grasses in Appendix 2). On 22 February 1868, the *Otago Witness* reprinted an article, 'Growing grass for sheep' from the *Canterbury Times*, which noted the almost invariable mix of perennial ryegrass and white clover in sown pastures. However, it went on to declare:

> What we want here [in Canterbury] for pasturing in summer is a grass that will send down its roots deep into the subsoil so that it will not be affected by the often long-continued droughts and hot winds. The cocksfoot grass seems to answer all requirements ... sow more cocksfoot and less ryegrass, and don't be niggardly with the clover seed, and don't overstock for the first year.

The author was confident that such a pasture would support a year-round average of three sheep per acre (seven or eight sheep per hectare). Cocksfoot was one of a number of grasses that came into fashion from the 1880s, when the reputation of perennial ryegrass as the dominant species in permanent pastures came under attack.

PAYING FOR LOST NUTRIENTS

Settlers tried a variety of methods to cope with unanticipated problems relating to New Zealand's relatively infertile soils. In Britain such soils would have been treated with copious amounts of farmyard manure, but in colonial New Zealand stall or yard feeding was uncommon, skilled labour scarce, and the cost of collecting and spreading animal manure on a large scale prohibitive.[43] Farmers made use of what was at hand. The pioneer residents of The Point station mucked out pigsties and cow byres for manure to spread around young potato plants. Other attempts to maintain or improve soil fertility in sown pasture involved soil amendments and mineral fertilisers. The first of these was lime, and as early as 3 December 1842 the *Nelson Examiner* was extolling it as a remedy for the 'sourness' suffered by pastoral land previously covered by bracken.

Farmers later discovered that nitrogen impoverishment was caused by rotting fern root, and the problem was temporary.[44] By the 1880s and 1890s ground limestone was being spread on pastures to neutralise soil acidity, enhance the growth of perennial ryegrass and white clover, and inhibit acid-loving weeds. A letter to the *Southland News*, published on 8 February 1868, detailed the efforts of 'Timothy' of Waikiwi to eradicate sorrel: 'I have recently been trying experiments with lime, but it is desirable that the experiment should be tried on a variety of soils, and in a variety of positions.' He called for 20 farmers each to buy a bag of lime, spread it where sorrel was dominant, and record the effects. Perhaps the most prominent early advocate of liming was Thomas Brydone, who superintended its use to great effect on 200 acres (80 hectares) of pasture at the New Zealand and Australian Land Company's estate at Edendale, Southland in 1890.[45]

The first 'artificial' fertiliser (a term signifying fertilisers of any type from sources beyond the farm)[46] to be tried was guano. Small cargoes of Peruvian guano reached Nelson via Australia in 1854, and guano was sold in Wellington, New Plymouth and Auckland the following year. One ton (about 1,000 kilograms) of imported guano cost the equivalent of several months' wages for an agricultural labourer, and its use was only economical in the low-fertility clay podzols of North Auckland,[47] where it was employed on formerly forested land to ensure a good first crop.[48] Cheaper guano from islands in the mid-Pacific,[49] along with locally manufactured bone dust, could supply the phosphorus needed for pasture establishment.[50] Various types of guano were used on South Island grassland farms during the Otago and West Coast gold rushes, with Thomas Murray of Mount Stuart Station reporting that an application rate of one hundredweight per acre (about 125 kilograms per hectare) had produced a 'quite extraordinary growth of grass', so much so, in fact, that perennial ryegrass seed germinated too thickly.[51] By 1867, there were bone mills in Canterbury and Otago, selling bone dust to farmers for use in fields of turnips grown for winter feed, to prepare the soil for permanent pasture or support the normal crop rotation.[52] Root crops, as John Beharrell told members of the Kaiapoi Farmers' Club in 1875, were 'most likely to repay' the use of artificial fertilisers.[53]

By the mid-1870s small quantities of superphosphate were being imported. This mineral fertiliser seems to have been manufactured by Goldsmith and Company in Dunedin in 1876,[54] and J.A. Wilson of Auckland dissolved animal bones in sulphuric acid pools on White Island in 1879.[55] The first commercial-scale production of superphosphate was in 1882 at T.C. Moorhouse's works at Belfast north of Christchurch and at Kempthorne Prosser's in Burnside south of Dunedin.[56] By 1887 the latter was making superphosphate at its Westfield plant in Auckland. Nearby meat freezing works provided a steady stream of bones for grinding, but this was not their only connection with agricultural fertilisers. In the words of one reporter 'the impetus which the frozen meat trade must undoubtedly give to the rearing and fattening of stock', and the coincident 'establishment of the manufacture of superphosphate of lime', meant that 'the attention of farmers' was now 'often engaged' by the question of superphosphate's employment on turnip crops.[57] The Waikato Farmers' Club, for instance, was by 1889 experimenting with artificial fertilisers and lobbying business and government to improve their quality and availability.[58]

James Belich has described how the transport of meat and dairy produce from New Zealand to Britain replaced 'an extractive economy [i.e. one based on the export of gold and kauri timber] with a more sustainable one',[59] but even in the late nineteenth century grassland farming was considered extractive. The *Otago Witness* noted on 11 November 1882 that the establishment of the Belfast superphosphate works was a welcome development 'in consequence of the attention which is being paid to the meat-preserving industry ... [since] every cargo of produce that leaves our shores represents a loss to the soil and our present system of agriculture does but little to restore the deficiency'. In 1891, Sir James Hector estimated that the country's annual meat exports resulted in the loss of one million pounds (450 tonnes) of plant nutrients, most of which had to be replaced by application of locally produced and imported mineral fertiliser.[60] Nutrient accounting had been anticipated by Justus von Liebig in his *Familiar Letters on Chemistry*, published in 1845. To Liebig, knowledge of the chemical composition of farm outputs, given by ash analyses, enabled the farmer 'by simple calculation [to] determine precisely the substances he must supply to each field, and the quantity of these, in order to restore their fertility'.[61] Nevertheless, imported guano and rock phosphate came at a cost to producer and consumer alike,[62] and it was several decades before the true cost to the New Zealand environment was recognised.

Ironically, just when mineral fertilisers and advanced farming techniques were allowing achievement of the goal of semi-permanent pasture in many parts of New Zealand, there had been a decline in the use of working knowledge gained earlier in the nineteenth century. Forest clearance for pasture accelerated in the 1880s and 1890s, triggering episodes of flooding, drought and soil erosion. Serious though they were, these effects were less frequently noted in the press and official documents than the upsurge of livestock diseases and growth in numbers of pest plants and animals. Amongst new diseases capturing attention were ryegrass staggers and facial eczema, two pasture-sourced afflictions which affected grazing sheep. Various legislative measures were initiated, notably the Rabbit Nuisance Act 1876 and subsequent amendments, the Small Birds Nuisance Act 1882, and the Codlin Moth Act 1884. The noxious weed clauses in the Public Works Act 1888 were, however, opposed by grassland farmers as too draconian. Regional differences over which sown grasses were weedy were also evident. In a published letter, one North Island farmer recommended blue grass for permanent pasture, to which the editor appended a note describing it as 'a troublesome weed' in Canterbury.[63] Similarly, in 1886 some of Otago's wealthiest families took to the Supreme Court a case centred on whether or not sowing blue grass had ruined the value of a leasehold property.[64]

CONCLUSION

Until the turn of the century, wool was New Zealand's main primary sector export (Table 1.1). After local demand for sheep meat had been met, carcasses were rendered for tallow and bones. From the mid-1880s, refrigerated shipping provided access to distant markets for meat and dairy products, as chapter 6 demonstrates. New economic opportunities drove the shift to multi-purpose animals and increased local demand for breeding stock, topics explored in chapter 5.[65] New sheep breeds required high-yielding nutritious pastures. During the 1880s, the area of sown pasture doubled from 1.44 million to 2.82 million hectares as new land was taken up (Figure 1.1), and its inherent fertility was rapidly depleted.[66] This change was particularly apparent in the North Island, where sheep numbers nearly doubled in the 1880s and cattle numbers expanded by 50 per cent. In the 1890s, these figures continued to grow, but those in the South Island stayed more or less the same.[67]

John Grigg wrote to James Wilson that he had not seen 'permanent pasture in New Zealand – all grassland has a tendency to deteriorate so far as I have been able to observe'.[68] Southland farmers had come the closest to achieving such permanence, not having experienced die-back in perennial ryegrass until the drought years of the mid-1880s.[69] However, with the expansion of North Island farming into cut-over and burnt-forest areas, it became a pressing need. Farmers aspired to artificial pastures of palatable grasses and broad-leaved herbs that would not need cultivation or resowing for at least a decade, but the poor quality of commercial seed, weed infestation, and variable soil moisture undermined these ends. Nonetheless, the implicit goal was a comprehensive makeover of ecological systems that had evolved in isolation from people, replacing them with largely artificial systems assembled from introduced plant and animal species. In part pragmatic, in part drawing on experience elsewhere, and in part guided by scientific principles, settlers' direct and indirect transformative actions entrenched an alien model for the emerging artificial landscapes of rural New Zealand for decades to come.

5 Pastoralism and the Transformation of the Open Grasslands

Robert Peden

INTRODUCTION

The first large-scale transformation of New Zealand's landscape by Europeans took place in the open country of the South Island between 1841, when organised settlement began, and the turn of the twentieth century. This transformation had a profound impact not only on these grassland environments, but also on the shaping of New Zealand. Apart from a decade from the mid-1860s to the mid-1870s, when gold was the most export-valuable commodity, returns from products grown on the South Island tussock grasslands – fine Merino wool, grain, and later half-bred and cross-bred wool, and sheep meat – provided the stimulus for the growth of the New Zealand economy in the colonial period (Table 1.1).[1]

Contrasted with the South Island, most of the North Island developed much more slowly. There was some open country in the Wairarapa and Hawke's Bay that was opened early for sheep farming, but large areas of land only became available after it had been confiscated from Māori following the bitter wars of the 1860s. Much of this was in fern and bush, or thick forest, and difficult to develop into farmland. In the South Island all of the eastern region was purchased from Māori between 1841 and 1857, which opened up this huge tract of land to Pākehā settlement. By 1865 pastoralists had explored and claimed extensive runs covering virtually everywhere up to the main divide of the Southern Alps. The dominant vegetation of this region at the beginning of colonisation was a mixed shrub–grassland complex. Burning soon turned it into tussock grassland for grazing sheep.

73

This chapter focuses on the ways in which pastoralists experimented in order to adapt their approaches and methods to the conditions of New Zealand's grasslands. They introduced animals, plants, ideas, techniques and technologies that irrevocably changed the open country of the region. In turn, the characteristics of the environment and the requirements of the international agricultural commodities market encouraged pastoralists to refashion their animals, plants and methods. They learned by trial and error how to manage their stock and the variable resource endowments of the land. By the early twentieth century they had developed different production systems to suit different types of country. On the plains and easy downlands a mixed farming system of cropping and sheep fattening was well established; on the easy hill country a semi-intensive pastoral farming had been developed.[2] The original system of land management, extensive pastoralism, remained only on the semi-arid valleys and basins in the lee of the mountains and the hard hills and alpine 'high country'.

The argument of the chapter is that the first generation of pastoralists transformed the open country of New Zealand in the second half of the nineteenth century with a considerable degree of deliberation. Using Mt Peel Station in the foothills of central Canterbury as a case study, it will examine the pastoralists' methods, including tussock burning, stocking the land, and sheep breeding, as well as exploring the unintended consequences of the liberation of exotic animals and plants into the open country, in particular the spread of rabbits. It will also assess long-standing criticisms of the pastoralists' methods by a variety of commentators. The discussion will illustrate that a distinctive feature of the open country was, and remains, the variety of landscapes and climate zones across the region. This had considerable influence on the way pastoralism developed and on the different outcomes in different districts.

ASSESSMENT AND OCCUPATION OF THE OPEN COUNTRY

Charles Clifford and Frederick Weld were among the earliest pastoralists to take up land in New Zealand. They started out in the Wairarapa in the North Island in 1843, but soon realised the potential of the open lands of the South Island. In 1847 they leased a huge block of land in the Cape Campbell area, where they established Flaxbourne Station. Others soon followed and by the end of 1850 most of the land in the Wairau and Awatere Valleys had been claimed by pastoralists. In Canterbury the Greenwood brothers established Motunau Station in 1847. However, the real scramble for runs in the region did not begin until February 1852 when a formal system for leasing what was called 'waste land' (that which belonged to the Crown but had not been freeholded) was established. Within three years all the plains and downs, from the Hurunui River to the Waitaki River, were claimed for sheep runs. Pastoralists then moved into the mountains to the west and finally into the inland basins and mountains of the Mackenzie Country and Central Otago. The last run to be applied for was Birch Hill, at the foot of Mount Cook, in 1865 (Figure 5.1).

There were considerable variations over quite short distances in the landscapes and climates of this vast area. This meant that there were marked differences between the resource endowments of stations that were taken up.[3] This was the case even on the plains, with some runs having better and deeper soils while others had only shallow and stony soils that were both less fertile and more prone to drought. After Christchurch was established, nearby land was occupied first, any newcomers generally having to move further and further out. That nearest to Christchurch was occupied first, with newcomers generally having to move further and further out. There were some exceptions. In 1853 land hunters passed over the light and stony land on the plains between the Ashburton and Rangitata Rivers to take up heavier land in South Canterbury. However, the following year all the plains between the Ashburton and Rangitata were claimed, regardless of their characteristics.

The establishment of Mt Peel Station by John Barton Arundel Acland and Charles George Tripp provides an example of how pastoralists assessed and occupied the South Island grasslands.[4]

The two Devonshire men made several journeys to the Mount Peel area in 1855 and early 1856 exploring and burning the country. Tripp recalled their first visit to the place saying 'we thought, if it could produce such coarse herbage, with that burnt off regularly, and well stocked, it must produce fine grass in time'.[5] People laughed at them when they decided to explore this mountainous landscape, and one runholder recalled that Acland was thought a 'harmless maniac' for taking up Mt Peel.[6] Nonetheless, Mt Peel proved to be a very productive station. It had nearly 50 kilometres of sunny country between the Rangitata River and the Mount Peel Range. Land that lies into the sun grows feed earlier in the spring and later in the autumn than flat land or south-facing country. Snow thaws quickly off sunny faces but can lie for long periods on cold country. Compared with most high country properties this is low-altitude land, with the homestead at 300 metres above sea level, and the western boundary at 450 metres. The lower the altitude, the longer the growing season (Figure 5.2).

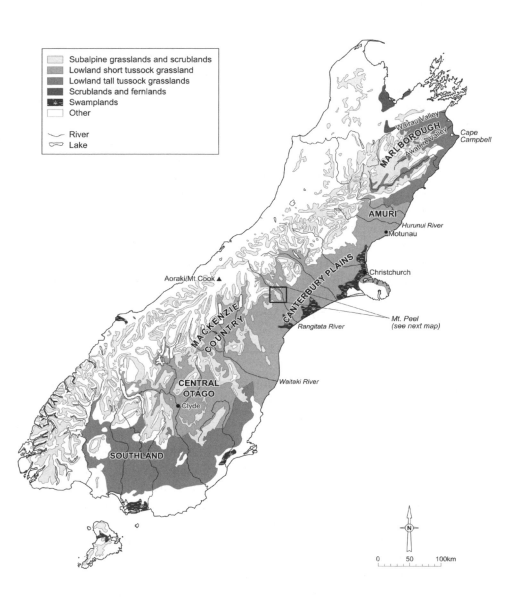

Figure 5.1: Map showing the distribution of South Island tussock grassland environments, c. 1850, and names of places and features used in this chapter. *Source*: McLintock, A.H., *A Descriptive Atlas of New Zealand* (Wellington, 1960), Map 15.

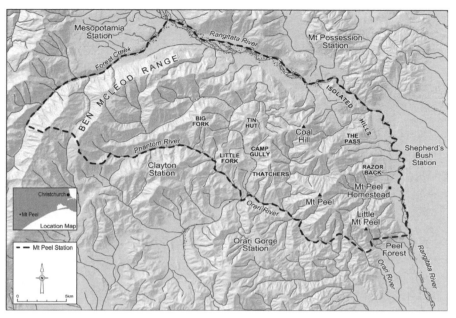

Figure 5.2: Map of Mt Peel Station, 1889. Numerous rivers and creeks provided stock water and water for other uses on the station. The long stretch of sunny, low-altitude country fronting the Rangitata River that helped make Mt Peel such a productive property is clearly evident here. *Source*: redrawn from part of South Canterbury Runs Map, Acland Family Papers, Box 89, 1889, Macmillan Brown Library, University of Canterbury, Christchurch.

Mt Peel had another advantage over many other stations: the variety and balance of its land types. The lower country along the Rangitata valley comprises river flats, fertile terraces and easy hills, with the higher parts being steep hills rising to 2,133 metres. The back side of the Mount Peel and Ben McLeod ranges took in the Orari country consisting of about 16,000 hectares of steep tussock hills. Most of this lies away from the sun, so it is cold country, but it does not dry up in warm weather and provides ample feed for sheep in summer and autumn. Mt Peel also lies in a high-rainfall zone, albeit with considerable variation, with the homestead area receiving, on average, 1,140 millimetres annually compared to 756 millimetres at the western boundary at Forest Creek. This ensured that drought was a rare occurrence and in conjunction with the extensive area of sunny country made the station highly productive (see Figure 5.3).[7]

Figure 5.3: Photograph of Mt Peel station, 1867. This photograph was taken early in 1867, just after the house was built. Round Hill is covered in native bush; in the background are the open tussock hills of the Mount Peel Range. There is a post and rail fence and gorse hedge in the foreground. *Source*: 1995/2, Neg. 3-23A, Macmillan Brown Library, University of Canterbury, Christchurch.

A mountain run is, however, subject to occasional extreme weather events, and over the station's history wind, rain, flood and snow have all taken a toll. The station is situated in a gorge which channels the prevailing northwest wind off the Southern Alps, increasing its intensity. Acland often referred to the northwesters in his diary, describing them as 'furious', 'frightful', 'violent' and 'extreme'.[8] Episodes of intense rainfall are often associated with severe northwest storms and Mt Peel suffered considerable damage from floods. There were also extreme snow events over the years, notably in 1862, 1867, 1887, 1888, 1895, 1903 and 1908.[9] In 1867 Mt Peel lost one third of its flock: 10,000 out of 31,000 sheep.[10] In 1895, the worst snow in Canterbury's recorded history, 18,200 sheep were killed on Mt Peel, which was 35 per cent of the station's flock.[11]

Despite such losses Mt Peel was able to maintain sheep numbers over a long period of time. The station was first stocked in 1856 and by 1873–4 the flock reached 40,000. With careful burning, fencing, oversowing and cultivation, numbers were maintained at this level until the property was subdivided by the Crown in 1912.[12] Moreover, the productivity of the sheep increased over that period. This history is at odds with orthodox accounts of the impact of pastoralism: that of declining productivity and vegetation depletion over time. So what was the experience of most pastoralists and what methods did they employ?

BURNING AS A MANAGEMENT TOOL

When Europeans arrived, the vegetation of the eastern South Island was a tangle of tall tussock, woody plants, herbs and other grasses. John Buchanan, who was employed on the survey of Otago, described the vegetation in some areas as 'an impenetrable growth'.[13] Consequently, people exploring new run country burned to make travel easier and to open it up for sheep. Buchanan also noted that after these initial burns 'a luxuriant growth of native grasses appeared without a seed being sown'. Buchanan's observations reflected Tripp's perception that burning would help to reduce the 'coarse herbage' to 'fine grass' pasturage.

Burning was one of many traditional practices introduced to New Zealand from Britain. Typically, shepherds burned a tenth of moor and heath lands each year in spring to promote the growth of palatable young shoots and to maintain open grazing for their sheep. The historian of human fire use, Stephen Pyne, has commented that in upland Britain 'the torch was as much a complement of the flock as was the shepherd's staff'.[14] Prospective pastoralists in New Zealand knew that the overgrown tangle of vegetation that they initially found would not sustain sheep. However, once the early fires reduced this rank growth they discovered that the short-tussock grassland pasturage included a number of succulent plants that sheep found particularly palatable, including blue tussock, blue wheat grass, anise and plants that they knew as 'wild turnip' and 'wild parsnip'.[15] Subsequent burning, after the initial firing to open up the country, was used as a management tool to maintain this short-tussock pasturage for grazing.

Even at the time, these burning practices were contentious. The Otago surveyor Alex Garvie complained about the impact of 'reckless and unseasonable burnings' in a report he wrote in 1857–8, and in 1865 Buchanan criticised burning in the very dry inland districts of Central Otago.[16] The expression 'indiscriminate burning' was coined by the politician-naturalist

W.T.L. Travers in parliament in 1868 to describe the use of fire by pastoralists.[17] Such views have been repeated many times since, assuming the status almost of dogma in New Zealand's environmental history. Pastoralists have been criticised for firing the country all year round; burning annually; burning for no apparent reason; and so depleting the vegetation by burning that it opened up the country to invasion by rabbits.[18]

Documentary evidence, however, demonstrates that pastoralists practised burning with considerable discrimination, burning on particular sites, for particular reasons, and in a particular season. Research based on diaries and memoirs from ten stations, covering the years from 1853 to 1912, shows that only one station, Mt Peel, burned annually, but the same country was not burned repeatedly, year after year.[19] Mt Peel is in a high-rainfall area and woody weeds grow readily, so annual burning took place to keep the pastures open for sheep. There were, on average, 19 references to burning each year over a ten-year period from January 1877 to December 1886.[20] Clearly the vigorous growth at Mt Peel necessitated regular burning. In contrast, Waitangi Station was a dry run on the north bank of the Waitaki River in South Canterbury, with an annual average rainfall of 559 millimetres. Its records show that burning took place on only 20 days over 16 years between 1887 and 1912.[21] All of this burning was to control and clear weeds, especially sweet briar. These findings fit with work done in the 1940s that drew attention to these environmental factors, concluding that 'In the drier areas burning is very limited; it is more frequently and widely resorted to in damper situations.'[22]

The station records also reveal that apart from the initial firing of the country when it was first explored, burning took place in late winter and spring. Other researchers have found the same seasonal pattern.[23] Spring burning had several advantages. There was usually plenty of moisture in the soil for plants to recover quickly after the fire. Also, in spring the days are short and the early onset of dew prevented the fires from getting out of control. The majority of burns at Mt Peel were small-scale and localised. Fires were lit on blocks where sheep were still grazing. These were not to clear off large areas or the stock would have been at risk. Fires were often lit soon after rain and snow, when it would have been difficult to light them, let alone burn large tracts of land.

It has been claimed that pastoralists burned for no apparent reason, these claims perhaps encouraged by the vivid descriptions of the activity in Lady Barker's journals.[24] The Mt Peel diaries provide a dozen reasons for burning, ranging from opening up new country for stock to clearing scrub to make mustering (rounding up sheep on open country) easier (Table 5.1). Samuel

Butler, who held Mesopotamia Station in the upper Rangitata Valley of South Canterbury between 1860 and 1864, added another reason. This was that on a well-burned run a neighbour's fire could not spread easily onto one's own property and burn stock. Butler wrote that burning made for contented and well-conditioned sheep. 'Burn … you must', he wrote. 'So do it carefully.'[25] He went on to prescribe how to burn firebreaks around the area to be burned to prevent the main fire spreading.

Table 5.1: Reasons for burning country at Mt Peel Station.

• To open up new country for stock
• To remove rank and overgrown vegetation
• To attract sheep into areas that they would not otherwise graze
• To control the regrowth of scrubby weeds
• To clear ground before sowing grass seed
• To clear ground before erecting fences
• To clear ground before draining
• To keep existing drains clear
• To clear ground before ploughing
• To clear stubble after harvest
• To clear scrub to make mustering easier
• To clear scrub to open sheep tracks

Source: Peden, R., 'Pastoralism and the transformation of the rangelands of the South Island of New Zealand, 1841–1912: Mt Peel Station, a case study', PhD thesis, University of Otago, 2007, p. 107, drawn from the Acland diaries, MB 44, Macmillan Brown Library, University of Canterbury.

Successful burning took a good deal of skill and experience. It was preferable not to burn the vegetation into the ground, but for the fire to scorch the tops of the big tussocks to open spaces between them where other plants could benefit from sun and rain. Under-burning, however, led to overgrazing, with sheep crowding onto the burned ground, grazing out the growing plants. Judicious burning attracted sheep into parts of a run where they would otherwise not graze, preventing the overgrazing of parts that stock normally found preferable. The practice allowed for the grazing of a larger area of a station.[26]

Burning was a potent tool in the hands of pastoralists. They used it to turn the mixed grass and shrub lands of the open country into grasslands for grazing sheep. Thereafter it was used to manage the pasturage to prevent the infestation of woody plants and to maintain the quality of the feed, through the production of sweet young shoots that sheep prefer to older rank growth. The evidence from station diaries demonstrates that pastoralists were far more judicious in their use of fire than critics have allowed. Yet some still claim that burning opened up the tussock grasslands to the rabbit irruption in the nineteenth century.[27]

THE IMPACT OF RABBITS

Numerous animals and plants were released, both intentionally and unintentionally, by early settlers and have become major threats to New Zealand landscape and to the indigenous flora and fauna.[28] Plants like gorse and broom were introduced for live fencing and have since taken over thousands of hectares of land.[29] Rabbits were released in Marlborough and Southland in the late 1850s and the early 1860s, to provide food and sport. They had formed established populations by the late 1860s. During a series of dry years beginning in 1871 the Southland rabbits began moving inland. With plentiful feed there would have been high levels of reproduction and with a high survival rate the rabbit population entered a high-growth phase. By the mid-1870s rabbits reached Central Otago. They had crossed the Waitaki River into Canterbury by 1887 and in the early 1890s they devastated the dry Mackenzie Country to the east of Aoraki/Mount Cook. The Marlborough rabbit population underwent a similar increase about the same time and by the late 1880s had spread into the Amuri District of North Canterbury. By the early 1890s, only central Canterbury remained relatively free of the pest.

By this time, rabbits had extended their range well beyond their preferred habitats with some populations even crossing the Southern Alps to live in high-rainfall river valleys on the West Coast that had never been burned or grazed by sheep.[30] Numbers peaked in the early 1890s. A wet year in 1894 and the worst snow year in recorded history in 1895 caused high death rates and saw rabbits withdraw from less favoured habitats and survive in their greatest numbers in semi-arid districts. These places – Central Otago, the upper Waitaki, the Mackenzie Country and inland Marlborough – never recovered from the damage that occurred in the two decades from the early 1870s, and from subsequent rabbit plagues. In the worst-affected areas the tussock cover disappeared almost entirely, leaving bare ground, scabweed, sorrel and later hawkweeds.[31]

The damage to the landscape caused by rabbits is impossible to quantify; it is usually described in terms of the decline in the production of affected stations. Earnscleugh Station near Clyde is an example from the most rabbit-prone part of Central Otago. Rabbits were first seen on the run about 1874 and in 1876 the runholder, Captain William Fraser, began his 'war' on the pest. In that year 5,000 rabbits were killed; in consecutive years, these numbers rose to 20,000, 40,000 and 60,000. In 1880 Fraser took 160,000 rabbit skins off Earnscleugh, but estimated that it was more likely that 400,000 had been killed, as many poisoned rabbits died in their burrows.[32] The station had carried around 24,000 sheep at the start of the outbreak but by 1894 Fraser was bankrupted by the cost of rabbit control and the declining productivity of his flock. W.S. Laidlaw took over Earnscleugh; in 1897, with his flock down to 12,500 sheep he gave up the lease.

The station remained unstocked until 1902 when S.T. Spain took up the lease, at first grazing only 1,455 sheep. By 1907 he had increased sheep numbers to 12,000 and was able to hold them at that figure. In contrast to Central Otago, stations in the less arid parts of Otago and Southland outside the rabbits' preferred habitat recovered quickly once rabbit numbers declined. Although sheep numbers often did not get back to earlier levels in these areas, they did increase and at the same time the productivity of the sheep often far exceeded pre-rabbit levels. Runs in central Canterbury, like Mt Peel, that were barely affected by rabbits maintained and even increased their sheep numbers (with some even improving their productivity) through this period.[33]

In the 1930s, New Zealand-trained botanist V.D. Zotov, after a nine-week tour of the South Island, concluded that the management practices of the early pastoralists were to blame for rabbit irruptions. He claimed that 'indiscriminate' burning and overgrazing with sheep had depleted the grasslands, turning them into an ideal environment in which rabbits could thrive. He wrote that 'the rabbit is not itself a major agent of depletion, and that at least without the aid of sheep and especially of fire it would not have exerted any significant influence on the vegetation'.[34] There is, however, no evidence to support his idea that rabbits need pre-existing bare ground in order to colonise new country, nor that rabbits do not invade, and barely maintain their existence in 'normal grassland vegetation'.[35]

The cause of the first rabbit plague was, rather, biological. Rabbits are adapted to take advantage of good seasons and to survive during times of food scarcity. When conditions are suitable they breed prolifically – a female can produce over 40 young in a breeding season and those born early may themselves breed late in the season. The pattern of increase seen during the first rabbit plague followed the logistic curve seen in many wild animal populations.[36] A slow initial increase as the population struggled to adapt environmentally was followed by one of rapid increase until the population encountered 'environmental resistance'. On the Iberian Peninsula where rabbits originated, predation and disease control their numbers. In New Zealand wet seasons provide the major constraint, with many young drowning in flooded burrows or as their resistance to disease declines.

Rabbits were a key agent in the depletion of the tussock grasslands across much of the South Island between the early 1870s and mid-1890s. The fall in sheep numbers on affected runs began soon after the arrival of rabbits, whereas stations in unaffected areas showed little or no decline. In semi-arid places, even after the peak of the plague subsided, the rabbit population remained high. This, along with sheep grazing, albeit at a lower level than before, prevented the recovery of the vegetation. Elsewhere, once rabbits came under control, vegetation recovered, though not necessarily to its pre-rabbit condition. But rabbits are pre-adapted to the feast-and-famine regimes of the South Island's semi-arid zones, where there is a high survival rate in their young in normal and dry seasons. They remain a threat to the landscape of those regions.

OVERSTOCKING AND OVERGRAZING

Along with burning and rabbits, it has often been argued that overstocking with sheep led to the deterioration of the grasslands during the pastoral era. The evidence for the case of overstocking is derived largely from an analysis of sheep numbers. In Canterbury these reached nearly 5 million in 1886 and did not surpass that figure until the early 1930s. In Otago and Southland the sheep population was nearly 4.5 million in 1886 and did not pass that until 1911.[37] The conclusion that has been drawn from this is that the early pastoralists, faced with an apparent abundance of pasturage, overestimated the carrying capacity of the country and failed to adjust their stock numbers as the pasturage declined. Overstocking, it has been said, resulted in overgrazing which led to the depletion of the vegetation, the rabbit invasion and the degradation of the land.[38]

The apparent stagnation in sheep numbers in the South Island after 1886 has, however, to be interpreted with care. Indeed, the use of sheep numbers alone is an unsatisfactory tool for assessing the productivity of grazing land. Changing to more productive breeds, or increasing the size of sheep, or changing the structure of the flock, can change the stock loading on the land. The development of the frozen meat trade in the late 1880s and 1890s encouraged pastoralists and farmers to change their systems of production and the way they managed their sheep.

In the 1960s Ian Coop, a New Zealand agricultural scientist, developed a method of assessing the stock load of any property based on a ewe with a liveweight of 120 pounds (55 kilograms) that rears one lamb through to weaning.[39] This is known as a ewe equivalent or one stock unit. Other classes of stock are assessed against this standard (Table 5.2). Coop sought to account for differences in feeding levels required to maintain different classes of stock according to their liveweight and productivity. His method, with adjustments over time, has been widely used in New Zealand ever since.

Table 5.2: I.E. Coop – table of ewe equivalents.

Class of stock	Liveweight in lbs	Ewe equivalents
Ewe (Merino)	80	0.8
Ewe	100	0.9
Ewe (Standard)	120	1.0
Ewe	140	1.1
Wether	80–90	0.6
Hogget	50–90	0.7
Ram	160	0.8
Beef cow	1,000	6.0

Source: Coop, I.E., 'A table of ewe equivalents', *Tussock Grassland and Mountain Lands Institute Review* 13 (1967), pp. 46–47. *Terms*: A ewe is a female sheep; a wether is a neutered male, usually kept for wool production and able to be run in harsher environments than breeding ewes; a hogget is a young sheep, usually between 6 and 18 months old, before it cuts its first adult teeth; a ram is a male and is kept only for breeding.

Using Coop's system the stock loading on three different farms running 3,000 sheep can vary considerably, as is shown in Table 5.3.

Table 5.3: Example of three stocking loads using ewe equivalents for different classes of stock.

	3,000 sheep	3,000 sheep	3,000 sheep
Ewes = 1 su	2,000 = 2,000 su	1,000 = 1,000 su	Nil
Wethers = 0.6 su	Nil	1,000 = 600 su	3,000 = 1,800 su
Hoggets = 0.7 su	1,000 = 700 su	1,000 = 700 su	Nil
	2,700 stock units	2,300 stock units	1,800 stock units

The application of Coop's stock unit method to Mt Peel Station between 1875 and 1911 shows how misleading it is to rely on sheep numbers to assess changes in the stock loading of sheep stations. In 1875–6 Mt Peel ran 44,076 sheep; by 1910–11 the number was 41,195, a decline of 2,881.[40] Yet, taking into account the increase in liveweight of the sheep, their increased wool cut, increased lambing percentage, and the shift from a flock based on wethers to a flock dominated by breeding ewes, it can be estimated that the stock units run on Mt Peel went from 23,004 in 1875–6 to 31,361 in 1910–11.[41] This is an increase in the stock loading of over 36 per cent, compared with a decline in sheep numbers of 6.5 per cent. The productivity of the station did not decline, but rather increased over time.

The development of the refrigerated meat export industry changed the production system on Mt Peel from a focus on growing fine Merino wool to growing half-bred and cross-bred lambs for the meat trade, as well as wool. A similar shift took place across the South Island, which, until the First World War, dominated the frozen meat trade. In 1900 the South Island accounted for 68 per cent of all frozen sheep carcasses exported from New Zealand; in 1911 it still stood at 56.6 per cent.[42] Canterbury was pre-eminent in the business. In 1899, 48.7 per cent of all mutton and lamb carcasses exported from New Zealand to Britain came from the region. In the first six months of 1900 Canterbury produced 51 per cent of all frozen carcasses exported from New Zealand.[43] The high number of sheep exported from Canterbury taxed the ability of the region's sheep population to maintain itself. The numbers of non-stud breeding ewes increased from 2,500,000 in 1900 to 2,850,000 in 1905, but remained at that level through to 1912 when 2,835,000 were recorded.[44]

From 1900, sheep were regularly imported from other districts to be fattened on Canterbury's improved pastures and crops on the downlands and plains.[45] 'Tens of thousands' of sheep were brought in from the North

Island in 1901 and many thousands entered the province from Otago and Southland.[46] In 1905 the *Otago Witness* reported that Canterbury farmers imported from the North Island, on average, 20,000 sheep a week for a period of over two months to maintain sheep numbers and to meet the demand of the frozen meat trade.[47] It was not any depletion of the vegetation that accounted for the lack of increase in Canterbury's sheep numbers; rather it was the drive to profit from the frozen meat trade through adaptation in production systems.

There was undoubtedly short-term overstocking during periods of drought when pastoralists and farmers were slow to make adjustments for feed shortages or when there were no outlets for surplus sheep. In semi-arid districts the rabbit plague led to overstocking of the pasturage, resulting in long-term deterioration of the vegetation. Yet elsewhere there is strong evidence that the productivity of sheep increased over time. Moreover, the rapid expansion of the frozen meat trade was based on production off the South Island grasslands, with hill and high country stations, e.g. Mt Peel, selling their surplus sheep to downland and plains farmers who finished them for export.[48]

SHAPING SHEEP TO SUIT THE LAND

The dominance of the sheep industry was established in New Zealand by the mid-1850s. Until the 1980s most rural land was given over to sheep farming, and it was commonly noted that the country 'rode on a sheep's back'. It was only in high-rainfall regions, swamps and bush country where sheep did not thrive that cattle predominated. In the North Island regions of the Waikato and Taranaki, dairying flourished after the development of refrigerated shipping. Cattle stations in the South Island were profitable in the 1860s during the gold rush when large mobs were driven to Otago and the West Coast to supply meat to miners. But the large export market for wool and later sheep meat and the nature of the land meant that sheep were by far the most profitable farm animals in the country until wool prices declined in the face of competition from cheap cotton and synthetic fabrics in the 1970s.

From the outset, pastoralists deliberately modified landscapes to facilitate sheep production: burning provided access to the land for sheep; fencing improved the management of sheep; while, on the downlands and plains in particular, cultivation to grow fodder crops and pasture, and oversowing, improved the quantity and quality of feed. They also modified their sheep to better suit local conditions. It has been claimed that changes in sheep breeding were made in response to economic factors, in particular the introduction of the frozen meat trade.[49] Market demand did have a profound influence in shaping sheep breeding, but pastoralists also soon became aware that different types of sheep did better in different environments. Sheep breeds that were run in places to which they were ill-suited suffered from health problems and were less productive than when run in those for which they had been bred. As a result, by 1914 different breeds had become established in different areas.

Pastoralism in New Zealand began with Merino sheep imported from the Australian colonies. Early on, sheep breeders recognised that South Island conditions changed the physical characteristics of these sheep. In 1851 Frederick Weld wrote that Merinos in New Zealand did not grow wool as fine as those in New South Wales, but that they grew more – 4 pounds (1.8 kilograms) compared with 2.5 pounds (1.1 kilograms) – and the animals themselves were bigger and stronger.[50] He ascribed this to the 'equability of the climate', the unlimited supply of the 'purest water', and the fact that 'the growth of grass is never sufficiently checked to affect seriously the condition of stock'.[51] Merino breeders were also set on further improving their sheep. From the late 1850s superior animals were introduced from Saxony, Prussia, Silesia, France, Russia, Britain, the USA and Australia. The combined effect of environment and breed improvement produced marked changes to the original sheep, so that by the early 1880s it was recognised that 'New Zealand merinos [had] acquired a distinct type'.[52]

By the 1890s, however, pure Merino sheep were declining as a proportion of the South Island sheep flock. In 1895 there were nearly 4 million Merinos making up 35 per cent of all sheep in the South Island; by 1905 that had declined to just over 2 million or 22 per cent; and by 1912 there were only 1.5 million Merinos making up just under 14 per cent of the South Island sheep flock.[53] This change was the outcome of the response of farmers and pastoralists to economic and environmental changes taking place at the time. The intensification of farming practices led to native vegetation being replaced with introduced grasses, legumes and other crops. These enabled the increase of stocking rates from perhaps a sheep to three acres (one sheep to 1.2 hectares) to a sheep to the acre (one sheep to 0.4 hectares) or better. In wet seasons this resulted in footrot epidemics, where sheep crippled with pain lost condition and, in the worst cases, died. To overcome this problem, sheep breeders began cross-breeding experiments using British breeds that were less susceptible to the disease.

There was also an appreciation that sheep needed to be suited to the country on which they were run. As early as 1859 a letter published in the *Lyttelton Times* suggested that crossing Cheviot rams over Merino ewes would produce a hardier sheep that would be 'better adapted for the cold, wet country south of Dunedin, than the pure merino'.[54] In the 1870s there was much discussion in the farming press about creating breeds to suit different districts, with one writer suggesting that the Merino was the best sheep for hilly country, the first cross English Leicester/Merino half-bred was ideal for English grasses, while for heavy low-lying pasture the half-bred should be mated to a Lincoln to produce a three-quarter-bred.[55]

There were considerable economic pressures to change from the pure Merino. In Britain, Europe and America worsted fabrics became fashionable and replaced the thicker woollen cloth that had been made from fine Merino. Early processing machinery used in the worsted process could not handle the short fine wool grown by Merinos, whereas wool from half-breds was ideal. From the 1860s half-bred wool attracted a premium over fine Merino.[56] Merinos were also not suited for meat production, being slow to mature and producing a small, lean carcass. Small farmers near towns began cross-breeding in the 1850s to produce animals for local butchers' markets. In the late 1860s the main outlet for sheep fell away once the runs were stocked up and pastoralists looked to boiling down surplus animals for tallow to provide a return. Some turned to cross-breeding to produce animals that would make business more profitable.[57] By the early 1880s cross-breeding was already well established; the development of the frozen meat export trade increased the practice.

Experiments in cross-breeding led to the development of a new breed and new types of sheep by 1914 (see Figure 5.4). The Corriedale originated with James Little's experiments crossing Merino and Romney sheep in 1868 and from similar experiments with Merinos and Lincolns on The Levels station in coastal Canterbury in 1874.[58] By the late 1890s the name 'Corriedale' was commonly applied to the inbred half-bred that resulted from these breeding programmes. Although not recognised as a separate breed at that time, the 'colonial' Halfbred originated from the same sort of experimentation as the Corriedale. However, where the Corriedale was developed by continually inbreeding after the first cross between the Merino and a British longwool, the Halfbred is bred by out-crossing. Here, first cross Merino/British longwool rams are used over half-bred ewes. Continually reintroducing a Merino influence makes the Halfbred able to cope with harsher conditions than the Corriedale and it is found in the harder hill and high country.

Figure 5.4: Sheep breeds. In the left-hand column: Merino, English Leicester and Corriedale; in the right-hand column: Lincoln, Halfbred and Romney.
Source: images reproduced from William Perry, *Sheep Farming in New Zealand* (Auckland, 1923).

In the North Island a similar system of experimentation took place, but resulted in one breed, the Romney, becoming by far the most popular sheep type.[59] Early pastoralists in the Wairarapa soon found that their Merinos succumbed to footrot and by 1850 they had begun to import British breeds. Similarly, small farmers in the wet regions of the west coast of the North Island and humid Auckland could not maintain Merinos in a healthy condition: they too imported English breeds. The English Leicester, Lincoln and Romney Marsh were three of the most popular, but there were numerous others. From the 1870s, with the beginnings of conversion of large areas of bush land to pasture, the Lincoln became the dominant breed.[60] It was a large sheep with a heavy coarse fleece that withstood being torn by and pulled on the rough stumps and limbs of the burned bush.

The Romney is an active sheep with a finer and more valuable fleece than the Lincoln and it is more resistant to footrot than any other sheep breed in New Zealand. Consequently, by the turn of the twentieth century the Romney and Romney cross had replaced most other breeds in the North Island. Farming writers noted that the New Zealand Romney had become a different type from the English Romney Marsh. Bred as a dual-purpose sheep, farmed for its wool as well as for meat production, the New Zealand Romney was also produced to cope with the steep hill country found in both the North and South Islands.[61]

By 1914 a clear pattern of differentiation of sheep types had taken place according to local environmental conditions as well as economic considerations. The Merino that had been the early dominant breed was pushed back to the semi-arid and high country and replaced by the Halfbred and the Corriedale on the easier high country, dry hill country and light plains of Marlborough, Canterbury and Otago. Elsewhere, crossing dominated sheep breeding. In Southland and the wetter parts of Otago the Romney Marsh cross had superseded the Merino because of its hardiness and resistance to footrot. In Canterbury the English Leicester had been the preferred sheep to put over the Merino because it produced a cross that grew a finer fleece. The English Leicester did well on lighter land, which accounted for its popularity on the Canterbury Plains. The Border Leicester was hardier than the English Leicester, having been bred in the Border hills of England and Scotland, making it better suited for the high plains and hills of Canterbury, the drier parts of Otago, and the lighter soils in Southland. The Lincoln had fallen out of favour as it produced the coarsest wool of the longwool breeds: the Romney and the Leicester breeds replaced it.[62]

CONCLUSION

In the early years of the pastoral expansion in the South Island all tussock grassland properties began with the simple practices of burning and stocking of the land. Thereafter, the extent and pace of development on the stations of the region depended on a variety of circumstances, including the abilities and drive of individual pastoralists. The resource endowments of the different runs were a significant influence on landholders' motivation to apply inputs. On the plains, downlands and easier hill country they became pastoral farmers. Pastoralism reached its ecological limits in the semi-arid and hard mountain country. Contemporary technological and scientific knowledge could not solve the problems that restricted production in these areas, and economic and biological constraints turned pastoralists in the high country from improvement to survival. Aridity and rabbits inhibited pastoral farming in inland Marlborough, the Mackenzie Country, the Upper Waitaki, and parts of Central Otago; they still do. Critics of pastoralism focus on these regions and choose to ignore the successes of pastoral farming elsewhere in the rangelands.

By the 1890s a differentiation between the largely freehold low country and the largely leasehold high country had already been established. In fact the term 'high country' for the semi-arid and mountain lands began to appear in common usage about this time.[63] The breakup of the great estates from 1893 and the settlement of small farmers on the low country intensified this division between pastoralism and farming. However, in the hills of the Amuri District, on the foothills adjoining the Canterbury Plains, and in the hill districts of Otago and Southland the distinction between the two systems remained blurred.

An improvement ethos underpinned the pastoral era: it was characterised by enterprise, enthusiasm and energy. Improving pastoralists applied scientific ideas and technology from around the world to their farming systems. As practical men, they bred improved livestock, trialled the use of artificial fertilisers on turnip crops, and experimented with different pasture plants in an effort to develop better permanent pastures.[64] Improving pastoralists developed the frozen meat trade and lobbied in Britain to advance its marketing.[65] The established account that their methods led to degraded landscapes does not take into consideration differences in land use and in its intensification. The evidence from Mt Peel and other runs outside the semi-arid and hard mountainous areas is that, up to the time of their subdivision at the turn of the century, productivity remained high and had even continued to increase. By 1914, systems of production were established on different types of country – mixed crop and livestock farming on the plains and downlands, pastoral farming on hill country, and extensive pastoralism in the mountains and semi-arid lands – that have lasted to the present day.

Nonetheless, by this time livestock farmers had been forced to confront major obstacles that constrained productivity. Internal and external parasites and trace element deficiencies in soils and pastures led to poor health and high stock losses, particularly among young stock, and reduced productivity in adult animals. As an example, by the late 1880s lungworm had become endemic (see Box 5.1) and until proprietary anthelmintics were developed in the 1950s it was hard to keep alive young sheep infested with the parasites. Declining soil fertility and trace element deficiencies also showed up in poor pasture productivity, the reversion of large areas of grassland to scrub and weeds, and the difficulty of maintaining permanent pastures without regular recourse to the plough. Many of these problems remained until after the Second World War, when scientific developments, agro-chemicals and aerial top-dressing with superphosphate appeared to provide a solution.

Oh, boys, I'll long remember, *Of course the boss was worried.*
The year of thirty-four.   *He did not have it on his own.*
The hoggets, they were sickly, *I was working day and night,*
They were dying by the score. *And was but skin and bone.*
The boss would blow along,   *They wouldn't live to please us,*
'Well, how's things here today? *You could see it in their eye,*
'Another 14 more to skin?   *And if you coughed a little loud,*
'Oh, hell,' was what he'd say. *They would stiffen out and die.*[66]

Doggerel describing the frustrating job of treating an outbreak of lungworm in hoggets, written by Fred Stevenson, a shepherd at Mt Peel in the 1930s.

The orthodox analysis of the impact of pastoralism on the grasslands has been largely negative. This chapter has argued that pastoralists did not merely impose an alien system of land use in the open grasslands, but that they learned to adapt their methods and their animals to suit the range of environments that they found across the region. There were unintended consequences of their trial-and-error methods and the introduction of exotic animals and plants, such as the rabbit plagues and the spread of invasive weeds. However, pastoralism and pastoral farming provided the economic impetus for the country's growth during the colonial era. The country was transformed to produce wool and later meat for the export trade. The economic benefit that New Zealand enjoyed, initially from pastoralism and later from pastoral farming, has been profound.

6 Mobilising Capital and Trade

Jim McAloon

INTRODUCTION

The environmental changes with which this book is concerned were part of a worldwide economic transformation and it is the purpose of this chapter to explore some of those dimensions, in particular 'the revolutionary effects of capital in simultaneously reshaping landscapes and economies in various parts of the globe'.[1] Grass was converted into commodities – wool, meat, butter and cheese. Grassland improvement required capital; markets for the commodities had to be developed, which in turn required the communication of the requirements of manufacturers, brokers and consumers. Nothing about the transformation of the New Zealand grasslands was inevitable. Against alternative sources of pastoral commodities that were variously larger, better endowed, or closer to Britain, 'an active capitalist class, sometimes working at cross-purposes, strove mightily to bring about' New Zealand's favoured position within British markets.[2] This chapter will discuss some dimensions of that capitalism, and particularly the relationship of New Zealand pastoral entrepreneurs to British markets. Flows of capital and trade were complex and multi-dimensional, and New Zealand farmers, their mercantile allies and the state endeavoured not only to meet the demands of British markets but in some important instances to create those markets.

This approach to the transformation of the New Zealand grasslands suggests that grass was both a vehicle and a product of capitalist globalisation. The simplification of ecosystems was part of 'an integrated economy ... that bound city and country into a powerful national and international market that forever altered human relationships to the ... land' and entailed 'the expansion of a metropolitan economy into regions that had not previously been tightly bound to its markets, and the absorption of new peripheral areas into a capitalist orbit'.[3] For example, the position which wool from all the Australasian colonies came to enjoy in overseas markets was hard won and even once Australasian wool 'occupied a dominant place in the London market ... maintaining a high quality reputation was more important than in ... earlier decades ... when it was no more than a marginal supplement to European suppliers'. This in turn required 'knowledge of the latest breeding, herding, and produce handling practices designed to improve wool quality'.[4]

Recent work in business history has emphasised the importance of stock and station agents in these relationships. In regions of recent European settlement, the 'greatest problem for the inexperienced, industrious yet isolated farmer was the scarcity of information and the high cost of acquiring it'.[5] As a rule, the necessary tasks of 'investment ... finance, technical expertise, and marketing' were by the 1860s 'beyond the capacity of all but the largest and most experienced of colonial farmers'.[6] Meeting those needs was the essential reason for the development of the 'quintessentially Australasian' enterprise, the stock and station agency, although its role was complemented by colonial newspapers, by farmer organisations, and eventually by the state, as well as by end-users of colonial commodities.

FINANCING PASTORAL DEVELOPMENT

Until the introduction of refrigerated shipping in the early 1880s, New Zealand pastoralism was based on the export of wool to Britain. The major market for New Zealand wool was the worsted trade in Yorkshire's West Riding, particularly in Bradford. Manufacturers and merchants in and around Bradford put considerable effort into disseminating information about their requirements. Their emphasis was usually on the quality of fleece, which in turn implied good pasture management. Sometimes explicit advice was given on this topic. Although Bradford explored alternative sources of supply, particularly from Central and South Asia, the settler colonies, including New Zealand, had significant advantages, not least compatible language, law, institutions, currency and webs of personal connections. Even so, nothing was guaranteed. It is

> misleading to imagine an ... output that was absorbed by a ready-made demand which merely grew year after year ... When considering the

markets for … wool what matters is not the general interdependence between pastoral production and manufacturing activity but the changes in the extent, the nature and the sources of the demand.[7]

There was not, in Britain, a simple and perpetual expansion of demand, whatever wool merchants and manufacturers might have said by way of encouragement to colonial pastoralists, but 'a complex pattern of adaptation and a changing utilization'.[8]

The sources of finance for grassland development were varied. In the 1840s, the Deans brothers, on New Zealand's Canterbury Plains, relied on advances from their family in Ayrshire which were repaid with the proceeds of wool sold in London.[9] The family took a close interest. James Deans, the settlers' brother, enquired in 1849 'if the natural pastures have improved as much as we anticipated'. He was informed that despite the difficulties

all the land we break up is regularly sown down with grass seeds after the first green crop, and the change which that makes is very great. Near to the house, which was, when we came here, entirely covered with fern or brackins, we have sown grass and lucerne seeds after burning off the fern, and the pasture will now carry as much stock per acre as the bank in front of your house.[10]

Twenty-five years later, and on a larger scale, the Dunedin stock and station agent and pastoralist, John Roberts, invested family money in land at Cape Turnagain, in Hawke's Bay. From Selkirk, his brother Thomas demanded full details of intended pasture development. John Roberts was the conduit for large sums of Scottish money into New Zealand grassland development, as other syndicates involving relations and colleagues from the Borders textile district also relied on him.[11]

Alongside family money, much transformation was financed by the reinvestment of profit. In some places, such as Banks Peninsula, and Geraldine and Waimate in South Canterbury, bush-felling provided the capital to turn the cleared land into exotic grasslands. In other cases, such as the stations held by the Rutherford family and William Robinson in the Amuri in North Canterbury, profits from Australian mercantile business and squatting funded New Zealand development. Finance companies, banks and stock and station agents often provided loan finance. From the 1870s, London-based companies like the New Zealand Loan and Mercantile Co. and the National Mortgage and Agency Co. (NMA) relied on debentures held by the genteel rentiers of the Home Counties and central Scotland;

these offered security rather than high interest.[12] Later in the century, wise directors increased the proportion of paid-up capital from the same sources. Smaller firms such as Levin, Gould, Wright Stephenson, and Donald Reid, depended on accommodation from local banks or even larger stock and station agencies. The sources of the banks' money varied too, from local depositors to the same rentiers that funded the larger mercantile concerns.

By 1860, after a decade of rapid expansion, with a simultaneous decline in the local wool supply, British manufacturers were seeking new sources of wool. The role of the Bradford Chamber of Commerce in encouraging, on a global scale, the supply of suitable wool for worsted spinning and manufacture was critical in the development of New Zealand pastoralism, and particularly in integrating it into West Riding manufacturing. In turn, as chapter 5 has shown, New Zealand pastoralists went to considerable lengths to meet the requirements of their distant markets.

THE BRITISH WOOL MARKET

The Chamber of Commerce for Bradford and the Worsted District was established in 1851. Membership was open to 'Bankers, Merchants, Spinners, Manufacturers, and others interested in the Trade of the Town of Bradford and its Neighbourhood, and the Worsted Trade generally'. The Chamber initially concerned itself with postal and railway communication and the legal environment for business. Desultory attention was paid to improving the quality of manufactured goods, to the potential of recently annexed parts of the Empire as a market for British manufactures, and to free trade.[13] Free trade after 1846 had allowed high-quality French woollens into Britain, and as Bradford manufacturers could not compete they oriented themselves explicitly to the mass market. By technical improvement in dyeing and machinery 'a great variety of articles were successively produced which combined great beauty and usefulness with remarkably low price ... for the use of the working and middle classes'. Demand soared, and as raw materials became short 'the whole world had to be ransacked to supply the ever growing demands of our machinery'.[14] It was not inevitable that New Zealand pastoralists would secure a position in this trade, nor therefore that New Zealand grassland environments would be so influenced by distant markets for their produce.

The Bradford Chamber considered many possible sources of supply. Relatively close to home, Silesia and Austria supplied considerable quantities of wool.[15] The Mayor of Halifax, emphasising the importance of 'the cheapness of the raw material', suggested India as a source of wool as well as cotton. A Bradford alderman thought Argentine wools 'might by improvement in culture be rendered suitable to the trade of this district' although 'the unsettled state of that country very frequently interfered … with any attempt to introduce improved modes of culture'. Others, noting the idle capacity in Bradford, suggested sourcing wool 'from our own Colonies'.[16] In February 1859 the Chamber appointed a Wool Supply Committee to encourage the increased supply of long or combing wool. The committee would 'offer suggestions and … give information to the Growers of Wool (more particularly in our colonies)' on the basis that 'no large additional supply can be expected from our Home Growers, but there are countries, such as New Zealand, Australia, India, and the Cape District of Southern Africa, where the Growth of Wool may be extended to an almost unlimited amount, and its character generally improved'[17] (Figure 6.1).

The committee would disseminate to growers 'the information and modes of management already at the command of more advanced communities'.[18] A circular to the trade noted that 'the peculiar excellencies of our [English] Long Wools are dependent upon our temperate and humid climate and succulent grasses: but those are partially to be found in New Zealand, Australia, and the Cape District of Southern Africa; not to mention other countries'. Local and overseas growers were addressed: 'in all the present Wool Growing District great improvements may be made, by … adopting improved breeds of sheep, by judicious crosses, and by taking care to secure a continuous supply of food through the year, to prevent the Wool becoming tender or cotted at any period of insufficient nutrition'.[19] This circular, with its message about grassland management, was widely distributed overseas, being copied from the Melbourne *Argus* to New Zealand newspapers.[20]

From the mid-1850s New Zealand newspapers had regularly included information on the British wool market.[21] Reports on the London sales were usually contributed by wool brokers via local merchants or sometimes directly from London. In 1859, 'for really choice combing descriptions the competition for foreign accounts against Bradford specimens led to a high range of prices and many flocks presenting all the features required were bought with great eagerness at long prices'. However, perhaps because easy markets had encouraged laziness, 'fine Australian flocks appear to have retrograded both in breed and condition, whilst burrs and carrot seeds have reduced the prices of many from those of former years'. There was encouragement for New Zealand pastoralists: 'Many flocks from the Canterbury and Otago settlements give great promise. Auckland and Wellington flocks, however, for the most part show heavy condition and

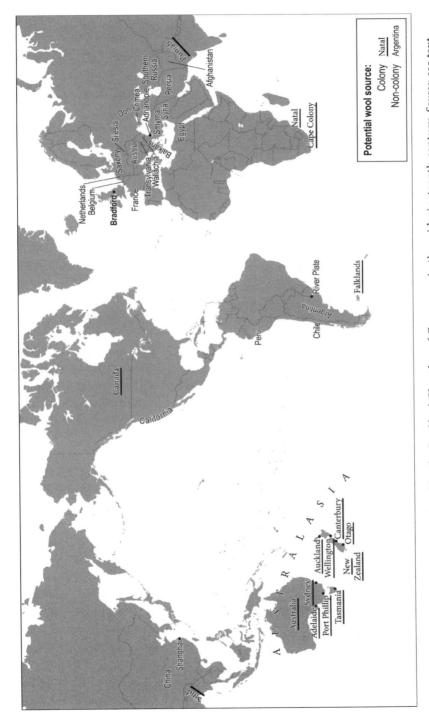

Figure 6.1: Sources of wool considered by the Bradford Chamber of Commerce in the mid-nineteenth century. *Source:* see text.

irregularity of classification, which may be easily improved.'[22] There was no room for complacency, though, for a few weeks later another broker noted 'no improvement in classification, packing, or condition' and a decline in the quantity of New Zealand combing wool in the August sales. There was an implicit warning that Cape wools 'were in good condition, and showed great improvement'.[23]

In any case, Bradford was looking well beyond the settler colonies. In 1857 the Chamber had received sample fleeces from a small Chinese breed and one member spent considerable sums experimenting unsuccessfully with crosses from that breed.[24] Between 1840 and 1857 the share of British wool imports arriving from India had greatly increased but the Chamber advised the Indian Chancellor of the Exchequer that quality needed considerable improvement. The key to the increased supply had been the opening, in 1851, of the port of Karachi, and the establishment by the British resident of an annual trade fair for caravans from Kabul and elsewhere. The Chancellor, who hoped that 'English enterprise, which was never wanting on these occasions' would establish firms for direct trade with Karachi instead of going through Bombay, was asked to get word through the Karachi customs office that long wool was particularly wanted, and the Bombay Chamber of Commerce would be asked to encourage annual shearing only. The Chancellor was given samples of East Indian wool and longstapled English wool for comparison, and the suggestion that Indian sheep be crossed with Leicestershire rams. He promised that 'nothing shall be wanting on the part of the authorities in India to give effect ... to ... suggestions as to the improvement of the quality of the Wool shipped from India, and to increase its quantity'.[25]

The wool committee also met P.M. Dalziel, the Karachi collector of customs, when he was home in Edinburgh on leave. Dalziel noted that wool exports from Sind were ultimately sourced from Afghanistan, and the increase during the 1850s had largely resulted from the abolition of internal duties in Sind and Punjab. He observed that there were still heavy duties levied by Afghan chiefs and at the port; abolition of the port duties might encourage the chiefs to follow suit and would allow direct shipping from Karachi. Dalziel also reported that the Punjab Government had made sporadic efforts to encourage cross-breeding, and that he had tried to persuade the government to import suitable sheep from Persia to Afghanistan, where '[e]xcellent pasture lands are found in the more elevated regions, whose climate is not inimical to the European Constitution; an admirable field, therefore, seems open to the Capitalist for a profitable cultivation of the Golden Fleece'.[26] During the first part of 1860, Dalziel visited Bradford, addressed a meeting, and was provided with ten Leicester rams to take back to Karachi. In the event, Afghanistan was too unpredictable a source, but the precedent was followed with regard to other wool-growing countries. During 1861 the chamber sent suggestions on improving wool to the Board of Trade, the India Office, and the Colonial Office for circulation to all wool-producing countries with which the United Kingdom had diplomatic relations.[27]

G.F. Bowen, the Governor of Queensland (and later of New Zealand), had this material published in the government gazette and visited Bradford, promising all assistance.[28] The letter and attached specifications were printed in the New Zealand government gazette in September 1861 and subsequently copied in a number of New Zealand newspapers.[29] What was wanted was

> a staple from four to seven inches long, according to its fineness, and [it] should, as far as possible, be uniform in quality throughout its whole length, bright and lustrous in appearance, *or* soft and kind to the touch, of good spinning properties, free from burrs or other vegetable fibre.

Naturally classing and packing had to be 'thoroughly trustworthy and fair'. Some improvement had already been noted and this 'might be made general if proper care were taken in the selection of breeding sheep, particularly of the rams, and, where necessary, by the introduction of new blood'. In particular, 'flocks should, as much as possible, be pastured upon succulent grasses, similar to those grown in Great Britain', with 'constant supply of food throughout the year'. The committee offered to give advice and assistance, and 'to facilitate the export of breeding sheep suitable for crossing and improving the inferior foreign breeds'.[30] To their advantage, settler colonies like New Zealand found it much easier to encourage the sowing of exotic grasses than was the case in the remoter regions of South Asia.

Wool from numerous sources across the five continents was discussed in considerable detail. Most was of poor quality, with some exceptions in India, Persia, and southern Russia; and 'large supplies' of New Zealand wool 'have already come to England, and we believe the country is peculiarly adapted to produce the long combing wools required, from its soil and climate, and an unlimited market is open here for such wools'. Australian wools were more mixed but were generally fine 'and, for certain purposes, are exceedingly valuable'.[31]

A Hawke's Bay pastoralist, H.S. Tiffen, had commented in 1857 that little consideration had been given to the best sheep for New Zealand conditions. Stock had been imported from Australia simply because it was easy to do so; it was only luck that the better conditions in New Zealand had resulted in a longer staple.

[The] effect of good feed and a humid climate is to increase the length and strength of the wool, while in a dry climate like New South Wales, if the wool is finer, it is shorter in staple and the fleece is consequently less in weight and not equal in elasticity and strength to New Zealand wool.[32]

Yet the connections with the colonies on the other side of the Tasman meant that much advice on breeding and pasture came at least indirectly from Australia, whether articles copied from Australian periodicals or individual pastoralists sharing experiences; pastoralism has, after all, been part of the Tasman world for a long time.[33] An East Taieri farmer recounted successful experiments by friends in Tasmania crossing Cheviot rams with Merino ewes. Mercantile advice was quoted, that this wool could be 'the very thing wanted' and warning against trying to get it too fine, for that was done at the expense of weight of the fleece and was therefore counterproductive.[34]

Farmers also shared their experiences through local newspapers. James Gardiner, in North Otago, discussed the introduction and refinement of Australian Merinos in the district, and the declining usefulness of German rams:

now that our ewes are finer, it is certain that carefully-bred and well-culled rams of New Zealand or Australian breed will pay us better than any rams in all Germany. We ought to breed sheep that will yield strong second-combing fleeces – they pay best.[35]

W.H. Poole of Popotunoa in Otago gave lengthy advice, noting that Merino might be thought to be suitable for native grasses in a relatively undeveloped state but there was room for improvement with introduced grasses. In crossing, 'never lose sight of the more important object you are endeavouring to arrive at – the length and quality of the staple of your wool'. Successful crossing required good enclosed paddocks in good English grass, and rape for winter feed 'for the country, in its natural state, will not feed Leicester, Lincoln, Cotswolds, or South Downs, without artificial aid … Good feeding is half the battle.'[36]

West Riding interests sometimes communicated directly with Australasian pastoralists. H.S. Tiffen had visited Europe and, advised by a Huddersfield merchant, James Beardsell, had brought some stud rams back to New Zealand. Beardsell later commented that earlier trials of Spanish Merino had been unsuccessful in producing long heavy fleeces in the British climate.

From what I know of your climate and soil, and from what I have seen of the wool from your colony (and I have seen and worked up a good deal of it) I am confident that to attempt to grow a fine clothing wool, or 'carding wool' as you call it, would be the most unprofitable wool you could grow, and if attempted, the results are sure to prove unsatisfactory. Your colony is peculiarly adapted for growing a middle quality of combing wool, a kind of wool for which there is a good demand, and has been for years, and likely to continue for many years to come.[37]

In 1863 S.M. Curl of Wanganui sent samples of New Zealand combing wool to the Bradford Chamber and was advised by the Wool Supply Committee that they

were not unacquainted with the varieties and properties of New Zealand wool, but have long held it in high esteem, and believe the colony of New Zealand to promise, more than any other, a future large supply of long-stapled fleeces, of a medium quality and length, between the fine Merinos of Australia and the long-grown Leicester of this country.

Bradford expressed 'much satisfaction, that the area of cultivated grass land is on the increase, as upon that, they believe, depends to a large extent the supply of nutritive provender necessary for the support of long-woolled sheep', particularly as more intensively cultivated grasses could provide the sheep with more food for less effort. The committee concluded that while it was 'for the colonists to determine what use to make of the hints [it had] given', it believed that the direction which should be taken was clear.[38]

By the end of the 1860s the Wool Supply Committee was fully occupied evaluating samples of imported wool from over two dozen countries or regions, and sending out exemplary samples of English wool to overseas growers. Circulars repeated the advice and specifications of a decade earlier and continued to be printed in New Zealand newspapers.[39] Some Australian commentators whose views appeared in North Otago thought Bradford was being a little exacting in its prescriptions, and wanted minimum acceptable standards as well as the ideal, so that pastoralists could decide whether it was even worth trying to raise combing wool, or clothing wool should be grown.[40] Conversely, Bradford frequently balanced its enthusiasm with observations that Australia and New Zealand had much yet to do in producing good combing wool, in terms of weight of fleece, length of staple, and fineness. The committee again conceded that it 'must submit to the superior judgment of the graziers in the colonies, as to the best breed of sheep for the certain class of land, but where the climate and land will produce deep stapled wool, it will find a readier and better market in this country'.[41] London and Australian merchants echoed the concern and warned that quality was already deteriorating after a promising beginning.[42]

By 1873, the Wool Supply Committee could report 'marked success' in encouraging colonial growers to concentrate on longstapled combing wool.[43] This was evident on a grand scale at the 1876 Philadelphia Exhibition, where Bradford judges reported favourably on Australasian wool. The Australasian colonies put up several hundred exhibits of both combing and clothing wool from a great variety of breeds and crosses. The Bradford judges enthused that there had

> never been such a fine collection of Wool brought together as that shewn by the Australian Colonies … while Saxony, Silesia and some parts of Russia produce wool of the finest qualities adapted for the manufacture of the best woollen cloth, Australia and New Zealand produce a much greater variety suited for combing and clothing purposes, of medium and fine qualities, and are making greater progress in cultivating the growth of these wools than any other country in the world … No part of the Exhibition was more striking or impressive than that of the British Colonies, the space occupied being quite as large as that allotted to the mother country.[44]

Philadelphia marked a transition. Looking back in 1887, the Wool Supply Committee recalled that in 1851 the industry had relied largely on local wool, but as demand grew, it had 'spent much time and money sending out long-woolled sheep to the Colonies, as well as freely giving its advice to Colonial breeders as to the best methods of producing the now well-known cross-bred sheep'. The supply of combing wools increased rapidly, and by the 1880s colonial wool-growing was more than established. In New Zealand, Merino had largely been replaced by cross-breds except in the high country. With improved transport and communication, and many smaller growers, the major sales were relocating from Britain to the colonies.[45] Philadelphia anticipated another transition too, in that within a few years Australasian economies and their relationship with Britain would be transformed by refrigeration.

REFRIGERATION AND DAIRYING

From the early 1880s New Zealand farming became increasingly oriented to supplying frozen or chilled meat, butter and cheese to Britain (Figure 6.2). With rising incomes and an increasing population, the British demand for these products, especially among the middle classes and better-off sections of the working class, was implicated in environmental transformation on a global scale.[46] Refrigeration brought far-reaching changes to New Zealand's agro-ecology.[47] Networks of information changed as well. Whereas these networks had been almost entirely in the private sector during the 1850s, 1860s and 1870s, the intensification of the refrigerated economy after 1890 saw an increasing emphasis on the role of the state in providing advice on grassland development, particularly through the Department of Agriculture (see chapter 9). Simultaneously, dairy and meat brokers provided frequent updates from Britain through New Zealand merchants and stock and station agents to local farmers.

Although it was by no means absent from the South Island, from the 1880s dairying was more intensively developed in the North Island. An essential prerequisite was the remorseless alienation of Māori territory.[48] Sometimes the link between exotic grass and the expropriation of Māori was made all too clear. In April 1881 a Taranaki newspaper reported that land sales in the Parihaka Block were proceeding rapidly. Parihaka, now well known for the passive resistance espoused by its leader, Te Whiti o Rongomai, was a thriving Māori community south of New Plymouth, in the middle of land notionally confiscated during the war of 1863–4 but in practice not secured by the state. By the late 1870s, the state was promoting European settlement in the area, to secure the revenue from land sales and to break an example of Māori autonomy. The newspaper noted with approval that recent purchasers had 'already commenced burning off the land and sowing it for pasture' and a local merchant 'forwarded a large quantity of English grass seed to them on Thursday morning'. The hope was that European occupation would rapidly intensify after this good example and 'if settlement at Te Whiti's doors proceeds unchecked, Te Whiti-ism will quickly die a natural death'.[49]

Even in the mid-1860s, there was frequent discussion of suitable grasses for the North Island. As in the south, local newspapers played a critical role in promoting the economic development of their districts. In 1864 the *Taranaki Herald* was two weeks ahead of *The Press* of Christchurch in reprinting an article promoting Californian prairie grass as a wonder crop, not only increasing milk yields but thriving on poor soil.[50] Australian sources were

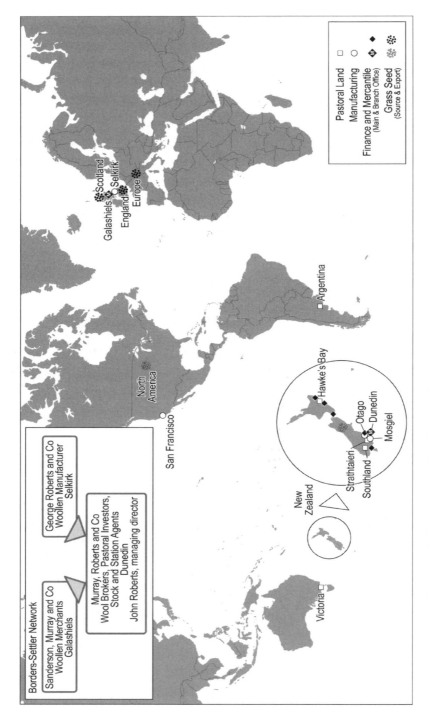

Figure 6.2: Some commodity flows in the international grasslands economy. *Source:* see text.

often relied on for the information of dairy farmers as they had been for sheep farmers. 'Good milk cannot be made without good grass' introduced a lengthy article from the *The Australasian* advocating the use of Italian ryegrass well irrigated and fertilised with liquid sewage, citing in support of this contention experiments at Rugby in England. Readers were also advised of the importance of fodder crops to carry herds through the winter.[51]

By the later 1860s the Taranaki Agricultural Society was discussing exotic grasses, although not from a position of great knowledge. As the president admitted, 'his experience of grasses was not very extensive' but he had in 15 years found ryegrass and clover to work well. Farmers retailed their own experiences, so debate was of an anecdotal quality. However, they demonstrated considerable willingness to experiment and pay attention to reported developments.[52] In this respect, little changed in the next 15 years.[53] In the 1880s, appropriate grasses for the North and South Islands were frequently discussed in the Canterbury Agricultural and Pastoral Association's *New Zealand Country Journal*. One of the main movers behind both the Association and its journal was the Dumfriesshire-born merchant, Robert Wilkin; like some of his colleagues, Wilkin published detailed advice on suitable grasses for various environments.[54]

Supplementary feeding was often debated. The National Dairy Association noted in 1895 that allowing cows to dry off in the winter because of a reduction in feed was unwise because of the amount of time it then took the animals to recover condition. Maximising each cow's output was advocated as a hedge against an anticipated fall in prices.[55] One Taranaki newspaper drew unfavourable contrasts between local farms and those in Victoria in Australia. The latter relied heavily on fodder crops in the winter months and were able to keep their stock in excellent condition throughout the winter; Taranaki farms tended to be almost entirely in grass and thus to run low on feed in the winter months. Cattle, once losing milking condition, found it almost impossible to get it back. Fodder crops allowed stock and pasture alike to survive the winter.[56] Although it has been said that this reflected an inappropriately British model, the merits of such advice and debate are less significant than that advice and discussion were so frequent and prolific.[57] Certainly an authoritative publication in 1889 pointed out that British experience in dairy pastures was not necessarily to be transplanted wholesale but might be useful.[58]

An important dimension of the state's involvement in the refrigerated economy was taking on a major role in advice and information, and indeed in marketing, thus complementing the role of stock and station agents. In 1888 the New Zealand Agent-General in London, Francis Dillon Bell, reported on the dairy industry. He had been in frequent contact with James Long, a professor at the Royal Agricultural College, Cirencester, who had been following developments in New Zealand with interest. Bell had much to say about the importance of consistent quality, and the need to cater to the existing tastes of the market. He also noted that 'a country ... which can grow English grasses as New Zealand does ... may well rival England and Europe' in butter production.[59] Bell's relationship with Long paid off when Long wrote a substantial booklet on dairy production for New Zealand farmers. This booklet was made available free of charge to anyone; many dairy farmers must have profited by it. Long's points about consistent quality were repeated in various parliamentary papers in the next few years.

From 1892 the Department of Agriculture was the major state agency providing such information to farmers, and its role became increasingly significant. Later chapters discuss this in more detail. If information was money, as Simon Ville has suggested, then the state provided some very major subsidies to emerging and, indeed, more established farmers.[60] Of equal importance was the often-cited dimension of cheap state-provided finance to Pākehā farmers through the Advances to Settlers Act system after 1894, and indeed the concessionary tenures which were expanded from 1892. Much of this, again, relied on the invested funds of British rentiers.

Despite the increasing role of the state, stock and station agents continued to be of importance. John Macfarlane Ritchie, the Dunedin-based General Manager of NMA, was a persistent advocate of smaller-scale and more intensive pastoral farming (indeed, he had an important role in reassuring overseas investors that the land policies of the Liberal governments of 1892–1912 did not herald socialist collectivisation). As early as 1877 he told Captain Kitchener that the latter's South Canterbury run needed to be improved beyond simple grazing, and had had too little spent on it, not too much.[61] More generally, Ritchie thought, too many landowners had borrowed heavily in order to substantially increase their holdings, instead of borrowing more moderately to develop what they had.[62]

The reluctance of such pastoralists to sell at less than their inflated book values was an additional reason for a blocked land market.[63] When the development of dairy and frozen meat exports finally did prompt subdivision, there was very rapid change in some previously marginal areas such as Western Southland. There, individual landowners and syndicates divided an area of around 120,000 hectares into farms of a hundred or so hectares, each which were then sold and progressively drained and cultivated by the new owners.[64] Stock and station agencies financed much of this continuing development. Ritchie noted that:

there is a very marked improvement going on yearly in the land in Southland, many farms having been made of greatly increased value entirely by the draining, fencing, and tilling done by the owners. Therefore, although many of our accounts tend to stand still or even increase in amount year by year, their position is quite different and greatly better by this fact. So long as this can be done – and it is peculiar to Southland which was especially a district of swamps or coldish clay land originally – the farmers are rarely keen to pay off land for the sake of doing so, but prefer to add field to field and thus provide land for their families.[65]

Similar processes were evident across the South Island. In 1914 one large mid-Canterbury estate was divided for sale into 20 blocks, mostly 'good sweet sheep country, and a large acreage is still in the tussock ... With the present trouble in finding labour &c, this is the class of land that is finding favour in this country.'[66] The rapid improvement in pasture was evidently the cause of 'more wool, consequent on the cutting up of the larger estates in the district ... being offered yearly at our local auctions and the Company is getting its full share of the business which pays very well'.[67]

Financing such activity, however, required at least tacit consent from London in those numerous cases where British rentiers provided the capital. J.M. Ritchie had to argue strenuously for the latitude to finance intensive development of smaller farms; head office in London was wedded to the older emphasis on lending to large pastoral clients on mortgage. Ritchie's response was to point out that the company's money was developing a country, a task not achieved in five minutes:

As I have frequently said to you ... we cannot escape from being more or less tied to the fortunes of our farmer clients, and that our advances, to a considerable extent at least, are not to be promptly called in without almost as much harm to ourselves as to our clients. The reason is that this southern country is largely in the process of being improved into full production power, and the process is slow and expensive.[68]

Some years later, in a brief economic contraction, London issued strict orders to NMA and its subsidiary Levin and Co. to limit advances to farmers. Inevitably this constrained development of grass, and similar pressures were evident during the First World War. In 1916 a Levin client in the Manawatu wished to increase his normal credit limit of £2,500 to £3,500, in order to clear and fence 100 hectares of bush land. The branch manager was not

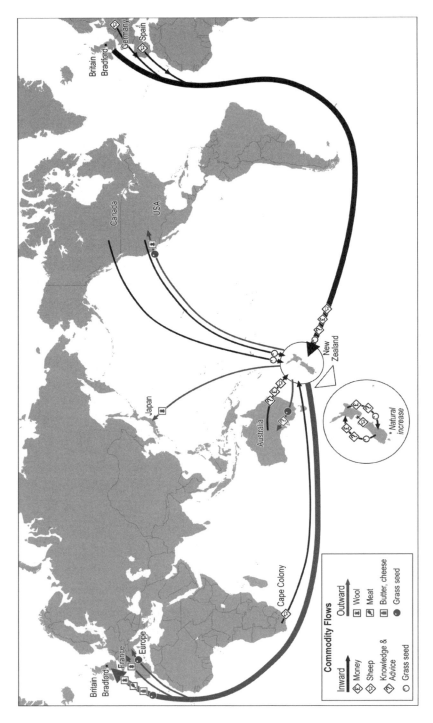

Figure 6.3: A grasslands network based in the Scottish Borders: Sanderson, Murray, and Roberts of Galashiels and Selkirk.

Source: see text.

at all keen to increase the account, as little business would result for some time: in other words, quick returns were what counted.[69]

Stock and station agents were also directly involved in the grass seed trade, particularly in the newer pastures of the North Island. (This trade is also discussed in chapter 7.) In the 1890s Levin emphasised that North Island farmers had a good deal of catching up to do in stock and pasture alike. Hoping to influence matters directly, Levin had advised Dalgety's on the quality of grass seed to be sent from Britain to Wellington.[70] At the same time Murray Roberts and Co. had a thriving grass seed business. Although that firm was closely identified with the woollen interests of its founders in the Scottish Borders, their emphasis in grass seed was on North America (Figure 6.3). The firm also speculated in grass seed for the British market, buying both opportunistically and to order and engaging in a regular trade with European, British and particularly Scottish houses.[71]

Strikingly, Murray Roberts and Co.'s trade in grass seed was diverse and involved both import and export. In other words, although occupying a small niche, this firm's trade did not adhere to a simple model of importing the inputs from the metropolitan economy and shipping out wool, meat and butter. Nor was Roberts particularly innovative; 20 years earlier Levin and the New Zealand Loan and Mercantile Co. were shipping copious quantities of grass seed to London.[72] In the developing area of Taranaki, however, it seems that the trade was one way. The local stock and station agent Newton King had a very large seed business across the North Island, but seems not to have exported. All King's imported seed was from one London firm, with certification by both English and New Zealand government botanists.[73] In other regions, such as the western Bay of Plenty, where settler farming was a recent development, the cultivation of grass seed was a short-lived affair and the seed was apparently sold locally for recently cleared land. Such small-scale efforts, lacking the advantages of established suppliers, could rely on poor sources of seed with the resulting risk of contamination by ragwort and other weeds.[74]

THE FROZEN MEAT INDUSTRY

As the frozen meat industry began to gather strength it was quickly evident, as one columnist noted in 1889, that the stocking capacity of indigenous grasslands had been reached, and thus 'any expansion ... must be due mainly to cultivation and increased carrying capacity'.[75] The economics of meat-growing meant that it was particularly important to ensure fast growth of stock: 'the farmer cannot afford to spend from 18 months to two years in growing a sheep fit for the butcher or the refrigerator ... each year must furnish the year's supply of mutton'.[76]

As in the case of wool and dairy produce, information about the state and requirements of the British market for frozen meat was an essential component of New Zealand grassland development. In contrast to wool, however, where New Zealand producers largely met the specifications of an overseas market, New Zealand meat exporters to some extent had to create a market in Britain for their produce:

> Hitherto the British public have been more a beef than a mutton eating people, but with a plentiful supply of good and cheap mutton brought to their doors, they are cultivating a taste for mutton ... A very slight change of taste in a population of 37,000,000 amounts to much.[77]

That was something of an exaggeration: mutton had never been unimportant in the British diet, but if New Zealand meat exporters 'did not invent lamb consumption in London, [they] did invent the Sunday lamb roast on the average table'.[78] Given the variations in regional and local taste in Britain, New Zealand growers had to attempt to standardise demand or, as it was put, 'in the course of time, educate the British taste up to a uniform standard' relying on well-conditioned smaller and finer carcasses.[79] This meant, among other things, constant renewal of pasture: 'Old pastures and early maturity will seldom, if ever, be found to go together, and neither are healthy well-grown lambs and old pastures usually found in conjunction.'[80]

For both meat and dairy produce, an important conduit of information was New Zealand's Agent-General in London (from 1905, the 'High Commissioner'). The Frozen Meat Trade Association (in 1909 renamed as the Incorporated Society of Meat Importers) worked closely with the colonial Agents-General, sent weekly summaries of prices to the colonies, and organised occasional conferences of importers and ship-owners on matters of concern. From 1895 until 1908 William Pember Reeves was Agent-General; his reports often reinforced those of the produce brokers, comparing New Zealand meat with Australian and River Plate, and commenting on the quality of butter. Reeves suggested that only factory-made butter should be exported; butter from the farm dairy was too erratic in quality. As for meat, 'the nearer our mutton could be bred to resemble the Hampshire Down sheep here the better price it would fetch: failing that then Border Leicester cross seems better liked than Lincoln'.[81]

Quality was often a problem. As Reeves warned, 'if this sending over of badly-frozen and inferior sheep goes on, added to accidents and mistakes during the voyage and want of cooperation among the big consignees here it is doubtful whether the industry will ever get into a healthy state'. Dairy factories had to

> take care that their stuff comes to people here who can be trusted to take it away instantly and store it in cool chambers: if it cannot be sold at once on favourable terms they had better keep the stuff in N.Z. I think there can be no doubt that much of our produce does not come to the right people.

He also wanted greater publicity given to the fact that the New Zealand Government graded all dairy exports, a fact 'not nearly widely enough known'.[82] Reeves emphasised that – just, incidentally, as had been the case with the worsted goods manufactured out of New Zealand wool – the market for New Zealand meat was 'neither with the very rich and fastidious nor with the masses of the poor ... It is in the middle class in which our customers are for the most part found.'[83]

Reeves was particularly concerned about 'passing-off', that is, where meat from one source was represented as being of another provenance. Generally, he thought, most frozen mutton from whatever source was passed off by unscrupulous butchers as New Zealand, which meant that New Zealand's reputation suffered badly from being associated with inferior Argentine meat. Conversely, the best New Zealand meat was passed off as Scottish, which meant New Zealand was robbed of the reputation such good meat should have earned it.[84] This of course had serious implications.[85] For someone with the image and reputation of a fastidious intellectual, Reeves was an advertising agent manqué: having persuaded the Premier, Richard Seddon, to consider an advertising campaign, Reeves wanted not an exhibition of New Zealand produce but 'canvassing, sample rooms, tasteful displays in good shops, lectures, photographs, pamphlets, illustrated interviews are my notion. Give me the sinews of war and I will boom New Zealand'[86] (Figure 6.4).

London meat brokers supplied frequent and comprehensive reports to New Zealand mercantile firms, from where the information obtained wide circulation. Much of the commentary in brokers' reports concerned timing of sales, storage facilities, and similar issues. Quality was a paramount issue, just as it had been in the development of the wool market. In 1899 it was observed that much very poor Australian mutton had been shipped 'under the mistaken impression that anything is good enough for this market' and with consequent damage to the Australian reputation. The quality of

New Zealand mutton had been adequate but not as consistent as it needed to be, and Australasian growers and shippers would need to work towards 'continuous supplies of evenly-graded meat'.[87] So far as beef was concerned, New Zealand would have to produce for the top end of the market as the River Plate sent plenty of average quality.[88]

Figure 6.4: Display of frozen meat carcasses at the British New Zealand Meat Company in Christchurch. At its first annual meeting in 1905, the company reported that it had purchased four shops in London for the sale of New Zealand meat. *Source*: *Feilding Star*, 17 June 1905. Photograph: 1/1-009113-G, Steffano Webb Collection, Alexander Turnbull Library, Wellington.

It did seem in the following years that New Zealand farmers did not make beef a priority. In 1910–11 a considerable quantity was imported from New Zealand 'which ought never to have left the Dominion', being only good for canning.[89] The importance of predictability, and therefore by implication a sustained approach to pasture development, was frequently emphasised. New Zealand shippers were reproved in 1901 for excessively large mutton carcasses with much fat on them.[90] Although 'much ha[d] been done in the way of educating consumers to use a larger weight of carcass than it was possible to sell in this country ten years ago' the preference was still for 'young meaty carcasses' under 56 pounds (25.4 kilograms) in weight, and lamb under 36 pounds (16.3 kilograms), despite the breeders continuing to produce large-framed and fat sheep.[91] A warning that New Zealand lamb was often, if not too large in the carcass, thin and plain, or second-class, was an implicit reflection on the quality of pasture.[92]

CONCLUSION

The integration of colonial pastoralism with the requirements of metropolitan manufacturers and consumers was not automatic, but was a process extending over a considerable period and one that depended upon the extension of webs of connection (Figure 6.4). While New Zealand wool exporters achieved significant success in supplying the manufacturing industry in Bradford and surrounding districts in the West Riding, the Bradford trade had considered and encouraged many other sources of supply, which for various reasons proved less satisfactory than the Australasian colonies and, later, South Africa. Pastoralists in the River Plate region tended not to produce wool of sufficient quality for British manufacturers but the lower quality of their wares was no barrier to finding markets in continental Europe. In view of this wide range of potential sources of wool, we must, therefore, modify Barnard's observation that 'the intimate economic, social and political bonds between the colonies and the mother-country dictated that Britain was to be the consumer of colonial wools'.[93]

So far as meat and dairy produce were concerned, the emphasis was to some extent more upon creating a demand than meeting an existing market, although this point can be exaggerated. New Zealand meat and dairy exporters did devote considerable energy to persuading British consumers of the desirability of eating New Zealand meat, butter and cheese, but the mass British market for better food was expanding anyway. What New Zealand's exporters did was to persuade that market to direct its spending towards New Zealand-sourced food.

New Zealand's economic development in the mid-nineteenth century was to a large extent related to the requirements of British industrial manufacturers and domestic consumers: not, primarily, as a market for manufactured goods, but as a source of raw materials and foodstuffs. It is also evident, as has long been recognised, that there was little of a grand plan in the development of settler colonies like New Zealand. Rather, it was fortuitous that the demand in the West Riding for good combing wool expanded shortly after New Zealand pastoral settlement began, and that the technology to transfer perishable foods from New Zealand to Britain was developed relatively soon after the limits of a wool-oriented pastoralism were reached. In the case of both wool and foodstuffs exports, meeting an existing demand and creating or channelling that demand were closely linked. This consideration might modify accounts that locate the ultimate forces in the development of settler colonies among the gentlemanly capitalists of the City of London.[94]

A striking aspect of pastoral history is the openness with which advice was shared by farmers and other interested parties. Pastoralists and stock and station agents had few reservations about publishing their recommendations. Information on British markets was in the colonial press for all to read, and stock and station agents often published free circulars.[95] Much of the literature on entrepreneurship emphasises the importance of innovation, but there is a particular dimension to entrepreneurship in primary commodities. That dimension lies in the importance of place of origin as an indicator of quality. In wool, as later with dairy and meat exporting, 'Port Phillip' or 'New Zealand' had to be a recognisable symbol of quality and the interest of any individual pastoral entrepreneur was advanced by widespread and collective attention to quality.

Many theoretical approaches to entrepreneurship stress the individual entrepreneur and some suggest that information that is the basis of the entrepreneur's judgement should remain secret, that is, a monopoly. In the case of improved farming practices a widespread dispersal of the information was much more efficacious.[96] If a single New Zealand farmer improved his pasture and stock to the point that the highest-quality wool or meat and butter was the result, that would avail him little if New Zealand produce generally had a reputation for inferiority.[97] Indeed, the pastoral finance sector could conceivably compel a laggard to improve his performance. The importance of this collective dimension, in terms of the mass marketing by national or regional origin, may be another way in which farming entrepreneurship differs from commercial or manufacturing varieties. Innovation and judgement are critical, but monopoly much less so.[98] These dimensions go far to explain the role of the state, which complemented private sector efforts in finance and information, after the mid-1880s.

Finally, this chapter suggests the importance of integrated perspectives. If traditional economic analyses of capitalist imperialism have 'emphasised economic drivers of imperial expansion, barely acknowledging environmental variability or transformation, including grasslands' it is certainly worthwhile expanding the perspective of imperial history to that extent.[99] We need to consider the wool, dairy and meat trades, as well as that in grass seed from which pastures were produced. If imperial history without grass is in the New Zealand context an incomplete account, an account of grass without imperial and economic history is at least as unsatisfactory.

7 *The Grass Seed Trade*

Eric Pawson and Vaughan Wood

INTRODUCTION

At the New Zealand International Exhibition held in Christchurch in the summer of 1906–7, 'The Department of Agriculture occupied, as was fitting, the premier place amongst the Government departmental courts.' The indoor display was complemented by 'a space of little over an acre, enclosed for the purpose of cultivation as a garden of grasses and forage-plants'.[1] A contemporary photograph indicates the neatly packaged way in which the demonstration plots were laid out, so that visitors could see the wide range of grasses that would grow in the country, and be able to learn more about them (Figure 7.1). Amongst the many useful grasses from all over the world, some with weedy characteristics like sweet vernal were included so as to discourage their use.

The timing of this exercise in public education is significant. By this time, Alfred Cockayne, then assistant biologist in the Department of Agriculture (and later, director of its Fields Division, and later still, director-general), was coming out against the belief that cheap grass seed was a cost saver. He wrote of the 'erroneous conception' that grass could be left to take care of itself, pointing to the presence of weeds in seed mixtures. 'There are no "bargains" in the seed trade', he said, calculating that weeds diminished the 'annual producing power of our land by at least 5 percent'. This translated into a loss of nearly one million pounds in agricultural exports.[2] It was not long before he and the Department were focusing not only on weeds, but also on seed quality, plant persistence and (as was apparent at the Christchurch Exhibition) the suitability of particular pasture plants for specific purposes and places. It was only to be expected that, given the intensification of pasture-based farming from the 1890s, 'improvement' of seed stock and quality-control measures would become of increasing importance across the world, in New Zealand no less than anywhere.

Figure 7.1: The Department of Agriculture's display of pasture and forage crops at the New Zealand International Exhibition, Christchurch, 1906–7.
Source: Steffano Webb Collection, Alexander Turnbull Library, Wellington.

The background to the emergence of this increasingly calculative approach to grass seed production and usage is the focus of this chapter. It considers the development of seed commodity chains, in terms of the international networks within which the seed trade in New Zealand was embedded. It examines the agents of this trade, the seed companies, importers and exporters, and nurseries. By the 1880s, domestic seed production was of growing importance in a number of districts for a small range of pasture plants, of which cocksfoot, ryegrass and white clover were the most significant. Between then and the 1920s, quite large quantities were exported, with some New Zealand seed gaining a high reputation in new pastoral frontier districts in Australia, North and South America, and South Africa, as well as amongst British farmers seeking to renew old pastures.[3] Grass seed commodity use and production in New Zealand therefore fits within a wider picture of the flexible webs and networks of biotic exchange of the imperial era.[4]

NETWORKS AND AGENTS

International networks of exchange shaped the developing profile of New Zealand's pastoral and agricultural outputs, as the preceding chapter has shown. In the same way, many of the inputs, notably capital, seed and information, were often sourced beyond immediate localities. Grass seed in particular was the product of a commodity chain with an international reach. Rapid landscape transformation required large quantities of seed, such as the 30 bushels (about 1,100 litres) of ryegrass and two hundredweight (about 100 kilograms) of hard fescue that James Wilson of Ngaio Station (see chapter 2) bought from Sutton and Sons of Reading in 1890.[5] Even established farmers usually lacked the means to harvest or clean sufficient seed of the right sort for their own use. Economies of scale dictated that it would be cheaper to buy from commercial suppliers.[6]

Farmers purchased seed directly from seed companies or agents overseas, or through local agents, stock and station agents, nurseries or domestic seed companies. Seed was sourced from a range of places, as farmers experimented with what would grow best on wet soils and dry, on reclaimed wetland, on bush-burn country, on ploughed tussock. There was, however, a common moniker given to pasture plants used in improvement, and that was 'English grasses'. The author of the first manual of grasses and forage plants published in New Zealand (in 1887) said, 'A new country begins of necessity by importing many commodities which require special skill in the production of them.' He referred to 'the great bulk of the seeds used [being] obtained from firms of seedsmen of the highest standing, specifically mentioning 'leading seedsmen at Home, such as Sutton, Carter, Webb and others'. 'But', he went on, 'that we should not be so largely dependent on them as we are at present is a matter that admits of no question.'[7]

At one level this portrayal of dependence on 'Home' sources very much accords with the discursive picture of imperial core and periphery that has framed much subsequent historical analysis. Although the real situation was more complex, the leading British seed companies played up to this image. Carters used an elaborate narrative brand, its byline of 'Seeds For All Climates' being displayed above a drawing of a sailing ship in dock, on which are several barrels and boxes of the firm's grass and clover seeds. Suttons' brand was even more dramatic (Figure 7.2). Its central image was of Demeter, goddess of corn, seeding the globe with 'Sutton's English Seeds for All Parts of the World', reinforced (as was Carters) by royal crests, as well as by more regionally specific endorsements in the form of exhibition medals and citations from leading settlers. There is plenty of incidental evidence, from advertisements in newspapers and directories, catalogues and letters, to support the reach that these companies claimed.

Suttons' *Farm Seed List* for 1865 states that they were 'constantly packing Farm and Garden Seeds for Australia, New Zealand, India, Africa and other Foreign Parts', whilst *Sutton's Autumnal Catalogue* for 1867 carries three endorsements from New Zealand, along with two from India and four from the Cape of Good Hope.[8] After Lincoln School of Agriculture was established in 1878 its first research report highlighted grass-plot experiments, 'the seed obtained from Messrs Suttons and Sons'.[9] Perhaps the most remarkable claim was one made on Suttons' behalf. It came from 'One of the earliest settlers in New Zealand', writing in the *Reading Mercury*, the newspaper in the firm's home town, in 1885. This person asserted that he had received

Figure 7.2: Suttons' brand. *Source: Wise's Post Office Directory*, 1890/91.

clover and ryegrass seeds from the company as early as 1841. These, he said, 'were the first English grasses sown in the Auckland district … the Colony since then has made rapid strides, and the Reading seed firm have shipped seed for most of the rich pastures of New Zealand'.[10]

On better lands, English grasses, like ryegrass, known for its nutritive value, were preferred. However, many pastures were far from 'rich', and required grasses that could thrive in marginal situations, such as the dry former tussock country of the South Island, or the hilly back country of the North. Most farmers were not rich either, and many, like Herbert Guthrie-Smith when he went to Tutira in 1882, used sacks of 'tailings and sweepings' rather than expensive premium branded seed.[11] It was these purchasers who were the target of Cockayne's campaign against cheap seed. But farmers tended to acquire information about seed from a range of sources, bought seed of a range of qualities, depending on available income as well as supplies, and ended up with pasture plants from a range of origins. For example, Sir James Wilson's biographer wrote that he looked for advice to 'Suttons the seed people, and to the Royal Agricultural Society' but that he spoke 'with keenest appreciation of Buchanan's *Manual of the Indigenous Grasses'.*[12]

Native grasses were the basis of New Zealand's early extensive pastoralism, which was dominated by Merino sheep. Tall tussocks however, with the exception of new leaves and flowering shoots, were unpalatable to stock. As chapter 5 has demonstrated, runholders burned tussock with discrimination, for reasons including the encouragement of new growth and succulent short-tussock pasturage. Samuel Butler commented on the 'delicately-green and juicy grass which springs up after burning'. On the plains and downlands, clover and English grass seeds were often scattered in the ashes, or sown after ploughing in order to provide better pasture for cross-breed sheep.[13] Elsewhere, some of the several species of danthonia – commonly known as oat grass – came to be highly regarded for use on poor hill country. While some danthonias were indigenous, many were naturalised from Australia: *Danthonia pilosa*, for example, which was regarded by Cockayne as having value for supplying at least some feed in such districts.[14] John Buchanan noted that it formed 'an important part of the pastures of New Zealand', highlighting its 'inherent regenerative power' (i.e. it could recover quickly from overgrazing) and its 'capacity of ripening abundance of seed'.[15]

In addition to native and Australian grasses, there were pasture plants sourced from countries other than Britain (like paspalum), and 'English' species that naturalised to produce characteristics that became highly valued in trade. *Paspalum dilatatum* is a sub-tropical grass of high nutritive value that prefers damp conditions such as those in Northland. By 1900, it was available from Auckland nurserymen and seed merchants as Louisiana grass (indicating a North American source), although it had also been imported earlier from Uruguay.[16] The best examples of naturalising 'English' species are Poverty Bay ryegrass, Chewings fescue, and Akaroa cocksfoot, the last-named being the basis of New Zealand's seed export trade from the 1880s. This will be discussed below; for the moment, the story of Chewings fescue is a good indication of how networks and agents intersected in the production and dissemination of seed.

About 1883, Robert Cleave, a nurseryman in Invercargill, imported seed from Hurst and Son of London. It was sold as hard fescue, one of the minor English species being tried at the time, as Wilson's later purchase (above) shows. Cleave sold the seed to local farmers wanting a grass that would grow on hard, stony ground. One sowed about ten hectares, selling the seed back to Cleave. George Chewings assumed ownership of the paddocks in 1887, supplying Cleave with more seed than he could handle. The balance was passed on to a seed merchant firm in Dunedin, J.E. Watson and Co., who gradually built up a national market, as well as selling it through Suttons to British, American and South African customers.[17]

In the North Island, Chewings fescue was championed by various landowners, as well as by Gerald Peacocke, editor of the Auckland-based agricultural journal, the *New Zealand Farmer*. He described it with enthusiasm in 1892 as a 'grass for pumice land',[18] meaning dry low-fertility soils. He was referring to the hill country in the southern Waikato and to the extensive ranges between the Thames Valley and Hawke's Bay. Mixed with danthonia, it was considered of potential value for these poor-quality lands, as well as for those in Taranaki, on the ridges behind Palmerston North and for surface sowing on the runs of the Mackenzie Country beneath the Southern Alps. Some of its promoters claimed it as an indigenous grass, in the sense of being a variety that had only emerged on New Zealand soils. This claim was ended in 1925, when the government seed analyst identified it as a variety of red fescue, well known in Europe, especially in Germany.[19]

Chewings fescue became widely available in the North Island through Auckland's leading seed merchant, Arthur Yates. Yates claimed to be 'the only firm in the colonial seed trade whose head-quarters are in England'. Arthur was a grandson of George Yates, who had established a seed business in Manchester in 1826. In 1883, Arthur moved to Auckland, and after being joined by his brother in 1887, he then moved on to Sydney to start a branch there. A list of accounts for the late 1880s shows that the Auckland firm had a very wide reach. It was dealing with individual purchasers, storekeeper agents, nurserymen and seedsmen not only in and around Auckland itself, but also in Northland, Tauranga, Cambridge (in the Waikato) and Gisborne. It had regular trade with the South Island, from Picton, to the West Coast and as far away as Invercargill. Yates sourced its seed in a number of ways: from Europe, from independent growers ('we are one of the largest buyers in the colonies'), and from farms at Mangere in Auckland, at Exeter in New South Wales, as well as Manchester.[20]

SEEDS AND SEED SPACES

The great bulk of the seed grown in New Zealand, and made available for domestic supply or export, was however grown by independent farmers and on-sold to nurseries, seed merchants or brokers. From contemporary seed catalogues, it is clear that, around 1900, the grass seed trade involved about 20 grass and 10 clover species (chapter 4). Up until the First World War, two species stood out above all others, because of their almost universal use in grass seed mixtures. These were ryegrass and cocksfoot. In the years before the First World War, seed production for each accounted for between 8,000 and 16,000 hectares, whereas the space given over to production of all other grasses and the clovers was only about 8,000 hectares. Ryegrass and cocksfoot accounted for more than £80,000 worth of trade for the Canterbury (NZ) Seed Company in 1910, whereas combined sales of all other grasses and clovers came to less than £30,000.[21]

Ryegrass in particular had a long history of prominence as a pasture plant in Britain. It was one of the principal components of the early grass seed trade (some sources say the only one),[22] being renowned for its abundant leaf growth and palatability to stock. After two centuries of being grown for seed, it was also possible to obtain cheap supplies that by nineteenth-century standards were relatively free of weeds and other grasses. Both factors endeared it to British farmers more used to gathering their grass seed from the sweepings of the hay barn. Ryegrass was even more of an early favourite within New Zealand owing to the difficulty of obtaining seed of other grasses that could be relied upon. Thus, when the mission farmer Richard Davis sought seed for sowing pastures in 1825, he asked for a combination of ryegrass together with white, red and trefoil clover.[23] Likewise, the Deans family, whose Riccarton farm served as a model for the first Canterbury settlers, sowed only ryegrass and clovers; they would have been well accustomed to this approach, coming from Ayrshire, a notable ryegrass seed-producing district.[24]

Merchants and farmers responded to this early demand for ryegrass, and by 1843, Auckland and Wellington newspapers were advertising both imported and locally grown seed for sale. White and red clovers were also available for purchase.[25] Later in the decade, cocksfoot, timothy, and some of the less extensively used grasses, such as sweet vernal, and meadow foxtail, were added to the mix; this was a consequence both of local seed growers and vendors diversifying, and of a developing seed trade with Tasmania.[26] At this point, the actual quantities of grass seed that merchants kept in store cannot have been large: when the Christchurch nurserymen William Wilson first tried to get some cocksfoot seed in 1851, having observed a flourishing stand of the grass in Auckland, he could procure none there and instead had to import it from Britain.[27]

Ryegrass had come to be known as 'perennial ryegrass' due to a widespread belief in its suitability as a persistent constituent of permanent pastures. It continued to be the main seed traded over the next few decades as the New Zealand grass seed industry established itself. Particular districts gradually emerged as producing preferred strains, of which Hawke's Bay and Poverty Bay (around Gisborne) were two. Ryegrass from these parts of the east coast of the North Island earned a price premium over other ryegrass seed because its perennial characteristics seemed more assured. The Poverty Bay appellation featured in advertisements from at least 1870, while by 1883 the genuine article was so sought after that perhaps half of the reputed stocks had been falsely labelled.[28] At the same time, other districts began to earn a name for themselves as producers of seed of different species, for example Southland for Chewings fescue and Banks Peninsula for Akaroa cocksfoot.

The period from the 1880s to the 1900s saw a marked change in the New Zealand seed trade, with Akaroa cocksfoot coming rapidly to prominence on not just the national but also the global stage. In part this was due to the ongoing 'ryegrass controversy' of the late nineteenth century. This began when a number of observers, prominent amongst them the Royal Agricultural Society's Consulting Botanist, William Carruthers, started to question the value of sowing apparently short-lived commercial varieties of ryegrass in long-term pastures. He published his concerns in the Society's *Journal* in 1882. These supported the detailed experiments of a Kent estate owner, Faunce de Laune, who advocated the replacement of perennial ryegrass in such pastures by a range of grasses (including timothy, cocksfoot and meadow fescue) and clovers.[29] The controversy raged for the next decade, 'till nearly every one [was] heartily sick of it'.[30] Gilbert Murray, in the *Agricultural Gazette*, asked why, if ryegrass was not perennial, it featured so prominently in the long-established and 'rich pastures of the Midlands', a point backed up by Dr Fream in the *Journal of the Royal Agricultural Society* in 1890. Murray considered that much of the opprobrium that ryegrass had received was due to 'bad management rather than a defect of the plant itself'. Others considered that poor seed was to blame.[31]

The questioning of ryegrass, however, led to a consideration of potential alternatives, of which cocksfoot was the main beneficiary, although many seedsmen and nurseries were by the 1880s offering quite complex seed mixtures for establishing pastures. The attributes of cocksfoot had been noted long before by the famous British writer on agricultural improvement, Arthur Young. Quoting a Hampshire farmer who in 1812 found his pastures far more productive under cocksfoot than ryegrass, Young considered 'that the exclusive attention that has been given to ryegrass has proved in a thousand instances most prejudicial'. He recommended cocksfoot 'in consequence of its earliness, largeness of produce, and yielding an ample rouen (aftermath)'.[32] It is a leafy plant and certain strains were also particularly long lived. The Akaroa strain, which had developed in pastures sown in the 1850s by seed supplied by William Wilson, had a longer life and better all-year-round growth than much of the cocksfoot produced in Europe and North America. Interest in sowing other grasses such as timothy, crested dogstail and meadow fescue increased at the same time. This was at least partly because the tufted nature of cocksfoot meant that companion planting was usually required to infill the patchiness of the sward.

At times, Banks Peninsula growers struggled to meet the demand from domestic as well as overseas buyers. Not only were New Zealand farmers well aware of the ryegrass controversy in Britain from information in the periodical literature and farming columns in newspapers, but cocksfoot was well suited to grassing the bush-burn districts of the North Island. The Akaroa strain had already proved its ability to bring about such a transformation on the previously forested slopes of Banks Peninsula. In the United States, the plant was known as 'orchard grass', reflecting its ability to cope with shade; it could also manage to survive in dry as well as damp periods. It was described in the 1893 catalogue of one Queen Street, Auckland grain and seed merchants as 'fast becoming the greatest favourite with farmers and stockholders in this colony ... it is one of the earliest, most productive, nutritious, and valuable of the cultivated grasses, and no grass comes sooner to perfection, or stands drought so well'.[33]

By the early part of the twentieth century, cocksfoot was often called 'the king of grasses'. In its 1918 catalogue, Yates described cocksfoot as 'perhaps the best known of all grasses', being 'found in all situations, on all varieties of soils'. It then added, in bold, 'It should be included in all mixtures for permanent pasture.' A similar conclusion had been reached by farmers overseas. Akaroa cocksfoot became popular in Australia and Europe in the 1880s, and ultimately in American markets. In the same decade, the clover seed industry was transformed by the successful acclimatisation of the bumblebee, with red clover becoming a significant local crop in parts of Canterbury. Ryegrass was, however, still extensively grown, and Yates again gave widely emulated advice: 'For good soils Perennial Ryegrass is

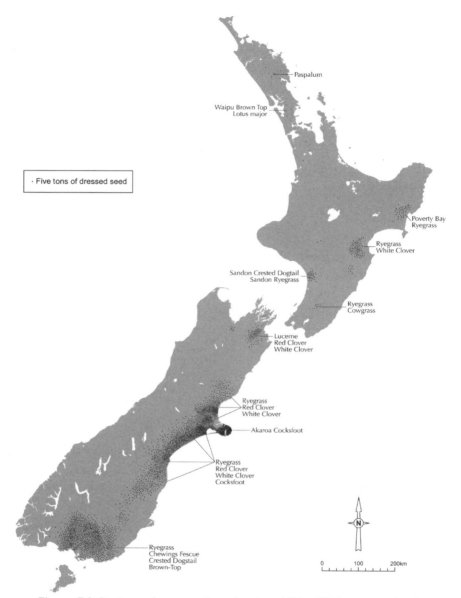

Figure 7.3: Regions of grass seed production, 1920s. Within a couple of generations, New Zealand farmers had identified regions associated with premium-quality seed, e.g. Poverty Bay ryegrass, and Akaroa cocksfoot. Two generations later these areas provided the 'mother seed' for the start of selective breeding efforts. *Source*: redrawn from N.R. Foy, 'The official seed-testing station: record of operations for 1926', *New Zealand Journal of Agriculture*, 21 March 1927, p. 189 (South Island) and p. 192 (North Island).

almost indispensable, and under favourable conditions affords permanent pasture of the highest feeding value.' Although advising that it died out 'sooner or later' on poorer soils, farmers were recommended to include it in all seed mixtures 'as it is beneficial in checking the growth of weeds and thus allowing slower grasses to develop'.[34]

Maps produced in the mid-1920s demonstrate clearly where grass seed was then being produced (Figure 7.3). These maps accompanied the printed 'Record of Operations for 1926' produced by the Seed Analyst at the Official Seed-Testing Station (which was located within the Department of Agriculture). The prominence of the Banks Peninsula cocksfoot growing area is clear. The analyst reported that amongst the 7,376 seed samples received 'from Merchants and Farmers' for testing that year, there were 15 named grasses and 6 named clovers. A quarter of these had come from Southland and another quarter from Wellington district (the latter covering the lower half of the North Island), and further significant amounts from Auckland district (18 per cent) and from Canterbury (16 per cent). Auckland accounted for the bulk of the imported samples (with Yates, for example, importing considerable quantities), whereas 'production and export [were] responsible for by far the greater portion' of the Southland and Canterbury samples.[35]

SEED EXPORTS

On 23 August 1879, the *Otago Witness* carried news in its trade columns that

> Messrs Law, Somner, and Co. made a shipment of Otago grown ryegrass to San Francisco, by last mail steamer. It was cleaned in the best manner by themselves. This is the fourth year that shipments of ryegrass seed have been made direct to California from Dunedin.[36]

Such reports are indicative of the early reach of the export seed industry. In the early decades of Pākehā settlement, the seed trade was based on importing, but this had reversed by the 1880s. Annual seed exports increased tenfold in that decade, and then continued to rise, as illustrated in Figure 7.4a. They reached a peak in 1911, before falling back during the First World War, then reached a second peak in 1923. The breakdown of destinations within the graph demonstrates the importance of the British and Australian markets before the war years, and the increasing significance

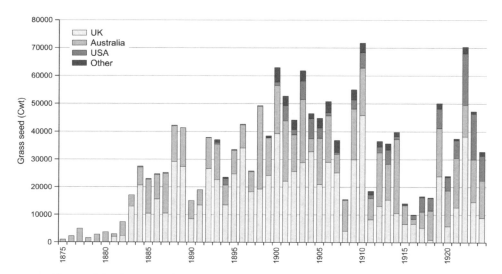

Figure 7.4a: Exports of grass and clover seeds, 1875–1924. The rise is largely reflective of the cocksfoot trade to Britain. *Source*: compiled from annual export data in the *Statistics of the Dominion of New Zealand*, 1875–1920, and *Statistical Report on the Trade and Shipping of the Dominion of New Zealand*, 1921–4.

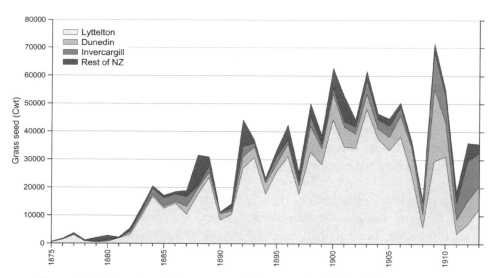

Figure 7.4b: Export ports for grass and clover seeds, 1875–1913. Lyttelton was the leader, again reflecting the trade in Akaroa cocksfoot. *Source*: compiled from quarterly export returns in the *New Zealand Gazette*, 1875–1913.

of American buyers in the 1920s. Figure 7.4b breaks the data down further, to illustrate the ports through which the seed was being exported. This stands as a useful proxy for which seed species were being traded.

The port data up to 1913 shows that the most significant point of origin by far was Lyttelton, the main port for Canterbury. Lyttelton is situated on the northern edge of Banks Peninsula. Written reporting on the Canterbury seed industry refers only to cocksfoot exporting (although other grasses were being grown for seed in the region). Furthermore, during the 1880s published shipping returns for Lyttelton used the category 'cocksfoot' rather than that of 'grass seed' as in the official statistics. The inclusion of cocksfoot in the Lyttelton returns, at a time when only six other commodities were identified in these, is indicative of the crop's importance in Canterbury's export economy when the cocksfoot trade was taking off.[37] Cocksfoot came only behind wool, wheat and mutton.[38] During the 1880s, New Zealand firms became the chief supplier in a British cocksfoot market that was rapidly expanding during the ryegrass controversy.[39]

Initially, the price of seed, from the values entered in the Lyttelton shipping returns, was high. There were a number of firms buying it from Banks Peninsula producers: in 1885, at least ten. By the 1890s, this had dropped to five or six and, with one or two exceptions, these were still the main buyers in 1910. One reason for this was the increased capital required to operate in the export trade, notably for mechanical seed-cleaning machinery.[40] Prominent examples were the Canterbury (NZ) Seed Co., based in Christchurch, and the Dunedin firm of Moritzson and Hopkin (which became A. Moritzson and Co.). Generally the seed sent overseas went to foreign seed merchants. If it was being sold in New Zealand, rather than going direct to farmers, it passed through seed suppliers, such as Nimmo and Blair of Dunedin, or stock and station agents, such as Dalgety and Co. A fair quantity of seed never entered into the formal market, however, instead going into the hands of indigent bush farmers from the North Island who came south to help with the cocksfoot harvest and to earn payment in kind.[41]

Adolph Moritzson is an important figure in the Peninsula export trade. He had migrated to New Zealand from Denmark (itself an important cocksfoot producer) in 1875, aged 22. He conducted his first business trip to the Peninsula in 1890, talking to no less than 258 growers over the space of a ten-day ride around its rugged hills and bays.[42] In a printed circular to the growers in 1891, he said that he was not able to give them 'a look up, as we have done last year', instead being bound on an 'extended tour' of the North Island, 'Napier and Taranaki especially', to see quantities of cocksfoot grown there. He added that after this tour, he would be better placed to advise on the season's prices. This points to the dependence of growers on such agents. In the meantime, his firm had sent lists to the principal growers in 'your Bays' to fill out with the quantities of seed grown that summer; and 'we are prepared to store your Seed in Lyttelton or Dunedin' and to ship it to London from either port. Significantly he then added that 'we wish to point out to you to stencil plate your bags "Akaroa Seed"'.[43] This is a good example of a strategy to capture value through place-specific marketing, like New Zealand-sourced meat at about the same time (as chapter 6 demonstrates).

The Banks Peninsula strain of cocksfoot was bulky, leafy, long lived and relatively persistent, and seemingly gave up seed year after year without cultivation, providing the paddocks were closed to stock as the plants matured.[44] It is these characteristics that found favour with overseas buyers, and encouraged both them, and brokers such as Moritzson, to brand the product by its geographical name of origin. This also enabled it to be distinguished from Danish cocksfoot, which was faster growing and shorter lived, and therefore less suited to the establishment of permanent pastures. This advertisement in the Welsh press on September 1890 is typical of those appearing in the United Kingdom at the time:

Seed: London, Wednesday Messrs John Shaw & Sons, seed merchants, of 37 Mark-lane, report that the clover seed market exhibits strong tone as regards value, but the demand is for the moment quiet, the only quotable advance being in white seed. Italian ryegrass is firm. For winter tares there is an improved sale at last week's rates. Sowing rye is without change. The new Essex white seed now coming to market exhibits for the most part poor quality ... New Zealand cocksfoot is getting dearer.[45]

The emergence of this localised industry into global prominence exemplifies not only how apparently peripheral places could assume central positions in value chains, but also how the local is constantly transformed by changing geographies of connection. Much of Banks Peninsula had been thickly forested until the 1860s. In 1869, a Canterbury district surveyor was of the view that 'as clearing bush lands for laying down grass is every year on the increase, I see nothing to prevent the total destruction of the bush in the Peninsula'.[46] This destruction only accelerated as the cocksfoot industry boomed in the 1880s. With the logging of big timber trees, and the firing of the residual timber, cocksfoot thrived when surface-sown in the fertile ash of the burn. Its production was not the only reason for bush removal, given the importance of timber in building the 'wooden world' of railway foundations, telegraph lines, houses and wharves. But cocksfoot was a significant factor in the transition described by a local historian of the time with the words: 'True gloomy Rembrandt like shadows have disappeared ... but in the stead of the past beauties are smiling slopes of grass.'[47]

The cocksfoot industry is also an example of the mutability of both the networks that constituted these geographies and of the objects (in this case, cocksfoot genetic material) that moved along them.[48] The seed that gave rise to the Banks Peninsula trade, having been imported by William Wilson in a two-hundredweight (about 100 kilogram) consignment, was part sown by him in Christchurch, with the balance sold to R.H. Rhodes, who sowed it at Purau on Banks Peninsula.[49] Given its characteristics, it is known to have been sourced from older grasslands and waste places of Britain.[50] Wilson then sold seed from the 1853 harvest to the family who were to become the most prominent early growers on the Peninsula, the Hays of Pigeon Bay. By the mid-1860s, they were on-selling seed to other farmers in the vicinity.[51] At this point, Peninsula cocksfoot became a tradeable commodity, and began to redraw the networks of which it was a product. Within 15 years, it shifted from being an English grass to a New Zealand one, and from being sourced in the English grasslands, to contributing, from afar, to the renewal of those same grasslands.

At the same time, it was being sold to buyers in the North Island of New Zealand and in Australia for new pasture establishment, and making headway into American markets for the same purpose. By the 1920s, America accounted for about one third of the sales of Peninsula seed. Some North Island seed was sold to both Australian and New Zealand buyers who would accept a lower standard; in Europe, Akaroa seed competed before the First World War with that sourced in France and Germany (which was not of great quality) as well as with American cocksfoot.[52] The significance of the branding of the New Zealand seed was that its attributes could be clearly identified and its price premium thereby justified. Between the 1900s and 1920s, American demand, which had previously been met largely from within, drew on Akaroa as well. This was perhaps the period of greatest reach of the New Zealand industry, but it occurred as the conditions that were to undermine its networks of exchange became increasingly apparent.

Denmark started to supply significant quantities of seed to European markets just before the First World War. At this point, a lower proportion of Akaroa seed seems to have been going overseas than previously: the proportion of its cocksfoot that the Canterbury (NZ) Seed Company sold to foreign buyers was only 31 per cent in 1910, compared to 64 per cent in

1898.[53] This shift was due to increasingly heavy demand in the North Island bush-burn areas with the growth of the dairy industry (see above, chapter 2). However the war disrupted the availability of labour for the harvest and, since the steep slopes of the Peninsula meant this had to be carried out by hand, the price of Akaroa cocksfoot began to rise sharply. Paddocks began to grow fern, as they were not being regularly opened to stock.[54] Local demand fell with the slowing of the New Zealand pastoral frontier in the 1920s, and with a new emphasis on creating temporary pastures on arable land, for which the Danish variety was better suited, New Zealand started once again to import cocksfoot.

By the 1930s, production was shifting off the Peninsula to the flatter fields of the Canterbury Plains, where machine harvesting could be used, and yields were higher.[55] At the same time, cheese and butter production was becoming more remunerative for Peninsula farmers. But George Stapledon, the Director of the Welsh Plant Breeding Station in Aberystwyth, who visited the district in 1926,[56] made sure that 'a very large number of the cocksfoot plants selected at Aberystwyth for breeding purposes emanated from seed received in New Zealand'. These included the S.37 and S.143 strains.[57] In New Zealand, the grassland scientist Bruce Levy, working with Stapledon's protégé William Davies, isolated the long-life strains that went into Poverty Bay ryegrass, thereby relegating the ryegrass controversy to history (see chapter 10). Nonetheless, grass and clover seed exports were still in the order of 2 million kilograms by 1930, the primary component of this being the perennial ryegrass trade to Australia. Production of Chewings fescue was also sustained by sales to the United States, where it was used as a lawn grass.

SEED QUALITY

The Welsh Plant Breeding Station had been established at Aberystwyth in 1919. One of Stapledon's first acts on taking up the directorship was to visit the German and Danish seed experiment stations.[58] Stations had been set up between 1869 and 1889 in Saxony, Denmark, Austria, Belgium, Sweden, Switzerland, Holland, Russia, Norway, France, Portugal and Romania. The USA had begun seed testing and plant breeding in 1875. This demonstrated how far ahead of Britain (and of New Zealand, which followed the British model) were other countries in the testing of seeds.[59] The gap explains Cockayne's concerns that were highlighted at the beginning of this chapter. Debate about the quality of seeds and seed mixtures had a long history.

Several aspects of quality were of concern to many – but not all – buyers.

One was the purity of seed stocks sold, i.e. the extent of contamination by weeds and seeds of other plants. A second was the risk of adulteration, i.e. whether samples were bulked up with dead or substitute seed. A third was the quality of the seeds themselves, i.e. the percentage of germination, and whether or not the seed was of the species or strain desired. In *The Clifton Park System of Farming*, a well-known book first published in Britain in 1898, and an inspiration to the young Stapledon, Robert Elliot compared wild local cocksfoot with New Zealand plants, observing that the former 'were very dwarf' and 'gave a much smaller amount of grass'. He also reported an experiment in a 20-acre (eight hectare) field,

> which was partly sown with seed supplied by a local seedsman, and partly supplied by one of the most eminent seedsman in England. The local seedsman knew that the comparison was to be made, and, no doubt, did his best, and there was no reason to complain of the germination or trueness of his seed, but the difference in the result was most marked, and the cattle declined to eat his plants so decidedly that one would imagine they had been fenced off the field.[60]

For such reasons, well-known seedsmen and companies guarded the integrity of their products and brands. Suttons, for example, announced in the New Zealand press that after 1 January 1886, their seeds would be supplied 'for sale in the Colonies IN SEALED PACKETS ONLY; which packets have been made up in our own Warehouses, and stamped with our Registered Trade Mark' (as illustrated in Figure 7.2). This assurance was for vegetable and flower seeds, but the same concern applied to grass seeds, namely that other suppliers were selling 'unreliable Seeds' under Suttons' name.[61] Yates, whose byline was 'Reliable Seeds', was aware of the same practices, as their 1904 catalogue indicated. It warned its customers that

> In procuring our Seeds from Agents and Storekeepers, make sure our name is on the bags or tickets enclosed. We are repeatedly hearing of Seeds being sold as Yates' which were never supplied by us. There are cheaper, inferior samples to be had at a lower cost, but good, clean Seeds are always worth the money asked for them.[62]

Concerns about seed quality emerged early in New Zealand. 'A bushman', writing to the *Southern Cross* in 1862, commented that when buying seed in Auckland, 'one often gets perfect rubbish ... and probably at the same time have the seed highly recommended by the seedsman'. He complained particularly about grass and clover seeds. 'Agriculturalist', writing in three days later, attributed some of the problems to seed germinating properties being 'dried up and exhausted by bad packing or by their being damaged by sea water'.[63] The more reputable firms tried to resolve such issues. For example, Suttons packed their export seeds in sealed zinc containers. This firm also produced its own seeds, either on its own land, or by contracting to growers, using Suttons' stock, who then delivered direct to the headquarters in Reading without the intervention of a third party. By the 1880s, it also had a comprehensive process for testing seed vitality. One observer of this noted that 'A most elaborate record is kept of all transactions.'[64]

Similarly, Yates in 1893 advertised that they followed 'the custom of TESTING THE GROWTHS of all the seeds we sell'. But it was not a widespread custom, being 'neglected by the trade generally'. Yates also emulated some of Suttons' approaches to vertical integration. They advertised: 'While others have to depend on intermediate merchants for their supplies of English and Continental seeds, we buy from the growers direct, in many cases the seeds being grown specially for us.' For testing these seeds, and 'for the growing of a large number of seeds which do not stand the sea voyage', the firm by 1893 had three 'extensive' farms, two south of Auckland and one outside Sydney. Here they saved 'pedigree' seeds to 'supply to the regular growers with whom we contract for our supplies', as well as putting in test plots of the seeds they sold: 'At one of our

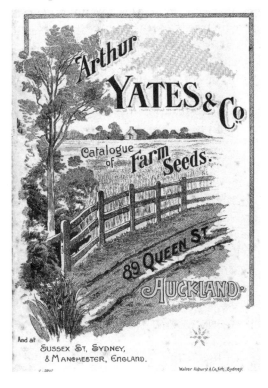

Figure 7.5: Cover of the Arthur Yates & Co. seed New Zealand catalogue, 1893. The cover was designed in Sydney, for a company established in Manchester whose first antipodean office was in Auckland. The farm scene is reminiscently English, albeit with an Australian eucalypt above the post-and-rail fence.

Mangere farms we are making very exhaustive trials of the various grasses.' This followed the thousands of trials that Martin Hope Sutton, who was regarded as a great 'improver', carried out in Reading. By 1917, the Wellington firm of F. Cooper Ltd claimed to be 'the largest growers of seeds in the Southern Hemisphere', with over 1,000 hectares 'under our immediate and direct control and personal supervision' in Marlborough.[65]

The emphasis on oversight in part reflects an increasingly calculative approach to production and an investment in brand awareness amongst larger seed suppliers. However, it cannot be properly understood without an appreciation of Victorian concerns about seed adulteration. The British Parliament passed the Adulteration of Seeds Act in 1869, in response to widespread concerns about practices whereby London seedsmen in particular were known to add dyed or dead seeds to samples, or even foreign matter. A few years later, these 'nefarious practices' re-emerged, drawing a swift response from companies such as Suttons and Carters. The latter wrote to the editor of *The Times* to say that 'The farmer need never fear getting adulterated seeds from respectable houses', because of the loss of reputation that they would suffer. Witnesses appearing before the Board of Agriculture's Committee on Agricultural Seeds in 1901 indicated that adulteration 'is not now practiced to any material extent'.[66]

These witnesses did however identify another long-running issue: 'carelessness in separating weed seeds from the bulk, and from want of care in cleaning and screening'.[67] This was exactly the case in New Zealand, as many people, from Herbert Guthrie-Smith to Alfred Cockayne, knew. When Guthrie-Smith arrived on Tutira in 1882, and bought the cheap seed of the sort that Cockayne subsequently decried, he ended up with hairgrass, crested dogstail, foxglove and common vetch in the first paddocks he developed.[68] Given the conditions under which seed was harvested, it is not surprising that it could be full of impurities. Akaroa cocksfoot, for example, was initially cut, threshed and cleaned by hand, using, respectively, sickles, flails and riddles (large wooden sieves). Lightweight portable threshing and seed-cleaning machines were adopted in time.[69] But at the start of the 1890s, export seed was still recleaned on receipt by British seed merchants.[70]

From then on, New Zealand suppliers began to take more responsibility for the cleanliness of their product. In 1894, Moritzson and Hopkin advised that 'we are starting Seed cleaning, and shall be ready for our farmer friends in January next'. A machine 'of the latest type' had been ordered capable of removing 'Hairgrass, Capeweed, Ergot, Yorkshire Fog, Sorrel, Clovers, Dock, Goosegrass etc.'. The following month the machine was constructed but the firm urged farmers 'to eradicate the Californian Thistle if it is growing on their land, as its presence in any seed makes the line almost unsaleable'.[71] The Canterbury (NZ) Seed Company was originally set up in 1889 to use patents developed for better cleaning grass seed. In an account in the *Weekly Press* in 1894, the secretary of the Canterbury Agricultural and Pastoral Association witnessed a sample before and after cleaning. He estimated that it contained 18 per cent Yorkshire fog beforehand, and many other impurities, with a germinating power 'in that state' of 65 per cent. Afterwards, he found 'practically nothing but clean seed', and a germinating power of 90 per cent, due to the elimination of light and immature seeds.[72]

Such evidence should be treated with caution. There was still plenty of cheap seed about and in 1912 Cockayne could assert that 'The desire for "bargains" in seed-buying is one that the farmer should sternly repress.' Many weeds originated in seed mixes (although some, such as blackberry, sweet briar, gorse and broom, were hedgerow escapees). By this point, the Department of Agriculture would test 'any seed received from farmers free of charge', and had also produced a 'Weed-Seed Reference Card' plus magnifying glass, covering 50 of the commonest weeds, for farm use. Cockayne saw the whole business of weeds in seed mixtures as 'one of the most serious problems for farmers'.[73]

As late as 1922, a significant range of impurities was found in cocksfoot samples tested by the Department's Biological Laboratory. There was an average 2.5 per cent of 'extraneous seeds', of which ryegrass, Yorkshire fog and goose grass were the most frequent. In addition, the germination rate of Akaroa cocksfoot, at 55 per cent, was found to be relatively low compared to imported Danish cocksfoot, at 75 per cent. This was attributed to the system of cultivating Danish cocksfoot in rows, as against shutting up paddocks on Bank Peninsula, and taking crops year in, year out, without returning nutrients to the soil.[74] By 1926, the Laboratory had become known as the 'Official Seed-Testing Station', and assessed 8,627 seed samples that year. The average percentage germination in the cocksfoot samples was 69, compared to 77 for perennial ryegrass, and figures in the 80s for Chewings fescue, Italian ryegrass and crested dogstail.[75]

CONCLUSION

The importance of the seed trade was due to the particular significance of pasture-based production in New Zealand. By the 1920s, this was more the case than ever. In Bruce Levy's vision, 'New Zealand is essentially a land of pastures, and the endeavour of its farmers is to grass every type of country from the seashore to the line of perpetual snow.' As an acolyte of Alfred Cockayne (who did so much to promote the scientific development of pastoral farming in New Zealand),[76] Levy's view was that 'The study of pastures is ... of national importance, and their improvement of national gain.'[77] One of his main contributions was to take up the ideas of Stapledon, who argued that there was much variation within pasture grass species, and that pasture could be improved by planting the best strains. By 1931, Levy and William Davies (a scientist seconded from Stapledon's plant-breeding station) had identified superior strains of ryegrass and white clover, which were to become the mainstay of productivity gains in pasture thereafter (see chapter 10).

The era of Levy and ryegrass is apt to obscure the interesting environmental histories of pasture production over the preceding century. At one level, this was a time of 'grassland silences', when too many farmers took grass for granted, bought cheap seed, and in effect connived in the practices of a seed trade that in Britain was known for the laxity of its practices. Yet ironically, it was 'English grasses' that had the greatest standing in New Zealand, being used to establish temporary and especially permanent pastures in a range of previously indigenous environments from wetland to bush. Through the geographies of connection of the seed trade, an increasing array of emergent grassland places began to coalesce as a pastoral fringe seeded by, and for, empire. But it was not only a fringe. The seed trade story shows how places can be simultaneously peripheral *and* nodal, with some of otherwise utter obscurity, like Banks Peninsula, emerging for a time as central to seed supply and pasture remaking in both the new and old worlds.

From the vantage point of the mid-twentieth century, it was easy to look back and decry the 'disquieting situation' of the 1920s before the introduction of official seed certification. There were then few good lines of perennial ryegrass, a great deal of unevenness amongst other grasses, and difficulties in demonstrating that cocksfoot lines were of the Banks Peninsula strain when so much Danish seed had been imported from time to time.[78] Nonetheless, the half-century before had been one of increasingly systematic practices in the seed industry, as those seedsmen seeking to build or protect their reputations applied an ethos of improvement to their trade. In this sense, seed companies became 'centres of calculation', or primary points through which materials were brought together, often from a wide geographical reach, and made to act together by a process of 'translation', or integration. This can be seen in the practices of Suttons, Yates and Moritzson and Hopkin. Each meets the criterion of a centre of calculation that acts at a distance on many other points.[79]

Ultimately, the best example of this was Stapledon's careful experimentation in Wales with Banks Peninsula cocksfoot. Through his incorporation of the Akaroa seed in the new strains that he developed there, he made available its best attributes for pasture production worldwide. Similarly, the work that his lieutenant, William Davies, did with Levy on perennial ryegrass in New Zealand had much wider significance. By the 1920s, the importance of the seed foundations of the imperial value chain in worked-up grass was becoming much more widely understood, and in this the systematic improvements of grass seed by nineteenth-century seed companies had played an important role.

8 Flows of Agricultural Information

Vaughan Wood and Eric Pawson

INTRODUCTION

Whilst large parts of New Zealand were being transformed into Britain's farm, (Western) European farming models were simultaneously undergoing significant changes. Like many other professions, early nineteenth-century farming was practised as an art, but by century's end it was also a science; where it differed say, from medicine and engineering, was that most of its workforce remained home taught, and without external qualifications.[1] These developments meant that New Zealand's settlers had a double learning task: in order to compete in international markets, they had to adapt the farming skills they had brought with them, as well as update these skills to keep up with both overseas and local innovations.

The lack of any pastoral farming tradition meant that it was critical that agricultural information networks were developed in New Zealand. Until the introduction of goats, pigs and sheep by Cook and de Surville between 1769 and 1777, it had the distinction amongst the world's temperate landmasses of being entirely bereft of grass-eating mammals.[2] As a result, there was no opportunity for the generation of pastoral farmers who established themselves in the 1840s and 1850s to be home taught (even by observing Māori) in the local environment. Traditional Māori agriculture only extended to sub-tropical tubers,[3] so New Zealand was effectively a tabula rasa when it came to cereal cultivation as well. Although Māori quickly adapted to European crops, as chapter 3 shows, only in the cultivation of potatoes was pre-contact Māori expertise readily transferable.[4]

If these features made the situation for New Zealand settlers difficult, the absence of preconceived notions gave plenty of scope for innovation.

Furthermore, by the time organised settlement began, formalised networks for the dissemination of new agricultural information were being established in Britain with the potential for replication elsewhere. Underpinning these networks was the principle that better farm practice would follow if farmers were better informed. In the fashion of recent scholarship on the movement of ideas around dynamic global networks,[5] this chapter examines how institutions from afar were propagated and reconfigured in order to instil better practices in New Zealand. A case study of an early agricultural periodical (the *New Zealand Country Journal*) illustrates the type of information that was circulating. The rise of the 'expert' (and thereby the centralisation of the production of information), and its implications for increasing state involvement in New Zealand farming, are also considered.

AGRICULTURAL INFORMATION NETWORKS IN THE BRITISH WORLD

In Britain at the start of the nineteenth century, most landlords and farmers drew their farming knowledge from direct experience and observation, and private communication with kith and kin. Innovations only diffused through the mobility of their practitioners.[6] But as Nicholas Goddard has documented, increasing numbers of British farmers began to tap into an expanding range of agricultural information sources during the next few decades.[7] The prospect of higher estate rentals, and the introduction of the 'tenant right' (which compensated tenants for their improvements), gave landlords, estate managers and tenant farmers alike a strong incentive to take an interest in new farming practices which might increase efficiency. Developing transport infrastructure was also a factor, as it situated the farmer in an ever-expanding market.[8]

In Britain and the United States the improving quality of agricultural information also had a significant bearing on how much notice farmers took of new information sources. 'Book farmers' had often been a figure of fun. But the production increases that followed from the introduction of 'artificial' fertilisers in particular convinced many farmers that the idea of combining 'practice with science' – which was chosen as the motto of the Royal Agricultural Society of England – had the potential to benefit them immediately, rather than being something to treat with derision.[9]

For the majority, the first new elements of the agricultural information network were agricultural shows, and the societies that organised them. These societies were readily embraced, being in effect public extensions of the traditional learning methods of private dialogue and direct observation. They began in Britain in the mid-eighteenth century and by 1835 there were around 90 in England and Wales, and more than 130 in Scotland.[10] Farmers' clubs, which put more emphasis on regular discussion and were less aristocratic than the societies, also appeared.[11] Agricultural shows extended into other events such as ploughing matches, and implement trials and demonstrations.[12] In that they relied on visual and oral interaction, such institutions and events were intrinsically local. Nevertheless, as transport networks improved it became increasingly feasible for observers to congregate within national institutions and at royal shows,[13] or for speakers or new implements to travel around different societies.[14] Increasing farmer mobility widened the diversity of views at events where private dialogue typically occurred, such as market days, livestock sales and horse races.[15]

Agricultural literature was also undergoing change by the end of the eighteenth century, with the emergence of, first, agricultural periodicals and then newspapers intended specifically for farmers. Most pre-nineteenth-century agricultural textbooks, with some exceptions, like Arthur Young's *The Farmer's Kalendar* (1770), had such indifferent content and limited readership that they had little effect on farming practice.[16] The new periodicals, such as Young's *Annals of Agriculture* (1784–1808), and the *Farmers' Magazine* (1800–26), and newspapers such as *Evans and Ruffy's Farmers Journal* (1807–32),[17] changed the nature of the agricultural information network, transcending space, and to some extent time. It was as easy to reprint advice from distant parts as it was to produce local copy, and their reports provided a widely accessible record of events such as shows and farmers' clubs meetings where previously there had been none.[18] By the mid-nineteenth century, gaining 'intelligence' in one's field by reading professional periodicals was also becoming commonplace.[19]

Agricultural societies in Britain were quick to exploit the new media, with the Bath and West publishing their own journal from 1780 to 1816, while in Scotland the Highland and Agricultural Society began publishing their *Prize Essays and Transactions* in 1799. The *Journal of the Royal Agricultural Society of England*, perhaps the most esteemed British periodical, did not start publication until 1840, but the RASE was itself established only two years previously.[20] Commercial firms such as seed merchants and implement manufacturers also benefited from the rise in periodicals and newspapers, as most contained advertising, allowing them to reach a wider client base. As postal services improved, the firms began producing their own circulars and catalogues, adding to the traffic in agricultural literature.[21]

Formalised agricultural education and instruction was the last major addition to nineteenth-century agricultural information networks. It combined oral, visual and written modes of communication. Edinburgh University established a Chair of Agriculture as early as 1790, but it was not until the 1840s that teaching of agriculture in British universities really took off. By this time, the Edinburgh course had been rejuvenated, and there were lectures on agriculture at Oxford, Durham and Aberdeen, and within Ireland's Queen's Colleges. The first of what became several independent agricultural colleges was established at Cirencester in 1845.[22] Like shows and societies, they relied on the physical presence of their students, but due to high fees and low numbers, they had little direct influence on farming.[23] It was only after 1890, when government funds for technical education became more freely available, that a number of British universities began to educate farmers through extension programmes.[24]

An illustration of how quickly such institutions could be adapted elsewhere is provided by the United States. There, the first agricultural societies were established in the 1780s, with the earliest agricultural periodicals, such as the *American Farmer*, dating from the 1810s.[25] These were not as direct an inspiration to New Zealand settlers as their British counterparts were, but the American agricultural college system, and its Department of Agriculture, founded in 1862, were seen as world leading. The Prussian agricultural education system was another model put forward as worth emulating.[26] In comparison, the Australian experience, despite its many commonalities with New Zealand, did not provide as significant an example. When addressing the Canterbury Agricultural and Pastoral Association in 1881, the *Melbourne Age*'s agricultural correspondent stated that he was sorry to say that it was questionable whether it had 'its equal in any part of Australia'.[27]

BUILDING NEW ZEALAND'S AGRICULTURAL
INFORMATION NETWORKS

Agricultural associations and societies were quickly established in New Zealand. Auckland, Wellington, Taranaki and Nelson all had such bodies by 1845 (within five years of organised settlement), and in Otago and Canterbury, where formal colonisation began in 1848 and 1850 respectively, they had been set up by 1852. Farmers' clubs followed, the first being in Auckland in 1853. Generally these survived for only a year or two, becoming defunct as soon as members dispersed onto farms beyond the immediate outskirts of the town.[28] Most did little more than organise a handful of shows, and produce reports on local farming conditions, which could be utilised as emigrant literature.[29] Some did host lectures and even essay competitions where practical information could be exchanged.[30]

Māori participation in shows seems only to have been encouraged at Auckland, even though they were the main produce suppliers in both the Auckland and Wellington markets at the time.[31] The success of Māori cultivation was a testament not only to their expertise at hand tillage, but also to the educational efforts of mission stations and church schools. Since the 1820s, these had provided some instruction on skills such as ploughing and handling livestock on what amounted to early model farms.[32] From the late 1840s, the colonial government also tried to promote sheep and dairy farming to Māori through its sponsorship of bilingual newspapers, but growing Māori distrust of settler intentions limited the success of this.[33]

A handful of schools and individuals also offered agricultural tuition to new settlers and their families. New Plymouth's Wesleyan-run 'Grey Institution' initially focused on training young Māori, but by the early 1850s took in Pākehā pupils as well.[34] Nelson also had an agricultural and industrial school, established by the land surveyor Alexander Ogg.[35] None of these endeavours seem to have made a lasting impression on farm education. A more enduring way of gaining instruction was the cadet system, whereby pastoral runholders provided food and lodgings for the term of an unpaid apprenticeship (usually about a year). However, this differed little in terms of information transfer from learning by direct observation and experience, and in the absence of any formal requirements was criticised by some as a waste of runholders' time and resources.[36]

With the settler population being small, and rural communications rudimentary, there was virtually no market for domestic agricultural publishing during the 1840s and 1850s. Some settlers brought British agricultural textbooks with them, and the New Zealand Company (which before 1850 was the main conveyor of British migrants) recommended in its *Handbook to New Zealand* that they should possess a copy of Stephens' *Book of the Farm* (1844).[37] This was one of a number of authoritative, almost encyclopaedic British textbooks that had been published in the mid-nineteenth century. These books, which were expensive to buy and bulky to transport, were sometimes donated to libraries in the new settlements,[38] but records of library issuing indicate that they were seldom borrowed.[39] Their value in New Zealand conditions was also doubtful; with the exception of *The Book of the Farm*, the Mahurangi correspondent of *the Auckland Weekly*

News opined in 1864 that 'works on farming written in England are not suitable for practical purposes in these colonies'.[40]

In contrast, high literacy levels and settler hunger for market and social information supported an abundance of colonial newspapers, which did carry agricultural items.[41] During 1865, aggregate New Zealand newspaper circulation amounted to 29 issues per head of population – a remarkable figure given that only a handful of newspapers were then published daily.[42] Local farming reports were particularly evident around harvest time, and copy from other parts of New Zealand and overseas was often used.[43] During the mid-1840s, the *Nelson Examiner* extracted material from publications as diverse as the *Transactions of the Highland and Agricultural Society of Scotland*, Western Australia's *Perth Gazette*, the *Philadelphia Saturday Courier* and Nova Scotia's *Colonial Farmer*.[44] In 1850 the *Otago News* reproduced a series of lectures on practical agriculture that had appeared in the *Sydney Morning Herald* two months previously.[45] The routing of such information could be complex. After first extracting a commentary on fern (bracken) land 'sourness' from Charles Hursthouse's *An Account of the Settlement of New Plymouth* (published in London in 1849), *Chambers' Emigrant's Manual for 1851* advised treating the soil with lime; both Hursthouse's commentary and the remedial advice were reprinted first in the Edinburgh-based *Journal of Agriculture*, and then in turn by the *Otago Witness*.[46]

From the first years of settlement, therefore, New Zealand farmers had links – even if these were dependent on the priorities of newspaper editors, and the content of postal correspondence – with agricultural information networks across the globe (the mapping of the connections in Joseph Munnings' diary in Figure 4:1 illustrates this high degree of connectivity in another way). The broad range of sources reflected the realisation that experience from other colonial or quasi-colonial settings could be as valuable as British experience. As Dr Curl, a founder of the Wellington Farmers' Club, observed, connections with other associations in both Europe and the United States, not to mention neighbouring colonies, would allow locals to take advantage of the American 'labor-economising machines, mode of culture, [and] manner of clearing forest land', and equally, of European improvements in cultivation and grazing practices.[47]

Not until the 1860s, however, did a stable information network begin to emerge. The best farmland around the main settlement centres had been taken up early and was by then under cultivation,[48] so those taking up new farms required greater skill to make up for this disadvantage. With a generation of local experience, some farmers were becoming recognised for expertise in areas such as livestock breeding.[49] Appreciation of the need to keep abreast of current market news was heightened by market volatility following the arrival of large numbers of gold miners in the South Island, and warfare in the North Island as Māori tribes attempted to retain their lands. Farming fortunes were further unsettled by falling wool prices and the saturation of the Australasian wheat market by the end of the decade.[50] Simultaneously, government (the provincial councils in the 1860s, and increasingly the colonial administration in Wellington in the 1870s) invested in new telegraph and rail systems, allowing the more effective circulation of price information, post and agricultural literature (Figure 8.1).[51]

Farmers now had both motive and opportunity to attend and participate in events like shows and ploughing matches. A new wave of agricultural institutions was established. Many of these, such as the Hawke's Bay, Canterbury and Southland Agricultural and Pastoral Associations (founded in 1858, 1863 and 1867 respectively),[52] are still in existence today. The first Canterbury Agricultural and Pastoral Show, held in 1863, was attended by 1,500 people, while by the time of the tenth in 1872, numbers had risen to 8,000 (or around 15 per cent of the province's population).[53] Some of the better-supported associations invested in libraries. Amongst the titles in the circulating library of the Auckland-based Otahuhu Agricultural Association were Morton's *Cyclopaedia of Agriculture*, Stephens' *Book of the Farm*, Johnston's *Chemistry of Common Life*, Liebig's *Principles of Agriculture*, and the *Journal of Agriculture*.[54] They also often represented the community interest in politics and commerce. The Ellesmere Farmers' Club, for example, having been set up to run the local ploughing match, arranged a successful trial shipment of wheat to Britain in 1870.[55]

Newspapers also reacted to changing conditions. Through most of the 1850s, agricultural content had been squeezed by domestic and foreign politics, but it started to return to prominence late in the decade. The *Taranaki Herald* published a series of 18 letters on agricultural chemistry in 1859,[56] despite warfare between British forces and local Māori over land being only a matter of months away; the Auckland-based *New Zealander* published a longer series on local farming two years later.[57] This interest may have reflected the shortage of quality farmland in Pākehā hands around the two settlements.[58] A shift to daily publication by most newspapers in the larger centres was mirrored by the inception of weekly versions tailored specifically for rural readers, published to coincide with market days. Examples such as the *Auckland Weekly News* (1863), *Weekly Press* (Christchurch) (1865) and *Canterbury Times* (1865) set aside pages for agricultural features. The *Otago Witness*, a weekly since 1851,[59] introduced farming pages in 1863, which included content not in its sister publication, the *Otago Daily Times* (founded in 1861).

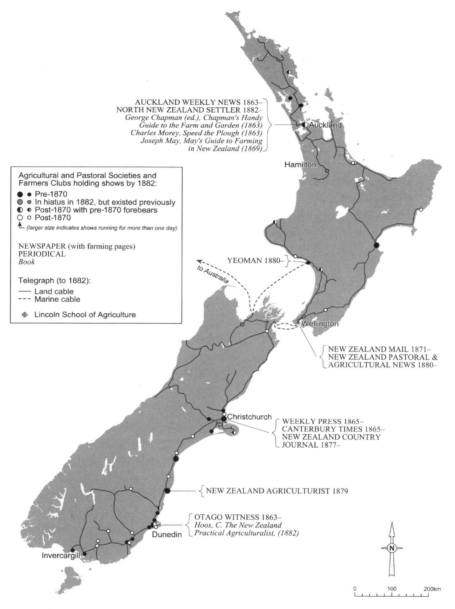

AUCKLAND WEEKLY NEWS 1863–
NORTH NEW ZEALAND SETTLER 1882–
George Chapman (ed.), Chapman's Handy
Guide to the Farm and Garden (1863)
Charles Morey, Speed the Plough (1863)
Joseph May, May's Guide to Farming
in New Zealand (1869)

Agricultural and Pastoral Societies and
Farmers Clubs holding shows by 1882:

● ● Pre-1870
◉ ◉ In hiatus in 1882, but existed previously
◐ ◑ Post-1870 with pre-1870 forebears
○ ○ Post-1870
↳ *(larger size indicates shows running for more than one day)*

NEWSPAPER (with farming pages)
PERIODICAL
Book

Telegraph (to 1882):

— Land cable
--- Marine cable

⊕ Lincoln School of Agriculture

YEOMAN 1880–

to Australia

NEW ZEALAND MAIL 1871–
NEW ZEALAND PASTORAL &
AGRICULTURAL NEWS 1880–

WEEKLY PRESS 1865–
CANTERBURY TIMES 1865–
NEW ZEALAND COUNTRY
JOURNAL 1877–

NEW ZEALAND AGRICULTURIST 1879

OTAGO WITNESS 1863–
Hoos, C. The New Zealand
Practical Agriculturalist, (1882)

Auckland

Hamilton

Wellington

Christchurch

Dunedin

Invercargill

N

0   100   200km

Figure 8.1: (facing page) Sources of agricultural information available to farmers
in 1882. In 1882, the development of farm production on the east coast of the
South Island was reflected in the extent of its agricultural information networks.
Many small communities were already holding their own shows, while the
telegraph network kept them in touch with market intelligence that might
otherwise have been the preserve of metropolitan newspapers. The   →

Most contributions to such newspapers were anonymous although some individuals, like the South Auckland farmer William Morgan, offered regular comment, becoming New Zealand's first agricultural journalists.[60]

Coupled with the rise of the rural weeklies, was the increasing use of circulars and catalogues to promote agricultural goods and services. Advertising literature was not new,[61] but improved postal and freight services allowed firms to move from point-of-sale information exchange to circulating such literature by mail order to distant potential customers.[62] To enhance their value, catalogues sometimes incorporated more general material too – the Dunedin seed firm of Thomas Allan, for instance, published a seed catalogue and gardening calendar.[63] As seen in chapter 7, this means of direct marketing proved a boon to companies offering farming inputs like seed or machinery where quality was important, and cartage costs relative to the lifetime of the product were low. Circulars could be just as useful for firms or organisations needing to instruct far-off suppliers, hence their use by the Bradford Wool Supply Committee described in chapter 6.

The third form of agricultural literature to appear during the 1860s was the locally produced agricultural textbook. Until then, the only advice available had been on sheep, from Frederick Weld's *Hints to Intending Sheep Farmers in New Zealand* (1851) and J.B. Acland's *Notes on Sheep Farming in New Zealand* (1858), both published in London. Acland's account drew from his initial experience at Mt Peel Station (described in chapter 5), and was based on his address to the Bath and West Agricultural Society; Acland's brother, Sir Thomas Dyke Acland, was one of the Bath and West's leading stalwarts.[64] Otherwise settlers had had to make do with chapters on farming in more general works such as Robert Bateman Paul's *Letters from Canterbury* (1857) and Charles Hursthouse's *New Zealand, or Zealandia, the Britain of the South* (1857).[65] In 1862, however, George Chapman of Auckland published *Chapman's Handbook to the Farm and Garden* (1862), which was followed

→ South Island main trunk railway already connected Christchurch, Timaru, Dunedin, and Invercargill (the venues for the four large South Island shows), and had a number of branch lines to smaller places; many North Island centres had rail but only in their immediate hinterland. *Source*: maps in the Post Office and Telegraph Department Annual Report for 1881–2, *Appendices to the Journals of the House of Representatives* 1882, F1; the list of textbooks and periodicals is from Wood, V. and Pawson, E., 'Information exchange and the making of the colonial farm', *Agricultural History* 82/3 (2008), pp. 337–65. The data on shows is from contemporary newspapers and local histories.

shortly by two other Auckland titles – *Speed the Plough* (1863), and *May's Guide to Farming in New Zealand* (1869).[66] Although the farming sector was then strongest in Canterbury and Otago, Auckland had the larger population. It also had a high percentage of novice farmers by virtue of its provincial immigration policy, whereby migrants who paid for their own voyage out were rewarded with small grants of land.[67]

It was another decade and a half before the first agricultural periodical appeared. Some short-lived general periodicals, such as the *New Zealand Magazine* and the *Hawke's Bay Monthly Manual*, had tried incorporating farming-related articles in the 1860s, but it was not until 1877 that the Canterbury Agricultural and Pastoral Association launched the first fully-fledged example, the *New Zealand Country Journal*.[68] There were good reasons for this timing. Large-scale immigration had occurred from the early 1870s due to a combination of agricultural depression in Britain, and the colonial government's policy of encouraging the opening up of the country to close settlement through public works. Canterbury, with a climate suitable for grain growing, and its extensive plains suitable for railways, took the lead. Canterbury's earliest Pākehā settlers had by then been farming for a generation, so felt able, even obliged, to instruct newcomers. As the *Country Journal's* editorial committee said in its second issue, 'the practice of agriculture in the Colony leaves a large margin for improvement, and it is this no doubt which has been the means of inducing a publication like the present to make its appearance'.[69]

Initially, the *Country Journal* hoped to become the national periodical. A meeting of Agricultural and Pastoral Association delegates in 1878 endorsed this aim, together with the establishment of a New Zealand-wide Association. This did not however occur, as local Associations themselves came under severe financial strain as the country sank into the lengthy economic depression that lasted throughout the 1880s. The City of Glasgow Bank failure in Scotland in 1878 rippled through the British and colonial banking systems. With the withdrawal of inter-bank credit, New Zealand farmers were subject to a wave of foreclosures and even bankruptcies.[70] The situation proved terminal for the Nelson and Hutt Valley Associations.

Instead, the *Country Journal* was joined in 1879 by the Oamaru-based *New Zealand Agriculturist*, and in 1880 by the Wellington-based *New Zealand Pastoral and Agricultural News, and Investor's Guide*. The Oamaru title lasted only a few issues, while its Wellington competitor was quickly incorporated into the *New Zealand Industrial Gazette, Pastoral and Agricultural News*. *The North New Zealand Settler*, published in Auckland from 1882, survived due to aggressive marketing, although with name and ownership changes.

It was eventually bought by the publisher Henry Brett (whose firm had produced the *Brett's Colonists' Guide*, a compendium of information for rural households, in 1883) and relaunched as *the New Zealand Farmer, Bee and Poultry Guide* in 1885. Over the next decade, the *Country Journal* and the *New Zealand Farmer*, both of which had national readerships, albeit concentrated in Canterbury and Auckland respectively, had the domestic market to themselves. In 1896, they were joined by New Zealand's first specialised publication, the *New Zealand Dairyman*.[71]

With the appearance of these periodicals, only one element was missing compared to the agricultural information networks of Britain and America – the agricultural college. Agricultural instruction by the state, through such means as farm advisors and model farm tours (described more fully in chapter 9), gained in significance from about 1900. Although the need for an agricultural college had been raised since the start of Pākehā colonisation, it was not until the mid-1870s that the University of New Zealand's Canterbury College moved to put the idea into practice. Provincial government was abolished in 1876, but a land endowment from the Canterbury provincial council in 1872 enabled an elaborately housed college to be opened at Lincoln (southwest of Christchurch) in 1878 (Figure 8.2).

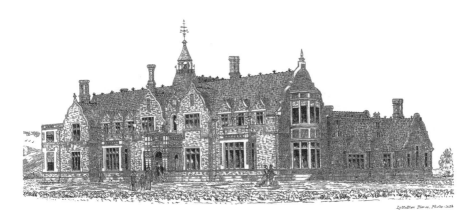

Figure 8.2: The elaborate buildings of the Lincoln School of Agriculture in 1880, the year it opened to students. *Source*: *New Zealand Country Journal* 4/5 (1880), facing p. 273.

Lincoln School of Agriculture was one of the earliest agricultural colleges in the British Empire after Cirencester, and the first teaching institution in Australasia.[72] The expense of its buildings made for high fees, however, and when its intake began in 1880, it struggled to attract students. Tuition cost £5 and board around £35 per year, ruling attendance out for the sons of almost all practising farmers. By 1894, just 43 had earned certificates in agriculture by passing the three-year course.[73] The onset of depression had not helped and there was adverse comment about the failure to reduce the fees accordingly. But the college developed a respected experimental programme and when lectures were given in rural communities they could draw sizeable crowds. In early 1878, for example, 150 people, most of them farmers, packed the town hall of Leeston to hear Professor Bickerton of Canterbury College give a talk on manures.[74]

This was also a significant time for agricultural education at primary school level. The 1877 Education Act had made it compulsory for all children to attend school between the ages of 7 and 13, and in 1878 a national curriculum was established. This stipulated that elementary science, including 'the simpler processes of agriculture, and the classification of animals and plants', should be taught in Standards Four to Six (that is, to 10- to 12-year-olds). Amongst the list of regulation textbooks that schools could use in their science programme were the *Irish Agricultural Class Book*, Johnston's *Agricultural Chemistry*, and Johnston's *Catechism of Agricultural Chemistry and Geology*; the latter, it was noted, 'should be studied, especially by teachers of country schools'.[75]

ASSESSING THE EFFECTIVENESS OF INFORMATION NETWORKS

By the mid-1880s, the architecture of agricultural information networks overseas had been largely replicated in New Zealand. As in British experience, it was newspapers tailored to farmer needs and agricultural periodicals that had the greatest potential to communicate information to the largest numbers. Newspapers were low in price, and some were widely circulated. For example, in 1896 the *Otago Witness* had a circulation of 9,650.[76] Newspaper contents were also often up to date, and allowed reader feedback and debate. They were, however, relatively ephemeral, which is where the more permanent record provided by periodicals was of value. These were more costly, and limited in circulation (the *New Zealand Farmer* had 2,000 subscribers in 1890),[77] although available to those who wanted to read them by subscription, sharing or through libraries. They also encouraged a certain amount of discussion in their pages, not as immediate as that which took place at shows or clubs, but mediated by peer review and increasingly the commentary of emerging experts. Robert Wilkin's article on 'Grasses and forage plants', the first to appear in the *Country Journal*, was, for example, used as the basis for organised discussion at the Cambridge Farmers' Club in the Waikato.[78]

In respect of New Zealand farming textbooks, several factors would have lessened their impact. Cost was one – *Brett's Colonists Guide*, for instance, was priced at £1, whereas an annual subscription to the *New Zealand Farmer* was half this amount.[79] Quality must have been an issue as well, given the telling remark by the Lincoln lecturer George Gray to the national conference of agricultural societies in 1898 that there were still 'no reliable textbooks that suited the requirements of farmers in New Zealand'.[80] They were also a virtually static source of information. Few were ever republished, and if they were there was usually a long wait; in the case of *Brett's Colonists Guide*, it took 14 years. When farming was subject to rapid technological advances (such as improved sowing and harvesting machinery, and new fertilisers), information soon became obsolete.

In contrast, New Zealand's newspapers and farming periodicals were connected in to the nineteenth-century world's rapidly evolving information networks described by writers such as Simon Potter and Alan Lester.[81] Copy from British, European and American sources could reappear within a matter of months. The first issue of the *New Zealand Country Journal* in January 1877 contained an article extracted from the *Agricultural Gazette* of the previous September, while an item which had appeared in the *American Farmer* in February 1885 was reprinted in the June issue of the *New Zealand Farmer*. After the linking of New Zealand with the international telegraphy network in 1876 (Figure 8.1), mercantile information was transmitted rapidly. The Grain and Produce Report of the January 1883 issue of the *New Zealand Country Journal* quoted a London cable dated 1 January.[82]

The provision of opportunities for feedback – much more so than in the *Journal of the Royal Agricultural Society of England* and the *Mark-Lane Express* (Britain's leading grain and seed trade journal) for example – was another factor that would have encouraged farmers to read rural newspapers and periodicals. Both the *New Zealand Country Journal* and *New Zealand Farmer* made a point of calling for the submission of articles from farmers, and set aside space for correspondence and queries. Through such contributions, farmers could float their own theories in front of a wide audience, including the observant sheep farmer, who despite the lack of assistance from textbooks recognised the relationship between perennial ryegrass, staggering sheep and heat almost exactly 100 years before the fungal cause of 'ryegrass staggers' was pinpointed.[83]

Queries could also give readers an indirect influence over content. For example, an article on liver fluke by the North Canterbury sheep inspector, Reginald Foster, in the March 1881 issue of the *Country Journal* was in response to a query four months earlier.[84] In a sense, newspapers and periodicals could act like a farmers' club meeting by post, albeit with editorial filtering. Textbooks (and by extension, textbook-based education in schools), in contrast, offered one-way communication from a few individuals at most.

THE *NEW ZEALAND COUNTRY JOURNAL*

The *New Zealand Country Journal* was published between 1877 and 1898, in its first year as a quarterly and thereafter bi-monthly. Its subscription income suggests its circulation was in mid-to-high hundreds.[85] Its lifespan coincided with the directional change in New Zealand farming brought about by the introduction of refrigerated shipping (as discussed in chapter 6), before the emergence of the state as the arbiter of good farming practice. In its early years, the cultivation of crops and pastures received just as much attention as the husbandry of livestock, with comparatively little focus on marketing of produce, other than through regular market reviews. At the time, the *Country Journal*'s aim of improving farming practice had plenty of scope, as its contributors tried to counter the perception of many that wheat was the only paying crop on newly cultivated land. This had become particularly prevalent once the onset of the depression in 1879 plunged those who had paid inflated land prices into debt.

The concern to improve the performance of intensive pastoralism on mixed arable and pastoral farms was reflected in the first article, Robert Wilkin's 'Grasses and forage plants'. His efforts to convey the merits and flaws of the different pasture species were greatly expanded upon by the eight-part series 'A short history of the grasses', by J.B. Armstrong of Christchurch's Botanic Gardens in 1880 and 1881. Soil-fertility issues also featured more prominently at this time than at any other, due to the overcropping of soils. Amongst articles on this subject was a 16-part series ('The chemistry of manures') contributed by George Gray between 1879 and 1882. Examination of queries that were submitted suggests that alternatives to continuous wheat cropping were at the forefront of readers' minds as well.[86] Almost half of the 32 queries received during 1879, for example, related to cultivating a variety of crops and sowing pastures. In keeping with the advocacy of Norfolk-style rotations from contributors like John Grigg of the Longbeach estate in mid-Canterbury, 5 of the 32 related to turnips or mangel cultivation, while 2 of the 6 livestock queries were about feeding stock on turnips and mangels.

Up until 1882, there was an eclectic mix of articles on livestock, the most active topic of discussion being the cross-breeding of sheep (see chapter 5). Once refrigerated shipping began in 1882, however, the number of animal husbandry articles increased threefold, reaching a maximum of 44 in 1884, around 30 per cent of the content in that year. There was also a marked shift in their focus, those on cattle outnumbering those on sheep by two to one. As rearing cattle was only just developing significant momentum in New Zealand – the first national herd books appeared at this time[87] – many of these articles were extracted from overseas sources such as the *Livestock Journal* and the *Irish Farmers' Gazette*. Increasing content on meat and dairy processing after 1882 also helped to keep farmers abreast of the needs of overseas markets; again, much of this content was derived from foreign literature.[88]

The fact that refrigeration had provided a viable alternative to growing wheat was also reflected in a declining emphasis on the potential of novel crops, such as beetroot and European flax. Nevertheless, the 'ryegrass controversy' (outlined in chapter 7) was prominent in the journal's pages in the 1880s. Extracts from the writings of British luminaries such as William Carruthers, Martin Sutton and Sir James Caird appeared alongside local contributions from farmers and agricultural commentators. An extract from Sutton's *Permanent and Temporary Pastures* (1886) described how his discussions with 'large flockmasters' from New Zealand had revealed the startling difference in reputation of Yorkshire fog and *Poa pratensis* in the two countries.[89] While the ryegrass controversy was largely exhausted by 1890, its practical effect was that farmers began questioning whether unfamiliar species had any value as pasture grasses; consequently, grass identification became a frequent query to the *Country Journal* from the mid-1880s.[90]

The identification and control of pests and diseases was the dominant theme of queries in its last decade. The main concern of reader correspondence moved from finding ways of combating rabbit numbers (see chapter 5) to the new opportunities that chemical treatment provided for controlling a variety of insect pests.[91] From the early 1890s, however, the journal pulled back on its efforts to educate farmers about pest and disease control, as the newly established Department of Agriculture began to take over this role with its farmer bulletins (some of which were supplied as inserts to readers).[92] At about the same time, improvement in the quality of dairy produce emerged as a major concern; a dedicated section entitled 'The dairy' was included in issues from 1893. This corresponded to the Department of Agriculture's early dairy instruction and regulation initiatives. Again, much of the dairy-related content was extracted from foreign publications. Nine articles were derived from the writings of James Long, the British dairy expert who had written a report for the New Zealand Government on the state of the British market in 1889.[93]

During its 22-year history, the *New Zealand Country Journal* published around 3,100 articles of around a page or more (not including those in the short regular sections on sports and horse racing), as well as about 600 farmer queries and letters. If these are classified into nine subject categories – Crops and pastures, Soils and manures, General survey, Livestock, Pests and diseases, Production and markets, Machinery, Shows and exhibitions, and Miscellaneous (including irrigation and drainage, ornamental horticulture, arboriculture, and natural history)[94] – then 'Production and markets', encompassing the content relating to outputs, such as milk and wool, accounted for the largest share of articles (21 per cent), with this total being split fairly evenly between stand-alone articles and regular market reports.

This figure is higher than in Nicholas Goddard's study of content in the *Journal of the Royal Agricultural Society of England* in the 1870s[95] (from which the categories used here were adapted), or for contemporary American agricultural periodicals,[96] but it reflects New Zealand's emerging dependence on distant markets. The relative importance of animal versus plant production, even in cropping country such as lowland Canterbury, was also suggested by the proportions for 'Livestock' (18 per cent) and 'Crops and pastures' (13 per cent, with farm and garden calendars included). The large proportion of 'Miscellaneous' articles – 17 per cent – was both a testament to the strong tradition of natural history observations, which the long-standing editor, Michael Murphy, sought to encourage, and to contributions on themes befitting a landscape in transformation, such as irrigation, acclimatisation, and arboriculture. When it came to queries, 'Pests and diseases' far outstripped all other categories, accounting for 34 per cent of the total.[97]

In the first five years of publication, around 85 per cent of the content was sourced domestically, but by the mid-1890s this figure had dropped to less than 50 per cent.[98] In contrast, the *New Zealand Farmer* seems to have held the proportion of domestic content at around 60 per cent. The *Country Journal* had a policy of reprinting content which New Zealand farmers would not be able to access elsewhere;[99] in the absence of extensive original contributions, it always stood to be beaten to press by more frequent publications (that is, the weekly rural newspapers and the monthly *New Zealand Farmer*). So rarely did the *Country Journal* or the *New Zealand Farmer* reprint material from each other that the latter was allowed to advertise in the committee room at the 1894 Canterbury Agricultural and Pastoral Association show.[100] Mapping of *New Zealand Farmer* subscribers, together with the stated origins of queries submitted to the *Country Journal*, indicates that in Canterbury, Hawke's Bay and Auckland there were probably a number of farmers who subscribed to both.[101]

The steady increase in foreign content in the *Country Journal* reflected the huge growth in the amount of overseas information. The first cheap, mass-produced British farming handbooks (by authors such as Robert Warrington, Eleanor Ormerod and James Long) appeared in the 1880s, while in the 1890s a number of Australian agricultural periodicals were established. About two-thirds of the *Journal*'s foreign articles were derived from British (including Irish) sources, with Australian and American literature accounting for most of the remainder. Occasionally material from Continental Europe, and other parts of the British Empire, such as Canada, was included. It might come via a circuitous route; in 1893, for example, a lecture on 'the profitable cow' to the Ontario Agricultural College was reprinted via the *South African Agricultural Almanac*. The most copied foreign periodical was *the Irish Farmers' Gazette*, which may have been a consequence of Michael Murphy's father being Professor of Agriculture at Queen's College, Cork, although a good number of its articles related to developments in England.[102] This reliance on British Empire publications was a reflection of both trading relationships and mail routes. In contrast, about half of the foreign content in the *New Zealand Farmer* was from American publications, but Auckland was on a regular mail route from San Francisco, whereas Canterbury was not.

THE RISE OF THE EXPERT

Irrespective of the geographic origins of their content, a feature strongly evident in both the *New Zealand Country Journal* and the *New Zealand Farmer* is the professionalisation of authorship, and the emergence of particular authors as 'authorities' or 'experts'. Similar trends have been observed with overseas periodicals, such as the *Journal of the Royal Agricultural Society of England*. In foreign-sourced material, this growing professionalisation was manifest in the increasing attribution of articles to individuals rather than just publications. Foreign experts, like the RASE consulting entomologist Eleanor Ormerod and consulting botanist William Carruthers, became so well known that they were quoted without affiliation.[103] In terms of the domestic content, however, practising farmers submitted less and less over time.

Both journals therefore become steadily dependent on contributions from two groups who emerged as 'authorities'. The first was the small number of agricultural journalists, such as Michael Murphy, and freelance contributors William Morgan and R.A. Wight. Murphy's obituary in 1914 observed that he was the arbiter of good farming practice in Canterbury prior to the Department of Agriculture's establishment: 'it was to him that most queries as to the best methods of agricultural practice were addressed'.[104] The freelance contributors provided an important linkage between publications. Morgan, for example, wrote articles for both the *Country Journal* and the *Auckland Weekly News*, while Wight submitted numerous articles and correspondence to the *Country Journal* under his own name, while writing for the *New Zealand Farmer* under the pseudonym 'Komata'.[105] Wight was a nodal individual for entomological information, with Eleanor Ormerod and C.V. Riley, Chief of the United States Bureau of Entomology, amongst his correspondents. Thanks in part to Wight, New Zealand provided the beetle that resolved California's cottony scale problem; he informed Albert Koebele, tasked with finding a natural predator from Australia, that this beetle had already eradicated cottony scale in Auckland.[106]

The second group was the agricultural scientists. Staff of the Lincoln School of Agriculture regularly published in the *Country Journal* (a college magazine did not appear until 1895), and because of its struggles to attract students, the *Country Journal* gave Lincoln its best chance of reaching out to the farming public. An informal history of the Canterbury Agricultural and Pastoral Association, which was closely associated with the college through its Board of Governors, credits George Gray's articles publicising analyses of manures as one of the reasons for the passing of the Manure Adulteration Act 1892.[107] In contrast, the *New Zealand Farmer* relied more on authors of Department of Agriculture publications such as the botanist Thomas Kirk. In 1894, it took the further step of engaging an English-qualified veterinarian to write a column, saying this would be 'of great practical value to our readers who have no opportunity of availing themselves of professional literary advice'.[108]

Farmer contributions to the *Country Journal* and *New Zealand Farmer* slipped away over time for a number of reasons. The rise of the expert probably diminished the value of observations from the field in readers' minds; as times became tighter in the 1880s, individual farmers had fewer resources for experimental ventures on which to report. The *New Zealand Farmer* maintained its local content by sending special reporters to visit notable farms and sites of agricultural industry, but this seems to have been beyond the financial resources of the *Country Journal*, which made do with supporting prize farm competitions.[109] The start of biennial national farmers' conferences in 1892 diminished the role that periodicals could play in transmitting information between disparate groups of farmers. So too did the increasing networking of exhibitions and shows, in which equipment, supplies and prize animals were displayed around the country (Figure 8.3). As discussed in chapter 9, the Department of Agriculture, with its significant political backing (and thus ultimately financial resourcing) also moved into this informational space.

Figure 8.3: Interested visitors amongst the agricultural implements at the Otago Agricultural and Pastoral Society show, Dunedin, 1903. *Source: Otago Witness*, 2 December 1903, p. 45. Hocken Collections, University of Otago.

While the Department first worked in tandem with the *New Zealand Farmer* and the *Country Journal*, the latter even helping to distribute its leaflets, ultimately it would go it alone. In February 1910, the *Canterbury Agricultural and Pastoral Association Journal* (from 1899 to 1912, the pared-down successor to the *New Zealand Country Journal*) reported on a new rule that 'officers of the Agricultural Department were forbidden to give information even of a technical kind to newspapers'.[110] Within five months, the Department would launch its own periodical for farmers, the *New Zealand Journal of Agriculture*.

CONCLUSION

There is little doubt of the commitment of the New Zealand farming community to the distribution of agricultural news. An effective network, relying primarily on newspapers and periodicals, and supported by local meetings of farmers' clubs and Agricultural and Pastoral Associations, had been established within a few decades of the start of organised settlement. Although linkages to Britain were very important, this network was interconnected, to varying degrees, with webs of information in various parts of the world. As a result, while New Zealand farmers were isolated geographically, there were not isolated educationally, a point that Rollo Arnold made of the late nineteenth-century New Zealand population more generally.[111] Information also flowed the other way, as the specific instances of Sutton's informants, and the resolution of California's cottony scale infestation demonstrate.

As communications improved, the locus of 'authority' when it came to agricultural information shifted from the farm, first to the Agricultural and Pastoral Associations or farmers' club hall, and then to the offices of the Department of Agriculture. Even so, connections with kith and kin could still modify the routes through which information travelled, as Acland's lecture and Murphy's use of Irish sources show. The growing influence of the state nevertheless marked a major change to the architecture of agricultural networks, as for the first time since the days of word-of-mouth it vertically integrated the production and distribution of information. As a result, the networks which had enabled farmers to share their experiences in farming a new land now had the potential to become a force for conformity.

9 The Farmer, Science and the State in New Zealand

Paul Star and Tom Brooking

INTRODUCTION

Between 1890 and 1930 the source of New Zealand's economic prosperity narrowed to an almost total dependence on the growth of grass for conversion by cattle and sheep into dairy produce, wool and meat. This much is well known. The role of farmers themselves in getting pasture development underway has never been properly explored, however, and is the first subject of this chapter. The second subject is the input of the state towards agricultural change through the utilisation of science. It seeks to assess the relative contributions of farmers and of officials and scientists in the transformation that occurred during these years.

New Zealand's agricultural history since the formation of the Department of Agriculture in 1892 has generally been presented in institutional terms.[1] This chapter, however, looks more at the human influences at work in pasture development that did *not* operate within an institutional framework. It sets out to review the field (*ager*) in a more fundamental way, to bring out the environmental history that lies around (*en viron*) the agricultural history.[2] This requires considerable reconstruction as the evidence comes from written primary sources that tend to be human- and stock-oriented rather than environment-oriented. With the striking exception of Herbert Guthrie-Smith's account of change on his Hawke's Bay sheep station, most interest in the environmental effects of farming dates to a later period.[3]

Local agricultural events should be positioned not only within their wider environmental setting, but also within the context of global changes in both primary production and governance. In 1967, Robert Wiebe characterised the history of the United States from 1877 to 1920 as

159

a 'search for order' directed by a new middle class that applied 'scientific method' to, amongst other things, the creation and distribution of agricultural produce.[4] Building on this theme, William Cronon, in his study of Chicago and the American West, described 'ever more elaborate and intimate linkages between city and country' based on grain, timber and meat[5] as he traced global commodity flows through a city of (in 1915) about 2.5 million people. Rollo Arnold revealed similar forces at work in the development of a small New Zealand farming township in the bush lands of south Taranaki in similar terms, despite the vast difference in scale. For the period up until 1900, Arnold portrays 'settlers bringing skills and dreams to the reshaping of a virgin landscape … with little interference'. Thereafter the outside world began to 'increasingly intrude', by way of interregional transport systems, sanitary reform, dairy inspections, meat marketing networks, and Department of Agriculture demonstrations of new farming techniques.[6]

James Scott, using scientific farming as a prime case study, pointed to the social and environmental consequences once European, American and African improvers began 'seeing like a state'. Scott identified 'consolidating the power of central institutions and diminishing the autonomy of cultivators and their communities' as 'the unspoken logic behind most of the state projects of agricultural modernisation'.[7] Similarly, Deborah Fitzgerald described 'farmers deskilled' through application of 'the industrial ideal in American agriculture', with 'every farm a factory' as the goal by about 1920.[8] With these analyses of other agricultural histories in mind, this chapter assesses the New Zealand situation up to that date, in terms of the role of farmers and of the state. It reveals many similar shifts. In turn, chapter 10 traces ongoing changes into the 1930s.

In most of the world, research into the role of science in agricultural development has centred on cereals and other human food crops. In New Zealand, however, the key crop was grass and a central concern has been pasture development.[9] The result of this development was a greatly increased carrying capacity for herbivorous stock, with particular emphasis on the dairy industry and production of sheep for lamb and mutton. By the 1920s, over 90 per cent of the country's entire export income was based on grass (Table 1.1).[10]

THE ROLE OF FARMERS IN PASTURE DEVELOPMENT

New Zealand's geographical position, topography, geology, climate and soils have all had a fundamental influence on the development of its pastures. Guthrie-Smith gave full consideration to such factors in 1921, and later scholars made a passing nod to them as 'general factors affecting land utilization'.[11] Beyond frequent and unsystematic commentary on the weather, however, the agricultural press of the time largely left such matters unstated. A picture emerges, rather, of the role people played in pasture development. It is a picture that includes seedsmen and other men of commerce, as well as scientific experts and government officials, but it was farmers who most clearly occupied the foreground in the 1890s.

In the late nineteenth century 'the priority for many struggling farmers was immediate survival rather than experimentation with new techniques', according to historian Tony Nightingale. He maintained that the creation of a Department of Agriculture in 1892 responded to a perceived 'need for experts able to translate scientific discoveries with the potential to increase production into practical advice to the farmer'.[12] True as far it goes, this assessment does not recognise either the attempts by individual farmers to inform themselves on these matters or the other, non-governmental, channels that dispersed new agricultural knowledge, as discussed in chapters 7 and 8. While the Department's annual reports catalogue state involvement in pasture, there is no easy way to assess the extent of farmer involvement. Patents lists, however, confirm the technical contribution of individuals, most of them farmers of whom only their names are known.[13] They invented no machine for pasture improvement quite as fundamental as the freezing chamber to meat export or the colonial plough to cultivation of rough land, though the seed drill and seed cleaner, both developed in the 1890s, played significant roles.[14]

By this time the majority of farmers and the agricultural press knew that, in most cases, lowland pasture carved out of bush land and sown in the most nutritious grasses did not have permanence. When the land could be ploughed, the traditional method of renewing pasture was to sow it afresh after first growing and harvesting other crops. One kind of farmer experimentation involved altering rotations to better suit local conditions. In Britain, pasture had also been renewed through application of natural fertiliser, but there was neither the intensity of agricultural practice nor the availability of labour to collect and redistribute animal manure in New Zealand. Already in the northern parts of the country in 1904, artificial fertilisers, more concentrated and ready for immediate application, had rendered rotation of 'comparatively less importance'.[15] Sowing other species along with the most nutritious grass could also increase a pasture's permanence. Some farmers sowed cocksfoot along with ryegrass, since cocksfoot would come to the fore in a few seasons as the ryegrass began to decline.

Scottish-born James Wilson, a progressive sheep farmer, large landowner and prominent rural politician who ran a successful property at Bulls near Palmerston North, and whose improvements are described in chapter 2, adopted a more innovative approach. He became an expert on grass at a time when no government assistance was available to extend his knowledge. Although he corresponded with other New Zealand farmers, he also utilised British sources. In 1889 he received advice and grass seed of superior quality from Suttons, the Reading seed merchants, and mailed the botanist of England's Royal Agricultural Society to identify grasses on his property. By the late 1890s, however, his local contacts had assumed greater significance, with Palmerston North's stock and station agents (representatives of large companies who supplied farmers with seed, stock and credit and sent their grain and stock to market[16]) offering him six different *regional* varieties of New Zealand-grown ryegrass with varying reputations for permanence.[17] Increasingly involved in agricultural development at a national level, Wilson remained receptive throughout to advice from other farmers, to scientific research, and to state participation.[18]

There is ample evidence from around 1900 of a growing awareness among farmers that a more scientific approach to pasture improvement had become necessary, for which cooperation with the state would be helpful. While the New Zealand Government held back, however, many farmers showed initiative in going it alone. As individuals, farmers around Kamo near Whangarei in Northland, for instance, in turn trialled ryegrass, rat's-tail (from 1840), Waipu browntop, cocksfoot (1860), tall fescue, *Poa brownii* (1886) and paspalum (1900), and by 1916 had turned 'waste lands to pasturage' for dairy cattle. In 1908 a Whangarei farmer successfully grew Garton's perennialised Italian ryegrass, one season after its introduction on the English market and in advance of Department of Agriculture trials.[19] The introduction of Chewings fescue and paspalum to New Zealand pastures has been traced in detail and reveals the crucial role played by farmers in Southland, Waikato and Northland, well before any state involvement with these grasses occurred.[20]

Results of most experimentation presumably spread first over the farm fence (where there was one) to the neighbour, and then in the stockyards at Agricultural and Pastoral Shows in conversations between farmers from the

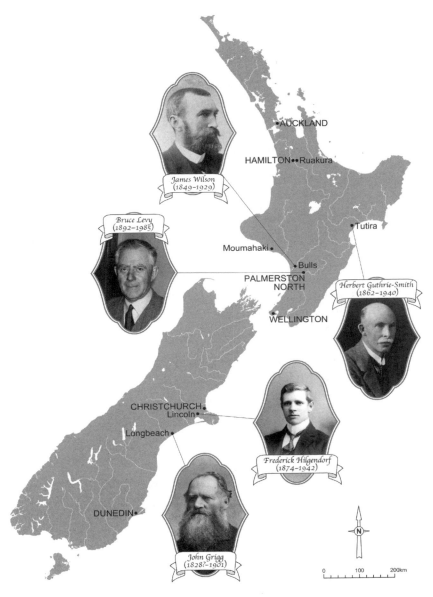

Figure 9.1: Early experiments with grass: people and places. John Grigg, James Wilson and Herbert Guthrie-Smith were farmers who showed a scientific approach to pasture improvement. While the early plant selection work of professional scientists Frederick Hilgendorf and Bruce Levy has received wide recognition, the pre-1914 grass trials conducted by A.W. Green and W.S. Hill at the state farms in Ruakura and Moumahaki are forgotten.

same locality. At a more formalised level, farmers publicised their findings through talks at Agricultural and Pastoral Association meetings and at farmers' clubs, both organizations growing in number and popularity during the 1890s (see chapter 8). Some, such as J.G. Carrie of Takapuna and Canterbury farmer J.R. Wilkinson, also published their results to reach audiences beyond these gatherings.[21]

Agricultural and Pastoral Associations had existed since the 1860s, but formal conference between Association delegates only commenced in 1892, when farmers successfully urged government to establish an agricultural department. Through ensuing conferences, a group of innovative farmers attained national prominence, including Wilson, Joseph Barugh of the Waikato Farmers' Club, and John Grigg, son and heir of the first John Grigg of Longbeach (Figure 9.1). The 1890s similarly witnessed the rise of farmers' unions. These were more concerned with political issues such as promotion of closer settlement and cheap credit, as well as pragmatic matters like the reduction of freight rates and the commission charged by middlemen. They wanted farming to be more efficient too, however, and promoted improved methods, agricultural education and state assistance with quality control.[22] Farmers also formed cooperatives, notably to run dairy factories, but sometimes to cut out middlemen. The United Farmers Co-operative Association in Palmerston North, initiated by Wilson in 1897, held 'large stocks of both English and colonial grown seeds, and ... stocks of crested dog's-tail, meadow foxtail, and cocksfoot'.[23]

Agricultural and Pastoral Winter Shows increasingly awarded prizes for the best grass seed. By 1908 the Hawke's Bay annual show included competitions for perennial ryegrass, Italian ryegrass, cocksfoot, prairie grass, ryegrass, Chewings fescue, crested dogstail, white clover, red clover, and alsike. Many similar examples indicate a vibrant agriculture community that, independent of the state, paid close attention to the quality of its grass seed.[24] In 1897 the Auckland Agricultural and Pastoral Association wrote to sister organisations around the country 'asking what kinds of grasses had proved most serviceable on the good and poor lands in [their] district', the precedent for a more thorough survey conducted by the New Zealand Agricultural Association (the umbrella group of Agricultural and Pastoral Associations) in 1907–9.[25] The same Association proposed a national 'bureau of agricultural information'. When the *New Zealand Farmer* tabulated details of 'a number of mixtures as more or less suitable for permanent grass on various classes of soil', prescribing broad seed mixes chosen from among 18 grasses for 7 different soil types, it provided a model for the Department of Agriculture's table of a decade later.[26]

The farmers who responded to the Association surveys were local experimenters in a way that later government-employed scientists were not. However, the working knowledge of New Zealand context which many farmers of European origin had acquired by then (as described in chapter 3) still fell far short of the 'traditional ecological knowledge' associated with indigenous people.[27] John Grigg senior, offering advice to James Wilson in 1889, wrote from the perspective of 26 years' experience at Longbeach, while Wilson had only 16 years' experience at Bulls. Although both had gained experience of local environmental conditions, neither possessed any 'traditional' knowledge beyond the British agricultural methods they had been brought up with, many of which proved inappropriate. Even the missionary Williams family, in Hawke's Bay, could not claim a century of local knowledge. Their territorial discourse, therefore, lacked the depth of attachment to the land that could be claimed by, for instance, a traditional small farmer in Ireland.[28] Pākehā who worked their land began at some mental distance from the object of their attention, and also had an eye on distant rather than local markets. Māori traditions were of hunting, gathering and gardening, rather than of farming in the Western sense, and, anyway (as chapter 3 also makes clear) their knowledge was often ignored.

New Zealand farmers around 1900 to 1910 sowed broader and more varied grass seed mixes in their pasture than either earlier or later (see chapter 4). In part, this practice reflected the greater availability of grass seed other than ryegrass and cocksfoot once farmers had experimented with niche species. Such learning, in turn, suggests that Pākehā farmers by this time (some of them New Zealand born) were more aware of the varying requirements of different regions, locations, soils and climates in the new land. Their newfound working knowledge supported a greater biodiversity in artificial pastures in 1910 than in the 1930s, when, as chapter 10 shows, government seed certification and promotion of fewer species encouraged simpler pastures sustained by higher technology.

There can be no doubt that many farmers around the turn of the century adopted practices in pasture improvement that reflected local environmental awareness. Some, however, regretted an emphasis on 'cocktail mixtures' rather than on 'thought to soil compositions and their requirements when deciding on seed mixture for any particular paddock'. Looking back on 'the numerous scourges ... that have been introduced', one writer argued that most grasses were 'valuable, given their natural habitat, but ... under certain conditions of soil and climate ... usurp the soil, destroying or driving out infinitely better sorts'.[29] Conclusions were increasingly tempered as the disadvantages of some new grasses became more evident. There was, therefore, a complex picture of diverse experimentation and opinion among farmers, which may have resulted in an environmentally healthy pastoral biodiversity as often by default as by intent.

Many farmers had used broad seed mixes out of ignorance about their particular soils, considering perhaps that this was the best approach to ensuring that at least some would thrive. Some confronted ground similar to that at Tutira in the 1880s (Figure 9.1), where Guthrie-Smith welcomed 'goose-grass, rat's tail fescue and fog ... damned in every respectable volume on British grasses ... [but] any plant that sheep would eat was an improvement on bracken'.[30] Some responded not so much to New Zealand soil conditions as to English and other weeds that threatened the quality of exotic pasture. A more complex pasture mix reduced the growth of weeds by introducing early-leafing grasses to outshade them. Meadow foxtail, for instance, was popular in Poverty Bay in 1901 for 'ridding new land of thistles in the second year'.[31]

FARMERS AND FERTILISERS

Articles in the *New Zealand Farmer* (a non-governmental publication) said little about the role of environment in facilitating or thwarting pasture improvement. Indeed, at the turn of the century in New Zealand, only the botanist Leonard Cockayne voiced an ecological knowledge of interrelationships between animals, plants and the land.[32] No doubt some farmers also had intuitive understanding of these links, but they did not have the words provided by ecological science to express it. There was, in consequence, a failure at the time to describe environmental impacts, other than in specific instances. This failure holds particularly for lowland New Zealand, where there was the highest level of transformation and the greatest extent of exotic pasture.

Farmers, departmental advisors and agricultural journalists scaled down emphasis on providing a range of grasses – at least in terms of the proportion of the land for which it remained the best option – as they talked up the benefits of artificial fertilisers. While the first formal trials with phosphatic manures on grassland occurred at Ruakura state farm in 1901, they were conducted under the auspices of the Auckland Agricultural Association. A discussion at Waikato Farmers' Club in 1905 revealed the width of members' independent 'experiences in topdressing grass': the chairman had trialled slag, bone phosphate and superphosphate on a four-hectare paddock of three-year-old grass; another member 'dressed a three year old pasture paddock with equal parts of bone phosphate and superphosphate'; a third 'tried top-dressing nine plots of young grass with manures of equal money value'.[33] In the southern parts of New Zealand, where it was colder and the season shorter, phosphates were tried more often on root crops.

Throughout the country, an expansion of dairy farming heightened appreciation of well-grassed paddocks, but dairying also often required a supplementary food supply during late summer drought and the chilly days of winter and early spring. There was, therefore, interest as well in fodder crops like maize, sorghum, vetches, mangolds, pumpkin, lucerne, Italian ryegrass, and crimson clover. A series of droughts in the early 1900s raised the question of American-style dry farming techniques in drier east coast areas, but artificial fertilisers arrived just in time to delay experimentation with such unfamiliar techniques.[34]

Continuing wheat production in Canterbury, well beyond the bonanza years of the late nineteenth century when overcropping had threatened its soil fertility, ensured an atypical approach to rotation in that region.[35] In general, New Zealand's agricultural future appeared to lie more with dairying than cereals, increasing the incentive to place most emphasis on keeping grass down as long as possible, rejuvenated by surface-sowing and artificial fertilisers, rather than operating crop rotation with cereals taking centre-stage. Where grass was the main crop, rotation seemed an inefficient way to boost productivity when, increasingly, the emphasis lay upon *speedy* improvement. Yet, as one South Canterbury farmer warned in 1912, 'so many of the fertilisers being quick stimulants, their too frequent use even on strong land is not wise', because 'succeeding crops on the same land must always be treated with a stimulant, otherwise partial failure in the crop will result'.[36]

Farmers in his region had long relied on the systematic rotation of temporary grass and crops, while North Islanders, many of them working recently forested ground that was hard or impossible to plough, more easily imagined increased production by applying artificial fertilisers to pasture alone. More farmers had money to buy them, the returns were better researched, and a variety of products were now available. According to a *New Zealand Farmer* editorial, 'With the advent of co-operative dairying and the accompanying benefits of the regular monthly cheque ... [farmers] recognise that the use of [artificial] manure should no longer be considered a matter of reproach to the quality of land, and that the better the land, the better returns will manure yield for the money so expended'.[37]

Seedsmen and stock and station agents became involved in pasture development through the supply of *both* external commodities – seed and artificial fertiliser – increasingly required by pastoral farmers. Farmers in districts such as Banks Peninsula and Taranaki grew local grass seed as a cash crop and sold it to seed companies for them to distribute. As chapter 7 describes, the most enterprising seedsmen were Yates of Auckland (Figure 9.2). In 1890 they bought about nine hectares at Mangere for 'a small seed farm, and also for the purpose of testing the merits of different kinds of vegetables, and the adaptability to our [New Zealand's] climate of certain subtropical plants'. This was experimental work, on a scale that individual farmers could not manage and of a kind the government was slow to initiate. Only Lincoln School of Agriculture[38] had similar scope for large-scale

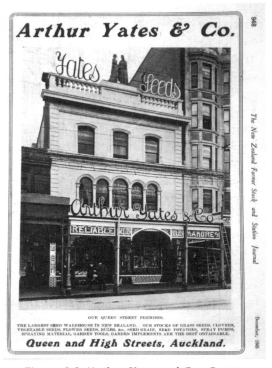

Figure 9.2: 'Arthur Yates and Co., Queen and High Streets, Auckland: The largest seed warehouse in NZ. Our stocks of grass seeds, clovers, vegetable seeds, flower seeds, bulbs etc., seed grain, seed potatoes, spray pumps, spraying materials, garden tools, garden implements are the best obtainable.' *Source: New Zealand Farmer* 30/12 (1909), p. 948.

experimentation, but in 1890 neither Yates nor Lincoln conducted trials with grass seed. In 1895, however, Yates leased a further 4.5 hectares to trial grasses suitable for poor clay soils. Later, they developed primarily as suppliers of garden seed, leaving agricultural and grass seed to stock and station agents and government plant breeders.[39]

THE ROLE OF THE STATE IN PASTURE DEVELOPMENT

The columns of the *New Zealand Farmer* confirm the limited extent of state participation in pasture development before 1900, but also indicate a wish among farmers that it would increase. A Masterton correspondent in 1893 regretted the Department was doing so little to promote 'scientific farming' even though New Zealand was, in other respects 'the most advanced country in the world'. Government offered a bonus of £200 in 1896 for the discovery of a local source of 'marketable mineral manure' and arranged through the Railways Department for free carriage of agricultural lime in 1898, both actions indirectly encouraging pasture improvement.[40] Moumahaki state farm also made a start on scientific research. Generally, however, the state remained more inclined to oppose poor practice than actively pursue anything better.

The 1900s saw a significant increase in direct involvement, principally through the expansion of the Department of Agriculture into experimental areas, through the activities of state experimental farms in the North Island and cooperative experiments with farmers on experimental plots throughout the country. While the greatest emphasis lay with testing the benefits of fertiliser usage (up to 1900 the state had conducted virtually *no* such trials), department-run farms also experimented with new grass varieties and species.

With or without the state, commerce and farmers worked together, but by the 1910s the state began to exert more influence on what seed was grown and sold. T.W. Kirk, the first director of the Biology Division within the Department of Agriculture from 1893 to 1909, continually stressed the importance of quality seed, and it was perhaps in response more to state input than farmer demand that seedsmen profited by offering it.[41] Already by 1912, every packet of seed from the New Zealand Loan and Mercantile Company in Palmerston North carried wording to 'certify that the contents are genuine, and have been tested by the Biologist of the Department of Agriculture'.[42]

While farmers led pasture development prior to 1914, the Department of Agriculture increasingly managed the *interpretation* of these advances, particularly after publication of an official *Journal of Agriculture* from 1910 provided a medium for syntheses by government employees. This was the first step both towards an official version of events that placed heavy emphasis on the state, and towards its actual assumption of a major role after 1918. Before the First World War the state provided some scientific input into farming and directly improved farm management. The early Department of Agriculture was, however, thinly staffed. It remained too

Figure 9.3: Key figures in the early years of the Department of Agriculture. Thomas Mackenzie, Minister of Agriculture is in the middle. Top left: T.W. Kirk, Director of Orchards, Gardens and Apiaries Division; top right: A.H. Cockayne, Biologist; bottom right: C.J. Reakes, Director of Livestock and Meat Division; bottom left: Edmund Clifton, Director of the Fields and Experimental Farms Division. *Source*: *New Zealand Farmer* 30/10 (1909), p. 757.

poorly equipped before 1914, and particularly before 1900, to do much research or to operate national or international linkages.

Until the First World War the Department concentrated on providing inspection, advice and, quality control, 'most notably for dairy factories', at a local level.[43] During these years few of its staff gave pasture improvement priority. In 1912 the Biology Division still only consisted of one biologist (Leonard Cockayne's son, Alfred) and three assistants. Their concerns were weeds, pests, seeds and grasses. The Chemistry Division began with Bernard Aston's employment in 1899; he had one assistant. Aston occupied himself with soil analysis and improvement through the application of fertiliser. Though there were experimental farms from the 1890s onwards there was no Fields Division until 1910. Its director from 1910 was Edmund Clifton, Chief Livestock Officer in Auckland from 1889 to 1906 and, from 1907, Chief Inspector of Stock for New Zealand. For his staff (30-strong by 1912) pasture improvement clearly *had* become a major concern[44] (Figure 9.3).

In 1910 the Department of Agriculture as a whole demonstrated openness towards promotion of plant and animal products in addition to those derived from grass. Departmental staff were optimistic about the future of production of native flax, poultry and honey, and in particular the fruit industry.[45] Interest in diversification suggests an awareness of the danger of becoming overspecialised or reliant on one crop. None of these industries, however, yielded anywhere near the export value of grass-based products. While it could be argued that realities of trade and environment perhaps predetermined a major reliance on grass, it is also evident that later governments closed doors that might have led to alternative agricultural developments in the 1920s and beyond.

PARTNERSHIP IN PASTURE DEVELOPMENT

In advance of any state encouragement, Wilson and the Wellington Farmers' Union initiated 'an up-to-date factory for the manufacture of superphosphate and sulphuric acid' in 1915, and farmers and growers formed a Pure Seeds Association in 1916 under the presidency of John Grigg junior.[46] Probably, pasture could not have reached higher levels of productivity, however, without greater involvement by the state thereafter, given the kind of scientific research required. As early as 1908, Leonard Cockayne remarked that plant breeding involved 'experiments on a large scale, which must be pursued with unbroken continuity, [and] could be carried on only by the State, or by some public Institution'.[47]

In the years immediately before the First World War, advances in pasture development were increasingly coming from active partnership *between* farmers and the state. In 1909, when 200 farmers cooperated with government in experiments in North Island alone, Clifton commented that while 'every farmer had to be his own experimenter ... the State was doing its best to assist'. He reported that for pasture top-dressing experiments in Marton, Feilding and Sandon, 'the Department finds the manure, and the official to conduct the experiments, and record the results, and the farmer finds the land and the necessary labour'. An experiment conducted at Guthrie-Smith's Hawke's Bay property, which traced the progress of 25 different grass species when sown with bonedust, was far from unique.[48] Such activity increased official participation in scientific work of this kind without distancing it from, or diminishing, direct farmer input. While more highly trained specialists later criticised these initiatives for a lack of published results, at the time the encouragement they provided for experimentation was considered important. A failure to publish did not rule out the possibility of success in practice.

The Department of Agriculture's Fields Division under Clifton from 1910 emphasised field experiments made in cooperation with farmers. Even though created largely as a sop to appease farmers' feelings of neglect, the state-sponsored Board of Agriculture under Wilson's leadership from 1914 did provide an official channel through which farmers could provide advice to government.[49] A framework was put in place to combine the strengths of those on the ground with those in the office or laboratory or, in other words, to draw upon both territorial and elite discourse. It posited a 'participatory' agriculture, 'farmers and other practitioners acting as partners with researchers' in a way that Jules Pretty and Norman Uphoff identify as the key to 'sustainable agro-ecological practices'.[50]

The establishment of a second state farm at Ruakura near Hamilton provided an early opportunity for experimentation with phosphatic manures. A paddock was prepared there in 1901 for grass-manuring experiments conducted under the auspices of the Auckland Agricultural Association, and Clifton planned a more complex three-year experiment dressing nine one-acre (0.4 hectare) plots of grass and oats with various combinations of basic slag, superphosphate and bones. Manurial experiments were also carried out at Moumahaki state farm north of Wanganui from 1907. Trials of fertiliser became more frequent from then on, and the Department of Agriculture's 1908 annual report claimed that:

From a financial point of view it will be found more remunerative to take time by the forelock and topdress pastures while the clovers and better grasses are fairly numerous in the sward, rather than wait until they have practically run out and have to be nursed back again by allowing the few such plants left to seed.[51]

Even so, for a time there was debate within government as well as farmer circles on how often it was worth top-dressing with artificial fertilisers. Clifton held that 'greater effort should be made to assist the latent fertility [of the soil] by a rotation of crops than by the application of expensive manures'.[52] In 1914, John Brown, as director of the Fields Division in succession to Clifton, provided a programme for the development of New Zealand farming. The final stage, as he saw it, would involve 'a definite rotation' and the cutting and carting of maize, lucerne, hay and ensilage for winter feed. His vision, like Clifton's, centred on increasing the area in temporary pasture and forage crops, not on increasing permanent pasture. Unlike some of his successors he considered that fertiliser inputs only provided a partial solution to increasing production. He wrote: 'Top-dressing cannot ... permanently replace cultivation', because '[a]t best it is an expedient for prolonging the life of a pasture for a year or two'.[53]

Lucerne (alfalfa) was one of many crops seriously investigated before 1914 but largely ignored after the war. Alexander Macpherson's 'personal record' provides a sense of this. In the 1913–14 season, as the Department of Agriculture's fields instructor for all the South Island, he directed a remarkable range of cooperative field experiments involving 4,613 plots on 428 farms. Some of these were experiments with cereals, some with grasses and clovers for permanent pastures, while other plots trialled forage crops of potential significance like maize and silverbeet (Swiss chard). His particular interest, however, lay in 1,322 plots of lucerne. The Fields Division's approach in applying science to agricultural development was then at its zenith. Macpherson and his superior, Clifton, sought to 'co-operate with the farmers on their own farms ... [to produce] higher yield per acre, of greater nutritive value ... not so subject to injurious weather effects, diseases or insect pests'.[54]

AGRICULTURE, SCIENCE AND THE FIRST WORLD WAR

Increasingly in the years before the First World War, gatherings instigated by agricultural associations had become a platform not just for farmers but also for the state. In 1911, Lord Islington became the first Governor to grace a national New Zealand agricultural conference. 'The time was not very far distant,' he said, 'when a hand-to-hand struggle would occur between all the agricultural countries in the world to secure the most favourable entry into the overseas markets, and it was the country which was furnished with the most scientific methods which would obtain first prize in that competition.'[55] Science, in other words, could give a country the edge.

At the Wellington Farmers' Union Conference of 1910, the Minister of Agriculture, Thomas Mackenzie, had already suggested that 'scientific research into the ways of securing better seeds for the various farm crops is ... going to be the feature of the present century'. However, the agricultural college at Lincoln (founded in 1878) had remained exceptional within New Zealand. By now New Zealand lagged behind Australia, which boasted 35 experimental farms and 5 agricultural colleges, including Hawkesbury (1891) in New South Wales. In 1914 there were six ex-Hawkesbury students in New Zealand's agricultural service, reinforcing a trend towards the professionalisation of agriculture.[56] Yet even Australia trailed well behind the USA, where land grant colleges had promoted the scientific development of agriculture since the 1890s. These institutions established active extension departments providing direct assistance to working farmers, albeit with modest result.[57]

By 1910 Mackenzie felt certain that New Zealand should concentrate on pasture rather than cereals. Most early plant-breeding work, however, did not centre on grasses. Selective plant breeding by the state began in New Zealand in the early 1900s with the work of A.W. Green at Ruakura, W.S. Hill at Moumahaki, and Frederick Hilgendorf at Lincoln (Figure 9.1). Hill produced an overview on plant selection in 1913 which prioritised local research, since 'varieties suited to one locality are entirely useless in many others, hence local selection is always of more economic value than working with types produced in a foreign country'. He thought this work would be furthered 'if the boys and girls of our country schools could be interested sufficiently to bring to the school-gardens any plants they see which show better growth than the average plant of that variety, [since] then thousands of pairs of eyes, instead of a dozen, would be searching for improved plants'. Hill clearly saw plant breeding as a combined project between specialists like himself and others – even children – who were not scientists or government employees. Green, in an article on 'co-operation in plant-improvement', named individual farmers who had contributed varieties worthy for selection and thus he, too, stressed the non-scientist's role.[58]

The war took both Hill and Green away from their work. No articles on plant-breeding appeared in the *Journal of Agriculture* during the war, and the main emphasis for some time afterwards was primarily on wheat, the only subject of Hilgendorf's paper on 'Methods of plant-breeding' of 1919.[59] Wartime shortages had led the government to promote self-sufficiency in wheat production through research and (until 1922) price control. By guaranteeing a market for local wheat, the war possibly delayed the adoption of an almost entirely pastoral future for the Dominion. In other respects, however, the war and its aftermath crystallised ideas on the way New Zealand farming should head. There were a number of reasons for this.

The first was the longer-term effect of the commandeering of New Zealand farm produce by the British Government. It bought all the meat (from 1915), wool and cheese (1916) and butter (1917) that New Zealand could produce at something like 55 per cent above the market rate. This not only brought about a brief post-war agricultural boom, but it normalised the state's close involvement in agriculture, rendering later extensions into research, marketing and certification both more likely and more acceptable.[60]

Second, the war, so nearly not won, led more people to think that Germany's greater openness to applied science, including agricultural science, was a major reason why it had so quickly grown to challenge the supremacy of the British Empire. Developer G.E. Alderton wrote in the *New Zealand Farmer* in 1916 of a need 'to induce the men on the land to follow a more scientific system of farming …[for,] if we would keep the Huns at heel, we must be just as scientific and intense or we shall be beaten by those who play the game better'.[61] The attempt to make scientific farmers of returned soldiers, though largely unsuccessful, symbolically indicated how the battle with the land should to be waged, once military victory over Germany had been accomplished.

The scientific approach came into international prominence at a time when state scientific work (as practised by the Department of Agriculture) still only operated at an elementary level. The Department's Biology Division no longer consisted of one biologist and three assistants operating out of a 'laboratory' in an upstairs room of Parliament House, as it had in 1912. Even so, in 1919 it had no library and only an inferior microscope.[62] Apart from Lincoln, this was New Zealand's only 'house of experiment' for pasture research,[63] and at first its staff lacked academic qualifications. When the laboratory shifted from Weraroa (near Levin) to Wellington in the 1920s, it gave them scope to attend evening lectures at Victoria University College, but 'after two lectures the Biologist [Alfred Cockayne] did not again honour the classes with his presence', and his assistant, Bruce Levy, only gained his degree after passing chemistry at the third attempt.[64]

Third, the war focused attention on the need not only for management and system, but for speedy result. Survival of the fittest, early endorsed in New Zealand as the aspect of Darwinism most relevant to colonisation, was now associated with pace of production.[65] In 1919 Leonard Cockayne obtained state funding to investigate native montane tussock grassland, but Levy 'dodged' work on these areas, believing that 'mesophytic grasslands of the lower altitude, warmer and higher rainfall belts, offered infinitely more scope for rapid development'.[66] Lord Moulton, introducing *Science and the Nation* in 1917, felt 'we [Britain] can no longer wait for the slow results of casual discovery'. Agriculture had 'hitherto reposed mainly on experience and tradition' but 'this must be changed and the teaching of Experimental Science must be listened to'.[67] Post-war Britain, made more aware of her earlier reliance on non-imperial produce, supported development of new state-led structures of scientific research and agricultural production throughout the Empire. It was a web into which New Zealand was readily drawn, facilitating the rise of Bruce Levy as the country's leading exponent of the 'glorious truth' of 'grassland advancement' (see chapter 10).[68]

Lastly, and specifically, the war precipitated access to an overseas, imperial source of phosphate for New Zealand at a time when scientific research was beginning to reveal and emphasise how artificial fertiliser induced rapid pasture development. As is also described more fully in the next chapter, New Zealand won 16 per cent of the phosphate from the formerly German-held island of Nauru (the rest going to Britain and Australia) and gained greater access to the phosphate of Ocean Island at cheaper prices.[69]

CONCLUSION

There had been an independence of thinking in New Zealand around 1900, even among the few scientists then employed by government. Together with an almost nationalistic pride in some of its indigenous and locally evolved grasses, this suggests a country less apt to play periphery to London's metropolis than might be expected.

A quarter of a century later, however, Levy's 'grasslands revolution' in 'Britain's farm' was initiated by government scientists working within a plant-breeding station and a Department of Scientific and Industrial Research, both copied from and working closely with their British models. This illustrates metropolitan influence rather better than the situation in

1900 and may, indeed, support the case made by James Belich for a degree of 'recolonisation' occurring in New Zealand after the First World War.[70]

'In the decade before 1914', according to Pat Stephens in 1960, 'the present-day pattern of New Zealand farming began to emerge, though not many people had a clear idea of just what form it would take'.[71] If a balanced contribution to the development of farming was emerging in that decade, however, based on fairly equal collaboration and communication between farmers and the state through the Fields Division and the Board of Agriculture, serious consideration of a wide range of primary produce, and reasoned rather than non-critical application of science, it was being broken down by the 1920s.

This chapter has described a period in the 1890s when the prime initiative came from farmers, followed by a period immediately before the First World War when farmers and government cooperated on an equal footing to improve the quantity and quality of grass. It identifies the aftermath of the war as the tipping point when the state was poised to play a greater role in pasture development. Previously, farmers had applied their knowledge of local and differing environmental conditions, and pasture improvement depended primarily upon sowing various, often broad, mixes of clean seed. Around 1920, however, greater emphasis came to be placed upon experimentation conducted at some distance from the farmer's field, employing government scientists influenced by overseas and imperial research.

This foreshadowed the situation appertaining by 1930, when the future lay firmly with development of the best strains of ryegrass and the clovers which, boosted by artificial phosphates, could produce nutritious pasture in, or in spite of, a wide range of soil conditions. From the early 1920s the state came to oversee agricultural development more directly and the industrialisation of New Zealand agriculture, already underway, accelerated noticeably despite severe economic problems. Farmers' working knowledge of the land thereby became less important as the state increasingly levied something close to pastoral totalitarianism.

10 *Remaking the Grasslands: the 1920s and 1930s*

Tom Brooking and Paul Star

INTRODUCTION

In New Zealand as elsewhere in the Western World the end of the First World War ushered in great hopes for the future. Like most nations which supported the Allied cause, New Zealand hoped to take advantage of a 'new dawn' and convert the self-governing Dominion into 'a land fit for heroes'.[1] Securing the rights to a 16 per cent share of the phosphate rock of Nauru in 1919 as a result of negotiations associated with the Versailles Conference underscored the prevailing sense of optimism.[2] From about 1900 environmental constraints in the South Island in general, and in the high country in particular, inhibited further expansion of farming activities (see chapter 5). Productivity began to dip in the North Island as well once the initial 'flush' induced by burning had passed. Many farmers had become aware even before the outbreak of war that they could not maintain soil fertility or productivity without the assistance of fertilisers.[3] Then, suddenly, at the end of the war to end all wars, agriculture's potential seemed almost limitless again.[4]

In the pre-war years, slag, rich in phosphate, along with other industrial fertilisers such as potash, which came predominantly from Germany, had helped to make up the fertility deficit, but these could not be obtained after August 1914.[5] Consequently, farming productivity fell away during the war years, despite the incentive provided by high prices and a guaranteed market for all the meat, wool, butter and cheese that New Zealand could produce under the commandeer system.[6] The return of recession for the first time in a generation in 1921 (sometimes described as a short, sharp depression) following close on the trauma caused by the influenza pandemic of

1918–19, which took the lives of around 8,600 New Zealanders,[7] then dampened expectations as the 1920s turned into a false dawn.

This chapter traces the ways in which such disillusionment helped accelerate the state's already increasing role in applying advances in scientific understanding to restore productivity in the hope that prosperity would thereby be regained. Major state efforts to address the farming problems described below have sometimes been summarised as 'the grasslands revolution' because applied science helped bring about significant increases in production on a virtually static area of land. Yet this interpretation in retrospect seems questionably celebratory, as well as condescending in its estimation of the efforts made by earlier generations of farmers to remake New Zealand into an English-style pastoral farm. In sum, this chapter builds on the reassessment of the whole notion of the grasslands revolution begun in the 1990s.[8]

POST-WAR PROBLEMS AND SOLUTIONS

The lag in artificial fertiliser supply highlighted that soils in some areas had become seriously depleted and that New Zealand's potential was, in fact, limited, rather than unlimited as earlier generations of settlers had hoped. This seemed to be the lesson of the Southern Pastoral Lands Commission of 1920, appointed to investigate concerns raised by the botanist Leonard Cockayne about the serious degradation of some high country farmland in Central and North Otago and North Canterbury, both in terms of 'deterioration' (defined as reversion to 'actual bare ground') and 'depletion' or 'reduction in palatability'. The Commissioners, whose ranks included Cockayne, generalised from the dramatic slide in carrying capacity that had occurred on some stations. They attributed this to erosion, supposedly caused by overgrazing, careless firing of tussock, and rabbit infestation. They concluded that recovery required the use of fire to be limited to spring only, more effective rabbit control, oversowing with exotic pastures and temporary retirement or 'spelling' of land denuded of vegetation; an analysis and set of recommendations[9] challenged by recent revisionist work represented by chapter 5.

A little later John McCaw, the very experienced Land Commissioner for the Auckland district, produced a report on the problems facing returned soldier settlers struggling on remote farms in the back country in the north as the recession caused increasing distress in 1922 and 1923. His report catches the sense of disillusionment that set in as commodity prices tumbled. McCaw claimed that far too many properties had been established on poor soils, lacked access to reliable water supplies and required high maintenance and fertiliser inputs to turn a profit. Heavily indebted and cash-strapped, they could not meet the hefty costs involved in clearing bush. Distance both from markets and from neighbours experienced in making farms from bush and swamp, added to their distress. Many soldier settlers on bush lands had to run dairy cattle on steep country to try and break in this land for more profitable sheep farming.

McCaw called for additional government financial assistance to enable farmers to purchase more manure, better-quality grass seed and beef cattle more suited to steep land. He also wanted roads, which became quite impassable in winter, to be improved so that stock could be moved to market more easily. Even in the warmer and wetter north, rabbits wrought havoc, and he called for the erection of rabbit-proof wire netting to control the pest. The weed ragwort had also become rampant as cleared land reverted to an unkempt state and failed to support continuing good pasture. McCaw intimated, as Kenneth Cumberland later put it, that nature was 'fighting back'.[10] He considered that only large-scale state investment could reverse this undesirable trend. If such financial help was forthcoming, he scrawled in long hand, then 80 per cent would 'make good', that is, a clear majority, but this figure conceded that there would be a significant proportion of failures.[11]

The scale of assistance recommended by McCaw did not eventuate. About a third of soldier settlers across the whole of New Zealand were unable to sustain a living on their marginal and underdeveloped farms. Many others who avoided outright failure struggled to move their operations beyond an uncomfortable subsistence. Even government seemed to lose its nerve by abandoning plans to develop soldier farms in the rugged and isolated Ureweras in the central North Island.[12] Recent work suggests that the scale of problems confronting the soldier settlement scheme has been exaggerated, but there is little doubt that many of these men and their families experienced genuine hardship.[13] The iconic 'bridge to nowhere' in the deserted Aotuhia settlement in the hard country at the back of Wanganui became a symbol of the failure of old-style frontier expansion (Figure 10.1). Rather, applying scientific advances to enable farming to be carried out in a more intensive manner came to represent the more modern approach. This soon won widespread support as it was accompanied by spectacular gains in productivity while reducing the amount of physical labour required to improve farmland.[14]

Figure 10.1: The 'bridge to nowhere'. This bridge provided access to a long since abandoned post-First World War soldier settlement in the hills behind Wanganui. *Source*: Department of Conservation.

Applied science came to play a much more important role in agricultural development through the foundation of institutions for research into how to increase productivity of both pasture and stock. Following the advice of British expert Sir Frank Heath, Gordon Coates (Prime Minister from 1925 to 1928) established the Department of Scientific and Industrial Research (DSIR) in 1926. He also set up Massey Agricultural College at Palmerston North and increased funding to Canterbury Agricultural College at Lincoln to modernise and expand its operations. The British at this time made a direct appeal to settler states within the Empire to increase their agricultural outputs, to ensure that Britain would not run short of food in the event of another war and, at the same time, to provide both materials and markets for British manufacturing.[15] The establishment of the Empire Marketing Board in 1926 was part of this drive.[16]

Also in 1926, Australia founded the Commonwealth Scientific and Industrial Research Organisation (CSIRO) to assist with repairing degraded land and to increase production of wool, wheat and minerals. Canada had established the National Research Council in 1916 and South Africa set up its Council for Scientific and Industrial Research (CSIR) soon after its unification in 1910 although it did not undertake any concerted action until the 1940s. In addition to agriculture, these Canadian and South African organisations also paid much attention to mining, geology, engineering, and in Canada's case, forestry.[17] These differences signalled a degree of imperial specialisation, with New Zealand left to produce meat and dairy products by turning the new science of ecology into 'a science of Empire'.[18]

Sir George Stapledon visited Australia and New Zealand in 1926. As head of the Welsh Plant Breeding Station in Aberystwyth and of the adjoining imperial bureau designated to communicate about herbage plants, Stapledon played a key role in the drive to lift food production throughout the Empire. In New Zealand, the Department of Agriculture, swayed by the director of the Fields Division Alfred Cockayne (son of botanist Leonard), also tried to address problems of declining productivity, farm failure and reversion of pasture land to native scrub and bush by turning to science for help. It was at this moment that Bruce Levy emerged to promote a simple solution to stock farming's difficulties: the application of an artificially boosted duoculture – a ground cover consisting of only ryegrass and clover – to increase grassland productivity.

Levy was already leading a grasslands research group in the Department's biological laboratories based in Wellington by the time that Stapledon visited. With Alfred Cockayne's support, in 1928, he took over as team leader of the Plant Research Station based in Palmerston North. This was located next to the new Massey Agricultural College and the Dairy Research Institute. The Empire Marketing Board, prompted by Stapledon and leading New Zealand scientist Dr Ernest Marsden (a physicist by training),[19] had provided funds to help establish a plant research station within the DSIR, but complications arose because of the British preference to separate pure scientists from departmental bureaucrats (the so-called 'Haldane principle'). Instead, Coates reached a compromise with the Department of Agriculture and the Council of the DSIR to permit scientists of both departments to work side by side. Dr Gordon Herriot Cunningham, a mycologist and expert in plant diseases who held much higher qualifications than either Alfred Cockayne or Levy, viewed this arrangement sceptically, but managed to work with Levy until 1936 when his plant-diseases team moved to Auckland, Levy then becoming director of a Grasslands Division in Palmerston North.[20]

This mixed group of scientists, dominated by those in the Department of Agriculture down to 1936, concentrated on two main ways of increasing farming productivity: first by studying and promoting greater inputs of artificial fertiliser; and second by selection of more productive and longer-lasting pasture plants. What happened between the mid-1920s and the late 1930s seemed to bear out Stapledon's answer to his rhetorical question, 'Who are the empire builders? ... Without a doubt the British breeds of cattle and sheep, and our British grasses and clovers.'[21]

POST-WAR PASTURE DEVELOPMENT, PHOSPHATE AND THE STATE

In 1916, when Edmund Clifton (see chapter 9) returned to New Zealand from America (where he had acted as New Zealand Resident Commissioner at the San Francisco Exposition), he found that his insistence on a balance between rotations and fertiliser inputs, as well as reliance upon trials in farmers' fields, no longer prevailed within the Department of Agriculture. The government had chosen John Brown, with 'an education in scientific agriculture to succeed [him] as director of the experimental farms', though Brown (with many views similar to Clifton's) did not last long. About the same time, A.W. Green was appointed manager at Ruakura near Hamilton in succession to Clifton's protégé, Primrose McConnell. McConnell, once he returned to private employ, became the loudest voice for the rotational approach increasingly abandoned by the Department. He accepted a place for artificial manures, but did so rather reluctantly, seeing 'no "clear-cut" to soil improvement'. Increased demand, he thought, 'cannot be satisfied when the greater part of the country is under permanent pasture'.[22] This view clashed with government agricultural chemist Bernard Aston's and Alfred Cockayne's emphasis towards artificial fertilisers and more permanent pasture.

By 1930 Cockayne, writing as director of the Fields Division and assistant director general of the Department of Agriculture, was able to affirm the new orthodoxy of New Zealand practice, retrospectively placing Clifton and McConnell in a cul-de-sac. He asserted that 'grassland farming ... in a country with the climatic advantages of New Zealand can be as highly technical and complicated an art as any farming where the plough plays a dominant part'. Emphasising pace, he spoke of recent improvements to pasture occurring 'with a rapidity that savours of the magical', thanks largely to top-dressing, 'the greatest factor at the present time', and, though 'at present barely recognised ... the question of [grass] strain'.[23] In the course of the 1920s, governmental promotion of these two factors had emerged as the key to further development.

This shift did not occur overnight but had emerged slowly from around 1914. Before the First World War and for some time after, the Department of Agriculture's advice to farmers spoke not so much of fertiliser usage as of matching grass seed mix to soil. It became the mission of Cockayne, when he was government biologist, and even more of his erstwhile assistant, Levy, to sort out all such advice into ordered guidelines. Cockayne in 1914 urged 'use of suitable mixtures in the first instance ... with top-dressing in those districts where the use of artificial manures becomes necessary'.[24] Fertilisers were clearly still not central to his picture at this time.

Levy wrote a long succession of articles on grasslands in the *New Zealand Journal of Agriculture* from 1921, emphasising that '[i]n no other country is the farmer more dependent – or, rather, more able to depend – on pastures for the sustenance of his stock'.[25] He followed up this work with more articles in 1924 in which he devised a 'preliminary ecological classification' of grasses. He listed 'factors that govern dominance or subjection of any one species, or set of species, in our pastures': soil fertility, soil-moisture content, intensity of light and shade, climatic conditions, growth-form of the plant, seasonal growth, and palatability.[26] This exercise constituted a rigorous classification of evidence and a method of applying it, by matching seed mix to the position of each species within sets of tables.

Levy at this stage made no mention of strain selection, and showed no indication that the potential for massive use of artificial fertilisers was about to be realised. Nevertheless, with increasing availability of phosphates and the enthusiasm of Aston and Cockayne as well as the Reform Government's determination to push for their use, state experiments in general centred more and more on how fertilisers affected different grasses, rather than on how different grasses grew in different soils. Numerous trials occurred on state experimental areas in North Island from 1918 onwards and increasingly found in favour of the use of rock phosphate or superphosphate, rather than slag. From this time on Aston also became a more and more successful advocate of much higher fertiliser inputs.

Until the First World War Aston promoted basic slag as 'the philosopher's stone of the pastoralist', claiming that this, 'of all substances, most nearly realizes the pastoralist's dream of a magic something, the touch of which should clothe the languishing earth with a perennial verdure'.[27] With the war, however, slag became largely unobtainable, encouraging a Cairo businessman to write to the Department of Agriculture suggesting a supply of rock phosphate for New Zealand from Egyptian mines. In rejecting his offer, the Cairo inquirer was informed, 'the government does not at present propose to take any steps in the matter, as it is considered more

a question for private than for Government enterprise'.[28] After the war
the situation became very different once William Massey (Prime Minister
from 1912 to 1925) negotiated the deal with the British and Australian
governments to secure a 16 per cent share of the phosphate available on
Nauru.[29] From 1920, the government employed businessman Albert Ellis,
who had already organised the extraction of phosphate from British- and
Australian-controlled Ocean Island (today known as Banaba, in the Kiribati
group), to supervise the flow of phosphate from Nauru to New Zealand
(Figure 10.2).[30]

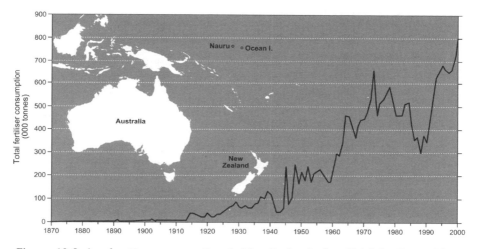

Figure 10.2: Accelerating consumption in New Zealand of artificial fertilisers. The
graph shows imports of phosphatic and nitrogenous fertiliser into New Zealand for
home use and the location of Nauru and Ocean Islands. There was a rapid increase
brought about by aerial top-dressing in the 1960s and 1970s and the dairy boom
in the 1990s. This latest rise has been based on nitrogenous fertiliser use. *Source*:
Statistics New Zealand (1870–1920), *Monthly Abstract of Statistics* (1921–60), *FAO
database* (1961–2000).

The recession in 1921 not only forced some soldier settlers off the land
but also halved imports of fertilisers, in particular rock phosphate, leaving
New Zealand with the option on more than it could cope with. 'Should
we fail to use our 16% quota during the first five years', noted Ellis with
more than a hint of panic, 'the Dominion would be entitled only to a
correspondingly reduced quantity for the subsequent period.'[31] Against this
background, a great many of the Department of Agriculture's experiments

seemed specifically designed to convince farmers that phosphate maximised production. In 1923 New Zealand absorbed its full quota, and by 1927 supply could not meet demand. Typically, trials like those at Puwera (near Whangarei) in 1922 still sought the best seed mix for pasture on that kind of land, but by 1927 departmental experts emphasised, rather, that any such land could be made into dairy farms with regular application of artificial fertiliser.[32]

State-sponsored trials on Charles Harrison's farm at Te Kuiti confirmed 'the response to top-dressing with phosphatic fertilisers is so marked that it undoubtedly pays to use such an immediate and effective means of improving pastures'. Experiments by the Fields Division in Canterbury found that 'soluble superphosphate [gave] quicker and more economical results' than its rivals.[33] Increasingly, emphasis was placed not just on artificial fertiliser rather than grass mix, or even on phosphates rather than other artificial fertilisers, but on superphosphate rather than basic slag or rock phosphate as the fertiliser producing the fastest return. Ellis, who now saw no end to phosphate use, enthused: 'southern farmers consider [lesser use] is evidence as to where the good land is situated, but their northern friends hold it is proof as to where the good farmers are!' 'Good' farming practice was increasingly associated not with reading the nature of the land but with rendering it irrelevant.[34]

Another dimension of this story often silenced is raised by Damon Salesa, an historian of Samoan heritage who works on the Pacific. He points out that:

> Nauru produced almost all of the phosphate that proved key to the domestic New Zealand agricultural revolution – the 'grasslands revolution' of the 1920s and 1930s ... This was dependent on an exploitative colonialism aimed not just at possessing the land, but also uplifting it and taking it away. In a strange irony these phosphates were then mixed with the soil of farms, themselves obtained in earlier iterations of New Zealand colonialism.[35]

In a further irony, the appropriated Nauru phosphate (and the island's wasted landscape) as well as the appropriated Māori soil did not so much contribute to feeding and clothing the Pākehā (at the centre of Salesa's 'New Zealand Empire') as to feeding and clothing the British who stayed at home, at the centre of the Empire, within which Pākehā were, in turn, considered peripheral. Although Nauru became the largest supplier, Ocean Island, and the Tuamotus group in the Society Islands near Tahiti, made significant contributions to supply as well (Table 10.1). The French Empire thereby also assisted in the feeding of its First World War ally.

Table 10.1: The origins of phosphatic fertiliser
(in imperial tons and by percentage).

	Imperial tons	Nauru	Ocean Island	Tuamotus Islands	Australia and rest of world
1920	49,145		23	60	17
1929	154,905	50	39		11
1938	264,003	71	29		
1948	309,902	46	4	50	
1958	486,292	63	10	27	

Source: Statistics of New Zealand.

The aptly named Percy Smallfield, trained by Levy and author of a major book on the grasslands revolution (the term he coined to capture the achievement of greatly increasing productivity on a virtually static land area), described the shift involved in employing much higher inputs of artificial fertiliser:

In the early 1930s farmers were able to exploit the full powers of fertilisers, lime and selected strains of grasses and clovers in pasture improvement. By, as it were, building a veneer of fertility on scrublands the apparent paradox was created of pastures which grew high-class milk-producing fodder being established on apparently unchanged and naturally sterile soils.[36]

Whether consciously or not, Smallfield, Levy and other agricultural scientists seemed determined to inflate the importance of their contribution to farming development by playing down the efforts of earlier farmers using different methods.

Disdainful comment also served to show older ways in the worst light in order to make newer methods appear even more successful. Levy made this clear in his book Grasslands of New Zealand when he wrote that the pioneer 'with his stout heart and virile body', knew nothing of the processes whereby the forest regenerated itself or of the forces at work in that regeneration; nor did he fully appreciate that the fight could be economically won only by the fire-stick and the correct use of appropriate grazing animals. He did not realise the insidious spread of secondary growth … He was ignorant of the correct grasses and clovers to use and was misled by the strong early growth of the coarser grasses which afterwards weakened and opened up as the temporary fertility of the bush burn declined. He did not know the part that a proper sward played in the competitive struggle against the return of the forest.[37]

Such a representation, however, cannot disguise the point that so-called 'rule of thumb' methods had laid down some 5.7 million hectares of English-style pasture by 1914 (Figure 1.2). Perennial ryegrass, despite its inadequacies, also covered 70 per cent of the improved pastures of the country by 1920, before Levy became its champion.[38] Reversion of forest, soil erosion, and infestation by weeds and secondary growth, were very real problems for farmers between the wars, but as scientists made clear in the 1980s and 1990s, such problems were not simply the fault of earlier generations of farmers.[39] Blame, however, helped prepare the way for the big shifts of the 1930s and the success of Levy's narrow suite of pasture plants.

THE IMPACT OF STAPLEDON'S VISIT

Both Frederick Hilgendorf at Lincoln and Bruce Levy in Wellington had been busy experimenting with grasses before George Stapledon arrived in 1926. When Stapledon visited Lincoln he claimed that he had come to the country 'with a view to learning something about the grasslands of New Zealand', not intending to give any lectures on tour.[40] Having changed his mind and engaged in an unofficial tour he reinforced the need for Britain to learn more about grasses by recommending to the Auckland Rotary Club that a scholarship scheme be introduced to send scholars throughout the Empire to 'comb' for 'new grasses in agriculture'.[41]

The influence of Levy, his guide around the North Island, can be seen in Stapledon's enthusiastic assessments of the potential of the North Island. When speaking to the Auckland University Agricultural Science Club, for example, he exclaimed that farms in the warmer areas had the potential to run two cows per acre (0.4 hectares), crediting this to the 'simply marvellous pasture conditions' created by 'sun and rain'. He added the interesting observation that the speed of landscape transformation provided better opportunity for grassland study than was the case in Britain.[42] In other words, experiments could be conducted more easily in a new country like New Zealand and with less complicated consequences.

Stapledon also 'paid a high tribute to the researches of Mr. E.B. Levy' in understanding this transformation.[43] Although he expressed admiration for Akaroa cocksfoot, he agreed with Levy that seed strains must be kept pure and advised 'seedsmen to keep the various grasses distinct from one another'.[44] As he travelled and observed New Zealand's pastures it seems that Stapledon helped persuade Levy that development of a truly perennial ryegrass would enable ecological simplification through concentration upon a narrow range of 'pure' and highly refined grass species. While Hilgendorf (who maintained a greater regard for cocksfoot) omitted ryegrass from three of his recommended mixes, Levy by 1928 had become a firm advocate of the advantages of the species if more perennial strains could be developed. '[T]he point I wish to make', said Levy, 'is that the rye-grass and white clover ideal is possible under nearly all grassland conditions in New Zealand ... maximum production will not be secured until such ideal is attained'.[45]

Levy noted that he had 'a good deal' to do with Stapledon's visit, in which the British expert's 'absorbing interest was centred on the part strain and breeding in pasture plants played in grassland improvement'.[46] Levy's approach until then had relied on switching the species in a grass mix or perhaps altering fertility, rather than artificially selecting from varieties of a particularly nutritious grass (like ryegrass or cocksfoot) that could function well in a broad range of environmental conditions. From 1926 onwards the science of genetics assumed a more important role in shaping Levy's work than the equally new science of ecology that had attracted him earlier. Stapledon's visit was, therefore, critical in redirecting his ideas.

This redirection was reflected in Levy's work with Stapledon's star student William Davies, who came to New Zealand and Australia as 'Empire grasslands investigator' on a two-year secondment from 1929–31, paid for by the Empire Marketing Board. The two men effectively brought to a conclusion once and for all the older 'ryegrass controversy' (see chapter 7), which stemmed from the fact that this grass had so often not proved perennial in either Britain or New Zealand. They removed these doubts by developing longer-lasting strains. Stapledon had already emphasised that improving the strain was more important than improving the soil (as in Levy's early so-called 'ecological' approach).[47] As a result, Levy's work with Davies concentrated almost exclusively on ryegrass. An exception was their development of a more vigorous variety of white clover which they called

'New Zealand Wild White no. 1'. Its success shifted the ratio of white to red clover dramatically, with white clover rising from a relatively minor 23 per cent of the total clover cover in 1918 to all but equal red clover by 1948 with 47 per cent[48] (Figure 10.3).

Figure 10.3: Alfred Cockayne, Bruce Levy, J.W. Dean and William Davies examining white clover plants in a trial in 1929, to find the most productive strain. *Source*: AgResearch Grasslands, Palmerston North.

Levy and Davies found that 'virtually the whole of the ryegrass of the South [Island] at present on the market is of the pseudo-perennial type' while 'the true perennial ryegrasses of the North [Island] are markedly superior'. The need was for 'detailed work to isolate the "super" strains, as it were, from the general mass of Hawke's Bay and other true perennial ryegrass types' and so select the cream of the cream. Only 'concerted action between the Department of Agriculture, the seed grower, and the seed trade' could 'right a position that was fast becoming untenable'.[49] Farmers' participation in such research would thereby be further reduced, implying that from then on farmers would be beneficiaries of research rather than partners in it.

Working with longer-lasting Hawke's Bay and Poverty Bay varieties of the grass, Levy and Davies demonstrated that ryegrass could be perennial *and* provide both more palatable feed and superior nutrition for stock. Ross Galbreath has suggested that Davies, with more formal training than Levy, was the better scientist who carried out the more significant part of this work.[50] But Levy was a much more effective publicist. As a result, even though Davies had been sent as a 'missionary' who would collect information and exchange ideas in the field, then 'bring all home to be sorted and shifted',[51] Levy claimed the lead in five of the six papers they wrote together and his distinctive voice booms off the page. By early 1931 he had converted both Davies and Stapledon to the superiority of ryegrass as opposed to the deeper-rooted cocksfoot or any other grass. Stapledon, indeed, vacillated because he had initially stressed the importance of broad mixes of grass seed.[52] After his visit and Levy's advocacy of a narrow and simple solution to grazing problems, Stapledon became very enthusiastic about the success of grasslands farming in New Zealand and held up the Dominion as a model which Britain and the rest of the Empire might follow.[53]

By the end of 1930, Levy and Davies had refined their preferred strain of perennial ryegrass sufficiently to commence state ryegrass certification with J.W. Hadfield – the Department of Agriculture agronomist who ran the seed certification service for wheat and potatoes from 1927 and pasture plants from 1929.[54] It was a development the three men felt could 'surpass in economic importance the stud-book of the stock-breeder and the milk test for the dairy cow'. The resulting certified seed, plus bags of fertiliser supplied by stock and station agents Wright Stephenson and others, became the stuff of the 'grasslands revolution'.[55] As Levy put it:

> The kinds and amounts of manure will vary according to the soil-type on which the experiment is laid down, and annual or twice-yearly applications will be made in order to keep ryegrass and white clover dominant on each soil-type. The object of this is to determine the amount of manure required to build up and maintain each soil-type to perennial-ryegrass and white clover standard ...[56]

Pasture development had become agricultural management from the top down. Utilising science as its tool, the state (through Levy) created a situation in which it became increasingly difficult for farmers to use anything other than the strains of ryegrass and the fertilisers prescribed to them.

The interactions between Stapledon, Levy and Davies exemplify arguments that imperial space was 'the sphere of a multiplicity of trajectories', rather than of core–periphery dichotomies.[57] Stapledon may have succeeded in persuading Levy to pay more attention to strain, but Levy brought Stapledon round to the view that a narrow focus on ryegrass and clover was preferable to a broad range of grasses. This attributed no importance to New Zealand's indigenous grasses; a view that diverged from Stapledon's earlier advocacy of grasses that had developed resilience over long periods of time in their place of origin to cope with the complexities of particular environments.[58]

In marked contrast to a New Zealand botanist like Leonard Cockayne, Stapledon had no time for the Dominion's indigenous vegetation, remarking that: 'We are concerned ... with the present and the future' and 'we can, therefore, make no more than passing reference to it ... features of the scenery, like the dense evergreen bush of New Zealand ... [are] rather of yesterday than today'. When he spoke of the importance of 'indigeneity' in grass strains in a New Zealand context, he did not mean New Zealand's indigenous grasses such as the native tussocks, but the number of seasons and the locations in which English grasses had grown in New Zealand. (Stapledon perhaps later realised the ambiguities in his use of the word, since he wrote, in 1938: 'The so-called indigenous strains! Badly called, and I am afraid that I have been largely responsible.'[59])

Similarly, rather than behaving as an orthodox missionary Davies returned home with new ideas.[60] The story is, therefore, complex. 'English' grasses did triumph in terms of serving the kinds of imperial ends prized by both Stapledon and Davies. On the other hand, Dominion scientists also changed the thinking of Stapledon and Davies in profound ways. It was an exchange driven by men working in the field together. Flows of influence and information were at least two-way, and tidy notions of core and periphery and gentlemanly capitalism do not adequately capture the complexities involved in either a descriptive or analytical sense. Much of the expertise required was developed locally in New Zealand and was often subsequently exchanged in apparently reverse fashion, to help remake the pastures of Britain and other parts of the world including the North West United States, Latin America and Australia.[61]

EVANGELISING THE LEVY SYSTEM

Levy still had to win over New Zealand farmers, especially as his was essentially a North Island system that suited farms on land cleared of bush. It did not hold immediate appeal to farmers in cooler areas like Southland or in longer established farming districts. Nonetheless, the self-proclaimed 'grasslands evangelist'[62] succeeded through his forceful public speaking and by employing able disciples like Peter Dill Sears in persuading the great majority of New Zealand farmers to implement his regime. Levy also benefited from his close association with Alfred Cockayne, whose influence and support enabled him to control the extension service by which the Department of Agriculture passed on information on the latest advances in farming techniques.[63] Displaying enormous energy, capacity for hard work and passionate oratory, Levy stumped the country with the enthusiasm of a populist politician, speaking to farmers at field days and sometimes on remote properties, winning over the great majority reasonably quickly. His ability as a writer also helped, even if in his later writings he lost the sense of proportion he demonstrated as a thoughtful young advisor and experimenter in the early 1920s.

Levy's increasing fundamentalism becomes clear when his early publications on grasslands in the *Journal of Agriculture* are compared with the first edition of *Grasslands of New Zealand*, published in 1951. In the early articles he demonstrated some ecological sensibility in allowing that native bush could usefully serve to moderate the effects of intense rainfall and runoff.[64] Thirty years on, however, he saw no place for any kind of forest other than exotic pine for pulp, paper and timber production in the North Island. Only in the most remote and mountainous parts of the South Island did he see remnant native forest as having scenic value. According to his simplified and more focused vision, every possible piece of land that could be covered in pasture, including that being locked up by expanding cities, should become a 'sward' of ryegrass and clovers. Any appreciation of biodiversity – which is now considered crucial to ecological sustainability – stopped at the paddock fence.

Levy justified his simple 'one system fits all' approach by appeal to a basic form of environmental determinism. New Zealand's relatively equitable climate and generally reliable rainfall enabled it to carry stock outside all year round. When compared with northern Europe or North America, annual grazing in outside paddocks constituted both a 'natural' and a 'comparative advantage'.[65] Pictures of stock overseas being fed inside reinforced the message with captions like 'Winter cold in Great Britain, Canada, U.S.A. and Europe necessitates the wintering of all dairy cows and fat cattle indoors for five to seven months.' A picture of a Swedish farm in summer reinforced his point with a caption proclaiming: 'The buildings required to house stock for seven months of the year may make up to 70 per cent of the capital value of the farm.' This tidy and easily understood reading of New Zealand's potential caught the imagination of public and politicians alike. Few pointed out that New Zealand lacked large areas of fertile soils, or that it grew trees (albeit of introduced species) faster than just about anywhere else.[66]

Success in bringing into production the 'gum lands' of the far north in the 1920s and the 'pumice lands' of the central plateau of the North Island from the late 1930s also aided Levy's cause. In both instances fertilisers played a key role. The apparently exhausted soils of the north, leached of fertility by the giant kauri tree but since cleared of its timber, responded well to the addition of superphosphate and lime when used in combination with newly certified ryegrass and clover. Smallfield remembered Alfred Cockayne's claim that this change bordered on the miraculous, as it brought new hope to the desperate farmers of this area.[67] On the central plateau, sheep and cattle experienced what was called 'bush sickness', or chronic loss of condition, due to the absence of cobalt and molybdenum in the soils. After 1949 this area became easier to develop when aerial top-dressing provided a means of spreading a mixture of superphosphate and cobalt. But it was Levy's suite of ryegrass and clover that then thrived in this formerly difficult environment.[68]

Even though farmers implemented Levy's regime unevenly, it taking a long time to establish in some areas,[69] the contributions of younger scientists ensured its survival. Levy handed over research on the efficacy of the 'dung and urine shower' to P.D. Sears, later director of the Grasslands Division of the DSIR. Sears carried out careful experiments to demonstrate that the other key component of Levy's system, the 'fertility shower' of stock, really did benefit pasture, with dung providing calcium and phosphorus, and urine adding nitrogen and potassium. Intensive stocking thereby supplemented the use of superphosphate. Sears' work provided Levy with the scientific justification he required to support his system, even if Sears himself later began to have second thoughts. More recent research has also suggested that Levy's emphasis upon this 'shower' greatly inflated the contribution of stock to either soil fertility or pasture improvement, and the superiority of New Zealand over other countries for pasture growth, but by then his system had become well entrenched.[70] His advocacy was so successful that by 1948 some 85 per cent of New Zealand's improved pasture was comprised of ryegrass.[71]

Levy was also successful in handing on the perpetration and expansion of his unbridled pasture system to latter-day charismatic evangelists such as W.M. (Mat) Hamilton and C.P. McMeekan. Both of these dynamic figures emerged in the 1940s to expand Levy's ideas, especially in relation to dairying. Hamilton, based at Massey Agricultural College, published *The Dairy Industry* in 1944 which proved influential, lending further credibility to Levy's approach.[72] McMeekan took over as director of Ruakura Research Station in the Waikato in 1943. The title of his popular survey – *Grass to Milk: A New Zealand Philosophy* (1960) – encapsulated Levy's conceptualisation of

New Zealand's role in the world, even if he tried to move experimentation back into the farm paddock. From the 1960s he also spent much energy on advocacy of increased research and development into agriculture to ensure that New Zealand did not slide towards the fate of Uruguay, once farming in that country failed to keep pace with developments elsewhere.[73]

The narrowing of grasses to be employed across a wide range of environments contrasted with trends in sheep breeding at the same time. Instead of trying to make the Romney fit all locations, Massey Agricultural College's Principal Geoffrey Peren set out to develop a specialist hardy sheep to flourish on the difficult arid and high country on the east coast of the North Island. The 'Perendale', crossed with the Cheviot and full of 'hybrid vigour', emerged from these endeavours while the specialist carpet wool sheep the 'Drysdale' rather emerged as unexpected outcomes from a series of breeding experiments to produce finer Romney wool.[74]

THE REJECTION OF ALTERNATIVE STRATEGIES

Before Levy won over doubters, however, some serious stock and environmental issues emerged in the late 1930s to challenge the ubiquity of his system. First, outbreaks of bloat caused by vigorous clover growth created problems for cattle. Very rich clover could (and still can) upset the digestive system of cattle, inhibiting the normal elimination of gas by belching. The pressure thereby built up can prove fatal. Not until the 1960s did scientists understand why cattle foamed at the mouth instead of belching and no final solution has yet been discovered. Reducing clover concentrations has been the easiest means of controlling the difficulty of over-rich pasture; this has led to increased use of nitrogenous fertilisers, as discussed in the final chapter.[75]

Second, stock could suffer from 'ryegrass staggers' when grazing pasture hard during dry summers. Only in the 1980s did scientists from the DSIR and the Ministry of Agriculture realise that this was due to a toxin in an endophytic fungus that co-existed with ryegrass. The endophyte protected the ryegrass against insect pests like the Argentine stem weevil, but affected stock as well. A return to work with the Aberystwyth research station, using its collection of pasture plants, enabled the identification of a strain of endophyte that warded off insects whilst apparently minimising staggers, although the problem was not entirely resolved.[76] Similarly, it took until the 1970s to fully understand and control outbreaks of facial eczema when heavy rain fell after a long period of warm, dry weather. Once again a fungus proved to be the toxic agent involved, one that flourished in ryegrass and clover.[77]

Environmental difficulties also slowed the implementation of Levy's vision. Erosion worsened as the Great Depression bit in the early 1930s creating a sense that deteriorating farmland led to increased soil loss, then really struck home in 1938 after the economy had begun to recover. This year remains something of an *annus horribilis* in New Zealand's environmental history, with major landslides and serious flooding afflicting the steeplands of the East Coast of the North Island. Kenneth Cumberland, newly arrived in New Zealand from Britain, like Lance McCaskill of Lincoln College, pushed the case for soil conservation after a comprehensive field-based assessment of the extent of the problem.[78] McCaskill, after travelling to the USA in 1939 to examine how the US Bureau of Agriculture and the Soil Bureau coped with the dust bowl, soon won over Prime Minister Peter Fraser to his cause. Labour established the Soils Conservation and Rivers Control Council in 1941 in recognition of the argument that the problems of flooding and soil erosion were related. Apparently powerful new regulatory forces were now aligned against indiscriminate pastoralism, but they were unevenly enforced and had only limited impact until tightened under the Water and Soil Conservation Act passed in 1967.[79]

From this point soil scientists and conservators never unanimously supported grassland scientists, with many adopting a critical rather than a celebratory attitude towards the grasslands revolution. But, because Levy and his supporters had already persuaded the Department of Agriculture and farmers that his approach held the key to future development, his system held sway, even though it was not implemented at the same rate in different places.[80] Alternative approaches to land use and farming development were also jettisoned despite the warnings of 1938, later summed up by Cumberland in his words: 'abused and exhausted, the land rebels'.[81] Levy also appeared to ignore DSIR soil scientist Norman Taylor's warning that even though '[i]n New Zealand, pasture is almost worshipped, and rightly so, since it is the foundation of our national wealth ... grasslands farming cannot be carried on everywhere regardless of natural conditions'.[82]

Levy's orthodoxy, pushed hard in editions of his *Grasslands of New Zealand*, undermined alternatives such as those expressed by Alexander Macpherson (see chapter 9). Lucerne (alfalfa), for example, was one of many crops seriously investigated pre-war but largely ignored afterwards because it struggles to cope with pest infestation in wetter areas and cannot withstand prolonged grazing. Macpherson's 'personal record' reveals a sense of the neglect of the hard work of a practical experimenter, even though written in old age when he despaired of the state's failure to pursue his very different vision. He ascribed the rejection of his farmer-centric approach after the First World War to a conspiracy organised by the 'Dictatorship'. By this he meant Reform Party leaders, the Department of Agriculture under C.J. Reakes and Alfred Cockayne, and seed merchants like Wright Stephenson. (He failed to mention Levy because he emerged as a major player after Macpherson had retired.) Their intention, he felt, was to 'annihilate and suppress any agricultural progress, stagnate production, and ... to hold the farming community as bonded slaves for all time'.[83] His disappointments resonate with some American interpretations of their agricultural history in the same period, marked by increased distance between state research and farmer input with consequent disempowerment of the farmer and deification of the state scientist. Recently, American historians working on the 1920s have also noted a decline in influence of individual American state governments through land grant colleges and the increasing impact of agricultural directives from Washington.[84] Similarly, government in Wellington played a much more important part in New Zealand's agricultural development after 1920.

Because 30 per cent of farms were under 50 acres (20.2 hectares) in 1940, there were still too many small units run on a part-time basis to argue that, in New Zealand, 'every farm was a factory', even if many larger operations had become increasingly 'industrial'.[85] According to productivist objectives, however, progress was impressive given that increases like the threefold lift in butterfat output between 1916 and 1934 had been achieved despite war, depression and environmental problems.[86] Some farms may still have been run in a rather old-fashioned and unscientific manner, but more balanced and diversified approaches to land use had been jettisoned. The form that the accelerating industrialisation of New Zealand agriculture assumed in the late 1920s and early 1930s would dictate the directions to be followed for the next two generations, and possibly beyond.

CONCLUSION

This narrowing of the farming vision ruled out any attempt at diversification of land-use strategies. As a result, at the outbreak of the Second World War, New Zealand was even more ensconced in its role as Britain's specialist sheep and dairy farm, producing more and more of a limited range of products with little attention to either the quality of those products or to their marketing. This position seemed to be legitimated by the return of the commandeer system during the war years. But thereafter, most New Zealand politicians, bureaucrats, agricultural scientists and farmers continued to assume that British consumers would go on buying New Zealand-produced butter, frozen sheep meat and wool out of a sense of Empire loyalty, no matter how unappealing it looked.

When Sir John Russell, Britain's leading agricultural scientist, had visited New Zealand in 1928, two years after Stapledon, he identified the crux of the problem from an economic if not from an environmental point of view: focusing so much attention on production had diverted attention away from the equally important task of marketing produce.[87] But Levy, like pretty much everyone else, assumed that British consumers wanted to eat New Zealand's particular brand of meat and dairy produce without ever inquiring as to whether they enjoyed doing so. With the British market being taken for granted, the productivist paradigm continued to dominate New Zealand's official approach to farming development.

Figure 10.4: Empire Marketing Board poster entitled 'New Zealand Dairy'. This was produced by an English artist, F.C. Herrick, and displayed in Britain in 1927 as part of the Board's campaign to encourage the home purchase of Empire goods. It portrays a dairy factory in Taranaki as it might have looked before the First World War rather than in the 1920s, by which time dairying was reliant upon motorised transport. *Source*: CO 956/3, National Archives, Kew, London.

Levy's attitudes and actions, like those of the Cockaynes, reflected a more widely held nationalistic sentiment and intent. After visiting Aberystwyth for a meeting of grassland scientists in 1937, Levy concluded that 'Britain did not have a great deal to teach us from its grassland farming.'[88] At much the same time the newly established Dairy Board set about building on the work of the Empire Marketing Board (Figure 10.4) by enthusiastically advertising New Zealand as the 'Empire's dairy farm'. Posters and films made by the Board to persuade British consumers (especially housewives) to purchase New Zealand products portrayed the Dominion as a farming idyll whose benign, grassy landscapes produced healthy settlers and even healthier food.[89]

The triumph of the ryegrass/clover duoculture, heavily reliant on inputs of artificial fertiliser and use of chemicals, encourages a reconsideration of the influence of the 'conservative' farmer-politicians William Massey and Gordon Coates on the setting of New Zealand's development strategies. Others have hinted that the leadership of these two prime ministers proved important in developing New Zealand into the Empire's specialist stock farm.[90] But Massey's enthusiastic support for greater use of phosphatic fertiliser and Coates' commitment to rescuing agricultural production through applied science literally reshaped the Dominion's geography as well as its history. These initiatives also appealed to the first Labour Government of 1935, given its commitment to state-controlled planning and utilisation of applied science.

11 *Conclusion*

Tom Brooking and Eric Pawson

INTRODUCTION

In this book, we have set out to answer a central question: how, why and with what consequences did the transformation of New Zealand into empires of grass occur? Our analysis has come down to an overarching theme, which is how one particular possibility for the future of the country was enacted. By the 1920s, grass-based products reigned supreme in the export profile, and were to remain so for a considerable time. Nonetheless, this was not a foregone conclusion, and there was nothing inevitable about it, as chapter 6 has demonstrated. In the 1860s, the Bradford Chamber of Commerce tried many places in search of suitable wool. Before the First World War, the English lamb roast had to be invented to create an outlet for New Zealand sheep meat.[1]

After the war, 'pastoral totalitarianism', built on a reliance on a chemically enhanced duoculture to support a narrow range of grass-based primary products, was the product of conscious choices and increasingly state-driven policy. The speed with which vineyards have replaced the sheep farms of the Wairau Valley in Marlborough since the 1980s, or with which farm-based tourism, wine and fine Merino wool for adventure wear have taken over on the formerly rabbit-infested runs of Central Otago, is another indicator that other choices existed. Indeed, chapter 2 shows that before the 1880s it was not clear which of several futures, perhaps to exist side by side, would prevail. By the 1920s, it was starkly clear. To Levy, it was a matter of common sense: 'Here are the world's best stock and the world's best grasses, clovers and fodders, with an environment to unfold all their latent qualities. What a heritage!'[2]

This final chapter will do two things. First, it will discuss what has happened to New Zealand farming under the Levy style of grassland management and pasture development from the 1930s down to the present. It will raise the matter of how the seeds of empire on which farming depended were used to produce moral landscapes that acted as powerful discursive features to cement Levy's self-described 'heritage' in place. Second, it will return to the central question, and the contextual themes within which it has been embedded (Figure 1.1), to suggest how our work informs new agricultural, imperial and environmental histories.

MORAL LANDSCAPES

During the hard years of the Great Depression farmers focused on economic problems and looked for assistance in terms of mortgage relief and devaluation of the currency. Their preoccupation was such that they paid little attention to matters other than increasing production and meeting their financial obligations. The majority, therefore, judged the noticeable reversion of pasture to scrub and bush as evidence of economic or even moral failure rather than as any kind of ecological or environmental problem.[3] Levy's insistence, as in a later set of radio talks, that his system could be applied 'irrespective' of the fertility of the soil helps explain this.[4] The work of David Matless in another context is illuminating. He describes moral landscapes as emerging in England in this period 'wherein structures are to embody moral principles and offenders are to be cleared out'. He is identifying behaviours ('[l]oudness, vulgarity, impertinence on the one side, dignity, composure, fitness on the other').[5] But the concept can as readily be applied to the form of landscape, and its fitness for purpose.

Levy said of George Stapledon that he 'repeatedly stressed the aesthetic and social values of an efficient countryside and a well-cared for countryside'. Stapledon himself related land degradation to 'spiritual' as well as moral decline.[6] Somewhat disingenuously, Levy wished for 'a like crusader in New Zealand to inspire a proper appreciation of these values'. He was clear enough what he meant by this: 'In our grasslands, studded with sheep, cattle and dairy herds, together with attractive homes and surrounds, we have a means to beautify our countryside unparalleled by any other country in the world ...'[7] The extent to which the countryside had been 'beautified' is reflected in Figure 11.1. The transformation of the North Island into sown pasture, much of it involving the prolonged hard labour of bush work on former Māori lands, is apparent. This is a considerable turnaround on the geography of pastoral farming up till the

1880s, when Agricultural and Pastoral Shows were rather more numerous in the South than in the North Island (Figure 8.1).

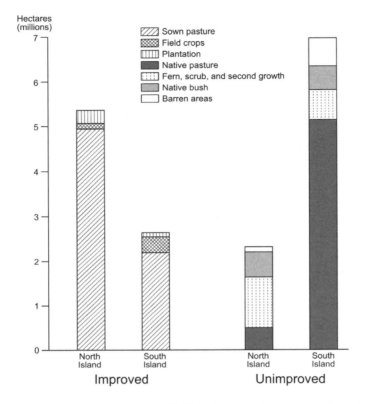

Figure 11.1: Land under occupation, 1946–7. *Source*: redrawn from Department of Agriculture, *Farming in New Zealand* (Wellington, 1950), p. 12.

Figure 11.1 illustrates the extent of different land uses on 'occupied land'; that is, the two-thirds of the country that in the late 1940s did not include urban areas, residual 'Maori communal land', forest and alpine regions 'unfit for settlement'.[8] Rather like those whom Samuel Butler sought to lampoon in the 1860s with his remark – quoted in chapter 2 – that 'a mountain here is only beautiful if it has good grass on it',[9] Levy felt that 'It is not right to have a vast area of land not producing its proper share'. Specifically he meant 'Crown land, Maori land, and much privately held land in poor pastures, in weeds and secondary growth or in gorse (the real menace of our hills) …'[10] Another take on this issue is revealed by the Royal Commission on Sheep Farming, which sat from 1947, travelled 70,000 kilometres, visited 2,027 farms and interviewed 6,479 witnesses before reporting in 1949.[11]

The Commissioners devoted a lot of space in their final report (over 47 pages out of 220) to the issues of high country degradation and reversion of pasture to scrub and bush. They argued that only abundant credit, expanded farm advisory services, more effective marketing, improved social amenities and expanded top-dressing would repair the damage caused by neglect during depression and war.[12] Levy's 'sward' would supposedly hold most country: the Commissioners wanted 'to have as much of our land as possible permanently available in such a condition that it will give the maximum production'.[13] Abandoned land represented a 'tragedy' to these farmers and their answer to deterioration was 'to raise fertility again'.[14] This perspective was very much in line with the prevailing view in New Zealand at the time that '[a]s a partner in the British Commonwealth of Nations, we have a boundless duty to produce food, and to produce it as cheaply as we can'.[15] A series of covers for the *Journal of Agriculture* in 1946 illustrates this very point (Figure 11.2).

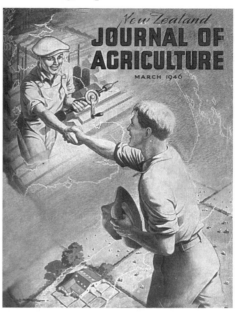

Figure 11.2: Cover of the *New Zealand Journal of Agriculture*, March 1946. This was one of seven produced that year focusing on the theme of feeding Britain after the war.

In the early 1950s, the Korean War triggered a boom in wool prices that saw another significant rise in production and the final phase of expansion of the farming frontier (Figure 1.2). Settlement pushed back into environmentally marginal areas through the 1950s, 60s and 70s. Specially modified military aircraft (and from 1957 the purpose-built 'Fletcher' light aeroplane) dropped over 27 million tonnes of super phosphate, rock phosphate, slag and trace elements such as cobalt and potash across New Zealand between 1949 and 1980.[16] This technology benefited the high country in particular so that sheep numbers climbed in the South Island from 14.8 to 32 million by 1980 and from 19 to 36.9 million in the North. This intensification was accompanied by the application of large numbers of chemicals, the use of which was promoted to produce a weed-free pastoral ideal, once again 'moralising' landscapes.[17] The 1950s also saw an acceleration of the industrialisation of farming as tanker collection of milk brought about consolidation of dairy factories resulting in the building of much larger but many fewer plants.[18]

The very high proportion of pastoral exports held steady until the 1950s, with Table 11.1 showing the effect of the Korean wool boom. Thereafter wool sales fell away, with a sharp decline in the late 1960s as prices collapsed in the face of competition from synthetic fabrics. A rise in the significance of meat production in part compensated for this, but even before the withdrawal in the mid-1980s of agricultural subsidies – introduced in the preceding decade to protect farm incomes – pastoral exports were well below the levels of the 1950s in overall significance. In part this reflected diversification within the primary products sector (towards horticulture, fishing and forestry); in part it was due to diversification beyond it to a range of industrial goods and raw materials, such as aluminium.[19] The overarching effect of the 1980s policy changes was, however, to put a stop to the expansion of the farming frontier and to reduce the national sum of stock units (Figure 1.2). Sheep numbers, which peaked at 70 million in 1982, had fallen to 38.5 million by 2007.[20]

Table 11.1: New Zealand exports by value (per cent), 1921–2001.

	1921	1931	1941	1951	1961	1971	1981	1991	2001
Wool	10	18	19	58	38	18	13	7	2
Meat	22	22	10	10	21	33	30	24	13
Butter	26	32	37	14	14	10	10	9	2
Cheese	18	12	17	8	7	4	4	3	4
Milk powder								5	8
Skins, tallow, casein	17	9	11	5	5	5	4	4	6
Subtotal: pastoral	93	93	94	95	85	70	61	52	37
Pulp and paper						5	5	5	3
Other	7	7	6	5	15	25	34	43	60

Source: *New Zealand Official Yearbook*, various dates.

This has not, however, meant the end of the productivist paradigm that has shaped the New Zealand countryside from before Levy's time. Since 2001, products of the dairy industry have become the leading source of export income (18 per cent of merchandise exports in 2006), the result of a 'dairy boom' that took off from the early 1990s.[21] The application of energy-hungry nitrogenous fertilisers has pushed the overall consumption of fertilisers, which had fallen in the 1980s, right back up again (Figure 10.1). The advent of intensive dairying into drier areas, where it is reliant on irrigation, has fuelled concern, particularly in Canterbury.[22] New Zealand's production of methane, stemming from ruminants, is about ten times the global per capita average,[23] and farm energy inputs have increased substantially since 1990.[24] A regional study of the Mataura River basin in Southland reveals that the older-style sheep farming had a substantially lower environmental footprint compared to new dairying farms.[25]

Levy would probably have had mixed feelings about these developments. He approved of more intensive usage, although he would not condone the loss of good soils to urban expansion. Nor would he look with favour on the withdrawal of the farming frontier and accompanying forest transition that is occurring in districts such as Banks Peninsula, where native forest is reclaiming former cocksfoot pastures.[26] He would also not be happy about the advent of stall farming for stock, as it is inconsistent with the advantages he saw of being able to farm outdoors all year round.[27] He would probably regret the move of corporate capital into agriculture: in Southland, for example, only 60 per cent of dairy farms are now owner operated.[28] He viewed the institution of the family farm as a bulwark against growing city influences.

REVISITING THE KEY THEMES

The dominance of New Zealand's export sector by agriculture and its role in transforming New Zealand's landscape and environment is not matched by the development of its agricultural history.[29] Much of what has been written is the preserve of agricultural scientists or is locked away in local and family histories, and ageing university theses. This state of affairs has not been conducive to the development of perspective, with the result that most accounts are either celebratory in nature or condemnatory. In the first, the proper use of landscape as Levy understood it is prominent; in the second, another sort of moralising emerges: that which decries not lack of use but poor practice.

Kenneth Cumberland, in his wartime reconnaissance of soil erosion in New Zealand, claimed that it sought 'to describe the regional variations in the extent and character of [the problem] and not to attach blame for its prevalence', shortly after describing it as the product of a national 'youth at times wantonly misspent'.[30] Much more recently, official reports on the state of New Zealand's environment or its farming practices focus on environmental costs, reflecting the politicization of resource management issues as well as a growing reliance on positive environmental branding in international marketplaces.[31] But whether positive or negative in tone, many assessments downplay or decry the past. Yet it is only an understanding of the past which can reveal that strategies adopted many generations ago mould patterns that are hard to break, even though such patterns were based on choices that were not in any way ordained.

These choices produced relatively straightforward landscapes. In common with settler societies elsewhere, the ideology of improvement aimed to simplify the environment and standardise production techniques. Chapter 4 draws on a model from the ecologist Pierre Dansereau which isolates the key factors in the establishment of agricultural property as the suppression of biodiversity and keeping production artificially high by supplementing nutrients not supplied by locally grown herbiage with minerals and fertilizers. The resulting production systems depend on young female animals. Chapter 6 expresses the same idea in the language of the economic historian: market opportunities 'brought far-reaching changes to New Zealand's agro-ecology'. Initially, settlers experimented with multiple species of 'English grasses', seeding the landscape as embodied in Suttons' brand (Figure 7.2). They then refined their choices down to a more manageable handful, even if ryegrass, white clover and cocksfoot were long the most popular. From Levy onwards, a duoculture of the first two alone was vigorously promoted.

Simplified though settler landscapes were, they were not uniform. They were constructed in environments that were originally richly varied. Tussock grasslands and bush intersected with extensive areas of wetland in low-altitude areas and with subalpine vegetation in upland regions. Landscapes were also made at different times, with large parts of the North Island in particular being beyond the reach of the Crown until the 1860s or later. There were differences in outcomes even within regions. Chapter 5 accounts for a clear divergence in the pathways of the South Island pastoral runs. Those on the Canterbury Plains and downlands were freeholded for mixed farming production. Those in the high country were variously affected by economic and ecological fortune, some increasing stock units over time, others declining. Similarly, it has been demonstrated that the later 'grasslands' revolution', so named by Percy Smallfield after the small battery of industrialised techniques propounded by Levy, was anything but evenly applied or adopted.[32]

The drive for improvement focused on property, production and productivity. Property required boundaries, and boundaries are rooted in abstract geometries of the sort illustrated in Figures 2.3 and 2.4. The finely attuned understandings of environment on which Māori depended were initially of value to settlers struggling to survive. But they were soon discarded in favour of more empirically based knowledge methods, as chapters 3 and 4 show. With these came a parcelling into paddocks, farms and stations. Describing the process in Canada, Northrop Frye wrote of 'the conquest of nature by an intelligence that does not love it'.[33] The landscapes of lowland Canterbury have been compared in consequence to a Mondrian painting.[34] Yet, with few exceptions, such as Christopher Perkins' representation of a Taranaki dairy factory, or Bill Sutton's plantation series, New Zealand painters of landscape seem rarely to see these human feats. It is as if they are simultaneously human and dehumanized. For spiritual (rather than material) nourishment, the artist has looked to the elemental land beneath.[35]

Social well-being was provided, at least to Pākehā settlers, by a high level of connectivity. Chapter 8 has discussed how a well-developed network of agricultural information was brought into being: even small settlements were remarkably well integrated into systems of communication, and market signals were widely distributed through newspapers and stock and station agents. Peter Hempenstall has observed that 'people live within their local communities, and their local histories, and find the meanings they give to their lives there'. This does not mean that places were isolated: far from it, but rather that historians and geographers seek today to 'trac[e] the messy entanglements of people and groups and ideas across local, regional, national and international boundaries'.[36] These entanglements *were* messy. Simple core-periphery models misrepresent the manner in which a settler society like colonial or nationalist New Zealand was integrated into the wider world.

Ideals of 'gentlemanly capitalism' centred in the City of London are similarly oversimplified.[37] The financing of pastoral development came from varied sources within New Zealand as well as from overseas, as chapter 6 has shown. Some was family money, some was reinvested, some came through complex routes like that of Murray Roberts, illustrated in Figure 6.2. The rentiers of the English Home Counties played an important role, through London-based companies like the New Zealand Loan and Mercantile Co. and the National Mortgage and Agency Co., but the point is that these were by no means the only sources. They were sufficiently important that the tightening of the British money market after the failure of the City of Glasgow Bank in 1879 had a sharp effect. At one level this contributed to the long depression that lasted till the mid-1890s; at another level however, New Zealand producers both managed to finance and to begin to create markets for the frozen meat trade in the 1880s.

The meat trade required new breeds of sheep, as had the wool trade before it, as chapter 5 has demonstrated. The Merino was ideal for neither, and fashionable worsted cloth of the type produced in Bradford was the stimulus for the development of the half-breed sheep. The introduction of the frozen meat export trade increased the practice of cross-breeding that by the early 1880s was already well established. The Corriedale was the product of cross-breeding; it has provided the most significant sheep breed exports from New Zealand. Breeders from around the world showed considerable interest in it from the time it was established, with the first exports to the USA taking place in 1914. By then, Corriedales had already been shipped to Australia; they have since gone to South Africa and eastern European countries. By far the largest market has been the South American countries of Argentina, Uruguay, Chile, Peru and Brazil, with both stud and flock sheep being exported from New Zealand. By 1937 there were 6 million Corriedales in Argentina and one third of the Uruguayan flock were from the same breed.[38] In the 1990s, Corriedales made up 60 per cent of Uruguay's national sheep flock.[39]

Such examples show that places could be simultaneously both peripheral and nodal. Akaroa cocksfoot was 'the first exotic commodity in which New Zealand gained global market dominance'.[40] It was of a localised strain that grew on Banks Peninsula, a place no larger than thirty kilometers north to south and forty from east to west. Yet, as chapter 7 reveals, this small district supplied much of the cocksfoot grass in international trade from the 1880s to the First World War. It rose to prominence at a time when the worth of ryegrass was doubted in some quarters, and sent seed to Australia, North America and northern Europe. In the 1920s, it attracted the attention of George Stapledon, who used Akaroa plants in the development of new cocksfoot strains at Aberystwyth. Stapledon and his pupil Davies, whose time in New Zealand is discussed in chapter 10, both learned from New Zealand grassland practice.

Stapledon subsequently wrote that

Nothing is more striking to one who has travelled fairly extensively overseas than the amazing extent to which in the more temperate parts of the Empire the country itself has been moulded to the appearance of this Greater Britain of ours. Nearly all the grasslands of New Zealand are man, cattle, and sheep made.[41]

This observation echoes that of Sir Walter Elliot, quoted in chapter 1, about the significance of grassland 'as one of the cornerstones on which the greatness of the British Empire has been built'.[42] Often however, its role has been taken for granted or shrouded in silence. One of the key findings of this book is laid out in chapters 3 and 4, concerning the extent to which grassland development was put in place by the three earliest but little-known generations of settler Pākehā farmers, those of the mid- to late nineteenth century. The extent of their experimentation is revealed in Figure 4.3, and the nature of their hard work is exemplified in Figure 2.5. The importance of their activities is reiterated in chapter 9.

The new generation of grassland scientists downplayed the accomplishments of these earlier pioneers, including their role in understanding the agency of grass in the transformation of landscape. But another message that comes through clearly is that even though, as latter chapters show, the twentieth century was increasingly the era of the expert, many other roles were significant in enabling a small remote country to capitalise on its chosen pathway. These included New Zealand politicians who served as Agent-Generals in London (or forerunners of later-day ambassadors) – William Pember Reeves and Thomas Mackenzie – along with Prime Ministers William Ferguson Massey and Gordon Coates. As a result, artificial grass was unquestionably seen as the fit and proper use of land. Although the Wellington-based *Evening Post* declared in 1922, 'Are there not already enough object-lessons of the consummate stupidity of the policy of growing one blade of grass where two trees grew before?' in commenting on the proposed development of the Waioeka and Waimana valleys[43] in the eastern Bay of Plenty, few commentators before Cumberland doubted the naturalising of such farming.

CONCLUSION

Just before the outbreak of the Second World War, the Primary Products Marketing Department began extensive advertising of New Zealand butter ('Ask for it by name') in the British press. To this end, a photograph of a young boy called 'Smiler' was used. Playing on the tropes of moral landscapes and healthy living prevalent in the 1930s, readers were told that:

> They call him 'Smiler' because he enjoys the happiness that springs from perfect health. His *Mother* realizes that good health springs from good feeding, so she spreads his bread freely with New Zealand butter, the finest of sunshine foods. This delicious golden butter from a country of fresh green pastures-lands has just the flavour to tempt 'Smiler's' appetite and is rich in those natural vitamins without which good health is left to chance.[44]

Shortly after the war, the large Marcus King painting[45] that provides the cover of this book also revealed much about moral landscapes of grass, but in a more literal sense. It was painted in the first half of the 1950s, at the height of the Korean wool boom, when large American cars still dominated roads that ran between paddocks full of cows and sheep. A streamlined train, more modern than anything actually seen in New Zealand, signifies speed and efficiency and suggests that 'machine technology is a proper part of the landscape'.[46] In the middle distance is a city, lying beneath the mountains that mark the border of humanised landscapes. Other than the mountains, everything portrayed in this painting is artificial, and gains its existence and meaning only in relation to the wider networks into which the activities portrayed are connected. And it leaves unanswered a deeper but related issue, posed by the former Waitangi Tribunal judge Eddie Durie, of whether settlers will truly settle until they come to accept the realities of the land in which they are living. Rather, that is, than continuously trying to make it into something different.[47]

It has been said that '[p]astoral science and perspiration rendered the mountaineous, forested land of New Zealand a land suitable for wool',[48] and for other grass-based products. The manner in which this happened, and the contexts within which it occurred, has been our focus. As William Cronon reminds us, a good story 'makes us care about its subject in a way that a chronicle does not' and 'expresses the ties between past and present in a way that lends deeper meaning to both ...'[49] even when that story relates to something as mundane and taken-for-granted as pasture grass.

Appendix 1:
Common and Formal
Names of Plants

Akaroa cocksfoot	*Dactylis glomerata*
alsike / alsyke clover	*Trifolium hybridum*
anise	*Pimpinella anisum*
barberry	*Berberis glaucocarpa*
birdsfoot trefoil	*Lotus* spp.
blackberry	*Rubus fruticosus*
bluegrass	*Poa alpina / Poa pratensis*
blue tussock	*Poa colensoi*
blue wheat grass	*Elymus* spp.
bracken	*Pteridium esculentum*
broom	*Cytisus scoparius*
Californian prairie grass	probably *Bromus* sp.
Californian thistle	*Cirsium arvense*
Cape weed / Capeweed	*Cryptostemma calendula*
Chewing's fescue	*Festuca rubra*
chicory	*Cichorium intybus*
clover	*Trifolium* spp.
cocksfoot	*Dactylis glomerata*
common vetch	*Vicia sativa*
cow grass	*Trifolium pratense*
crested dog's-tail	*Cynosurus cristatus*
crimson clover	*Trifolium incarnatum*
danthonia	*Rytidosperma* spp.
dock	*Rumex* spp.
fern / bracken fern	*Pteridium esculentum*

211

foxglove	*Digitalis* spp.
furze	*Ulex* spp.
goosegrass	*Galium aparine*
gorse	*Ulex europaeus*
hair-grass	*Deschampsia tenella*
hard fescue / hard tussock	*Festuca novae-zelandiae*
hawkweed	*Hieracium* spp.
hawthorn	*Crataegus monogyna*
Italian ryegrass	*Lolium multiflorum*
kahikatea	*Dacrycarpus dacrydioides*
kauri	*Agathis australis*
kūmara / kūmera	*Ipomoea batatas*
larch	*Larix* spp.
Louisiana grass	*Paspalum* sp.
lucerne	*Medicago sativa*
maize	*Zea mays*
manuka	*Leptospermum scoparium*
marigold	*Calendula officinalis* / *Tagetes* spp.
meadow foxtail	*Alopecurus pratensis*
New Zealand flax	*Phormium tenax*
niggerhead	*Carex secta*
oat grass	*Microlaena avenacea*
orchard grass	(common term for cocksfoot)
parsley	*Petroselinum crispum*
paspalum	*Paspalum dilatatum* / *Paspalum distichum*
perennial ryegrass	*Lolium perenne*
plantain	*Plantago* spp.
podocarp	member of the *Podocarpaceae*
Poverty Bay ryegrass	*Lolium perenne*
pumpkin	*Cucurbita maxima*
ragwort	*Senecio jacobaea*
rape	*Brassica* spp.
rata	*Metrosideros* spp.
rat's-tail	*Sporobolus africanus*
raupo	*Typha orientalis*
red clover	*Trifolium pratense*
red tussock	*Chionochloa rubra*
ryegrass	*Lolium* spp.
scabweed	*Raoulia* spp.
Scotch thistle	*Cirsium vulgare* / *Onopordum acanthium*

APPENDIX 1: COMMON AND FORMAL NAMES OF PLANTS

sheep's sorrel	*Rumex acetosella*
silver beet	*Beta vulgaris*
smooth meadow grass	*Poa pratensis*
sorghum	*Sorghum vulgare*
sorrel	*Rumex* spp.
speargrass	*Aciphylla* spp.
sweet brier	*Rosa* spp.
sweet vernal	*Anthoxanthum odoratum*
tall fescue	*Festuca* spp.
timothy	*Phleum pratense*
toetoe	*Cortaderia* spp.
Waipu browntop	*Agrostis capillaris*
wild turnip / turnip weed	*Rapistrum rugosum*
white clover	*Trifolium repens*
yarrow	*Achillea* spp.
Yorkshire fog	*Holcus lanatus*

Source: Nicol, E.R. (1997), *Common Names of Plants in New Zealand*, Manaaki Whenua Press, Lincoln.

Appendix 2:
Short Biographies of
Twelve Pasture Plants

Peter Holland, Vaughan Wood and Paul Star

During the second half of the nineteenth century, more than 60 introduced grasses and broad-leaved herbs were used for sown pastures throughout New Zealand, but the 12 detailed here were most commonly sown. Latin names are in brackets. The principal sources of information are as follows:

Armstrong, J.B. 'A short history of the grasses', *New Zealand Country Journal* 4/1–6 (1880), pp. 69–70, 120–25, 170–74, 219–22, 301–04 and 340–43, and 5/1–2 (1881), pp. 54–63 and 121–26.

Cockayne, A.H., 'The grasslands of New Zealand: component species', *New Zealand Journal of Agriculture* 16/4 (1918), pp. 210–20.

Dixon, M., 'On grasses', letter to the Editor of *The Press*, 19 August 1864.

Dixon, M., 'Permanent pasture grasses', *New Zealand Country Journal* 10/1 (1886), pp. 35–38.

Evans, B.L., 'Grassland research in New Zealand', *New Zealand Official Yearbook* (Wellington, 1960), pp. 1243–64.

Kelly, T., 'Taranaki forest and forest burning', *New Zealand Country Journal* 1/4 (1877), pp. 242–45.

Mackay, T., *A Manual of the Grasses and Forage-Plants Useful to New Zealand, Part I* (Wellington, (1887).

'Ruarata', 'Laying down permanent pasture on bush land', *New Zealand Country Journal* 9/2 (1885), pp. 125–28.

Simson, A., 'Pasturage', *New Zealand Country Journal* 10/4 and 5 (1886), pp. 291–95 and 360–63.

Steel, G., 'Meadow grasses', *New Zealand Country Journal* 13/2 (1889), pp. 124–26.

Stefferud, A., *Grass: The Yearbook of Agriculture 1948* (Washington, 1948).

Sutton, M.H., 'The selection of grasses and clovers', *New Zealand Country Journal* 11/3 (1887), pp. 201–03.

Tothill, G.C., *Laying Down Land in Permanent Grasses* (Invercargill, 1893).

Wilkin, R., 'Grasses and forage plants best adapted to New Zealand', *New Zealand Country Journal* 1/1 (1877), pp. 3–12.

These are supplemented by brief notes in nineteenth-century newspapers (including numbers of references to species in advertisements published by the *Otago Witness* between 1851 and 1900), farming magazines, farmers' diaries and letter books, official reports, and the scientific literature. With two exceptions, the illustrations come from Mackay, T., *A Manual of the Grasses and Forage Plants Useful to New Zealand, Part 1* (Wellington, 1887). The exceptions are *Paspalum dilitatum* and *Poa pratensis*, and the illustrations for these two come from Hitchcock, A.S., *A Text-book of Grasses with Especial Reference to the Economic Species of the United States* (New York, 1914).

The accounts describe the 12 pasture plants as nineteenth-century grassland farmers knew them. Progressively fewer species were sown during the twentieth century, and seed certification from the late 1920s onwards provided welcome assurance of quality to farmers. There was also a shift from the multi-species swards favoured by New Zealand farmers in the mid-nineteenth century to closely managed pastures dominated by named varieties of cocksfoot, Italian and perennial ryegrass, timothy, red and white clover.

Alsike clover (*Trifolium hybridum*), a perennial with upright growth, and well suited for sowing in damp acidic soils. It only persisted in dry sites if irrigated. The legume of choice on land where red clover did not grow well, alsike clover was a palatable and nutritious component of mixtures for temporary or permanent pastures, especially those dominated by timothy and cocksfoot. Unlike other recommended clovers, it was not preferentially eaten by livestock. In the USA it was chiefly known as an annual or biennial plant.

Cocksfoot (*Dactylis glomerata*) was one of the most common perennial pasture grasses on New Zealand farms. It was nutritious to sheep and cattle, a productive hay plant, and usually grown in combination with one or several of crested dog's-tail, Italian and perennial ryegrass, red clover and white clover. Establishment could extend over two or three years, by which time the plant's characteristic growth form provided shelter for palatable broad-leaved herbs and small grasses. Periods of intensive grazing were needed to control development of clumps. Its deep roots tapped water and nutrients, making it less likely than perennial ryegrass to deplete surface reserves of both. Its growth peaked in summer, when other pasture grasses were either growing slowly or were dormant, and it continued to grow until the first hard frosts of winter. Growth resumed early in spring. Although tolerant of sparingly fertile soils and heavy land, it did best on rich, moist but well-drained soils. By the 1860s good commercial lines – which often reached 95 per cent germination – had been established at Akaroa and in Taranaki, with occasional imports from Denmark after 1920 to refresh the gene pool. Regionally, it was the preferred species for oversowing tracts of burned tussock in Central Otago, for sowing in well-drained and occasionally droughty soils in Canterbury and Marlborough, for spreading on light virgin soils after bush-burns in the North Island provided that grazing could be postponed for a couple of years to allow the young plants time to develop a root run, and for sowing in former fernland after cattle had consolidated the topsoil. In Southland, with its almost ideal climate for grass growth, cocksfoot ranked after perennial ryegrass, meadow fescue, and crested dog's-tail, and it was sown with meadow foxtail where permanent pastures were desired.

Crested dog's-tail (*Cynosurus cristatus*) was the most important fine-leaf pasture grass across lowland New Zealand during the last two decades of the nineteenth century, especially in drier sites, and was a normal ingredient of seed mixtures for long-duration pastures. A smaller and finer plant than cocksfoot, crested dog's-tail was slower to establish in sown pasture and produced less herbage. It thrived in a variety of soils, and did well in admixture with hard fescue and sheep's fescue. In the late nineteenth century it was the third-ranking grass in Southland pastures, where it was one of the most palatable, but not the most productive, of the introduced pasture grasses. It, cocksfoot and white clover were the most successful introduced pasture plants in the almost continental climates of inland South Island. A nutritive turf-forming species that thrived on soils ranging from light sand to rich loams, it did not grow tall enough for hay. In North Canterbury it grew almost year round and was recognised as a valuable in-filling species between taller grasses. It persisted in sown pasture, where it seeded prolifically and spread spontaneously, yet did not suppress other valued species. Its compact short foliage was much relished by sheep, but livestock did not usually eat the seed heads. Its fibrous roots penetrated deep into the soil, enabling it to withstand extended spells of hot dry weather. Its needs for soil water and nutrients compared with those of cocksfoot, and it was a prominent element of sown pasture in second-class country until improved and certified strains of perennial ryegrass displaced it. Elsewhere, it retained its place as a valuable pasture grass because its early season growth began before that of perennial ryegrass. It did not thrive in shade, and could grow rank when in association with cocksfoot. One nineteenth-century commentator saw its prime merit as the ability to spread over unploughable country. By the end of the nineteenth century most of the seed was produced in New Zealand, with good-quality seed in commercial quantities coming from Otago, Southland and the Sandon District of southwestern North Island. It repaid a farmer's time and care, and was valued where footrot in sheep was a problem.

Italian ryegrass (*Lolium multiflorum*) had been recognised since the 1860s as a first-class, normally annual, nutritious pasture plant, albeit one that was much less persistent in sown pasture than perennial ryegrass. It was esteemed as a forage grass in moist areas but did not form as strong a turf as did perennial ryegrass, grew throughout the frost-free season, was highly palatable to sheep and cattle, and could withstand seasonal drought. Although suited to all classes of soil and most environmental situations in the cool temperate lowlands, it did best in moist fertile soils when sown in combination with perennial ryegrass, timothy, cocksfoot and a clover. It was one of the best grasses for a forage crop or a temporary pasture intended to last a couple of seasons, but plants lived longer when seed production was suppressed. When grown with red clover in temporary pastures, it progressively disappeared from the sward, allowing longer-lived grasses to take over. It yielded best in rich soils, but was the second most important pasture species in medium- to good-quality soils on the Canterbury Plains. If sown in February, it could provide herbage from early winter into the following summer. Its rapid spring growth could suppress late-season pasture plants.

Meadow fescue (*Festuca pratensis*) was widely recognised as a fine-leaf grass of first-class pasture value. It was recommended for sown pastures co-dominated by cocksfoot and perennial ryegrass because it yielded well during dry summers and withstood seasonal drought. It could be suppressed soon after germination by Italian ryegrass, but once established it was a strong permanent grass that produced abundant nutritious and palatable herbage. It was widely used in British pastures, and in New Zealand locally produced seeds were reasonably priced and germinated well. It flourished on well-drained soils and thrived across Southland, where it was second only to perennial ryegrass as a component of sown pastures. The value of meadow fescue in permanent pastures was realised after it had formed a sward, although that could take several years. Today, it is virtually unknown in sown pastures.

Meadow foxtail (*Alopecurus pratensis*) was one of the earliest and best fine-leaf grasses for permanent pastures on well-watered land. With short root stocks, it grew in loose tufts and formed a medium to dense sod as it matured. It responded well to irrigation, did best in cool moist conditions, yet was tolerant of episodes of hot or cold weather. It showed a spurt of growth in spring, but grew year round unless checked by the availability of soil moisture in the summer. In Canterbury it tended to be sown for pastures in dairying areas with heavy soils, but thrived in all soils except dry sands and gravels. As a soil binder it was superior to timothy. The plants could take three or four years to become fully established – a property it shared with cocksfoot and crested dog's-tail – when its rapid growth and palatable herbage made it a valued species for permanent pasture. It was seldom grown for hay. During the nineteenth century the high cost and low germination rate of imported seed meant that meadow foxtail had a lower ranking than its recognised merits might have suggested. Probably the most nutritious of the sown pasture grasses, especially in the fertile soils of drained swampland, in temperate conditions it could yield herbage year round.

Paspalum (*Paspalum* spp.) was grown in warm temperate parts of the North Island. Speculative introductions of *Paspalum* to New Zealand farms were made from Uruguay in 1881, and presumably from the USA in 1894 (when it was sold here as 'Louisiana Grass'). It was more widely adopted in the eastern Australian states, to which it had been introduced at about the same time. Thanks to the promotional activities of seed merchants in New South Wales, a New Zealand market for *Paspalum* (or 'Golden Crown Grass' as it was sometimes know) seed was built up from about 1905, with Australian imports supplemented by locally harvested seed from the South Auckland / Waikato region. In warmer parts of the North Island it was quickly regarded as a first-class pasture grass, but it was viewed less favourably south of Auckland city because its strong summer growth did not compensate for a tendency to displace grasses needed for winter forage. It was a deep-rooted, large-leaf grass that grew well on poorer soils unsuited to cocksfoot, but even there it tended to be a second-ranking pasture species. It required moist but not wet soil, seldom formed a dense sward, and was best sown in a mixture of grasses and legumes. Its seasonal growth peaked between late spring and early autumn, when it overtook perennial ryegrass, but in winter it grew less. In 1915, *Paspalum dilatatum* was known as a grass of recognised first-class pasture value, and a warm-climate species best sown in the north of the country. It needed hot summers and warm autumns, and yielded herbage when many other pasture grasses had ceased growing. It required a moist but not wet soil with ample organic matter, tended not to persist in monoculture but did best in a mixture of pasture plants, produced abundant seed with variable germination rates, and like perennial ryegrass was susceptible to infestation by ergot. It was effectively permanent on warm sites, ranging from sloping ground to drained wetlands. As a sod-forming species, its compact roots made ploughing difficult, and it was unsuited to short-term pastures. Mercer grass (*P. distichum*) had its place on grassland farms in northern New Zealand but was seen there as a pasture species of only secondary value.

Perennial ryegrass (*Lolium perenne*) had its supporters and its detractors, their stance often changing over time. From the earliest years of organised settlement, it was the dominant or co-dominant species in recommended seed mixtures for sown pastures because it germinated well, matured quickly, was highly productive, and sheltered other desirable pasture plants. It did not persist in the light soils of Canterbury, although farmers found that addition of a clover could sometimes extend pasture duration. It required carefully managed grazing to inhibit flowering and ensure new tillers, and its shallow roots could deplete surface soil reserves of nutrients and water. It may have been the first commercial agricultural grass in Britain, and the Pacey's, Russell's, Stickney's, Sutton's, Pollexfen's and Whitworth's commercial varieties were sown in nineteenth-century New Zealand. The British 'Devon Evergreen' strain, possibly the origin of the highly valued 'Hawke's Bay' and 'Poverty Bay' strains, may have been brought to New Zealand by the missionary, Samuel Marsden. As Alfred Cockayne reported in 1918, perennial ryegrass was popular with grassland farmers because its seeds were cheap and germinated well, it grew during mild winters, had a flush of growth in spring, yielded into summer, and was highly palatable to livestock. It was sown at rates of 14 to 25 pounds of seed per acre (16 to 28 kg per hectare). Amongst the problems associated with it was 'ryegrass staggers', which was caused by a fungal endophyte. Others included slow recovery after summer drought, and open patches of bare soil left by mature plants when they died creating opportunities for weeds and less valued pasture species to become established. Its most serious shortcoming was that not all commercially available material was perennial, despite vendors' protestations. For that reason, some nineteenth-century farmers selected for long-lived strains by harvesting seeds from old pastures. The nineteenth-century British agronomist and agricultural commentator, Faunce de Laune, supported use of perennial ryegrass during the 1860s and 1870s, but in 1882 criticised its involvement in seed mixtures, extravagantly describing it as 'the cause of so much evil'. In New Zealand, his views were supported by Alfred Cockayne who, in 1914, concluded that on New Zealand farms the species was virtually biennial. For that reason, he believed that it should not be a major component of seed mixtures for intended long-duration pastures. For several years perennial ryegrass was sidelined by advisors, but not by the majority of farmers. In the 1930s and 1940s, seed certification and varietal selection brought about a change in attitude. Since then, irrigation, aerial top-dressing with mineral fertilisers, selection of short- and long-lived varieties, and breeding for endophyte resistance, have ensured its prime position in grassland farming.

Red clover (*Trifolium pratense*) and cow grass (a longer-lived variety of *Trifolium pratense*) have been valued as fodder plants and nitrogen-fixing soil improvers since the earliest days of organised settlement. The shorter-lived red clover preferred deeper and richer soils than the perennial white clover, but it could survive seasonally dry conditions and was valued as a fodder species in short-rotation pastures expected to last less than two years. Farmers had to manage it differently from white clover, and it was well suited to areas with frequent summer dry spells or low summer rainfall. Cow grass was sown when a longer period between planting and re-establishment was possible. It was usually grown in admixture with either Italian or perennial ryegrass, and remained productive for about five years before dying out. An upright, short-lived perennial with an underground rootstock prone to attack by a root borer, cow grass survived when the water table in winter rose almost to the surface and could withstand summer dry spells because its deep roots tapped sub-surface supplies of water. It did best, however, in deep, rich and moist soils.

Smooth meadow grass (*Poa pratensis*) – also known as blue grass – was usually a minor component of seed mixtures for permanent pastures but it progressively dominated the sward. In the USA, on the other hand, it was known as a cool-weather turf species that formed a dense sod and yielded highly palatable herbage. In New Zealand it did best in cooler sites, where it could persist for decades. Rhizomatous and shallow-rooted, it was valued by farmers as an early and nutritious grass that kept green all year, formed a compact sward that helped protect against establishment of unwanted adventives, and yielded herbage liked by livestock. It tended to grow more rapidly in spring. Its weedy tendencies in New Zealand pastures were recognised early in the twentieth century, when it became known as a weed of arable land.

Timothy (*Phleum pratense*) was particularly valued for sown pastures on rich soils in damp situations, where it produced an abundance of nutritious herbage liked by sheep and cattle. It needed a fertile soil to grow well, and was not suitable for pastures in dry gravelly or sandy soil. Although one of the best grasses for dairy farms, its late start in spring meant that it was best sown with meadow foxtail. In warmer parts of northern New Zealand it gave way to *Paspalum*. Exceptionally palatable to livestock, and frequently grazed hard, it was often sown at rates of three to four pounds per acre (3.5 to 4.5 kg per hectare). Most of the seed first sown on New Zealand farms was imported from the USA, where timothy did not survive the cold winters. A fine Welsh strain grown in New Zealand progressively satisfied local need. A permanent grass, timothy was a component of almost every seed mixture recommended for permanent pasture during the second half of the nineteenth century, but rarely dominated the sward. In heavy North Canterbury soils it was more productive than perennial ryegrass, tended to flower later in the growing season, but was intolerant of trampling and persistent close cropping of its shoots. It ranked fifth amongst the pasture grasses and clovers sown in Southland.

White clover (*Trifolium repens*) has long been the principal nitrogen-fixing plant in New Zealand pastures and is highly palatable to sheep and cattle. Three decades after the start of organised settlement, one commentator stated that New Zealand owed more to white clover, with its high yield and propensity to self-seed, than to any other forage plant. Its combination of surface and deep roots enabled it to withstand water-logging as well as drought, and its spreading stems that rooted at the nodes could extend the life of a sown pasture by several years. White clover tended to dominate in summer and autumn when other pasture plants were growing only slowly, but its growth was checked when tall grasses overshaded it. It could also be crowded out soon after sowing by fast-growing grasses, a disadvantageous trait that called for careful pasture management, and it readily exhausted soil fertility. Since the mid-nineteenth century, white clover has been an indispensable component of long rotation and perennial pastures across New Zealand even though, as Alfred Cockayne observed, not all New Zealand soils are inherently suited to it. Of the commercial varieties sown by farmers, those that showed strong growth during late winter and early spring were preferred. In the nineteenth and early twentieth centuries, a true Dutch form was valued but the 'Webb's Giant White' and 'Ladino White' varieties did not do well. Initially imported, seeds harvested in New Zealand were soon favoured by local farmers, and some seed crops were exported. Once established, it rarely needed to be resown, a property that was to make it an environmental weed.

Notes

PREFACE

1   Pawson, E. and Brooking, T. (eds), *Environmental Histories of New Zealand* (Melbourne, 2002).
2   Newton, J., *The Roots of Civilisation: Plants that Changed the World* (Sydney, 2009).
3   Papers Past is available at: http://paperspast.natlib.govt.nz; Timeframes is at: http://timeframes.natlib.govt.nz; Te Ara is at: www.teara.govt.nz.

CHAPTER 1

1   Stapledon, R.G., *A Tour in Australia and New Zealand: Grassland and Other Studies* (London, 1928), p. v.
2   Matthew, H.G.C. and Harrison, B. (eds), *Oxford Dictionary of National Biography*, Vol. 18 (Oxford, 2004), pp. 187–90. The Empire Marketing Board tried to encourage British consumers to purchase products from throughout the Empire as an act of patriotism between 1926 and 1933 without much success. See Constantine, S., *Buy and Build: The Advertising Posters of the Empire Marketing Board* (London, 1986).
3   Elliott, W., 'Introduction', in Stapledon, *A Tour*, p. xii.
4   Perren, R., 'The North American beef and cattle trade with Great Britain, 1870–1914', *Economic History Review* 24/3 (1971), p. 430.
5   Vamplew, R. (ed.), *Australians: Historical Statistics* (Broadway, NSW, 1987), p. 195. Wheat farming and mining always earned more for Australia than New Zealand.
6   Pendle, G., *Uruguay* (Oxford, 1963); Cossley, C. and Greenhill, R., 'The River Plate beef trade', in D.C.M. Platt (ed.), *Business Imperialism, 1840–1930: An Enquiry Based on British Experience in Latin America* (Oxford, 1977); Denoon, D., *Settler Capitalism: The Dynamics of Dependent Development in the Southern Hemisphere* (Cambridge, 1983); Rock, D., *Argentina 1516–1982: From Spanish Colonization to the Falklands War* (London, 1986), pp. 162–213.
7   Kerr, D. and Holdsworth, D. (eds), *Historical Atlas of Canada, Vol. III* (Toronto, 1990), plates 3 and 5.
8   Elliot, W., 'Introduction', p. xii.
9   Weaver, J.C., *The Great Land Rush and The Making of the Modern World, 1650–1900* (Montreal and Kingston, 2003), *passim* and especially pp. 81–87.

224

10 McGlone, M.S. and Webb, C.J., 'Selective forces influencing the evolution of divaricating plants', *New Zealand Journal of Ecology* 4 (1981), pp. 20–28.

11 Brooking, T., Hodge, R. and Wood, V., 'The grasslands revolution reconsidered', in E. Pawson and T. Brooking (eds), *Environmental Histories of New Zealand* (Melbourne, 2002), pp. 170–71; *New Zealand Official Yearbook* 1919, p. 515; 1950, pp. 341–42 and 1990, pp. 435–37; *The State of the New Zealand Environment, 1997* (Wellington, 1997), 8: pp. 9 and 24–25; and 76; Robin, L., *How a Continent Created a Nation* (Sydney, 2007), pp. 63–64.

12 A paddock is a fenced area of land on a fence or station, a usage known as early as 1880. It can refer to anything from a small to a very large space (80–400 hectares or more): Bardsley, D., *In the Paddock and On the Run: The Language of Rural New Zealand* (Dunedin, 2009), p. 47.

13 Cumberland, K.B., 'A century's change: natural to cultural vegetation in New Zealand', *Geographical Review* 31/4 (1941), p. 529.

14 Urry, J., *Sociology Beyond Societies: Mobilities for the Twenty-first Century* (London, 2000); Cresswell, T., *On the Move: Mobility in the Modern Western World* (New York, 2006).

15 Blunt, A., 'Cultural geographies of migration: mobility, transnationality and diaspora', *Progress in Human Geography* 31/5 (2007), pp. 684–94; Hannam, K., Sheller, M. and Urry, J., 'Mobilities, immobilities and moorings', *Mobilities* 1/1 (2006), pp. 1–22.

16 Massey, D., *For Space* (London, 2005); Winder, G.M., 'Seafarers' gaze: Queen Street business and Auckland's archipelago, 1908', *New Zealand Geographer* 62/1 (2006), pp. 50–64.

17 Lester, A., *Imperial Networks: Creating Identities in Nineteenth Century South Africa and Britain* (London, 2001), pp. 5–8 and 189–92; Ballantyne, T., *Orientalism and Race: Aryanism in the British Empire* (Basingstoke, 2002); Schiebinger, L., 'The European colonial science complex', *Isis* 96/1 (2005), pp. 52–55; Lambert, D. and Lester, A., 'Introduction', in D. Lambert and A. Lester (eds), *Colonial Lives Across the British Empire: Imperial Careering in the Long Nineteenth Century* (Cambridge, 2006), pp. 1–10.

18 Beinart, W. and Middleton, K., 'Plant transfers in historical perspective: a review article', *Environment and History* 10/1 (2004), pp. 3–29; Pawson, E., 'Plants, mobilities and landscapes: environmental histories of botanical exchange', *Geography Compass* 2/5 (2008), pp. 1464–77.

19 Fieldhouse, D.K., *The Theory of Capitalist Imperialism* (London, 1969); and Arnold, D., *The Problem of Nature: Environment, Culture and European Expansion* (Oxford, 1996), pp. 13 and 24.

20 Crosby, A.W., *Ecological Imperialism: The Biological Expansion of Europe, 900–1900* (Cambridge, 1986).

21 Crosby, *Ecological Imperialism*, p. 7.

22 Crosby, *Ecological Imperialism*, pp. 217–68. On neo-Darwinism in New Zealand, see Livingstone, D.N., 'Science, text and space: thoughts on the geography of reading', *Transactions of the Institute of British Geographers*, NS 30/4 (2005), pp. 391–401.

23 Beinart and Middleton, 'Plant transfers'; Pawson, 'Plants, mobilities and landscapes'.

24 Cain. P. and Hopkins, A.G., *British Imperialism: Innovation and Expansion 1688–1914* (London, 1993) and *British Imperialism: Crisis and Deconstruction 1914–1990* (London, 1993); Dumett, R.E., *Gentlemanly Capitalism and British Imperialism: The New Debate on Empire* (Harlow, 1999); but see McAloon, J., 'Gentlemanly capitalism and settler capitalism: imperialism dependent development and colonial wealth in

the South Island of New Zealand', *Australian Economic History Review* 42/3 (2002), pp. 204–23.

25 Lester, A., 'Imperial circuits and networks: geographies of the British empire', *History Compass* 4/1 (2005), pp. 124–41; Lester, A. and Dussart, F., 'Trajectories of protection: protectorates of Aborigines in early 19th century Australia and Aotearoa New Zealand', *New Zealand Geographer* 64/3 (2008), pp. 205–20.

26 Wood, V. and Pawson, E., 'Information exchange and the making of the colonial farm: agricultural periodicals in late nineteenth-century New Zealand', *Agricultural History* 82/3 (2008), pp. 337–65.

27 Belich, J., *Making Peoples: A History of the New Zealanders from Polynesian Settlement to the End of the Nineteenth Century* (Auckland, 1996), pp. 278–337 and *Paradise Reforged: A History of the New Zealanders from the 1880s to the Year 2000* (Auckland, 2001), pp. 27–120.

28 Brooking, T. and Pawson, E., 'Silences of grass: retrieving the role of pasture plants in the development of New Zealand and the British Empire', *Journal of Commonwealth and Imperial History* 35/3 (2007), pp. 417–35.

29 Morgan-Richardson, C., 'The story of a grass farm on clay', *Journal of the Bath and West of England Society*, Fourth Series 10 (1900), pp. 34–43.

30 Swift, J., *Gulliver's Travels*, Part 2, in H. Davis (ed.), *The Prose Works of Jonathan Swift* (Oxford, 1941), pp. 119–20.

31 Foster, R.L., *Modern Ireland 1600–1972* (London, 1988), pp. 197–201.

32 Pawson, H.C., *Cockle Park Farm: An Account of the Work of the Cockle Park Experimental Station from 1856–1956* (London, 1960); and Russell, E.J., *A History of Agricultural Science in Great Britain* (London, 1966), pp. 143–98; Jenkin, T., *The Welsh Plant Breeding Station in 1937* (Welshpool, 1937), p. 2.

33 Canby, H.S., 'Redwood Canyon', *The Atlantic Monthly* (June 1914), p. 835.

34 Winter, J.M., *The Great War and the British People* (London, 1986), pp. 213–28; and De Groot, G., *Blighty: British Society in the Era of the Great War* (London, 1996), pp. 201–09.

35 *The Times*, 9 February 1920; *Nature*, 27 May 1920, p. 408.

36 Quoted in Palmer, P., 'Hilgendorf, Frederick William 1874–1942', *Dictionary of New Zealand Biography*, updated 16 December 2003, http://www.dnzb.govt.nz.

37 Brooking and Pawson, 'Silences of grass'.

38 Winks, R.W., 'The future of imperial history', in R.W. Winks (ed.), The *Oxford History of the British Empire – Vol. V: Historiography* (Oxford, 1999), pp. 653–68.

39 Beinart, W. and Hughes. L., *Environment and Empire* (Oxford, 2007).

40 Malone, M.P., 'Beyond the last frontier: towards a new approach to Western American History', in P.N. Limerick, C.A. Milner II and C.E. Rankin (eds), *Trails: Towards A New Western History* (Lawrence, 1991), pp. 139–60; Malin, J.C., *The Grassland of North America* (Lawrence, 1948).

41 Cronon, W., *Nature's Metropolis: Chicago and the Great West* (New York, 1991); Worster, D., *Dust Bowl: The Southern Plains in the 1930s* (New York, 1979).

42 Cunfer, G., *On the Great Plains: Agriculture and Environment* (Texas Station, 2005); Meinig, D.W., *On the Margins of the Good Earth: The South Australian Wheat Frontier, 1869–1884* (Chicago, 1962).

43 E.g. Morton, W., *Manitoba: A History* (Toronto, 1967); Owram, D., *Promise of Eden: The Canadian Expansionist Movement and the Idea of the West* (Toronto, 1980); Friesen, G.,

The Canadian Prairies: A History (Toronto, 1984); Voisey, P., *Vulcan: The Making of A Prairie Community* (Toronto, 1988).

44 For celebratory examples see Levy, E.B., *The Grasslands of New Zealand*, three edns (Wellington 1923, 1951, 1970); Smallfield, P.W., *The Grasslands Revolution in New Zealand* (Auckland, 1970); McCaskill, L., *Hold This Land: A History of Soil Conservation in New Zealand* (Wellington, 1973); Gould, J.D., *The Grassroots of New Zealand History* (Palmerston North, 1974) and Galbreath, R., 'A grassland utopia? Pastoral farming and grassland research in New Zealand', in *DSIR: Making Science Work for New Zealand, 1926–1992* (Wellington, 1998), pp. 58–79. For a more recent critical view see Brooking, Hodge and Wood, 'The grasslands revolution reconsidered'.

45 Byrnes, G., 'Surveying space: constructing the colonial landscape', in B. Dalley and B. Labrum (eds), *Fragments: New Zealand Social and Cultural History* (Auckland, 2000), pp. 54–75; Pratt, M.L., *Imperial Eyes: Travel Writing and Transculturation* (London, 1992).

46 King, J., 'Facing up to Fox: The colonial watercolours of William Fox', *Art New Zealand* 95 (2000), pp. 84–87 and 99.

47 Nicholas, J., *A Voyage to New Zealand* (London, 1817), quoted in J. Ward, *Information Relative to New Zealand Compiled for the Use of Colonists* (London, 1840), p. 23.

48 Mitchell, W.J.T., 'Imperial landscape', in W.J.T. Mitchell (ed.), *Landscape and Power* (Chicago, 1994), pp. 5–34; Brooking and Pawson, 'Silences of grass'.

49 Turnbull, D., 'Mapping encounters and (en)countering maps: a critical examination of cartographic resistance', *Knowledge and Society* 11 (1998), p. 17.

50 Beattie, J. and Stenhouse, J., 'God and the natural world in nineteenth-century New Zealand', in J. Stenhouse and G.A. Wood (eds), *Christianity, Modernity and Culture* (Adelaide, 2005), pp. 180–203; Shepard, P., *English Reaction to the New Zealand Landscape before 1850*, Pacific Viewpoint Monograph no. 4 (Wellington, 1969), pp. 3–5.

51 Irving, S., *Natural Science and the Origins of the British Empire* (London, 2008), p. 110.

52 Wolf, E.R., *Europe and the People Without History* (Berkeley, 1982).

53 Binney, J., 'Wars and survival' and 'The Native Land Court and the Maori communities, 1865–1890', in J. Binney, J. Bassett and E. Olssen, *The People and the Land Te Tangata me Te Whenua: An Illustrated History of New Zealand 1820–1920* (Wellington, 1990), pp. 123–64; Brooking, T., *Lands for the People? The Highland Clearances and the Colonisation of New Zealand – A Biography of John McKenzie* (Dunedin, 1996), pp. 131–56; Boast, R., *Buying The Land, Selling The Land: Governments and Māori Land in the North Island 1865–1921* (Wellington, 2008).

54 Levy, *The Grasslands of New Zealand*, 1970, p. xxx.

55 Roche, M.M., 'Failure deconstructed: histories and geographies of soldier settlement in New Zealand circa 1917–39, *New Zealand Geographer* 64/1 (2008), pp. 57–67.

56 Cumberland, K.B., *Soil Erosion in New Zealand: A Geographic Reconnaissance* (Wellington, 1944).

57 Schedvin, C.B., 'Staples and regions of Pax Britannica', *Economic History Review* 44/4 (1991), pp. 533–59.

CHAPTER 2

1   Two excellent sources for such background material are McKinnon, M. (ed.), *New Zealand Historical Atlas* (Auckland, 1997) and *Te Ara: The Encyclopaedia of New Zealand*, www.teara.govt.nz.

2   Figures on formed grassland taken from *New Zealand Official Yearbook* and Gould, J.D., *The Grassroots of New Zealand History: Pasture Formation and Improvement* (Palmerston North, 1974). On the impact of Nauru see Maslyn, W. and MacDonald, B., *The Phosphateers: A History of the British Phosphate Commissioners and the Christmas Island Phosphate Commissioners* (Carlton, 1985).

3   Stapledon, R.G., *A Tour in Australia and New Zealand: Grassland and Other Studies* (London: 1928), p. 2.

4   Stapledon, *A Tour*, p. 66.

5   Banks, J., March 1770 in J.C. Beaglehole (ed.), *The Endeavour Journal of Joseph Banks, 1768–1771, Vol. II* (Sydney, 1962), p. 3, cited in Wood, V., 'Soil fertility management in nineteenth century New Zealand agriculture', PhD thesis, University of Otago, 2003, p. 48.

6   Hawkesworth, J., *An Account of the Voyages Undertaken by the Order of his Present Majesty for Making Discoveries in the Southern Hemisphere, Vol. III* (London, 1773), pp. 437–38.

7   Darwin, C., 23 December 1835, 'Journals and Remarks, 1832–1836', in R. FitzRoy (ed.), *Narrative of the Surveying Voyages of His Majesty's Ships Adventure and Beagle between the Years 1826 and 1836, Vol. III* (London, 1839), p. 506, cited in Wood, 'Soil fertility management', p. 56 and in Stenhouse, J., 'The battle between science and religion over evolution in nineteenth century New Zealand', PhD thesis, Massey University, 1985, p. 11.

8   McDonnell, T., 'Extracts from Mr McDonnell's MS: Journal containing observations on New Zealand', in R.P. Hargreaves and T.J. Hearn (eds), *New Zealand in the 1830s* (Dunedin, 1979), p. 16.

9   Earle, A., *A Narrative of Nine Months' Residence in New Zealand* [1832] (Christchurch, 1909), pp. 110–11.

10   Wakefield, E.G., *The British Colonization of New Zealand* (London, 1837), p. 389.

11   Patterson, B., 'The grain mirage: ideal and reality in early Wellington agriculture', *Stout Centre Review* 2/3 (1992), pp. 14–26; Gardner, W., 'A colonial economy', in G. Rice (ed.), *The Oxford History of New Zealand*, 2nd edn (Auckland, 1993), pp. 62–64.

12   Grey, G., *New Zealand Parliamentary Debates* 42 (1882), pp. 6–8; and Gardner, 'A colonial economy', in Rice, *The Oxford History of New Zealand*, pp. 62–64.

13   Cochran, W., 'Tea and silk farming in New Zealand', *Chambers's Journal* (19 March 1881), pp. 181–84; (23 July 1881), pp. 468–72; (20 August 1881), pp. 538–41; (14 October 1882), pp. 660–61; Cochran, W., 'Tea and silk farming in New Zealand', *Transactions of the Highland and Agricultural Society*, 4th Series (1882), pp. 175–249.

14   Weaver, J., *The Great Land Rush and the Making of the Modern World* (Montreal, 2003).

15   Hargreaves, R.P., 'Changing Maori agriculture in pre-Waitangi New Zealand', *Journal of the Polynesian Society* 72/2 (1963), pp. 101–17, and 'The Maori agriculture of the Auckland province in the mid-nineteenth century', *Journal of the Polynesian Society* 68/1 (1959), pp. 61–79; Henare, M., 'The changing images of nineteenth century Māori society: from tribes to nation', PhD thesis, Victoria University of Wellington,

2003; and Petrie, H., *Chiefs of Industry: Maori Tribal Enterprise in Early Colonial New Zealand* (Auckland, 2006).

16   E.g. Binney, J., 'Wars and survival' and 'The Native Land Court and the Maori communities, 1865–1890', in J. Binney, J. Bassett and E. Olssen, *The People and the Land Te Tangata me Te Whenua: An Illustrated History of New Zealand 1820–1920* (Wellington, 1990), pp. 123–64; Brooking, T., *Lands for the People? The Highland Clearances and the Colonisation of New Zealand: A Biography of John McKenzie*, (Dunedin, 1996), pp. 131–56; Stokes, E., 'Contesting resources: Māori, Pākehā and a tenurial revolution', in E. Pawson and T. Brooking (eds), *Environmental Histories of New Zealand* (Melbourne, 2002), pp. 35–51.

17   The rise and fall of Māori farming has not been investigated in any systematic manner, although much is being revealed by investigations carried out for the Waitangi Tribunal; for example, see *The Ngai Tahu Report (Wai 27)* (Wellington, 1991), pp. 195–96, 841–919, 922, 935 and 1041; *The Taranaki Report: Kaupapa Tautahi (Wai 143)* (Wellington, 1996), pp. 3, 286 and 289; and *Ngati Awa Raupatu (Wai 46)* (Wellington, 1999), pp. 90, 92, 99, 101–02 and 107. Otherwise, see Parsonson, A., 'The challenge to mana Maori', in Rice, *The Oxford History of New Zealand*, pp. 167–200; Keenan, D., 'Bound to the land: Māori retention and assertion of land and identity', in Pawson and Brooking, *Environmental Histories*, pp. 246–60. On Māori shearers see Martin, J.E., *Tatau Tatau – One Big Union Altogether: The Shearers and the Early Years of the New Zealand Workers' Union* (Wellington, 1987).

18   Belich, J., *Paradise Reforged: A History of the New Zealanders from the 1880s to the Year 2000* (Auckland, 2001), pp. 54–86; and Brooking, *Lands for the People?*, pp. 97 and 157–58.

19   *New Zealand Official Yearbook* 14 (1905), p. 1; Arnold, R., *Settler Kaponga, 1881–1914: A Frontier Fragment of the Western World* (Wellington, 1997).

20   *Census of New Zealand*, 1911, Part 8, pp. 473. The actual figure is 21,486 but this includes some relatives assisting.

21   Based on Brooking, T., 'Economic transformation', in Rice (ed.), *The Oxford History of New Zealand*, pp. 230–53; Seal, B., 'Illusions of grandeur? A history of the New Zealand winemaking industry, 1895–1919', MA thesis, University of Otago, 2001; Cooper, M., *The Wines and Vineyards of New Zealand* (Auckland, 1984); and Roche, M., '"Wilderness to orchard": the export apple industry in Nelson, New Zealand 1908–1940', *Environment and History* 9/4 (2003), pp. 435–50.

22   Pearson, W., 'Southland Land Commissioner's Annual Report', *Appendices to the Journal of the House of Representatives*, 1879, C-7, pp. 1–2.

23   Twain, M., *Mark Twain in Australia and New Zealand* (Ringwood, Victoria), 1973, pp. 290 and 297.

24   Davitt, M., *Life and Progress in Australasia* (London, 1898), pp. 344–54.

25   Lloyd, H.D. *Newest England: Notes of a Democratic Traveller in New Zealand with some Australian Comparisons* (New York, 1900), *passim*, especially pp. 1–11.

26   George, H., *Poverty And Progress: An Inquiry Into The Causes Of Industrial Depressions, And Of Increase In Want With Increase In Wealth – The Remedy* (London, 1883); Brooking, *Lands for the People?*, *passim*.

27   Another leading American progressive, Frank Parsons, held similar views but never visited, drawing instead on Lloyd and on the New Zealand historian and political activist W.P. Reeves to provide an equally favourable endorsement in his tome:

Parsons, F., *The Story of New Zealand* (Philadelphia, 1904), *passim*, especially chapter 79: 'Causes and conditions', pp. 658–88.

28 Seddon, *New Zealand Parliamentary Debates* 86 (1894), p. 191.

29 Ministry for the Environment, *The State of New Zealand's Environment, 1997* (Wellington, 1997), 8, p. 30 on deforestation; Park, G., '"Swamps which might doubtless Easily be drained": Swamp drainage and its impact on the indigenous', in Pawson and Brooking, *Environmental Histories*, p. 151, and *Nga Uruora. The Groves of Life: Ecology and History in a New Zealand Landscape* (Wellington, 1995), pp. 19–56.

30 Gorst, J., *New Zealand Revisited: Recollections of the Days of My Youth* (London, 1908), pp. 51–53.

31 Star, P., 'Potts, Thomas Henry 1824–1888', *Dictionary of New Zealand Biography*, updated 22 June 2007, http://www.dnzb.govt.nz; Beattie, J., 'Alfred Sharpe, Australasia, and Ruskin', *Journal of New Zealand Art History* 27 (2006), pp. 38–56.

32 Grossman, J.P., *The Evils of Deforestation* (Auckland, 1909); and Scholefield, G., *New Zealand in Evolution: Industrial, Economic and Political* (London, 1909), pp. 51–52.

33 Reeves, W.P., *The Long White Cloud*, 1st and 3rd edns, 1898 and 1906 (reprinted Auckland, 1980), p. 382.

34 Guthrie-Smith, H., *Tutira: The Story of a New Zealand Sheep Station*, 4th edn (Wellington, 1969), p. xiii.

35 Cited in Petersen, G.C., *The Pioneering Days of Palmerston North* (Levin, 1952), p. 58.

36 Irvine, R.F. and Alpers, O.T.J., *The Progress of New Zealand in the Century* (London, 1901), pp. 438–39.

37 Reeves, *The Long White Cloud*, 1st edn, p. 35.

38 *New Zealand Official Yearbook* 14 (1905), pp. 1 and 607.

39 *New Zealand Official Yearbook* 20 (1911), p. 600; and 22 (1913), p. 569.

40 E.g. Levy, E.B., *The Grasslands of New Zealand* (Wellington, 1923); Cockayne, A.H., 'New Zealand agriculture: its trends in the past quarter century', *New Zealand Journal of Agriculture* 32/2 (1926), pp. 88–92; and Stapledon, *A Tour*.

41 Constantine, S., *Buy and Build: The Advertising Posters of the Empire Marketing Board* (London, 1986).

42 The term 'station' means 'a large landholding', or 'a building on a large landholding': Bardsley, *In the Paddock and On the Run: The Language of Rural New Zealand* (Dunedin, 2009), p. 56.

43 In Wild, L.J., *The Life and Times of Sir James Wilson of Bulls* (Christchurch, 1953), p. 48.

44 Star, P., 'On Southland farm dairies', unpublished paper (2004). Star found about ten farm dairies for Southland properties up to 1930, many of them for very short periods. A search in Canterbury by Vaughan Wood produced a similar result.

45 Olson, S. and Holland, P., 'Maintaining the rural landscape: expectations and costs of hedging', *New Zealand Geographer* 51/2 (1995), p. 23.

46 In Wild, *The Life and Times of Sir James Wilson*, p. 51.

47 Guthrie-Smith, *Tutira*, pp. vii–viii.

48 Wynn, G., 'Remapping Tutira: contours in the environmental history of New Zealand', *Journal of Historical Geography* 23/4 (1997), pp. 418–46.

49 Pawson, E. and Holland, P., 'People, environment and landscape since the 1840s', in M. Winterbourne, G. Knox, C.Burrows and I. Marsden (eds), *The Natural History of Canterbury*, 3rd edn (Christchurch, 2008), pp. 37–64.

50   These are illustrated in Figure 5.1.

51   Cant, R.G., 'The agricultural frontier in miniature: a microstudy on the Canterbury Plains, 1850–75', *New Zealand Geographer* 24/2 (1968), pp. 155–67.

52   Cant, 'The agricultural frontier'.

53   Blair, I.C., *Life and Work at Canterbury Agricultural College: The First Seventy-five Years of the Agricultural College at Lincoln New Zealand* (Christchurch, 1856), pp. 35 and 327.

54   Holland, P.G. and Hargreaves, R.P., 'The trivial round, the common task: work and leisure on a Canterbury hill run in the 1860s and 1870s', *New Zealand Geographer* 47/1 (1991), pp. 19–25.

55   Holland and Hargreaves, 'The trivial round', p. 21.

56   Holland, P., 'Plants and lowland South Canterbury landscapes', *New Zealand Geographer* 44/2 (1988), p. 52.

57   Holland and Hargreaves, 'The trivial round', pp. 22–23.

58   Dominy, M.D., *Calling the Station Home: Place and Identity in New Zealand's High Country* (Lanham, 2001), pp. 54–55 and 144–47.

59   Hargreaves, R.P., 'Farm fences in pioneer New Zealand', *New Zealand Geographer* 21/2 (1965), pp. 144–55. Contemporary plant nursery catalogues indicate the range of live hedging plants available. On the impact of wire fencing see Weaver, *The Great Land Rush*, pp. 81–87; Gardner, J., *The Amuri: A County History* (Culverden, 1893), pp. 229 and 275–79; Arnold, R., *New Zealand's Burning: The Settlers' World in the Mid 1880s* (Wellington, 1994), pp. 137, 145 and 170; and Peden, R., 'Pastoralism and the transformation of the rangelands of the South Island of New Zealand, 1841–1912', PhD Thesis, University of Otago, 2007, pp. 241–50.

60   Butler, S., *A First Year in Canterbury Settlement, with Other Early Essays* (London, 1914), p. 66.

61   Scrivener, R., 'The subdivision and closer settlement of Edendale estate, 1879–1914', BA Hons essay, University of Otago; Hawke, G.R., *The Making of New Zealand: An Economic History* (Cambridge, 1985), p. 88.

62   Paulin, K., Hall, I. and Hall, W., *The Story of John Hall and His Descendants* (Edendale, 1983).

63   *Otago Witness*, 1 January 1881, quoted in Scrivener, 'The subdivision and closer settlement of Edendale', p. 19.

64   Scrivener, 'The subdivision and closer settlement of Edendale', pp. 59–61; Wynn, G. and Cant, G., 'The bonanza wheat boom', in G. Cant and R. Kirkpatrick (eds), *Rural Canterbury: Celebrating its History* (Wellington, 2001), pp. 69–71; Hawke, *The Making of New Zealand*, pp. 35–36.

65   Wood, V. and Pawson, E., 'The Banks Peninsula forests and Akaroa cocksfoot: explaining a New Zealand forest transition', *Environment and History* 14/4 (2008), pp. 449–68.

66   Wood and Pawson, 'The Banks Peninsula forests'.

67   Petersen, G.C., 'Pioneering the North Island bush', in R.F. Watters (ed.), *Land and Society in New Zealand: Essays in Historical Geography* (Wellington, 1965), pp. 66–79; Warr, E.C.W., *From Bush Burn to Butter: A Journey in Words and Pictures* (Wellington, 1988); Arnold, *New Zealand's Burning*; Roche, M.M., 'From forest to pasture: the clearance of the lower North Island bush, 1870s to 1910s', in M. McKinnon (ed.), *New Zealand Historical Atlas*, plate 47; Wynn, G., 'Destruction under the guise of

improvement? The forest, 1840–1920', in Pawson and Brooking (eds), *Environmental Histories*, pp. 100–16.

68 Stokes, 'Contesting resources'; Waitangi Tribunal, *The Taranaki Report*.

69 Arnold, *Settler Kaponga*, pp. 15 and 38–39.

70 Johnston, W.B., 'Pioneering the bushland of lowland Taranaki: a case study', *New Zealand Geographer* 17/1 (1961), pp. 1–18.

71 Johnston, 'Pioneering the bushland', p. 8; Arnold, *Settler Kaponga*, pp. 57–63.

72 Wood, V., Brooking, T. and Perry, P., 'Pastoralism and politics: reinterpreting contests for territory in Auckland Province, New Zealand, 1853–1864', *Journal of Historical Geography* 34/2 (2008), pp. 220–41.

73 Swainson, W., *Auckland, The Capital of New Zealand, and the Country Adjacent* (London, 1853), pp. 36–37, quoted in Wood *et al.*, 'Pastoralism and politics', p. 224.

74 Cited in Ward, A., *A Show of Justice: Racial 'Amalgamation', in Nineteenth Century New Zealand* (Auckland, 1995), pp. 106–07.

75 Waterson, D.B., 'The Matamata estate, 1904–1959', *New Zealand Journal of History* 3/1 (1969), pp. 32–51; Winder, G., 'Development of the Waikato, 1860–1895: power structures and historical explanation in geography', MA thesis, University of Auckland (1982).

76 Park, *Nga Uruora*; Hatvany, M., 'Environmental failure, success and sustainable development: the Hauraki Plains wetlands through four generations of New Zealanders', *Environment and History* 14/4 (2008), pp. 469–95.

77 Report of the Royal Commission on Forestry (Wellington, 1913), p. xxiv.

78 Wood *et al.*, 'Pastoralism and politics', p. 241.

79 Schama, S., *Landscape and Memory* (London, 1995), p. 61.

80 Shepard, P., *English Reaction to the New Zealand Landscape before 1850*, Pacific Viewpoint Monograph 4 (Wellington, 1969), p. 14.

81 Colenso, W., 'Memorandum of an excursion made in the Northern Island of New Zealand', *The Tasmanian Journal* 2 (1846), p. 280, quoted in Crosby, A.W., *Ecological Imperialism: The Biological Expansion of Europe, 900–1900* (Cambridge, 1986), p. 253.

82 Hooker, J.D., 'Note on the replacement of species in the colonies and elsewhere', *The Natural History Review* (1864), p. 124, quoted in Crosby, *Ecological Imperialism*, p. 255.

83 Darwin, C., *The Origin of Species* (London, 1902), p. 483.

84 Livingstone, D.N., *Putting Science in its Place: Geographies of Scientific Knowledge* (Chicago, 2003), p. 4; Livingstone, D.N., 'Science, text and space: thoughts on the geography of reading', *Transactions of the Institute of British Geographers*, NS 30/4 (2005), pp. 391–401.

85 Armstrong, J.F., 'On the naturalized plants of the province of Canterbury', *Transactions of the New Zealand Institute* 4 (1871), p. 285.

CHAPTER 3

1 When an authorised member of a tribe applied tapu to an object or place it could not be used or freely accessed until that proscription was lifted. Tapu was applied for diverse reasons, including out of respect for the dead, to ensure hygiene, maintain water quality, and protect indigenous food sources from unsustainable exploitation.

2   For an account of Māori weather knowledge see King, D.N.T., Skipper, A. and Tawhai, W.B., 'Māori environmental knowledge of local weather and climate change in Aotearoa – New Zealand', *Climatic Change* 90/4 (2008), pp. 385–409; Māori traditions and sayings have been compiled in Mead, S.M. and Grove, N., *Nga Pepeha a Nga Tipuna* (Wellington, 2008); and Bawden, P., *The Years Before Waitangi: A Story of Early Maori/European Contact in New Zealand* (Auckland, n.d.), is informative about society and culture during the first three decades of the nineteenth century.

3   The inside walls of the meeting house on a marae (the traditional centre of a Māori community) are commonly lined with panels woven from dyed plant fibres. These panels, known as tukutuku, are more than mere decoration. They represent allegories or serve as reminders of important historical events.

4   Baddeley, A.D. and Hitch, G., 'Working memory', in G.H. Bower (ed.), *The Psychology of Learning and Motivation: Advances in Research and Theory*, Vol. 8 (New York, 1974); and a fuller account is in Baddeley, A., *Working Memory, Thought and Action* (Oxford, 2007). This model has also been used in assessing how early hominids responded to cultural and environmental challenges: Wynn, T. and Coolidge, F.L., 'A stone-age meeting of minds', *American Scientist* 96/1 (2008), pp. 44–51.

5   Earp, G.B., *Handbook for Intending Emigrants to the Southern Settlements of New Zealand* (London, 1849), p. 252. Earp's was one of several handbooks published for the guidance of intending settlers.

6   Holland, P.G. and Hargreaves, R.P., 'The trivial round, the common task: work and leisure on a Canterbury hill country run in the 1860s and 1870s', *New Zealand Geographer* 47/1 (1991), pp. 19–25.

7   Pawson, E. and Quigley, N.C., 'The circulation of information and frontier development: Canterbury 1850–1890', *New Zealand Geographer* 38/1 (1982), pp. 65–76.

8   King *et al.*, 'Māori environmental knowledge'.

9   At least 60 varieties of New Zealand flax were recognised by Māori, and information about the uses of 15 of them is in Harrison, P., Te Kanawa, K. and Higgins, R., 'Nga mahi toi: the arts', in T. Ka'ai, J.C. Moorfield, M.P.J. Reilly and S. Mosley, *Ki te Whaiao: An Introduction to Māori Culture and Society* (Auckland, 2004), pp. 116–32.

10   The original of the map by Tuki-Tahua was drawn in 1793, and reproduced in Milligan, R.R.D., *The Map Drawn by the Chief Tuki-Tahua in 1793* (Mangonui, 1964). The sketch map of southern New Zealand given by Huruhuru to Edward Shortland was drawn in January 1844 and reproduced in Shortland, E., *The Southern Districts of New Zealand: A Journal with Passing Notices of the Customs of the Aborigines* (London, 1851). For perceptions and representations of geographical knowledge in traditional Māori society see: Small, D. (ed.), *Map New Zealand: 100 Magnificent Maps from the Collection of the Alexander Turnbull Library* (Auckland, 2006), pp. 16–17, and Williams, J., 'Traditional Māori images of geographic space', in G.W. Kearsley and B.B. Fitzharris (eds), *Glimpses of a Gaian World: Essays in Honour of Peter Holland* (Dunedin, 2004), pp. 271–83.

11   Leach, H.M.K., *1000 Years of Gardening in New Zealand* (Wellington, 1984).

12   Cruise, R.A., *Journal of a Ten Months' Residence in New Zealand* (London, 1823), p. 195.

13   The sub-tropical food plant, kūmara – alternative spelling, kūmera – was brought to New Zealand by Polynesians and cultivated wherever the growing season was sufficiently long and warm. Sensitive to late-season frosts, its southern limit on

low-lying flat ground was in North Canterbury, but even there it was planted on low mounds of friable soil to which river gravel had been added to ensure a warm tilth and facilitate cold-air drainage. The cultivation of kūmara in lowland North Canterbury was described by Canon J. Stack in Travers, W.T.L. and Stack, J.W., *The Stirring Times of Te Rauparaha Chief of Ngatitoa* and Stack, J., *The Sacking of Kaiapohia*, bound in one volume (Christchurch, 1906). As far south as the Māori settlement near Temuka in South Canterbury, kūmara could occasionally yield a harvest of edible tubers. For a comprehensive account of Māori horticulture see Leach, *1000 Years of Gardening in New Zealand*.

14 Clark, A.H., *The Invasion of New Zealand by People, Plants, and Animals: The South Island* (New Brunswick, 1949).

15 *Nelson Examiner*, 7 January 1843, 29 March 1845.

16 *Hawke's Bay Herald*, 26 May 1868.

17 Ward, J., *Information Relative to New Zealand, Compiled for the Use of Colonists*, 2nd edn (London, 1840), p. 93.

18 Gillespie, O.A., *South Canterbury: A Record of Settlement* (Timaru, 1958).

19 Edward Shortland was Deputy Protector of Aborigines in New Zealand, and his book about southern and eastern New Zealand contains eyewitness accounts of life and landscape in an area that was soon to be colonised by European settlers: Shortland, *The Southern Districts of New Zealand*. See also Dann, C. and Barton, P., 'Exploring Pākehā gain knowledge of Te Wāi Pounamu', in M. McKinnon (ed.), *New Zealand Historical Atlas* (Auckland, 1997), Plate 34.

20 King, D.N.T., Goff, J. and Skipper, A., 'Māori environmental knowledge and natural hazards in Aotearoa–New Zealand', *Journal of the Royal Society of New Zealand* 37/2 (2007), pp. 59–73.

21 Greenwood's diary covers the period between 1 January 1841 and 31 May 1847: the handwritten original and a typed transcript, MS 0878, are held by the Alexander Turnbull Library, Wellington.

22 Gillespie, O.A., *South Canterbury: A Record of Settlement* (Timaru, 1958).

23 Acland, L.G.D., *The Early Canterbury Runs* (Christchurch, 1951).

24 McIntosh, A.D. (ed.), *Marlborough: A Provincial History* (Blenheim, 1940).

25 MS 0039, Alexander Turnbull Library, Wellington.

26 MS 1187, Takao, T.T. (n.d.) *Mahika Weka*, Alexander Turnbull Library, Wellington.

27 Barker, Lady Mary, *Station Life in New Zealand* (Christchurch, 1950), p. 173.

28 Broome, M. [Lady Barker], *Colonial Memories* (London, 1904), p. 23.

29 Shortland, *The Southern Districts of New Zealand*, p. 99.

30 Andersen, J.C., *Jubilee History of South Canterbury* (Auckland, 1916).

31 McIntyre, W.D. (ed.), *The Journal of Henry Sewell, 1853–7*, Vol. II (Christchurch, 1980), p. 208.

32 McIntyre, *The Journal of Henry Sewell*, pp. 210–11.

33 Hursthouse, C., *New Zealand, the 'Britain of the South'; with a Chapter on the Native War, and our Future Native Policy*, 2nd edn (London, 1861), p. 67.

34 Entry in the diary of F.W. Teschemaker, held by the Hocken Collections, University of Otago, Dunedin.

35 Gordon, M., *The Garden of Tane* (Wellington, n.d.), p. 67.

36 Richards, E.C. (ed.), *Diary of E.R. Chudleigh 1862–1921: Chatham Islands* (Christchurch, 1950), p. 40.

37 Studholme, E.C., *Te Waimate: Early Station Life in New Zealand*, 2nd edn (Wellington, 1954).

38 McIntyre, *The Journey of Henry Sewell*, p. 208.

39 Anon (ed.), Letter 21 in *Letters from Settlers and Labouring Emigrants in the New Zealand Company's Settlements of Wellington, Nelson, and New Plymouth, from February 1842 to January 1843* (London, 1843), pp. 39–43.

40 Sharp, C.A. (ed.), *The Dillon Letters: The Letters of the Hon. Constantine Dillon, 1842–1853* (Wellington, 1954), p. 38.

41 Anon, *Letters from Settlers and Labouring Emigrants*, Letter 36, p. 75.

42 Paul, R.B., *Letters from Canterbury, New Zealand* (London, 1857), p. 12.

43 McIntyre, *The Journal of Henry Sewell*, p. 121.

44 Diary of F.S. Pillans, Inch Clutha, 1850 to 1852: typed transcript, 10005.2, Hocken Collections, University of Otago, Dunedin.

45 *Otago Witness*, 4 September 1852.

46 Holland, P., Wood, V. and Dixon, P., 'Learning about the weather in early colonial New Zealand', *Weather and Climate* 29 (2009), pp. 3–23.

47 Anon, *Letters from Settlers and Labouring Emigrants*, Letter 58, p. 125.

48 Andersen, *Jubilee History of South Canterbury*, pp. 57–58.

49 He was probably referring to *Kunzea ericoides* rather than *Leptospermum scoparium*.

50 Weld, F.A., *Hints to Intending Sheep-Farmers in New Zealand* (London, 1851), p. 6.

51 A list of those consulted is in Holland *et al.*, 'Learning about the weather'.

52 In its publications, the New Zealand Company raised expectations of extraordinarily rich forest soils, but this proved to be a myth and was beginning to fade from settlers' minds by the early 1850s. It created the sense that ploughed soils did not require manuring or fallowing. It also steered rural settlement towards forested areas, such as the Hutt Valley and New Plymouth, and ensured that reserves set aside for Māori communities were too small to support them. See Wood, V., 'Appraising soil fertility in early colonial New Zealand: the "biometric fallacy" and beyond', *Environment and History* 9/4 (2003), pp. 393–405.

53 Ward, E., *The Journal of Edward Ward, 1850–51* (Christchurch, 1851), p. 181. The Deans family from Scotland began farming in the 1840s on the western edge of what would become the site of Christchurch.

54 Anderson, K., *Predicting the Weather: Victorians and the Science of Meteorology* (Chicago, 2005).

55 Diary of Joseph Munnings, Banks Peninsula and Christchurch: typed transcript, ARC 1990.50, Canterbury Museum, Christchurch.

56 Pawson, E., 'Confronting nature', in J. Cookson and G. Dunstall (eds), *Southern Capital: Christchurch – Towards a City Biography, 1858–2000* (Christchurch, 2000), pp. 60–84.

57 Andersen, *Jubilee History of South Canterbury*, pp. 556–58.

58 Acland, L.G.D., *The Early Canterbury Runs* (Christchurch, 1851).

59 Holland, P.G. and Mooney, W.J., 'Wind and water: environmental learning in early colonial New Zealand', *New Zealand Geographer* 62/1 (2006), pp. 39–49; and Holland *et al.*, 'Learning about the weather in early colonial New Zealand', pp. 3–23.

60 Holland, P.G. and Fitzharris, B.B., 'Wind in the tussock: the weather in the foothills of mid-Canterbury during 1866–1871', in G.W. Kearsley and B.B. Fitzharris (eds), *Southern Landscapes* (Dunedin, 1990), pp. 39–53.

61   Scotch thistle is *Cirsium vulgare* or *Onopordum acanthium*.

62   Clark, *The Invasion of New Zealand by People, Plants, and Animals*; and Crosby, A.W., *Ecological Imperialism: The Biological Expansion of Europe, 900–1900* (Cambridge, 1986).

CHAPTER 4

1   Dansereau, P., personal communication, October 1987.

2   Ondersteijn, C.J.M., Giesen, G.W.J. and Huirne, R.B.M., 'Perceived environmental uncertainty in Dutch dairy farming: the effect of external context on strategic choice', *Agricultural Systems* 88/2–3 (2006), pp. 205–26.

3   Botterill, L. and Mazur, N., *Risk and Risk Perception: A Literature Review* (Barton, 2004).

4   Brooking, T., *The History of New Zealand* (Westport, Conn., 2004); and King, M., *The Penguin History of New Zealand* (Auckland, 2003).

5   Alley, G.T. and Hall, D.O.W., *The Farmer in New Zealand* (Wellington, 1941).

6   Star, P., '"Nature's trump card": confronting the rabbit problem in southern New Zealand, 1867–1897', *Environment and Nature in New Zealand* 12 (2006), pp. 4–12; and Holland, P., Wood, V. and Dixon, P., 'Learning about the weather in early colonial New Zealand', *Weather and Climate* 29 (2009), pp. 3–23.

7   Meinig, D.W., *On the Margins of the Good Earth: The South Australian Wheat Frontier, 1869–1884* (Chicago, 1962), pp. 3, 17 and 19.

8   James Hector's words come from his lecture, 'The utility of natural science', to members of the Dunedin YMCA. It was reported by the *Otago Daily Times* on 24 October 1862, with sections apparently reproduced verbatim. The Governor's words were published in the first volume of the *Transactions of the New Zealand Institute*, and reported in the *Otago Witness* on 8 August 1868.

9   Anon, 'The experimental farm', *New Zealand Country Journal* 1/2 (1877), pp. 75–77.

10   Wild, L.J., *The Life and Times of Sir James Wilson of Bulls* (Christchurch, 1953).

11   Anon, 'The value of farm experiments', *New Zealand Farmer, Bee and Poultry Journal* 4 (1885), p. 114.

12   Wild, *The Life and Times of Sir James Wilson*. Also, in a letter to *The Press* on 27 December 1867, R.D. Burt urged greater attention to practical and scientific knowledge of farming and other enterprises as a way to lift the country out of economic depression. He saw a role for the Agricultural and Pastoral Societies, and praised the commitment of Otago to this task.

13   *New Zealand Herald*, 8 August 1876.

14   *Otago Witness*, 25 January 1868.

15   Wild, *The Life and Times of Sir James Wilson*, p. 117.

16   Alley and Hall, *The Farmer in New Zealand*.

17   Telegraph lines are mapped later, in Figure 8.1.

18   Wild, *The Life and Times of Sir James Wilson*.

19   Hunter, I., *Age of Enterprise: Rediscovering the New Zealand Entrepreneur, 1880–1910* (Auckland, 2007), pp. 166–68.

20   McAloon, J., 'Gentlemanly capitalism and settler capitalists: imperialism, dependent development and colonial wealth in the South Island of New Zealand', *Australian Economic History Review* 42/2 (2002), pp. 204–23.

21 Ville, S., *The Rural Entrepreneurs: A History of the Stock and Station Agent Industry in Australia and New Zealand* (Cambridge, 2000), p. 14.

22 A partial run of ledgers for the Studholme family property, Te Waimate in South Canterbury, is held by the Waimate Historical Society and Museum. Entries show that in 1878, when the last of the lowland tussock grassland on their property was being ploughed for wheat, the expenditure on wages was £6,700. In 1874 the wage bill was £9,500, two years later it was £5,400, and the following year it was £6,100. The payments recorded in these ledgers covered work associated with wheat cropping, contract ploughing and cultivation, shearing and other work with sheep, work with cattle, harvesting and storing hay, fencing, building construction and farm maintenance.

23 Holland, P.G. and Hargreaves, R.P., 'The trivial round, the common task: work and leisure on a Canterbury hill country run in the 1860s and 1870s', *New Zealand Geographer* 47/2 (1991), pp. 19–25.

24 See Winder, G.M., 'A trans-national machine on the world stage: representing McCormick's reaper through the world's fairs, 1851–1902', *Journal of Historical Geography* 33/2 (2007), pp. 352–76.

25 *Southland Times*, 21 November 1891.

26 Scotter, W.H., *Ashburton: A History of Town and County* (Ashburton, 1972), p. 98; McAloon, J., *No Idle Rich: The Wealthy in Canterbury and Otago, 1840–1914* (Dunedin, 2002), p. 51.

27 Holland, P., O'Connor, K. and Wearing, A., 'Remaking the grasslands of the open country', in E. Pawson and T. Brooking (eds), *Environmental Histories of New Zealand* (Melbourne, 2002), pp. 69–83.

28 'Science and farming', *The Press*, 4 January 1868. On 24 August 1867, *The Press* had reprinted a long article, originally published on 9 August 1867 in the Hobart, Tasmania *Mercury*, under the headline 'Agriculture in Denmark'. It was clear that the two editors saw scientifically based agriculture as the model for their respective countries.

29 Wood, V. and Pawson, E., 'The Banks Peninsula forests and Akaroa cocksfoot: explaining a New Zealand forest transition', *Environment and History* 14/4 (2008), pp. 449–68.

30 Wilson, B., 'Stock to fit the environment', *New Zealand Farmer* 103/15, (1982), pp. 184–206; see also 'Artificial grasses for New Zealand', *Otago Witness*, 31 January 1863.

31 Morgan, W., 'Grasses for permanent pasture', *New Zealand Country Journal* 7/2 (1883), p. 124.

32 Letter from Nugent Wade to W.H Teschemaker, 15 December 1875, South Canterbury Museum, Timaru.

33 'Ruarata', 'Laying down permanent pastures on bush land', *New Zealand Country Journal* 9/2 (1885), pp. 125–28.

34 Acland, L.G.D., *Early Canterbury Runs* (Christchurch, 1946); and Travers, W.T.L., 'Acclimatisation in Canterbury', *New Zealand Country Journal* 8/6 (1884), pp. 496–500. During the first four decades of organised settlement in Canterbury use of native grasses for improved pasture was advocated by several experts, amongst them Armstrong, J.B., 'The native grasses', *New Zealand Country Journal* 3/4 (1879), pp. 201–04 and Buchanan, J., *Manual of the Indigenous Grasses of New Zealand* (Wellington, 1880).

35 Anon, 'An extraordinary yield of seed', *New Zealand Country Journal* 3/2 (1879), p. 84.

36 Pattullo, P., 'Farming experiments', *New Zealand Country Journal* 22/4 (1898), pp. 374–79.

37 Wilkin, R., in *New Zealand Country Journal* 3/5 (1879), p. 294; *Auckland Weekly News*, 8 April 1876; and *New Zealand Herald*, 8 August 1876. Waugh's Invercargill trials were discussed in the 7 February 1889 issue of the *Otago Witness*, and Armstrong's series 'A short history of the grasses: Parts I to VIII' was published in the *New Zealand Country Journal* 4/1 (1880) to 5/2 (1881), *passim*.

38 W.T.L. Travers, cited in the *Lyttelton Times*, 2 April 1864. An editorial in *The Weekly Press* on 23 March 1867 included this sentence: 'This instance shows clearly that it is better to have pastures composed of a variety of grasses than [to] trust wholly to one sort', an observation that accords with ecological thinking a century later about ecosystem structure, composition and diversity.

39 'Philosophical Institute of Canterbury', *Transactions and Proceedings of the New Zealand Institute* 3 (1870), pp. 51–53.

40 Travers, 'Acclimatisation in Canterbury', p. 498.

41 Mackay, T., *A Manual of the Grasses and Forage-Plants Useful to New Zealand: Part 1* (Wellington, 1887), p. 2.

42 Cockayne, A.H., 'The grass-lands of New Zealand', *New Zealand Journal of Agriculture* 16/4 (1918), pp. 210–20.

43 Hargreaves, R.P., 'Speed the plough: an historical geography of New Zealand farming before the introduction of refrigeration', PhD thesis, University of Otago, 1966.

44 Wood, V., 'Appraising soil fertility in early colonial New Zealand: "the biometric fallacy" and beyond', *Environment and History* 9/4 (2003), pp. 393–405; and Wood, V., 'Soil fertility management in nineteenth century New Zealand agriculture', PhD thesis, University of Otago, 2002.

45 Hunt, W.D., 'Lime and liming in the south', *New Zealand Journal of Agriculture* 13/2 (1916), pp. 87–96.

46 Haxton, J., 'Manure', in J.C. Morton (ed.), *A Cyclopaedia of Agriculture, Practical and Scientific*, Vol. 2 (Edinburgh, 1855), p. 313.

47 Wood, 'Soil fertility management in nineteenth century New Zealand agriculture'; and Smallfield, P.W., *The Grasslands Revolution in New Zealand* (Auckland, 1970), pp. 13–15.

48 'Pioneer', *New Zealander*, 24 September 1859.

49 Smith, A.G., 'The beginnings of the New Zealand phosphate trade, 1855–1870', MA thesis, University of Otago, 1966.

50 Wood, 'Soil fertility management in nineteenth century New Zealand agriculture'; and Wood, V., Brooking, T. and Perry, P., 'Pastoralism and politics: reinterpreting contests for territory in Auckland Province, New Zealand', *Journal of Historical Geography* 34/3 (2008), pp. 220–41.

51 *Weekly Press*, 20 October 1866.

52 Wood, 'Soil fertility management in nineteenth century New Zealand agriculture'.

53 *Weekly Press*, 6 February 1875.

54 Wood, 'Soil fertility management in nineteenth century New Zealand agriculture'.

55 Bellamy, A.C., *BOP First in Fertiliser: A History of the Bay of Plenty Co-operative Fertiliser Company Limited* (Tauranga, 1991).

56   *Otago Witness*, 10 February 1883; and Tait, A.N., 'The growth of fertiliser use in New Zealand', *New Zealand Journal of Agriculture* 95/2 (1957), pp. 186–97.

57   Anon, 'Artificial manures for turnips', *New Zealand Country Journal* 7/4 (1883), pp. 292–93.

58   *New Zealand Farmer* 9/8 (1889), p. 323.

59   Belich, J., *Paradise Reforged: A History of the New Zealanders from the 1880s to the Year 2000* (Auckland, 2001), pp. 66 and 30.

60   Nathan, S. and Varnham, M. (eds), *The Amazing World of James Hector* (Wellington, 2008), p. 123.

61   Liebig, J., *Familiar Letters on Chemistry, and its Relations to Commerce, Physiology, and Agriculture*, 3rd edn (London, 1845), p. 173.

62   Goodman J., 'Guano happens (sometimes)', *Geographical* (November 2006), pp. 40–44.

63   Steel, G., 'Meadow grasses', *New Zealand Country Journal* 13/2 (1889), pp. 124–26.

64   *Otago Witness*, 16 January 1886.

65   Belshaw, H., Williams, D.O., Stephens, F.B., Fawcett, E.J. and Rodwell, R., *Agricultural Organization in New Zealand: A Survey of Land Utilization, Farm Organization, Finance and Marketing* (Melbourne, 1936), p. 623.

66   Gould, J.D., 'Pasture formation and improvement in New Zealand, 1871–1911', *Australian Economic History Review* 16/1 (1976), pp. 1–22.

67   Evans, B.L., *Agricultural and Pastoral Statistics of New Zealand, 1861–1954* (Wellington, 1966), pp. A31, A35.

68   Letter from John Grigg to J.G Wilson, 22 November 1889 in Wild, *The Life and Times of Sir James Wilson of Bulls*, p. 74.

69   Wallace, R.A., *The Rural Economy and Agriculture of Australia and New Zealand* (London, 1889), p. 304.

CHAPTER 5

1   The term 'tussock grasslands' is now used to describe the mountain and semi-arid pastoral country of the South Island high country. There is no catch-all term to describe the non-forested country of the eastern South Island at the time of settlement. Different authors have used a variety of terms, such as open country and rangelands. The whole region was clothed in tussock grasslands until about 1850, despite local differences in the composition of the vegetation, but by 1914 these remained largely in the semi-arid lands and hard hill and high country.

2   'Pastoralism' refers to the system of production where livestock were run on the open grasslands. When these were subdivided into farms, and the livestock run intensively, the system became one of 'livestock farming'. In the late 1870s and 1880s, with the opportunity to profit from cropping, pastoralists readily turned to agricultural production at the same time as maintaining large sheep flocks.

3   In the early years of pastoral expansion, the terms 'station' and 'run' had different meanings, but in time became interchangeable. A run was a geographically defined area of Crown land for which a runholder held a grazing licence. A station was the site on a run where a runholder was stationed and from which the property was worked. The larger stations were made up of several runs.

4   In this chapter I use Mount Peel for the mountain and its geographical region and Mt
    Peel for the name of the station.

5   Tripp, C.G., *Lecture given by the Late C.G. Tripp of Orari Gorge, Canterbury at Silverton,
    Devon 1862* (Wellington, 1926), p. 7.

6   Kennaway, L.J., *Crusts. A Settler's Fare Due South* (1874; reprinted Christchurch, 1970),
    p. 60.

7   Peden, R.L., 'Pastoralism and the transformation of the rangelands of the South Island
    of New Zealand, 1841 to 1912: Mt Peel Station, a case study', PhD thesis, University of
    Otago, 2007, pp. 71–75.

8   MB 44. Acland Family Papers, Box 7, 4 January 1855, Macmillan Brown Library,
    University of Canterbury, Christchurch, Box 4, J.B.A. Acland Diary, 3 February, 19
    March, 28 October, 4 November 1864; 31 July 1867.

9   Acland, L.G.D., *The Early Canterbury Runs*, 4th edn (Christchurch, 1975), p. 21.

10 Harte, G.W., *Mount Peel is a Hundred: The Story of the First High-country Sheep Station in
    Canterbury* (Timaru, 1956), p. 68.

11 Acland Papers, Box 52, 2 January 1896; 22 February 1896.

12 Peden, 'Pastoralism and the transformation of the rangelands', p. 311.

13 Buchanan, J., 'Sketch of the botany of Otago: written for the New Zealand
    Exhibition, 1865', *Transactions and Proceedings of the New Zealand Institute*, 1 (1868),
    p. 181.

14 Pyne, S.J., *Vestal Fire: An Environmental History, Told through Fire, of Europe's Encounter
    with the World* (Seattle, 1997), p. 352.

15 Acland, *The Early Canterbury Runs*, p. 17.

16 Garvie, A., 'Report on the reconnaissance survey of the south-eastern districts of
    the Province of Otago, executed during the months of October and November,
    also February, March, and part of April, 1857–8', *The Otago Provincial Government
    Gazette*, Vol. 3 (January 1856–December 1859), p. 280; Buchanan, 'Sketch of the
    botany of Otago', p. 182.

17 Travers, W.T.L., 7 October 1868, *New Zealand Parliamentary Debates*, Vol. 4 (25
    September to 20 October 1868), p. 191.

18 McGillivray, R., 'The Mackenzie Country grasslands: progress of natural regeneration and
    experimental sowings', *New Zealand Journal of Agriculture* 39/2 (1929), p. 73; Hilgendorf,
    F.W., 'The grasslands of the South Island of New Zealand: an ecological survey',
    Department of Scientific and Industrial Research Bulletin 47 (1935), p. 22; Cumberland,
    K.B., 'High-country "run": the geography of extensive pastoralism in New Zealand',
    Economic Geography 20/3 (1944), p. 148; Cumberland, 'Burning tussock grassland: a
    geographic survey', *New Zealand Geographer* 1/2 (1945), p. 150; Relph, R.H., 'A century
    of human influence on high country vegetation', *New Zealand Geographer* 14/2 (1958),
    p. 133; Mather, A.S., 'The desertification of Central Otago, New Zealand', *Environmental
    Conservation* 9/3 (1982), p. 215; Zotov, V.D., 'Survey of the tussock-grasslands of the
    South Island of New Zealand', *Department of Scientific and Industrial Research Bulletin*
    (1938); Egerton, R.E., 'Unconquerable enemy or bountiful resource? A new perspective
    on the rabbit in Central Otago', BA Hons long essay, University of Otago, 1993, p. 12.

19 The records used come from Mt Peel (MB 44. Acland Family Papers, Macmillan Brown
    Library, University of Canterbury, Christchurch), Waitangi (Waitangi Station, Kurow),
    The Levels, Grampian Hills and Holme Station (Typescript of Grampian Hills Station
    day book kept by Henry Ford until March 1866, the farm diaries of Pareora and Holme

Stations, October 1862–December 1873, Canterbury Museum Documentary Research Centre, Christchurch), Rockwood (Rockwood Station Diary, 1855–57, Transcript, Canterbury Museum Documentary Research Centre), Rakaia Terrace (Rakaia Terrace Station Journal, 30 June 1853 to 14 June 1854, Canterbury Museum Documentary Research Centre), Lake Coleridge, Rakaia Forks and Glenthorne station (Mathias, F., Journal, 1 October 1859 to 30 September 1861, Hocken Collections, University of Otago, Dunedin).

20 Peden, 'Pastoralism and the transformation of the rangelands', pp. 104–08.

21 Peden, 'Pastoralism and the transformation of the rangelands', p. 104.

22 Cumberland, 'Burning tussock grassland', pp. 153–54. Cumberland's survey covered 60 runs that took in over 400,000 hectares.

23 Hoy, J.F. and Isern, T.D., 'Bluestem and tussock: fire and pastoralism in the Flint Hills of Kansas and the tussock grasslands of New Zealand', *Great Plains Quarterly* (1995), pp. 173–74; Holland P.G. and Hargreaves, R.P., 'The trivial round, the common task: work and leisure on a Canterbury hill country run in the 1860s and 1870s', *New Zealand Geographer* 47/1 (1991), p. 22.

24 Hargreaves, R.P., 'The Golden Age: New Zealand about 1867', *New Zealand Geographer* 16 (1960), p. 3; Hargreaves, R.P., 'Speed the plough: an historical geography of New Zealand farming before the introduction of refrigeration', PhD thesis, University of Otago, 1966, p. 185. Barker, M.A., *Station Life in New Zealand* (1870; reprinted Christchurch, 2000), pp. 225–26. In her book Lady Barker called her husband's station Broomielaw; it was, in fact, Steventon. The run is situated in the foothills near the headwaters of the Selwyn River.

25 Butler, S., *A First Year in the Canterbury Settlement* (London, 1914), p. 133.

26 Peden, 'Pastoralism and the transformation of the rangelands', p. 101.

27 Zotov, 'Survey of the tussock-grasslands'; Mather, 'The desertification of Central Otago', p. 215; Office of the Parliamentary Commissioner for the Environment, *Investigation of the Proposal to Introduce Myxomatosis for Rabbit Control* (Wellington, 1987), p. 35.

28 Wynn, G., 'Remapping Tutira: contours in the environmental history of New Zealand', *Journal of Historical Geography* 23/4 (1997), pp. 418–46.

29 Allan, H.H., 'The vegetation of Mount Peel, Canterbury, N.Z.: Part 2 – The grasslands and other herbaceous communities', *Transactions and Proceedings of the New Zealand Institute* 57 (1927), pp. 86–87. Allan documented the spread of gorse on Mt Peel that originated from a gorse fence planted in 1862. See *Otago Witness*, 1 July 1887, p. 8 for reference to this phenomenon in south Otago.

30 Thomson, G.M., *The Naturalisation of Animals and Plants in New Zealand* (Cambridge), p. 90.

31 Wodzicki, K.A., 'Introduced mammals of New Zealand', *Department of Scientific and Industrial Research Bulletin* 28 (1950), p. 126.

32 *Appendix to the Journals of the House of Representatives of New Zealand*, 1881, I 6, p. 6.

33 Peden, 'Pastoralism and the transformation of the rangelands', pp. 199, 223.

34 Zotov, 'Survey of the tussock-grasslands', p. 228A.

35 Zotov, 'Survey of the tussock-grasslands', p. 228A.

36 Bull, P.C., 'Some facts and theories on the ecology of the wild rabbit', *New Zealand Science Review* 14/5 (1956), p. 56.

37 *Statistics of New Zealand for the Year 1912* (Wellington, 1913), p. 530.

38 Kerr, C., 'The high country in transition – some implications for occupiers and administrators', *Tussock Grasslands and Mountain Lands Institute Review* 49 (1992), pp. 32–33; Mather, 'The desertification of Central Otago', p. 215.

39 Coop, I.E., 'A table of ewe equivalents', *Tussock Grassland and Mountain Lands Institute Review* 13 (1967), pp. 46–47.

40 MB44, Acland Family Papers, Boxes 50, 52, 57, 63, 65 and 72.

41 Peden, 'Pastoralism and the transformation of the rangelands', p. 200.

42 *Statistics of New Zealand*, 1896, p. 420; 1905, p. 465; 1912, p. 577.

43 *Otago Witness*, 15 March 1900, p. 5; 24 July 1901, p. 16.

44 *Appendices to the Journal of the House of Representatives*, 1912, H-23B.

45 *Otago Witness*, 13 February 1900, p. 13; 2 August 1900, p. 7.

46 *Otago Witness*, 27 March 1901, p. 14; 24 April 1901, p. 5; 7 August 1901, p. 9.

47 *Otago Witness*, 26 April 1905, p. 20.

48 Peden, 'Pastoralism and the transformation of the rangelands'; *Timaru Herald*, 4 July 1873, p. 2.

49 Stevens, P.G.W., *James Little and his Corriedale Sheep* (Christchurch, n.d.), p. 8; Perry, W., *Sheep Farming in New Zealand* (Christchurch, 1923), p. 52; Simkin, C.G.F., *The Instability of a Dependent Economy: Economic Fluctuations in New Zealand 1840–1914* (Oxford, 1951), p. 169.

50 Weld, F., *Hints to Intending Sheep Farmers in New Zealand* (London, 1851), p. 2.

51 Weld, *Hints to Intending Sheep Farmers*, p. 2.

52 *Otago Witness*, 9 June 1883, p. 6.

53 *Appendices to the Journal of the House of Representatives*, 1895, H-23; 1905, H-28; 1912, H-23B.

54 *Lyttelton Times*, 12 October 1859.

55 *New Zealand Country Journal* 1/4 (1877), p. 267. In the early years of cross-breeding, the terms half-bred and cross-bred were used without distinction. However, as the practice became more widespread the term half-bred was increasingly used only for the first cross between a Merino and a longwool, and the term cross-bred was used for subsequent crosses, such as the three-quarter-bred and beyond. A longwool described British breeds such as the Leicester, Lincoln and Romney Marsh, in contrast to the Down breeds, such as the Southdown, which grew shorter and finer wool.

56 Andersen, J.C., *Jubilee History of South Canterbury* (Auckland, 1916), p. 95. Andersen gives an example from The Levels from 1868, when the station's first cross Merino/Leicester wool sold for 16 pence per pound while its Merino wool fetched 9 pence.

57 *Timaru Herald*, 7 December 1870, p. 2.

58 Stevens, *James Little and His Corriedale Sheep*, p. 7; Davidson, W.S., *William Soltau Davidson 1846–1924. A Sketch of his Life Covering a Period of Fifty-two Years, 1846–1916, in the Employment of the New Zealand and Australian Land Company Limited* (Edinburgh, 1930), pp. 24–25.

59 Perry, W., *Sheep Farming in New Zealand* (Auckland, 1923), p. 46.

60 Stevens, P.G., *Sheep: Part 2 – Sheep Farming Development and Sheep Breeds in New Zealand* (Christchurch, 1961), p. 83.

61 Stevens, *Sheep*, p. 45.

62 Peden, 'Pastoralism and the transformation of the rangelands', pp. 304–05.

63 MB 44. Acland Papers, Box 12, 11 July 1888, Letter from Acland to Mr Alexander. Acland described Mt Peel as a high country run, which is the first instance that I have

seen the term used; *Otago Witness*, 14 November 1895, p. 6, 'Drover' described some Merino sheep shown at the Christchurch Show as being very suitable for the high country as they were of a very robust type.

64 *New Zealand Country Journal* 18/4 (1894), p. 281.

65 Macdonald, G.R., *The Canterbury Frozen Meat Company Ltd: The First Seventy-five Years* (Christchurch, 1957), p. 90.

66 Stevenson, F., 1934, in Harte, *Mount Peel is a Hundred*, p. 59.

CHAPTER 6

1 Robbins, W.G., *Colony and Empire: The Capitalist Transformation of the American West* (Lawrence, 1994), p. 3.

2 Robbins, *Colony and Empire*, pp. 71 and 72.

3 Cronon, W., *Nature's Metropolis: Chicago and the Great West* (New York, 1991), pp. xvi, xviii.

4 Ville, S., *The Rural Entrepreneurs: A History of the Stock and Station Agent Industry in Australia and New Zealand* (Cambridge, 2000), pp. 9 and 10.

5 Ville, *Rural Entrepreneurs*, p. 150.

6 Ville, *Rural Entrepreneurs*, p. 10.

7 Barnard, A., *The Australian Wool Market 1840-1900* (Melbourne, 1958), p. 19.

8 Barnard, *Wool Market*, p. 20.

9 John Deans to John Deans Snr, 7 March 1850, in *Pioneers of Canterbury: Deans Letters 1840–1854* (Dunedin, 1937), p. 161.

10 John Deans to John Deans Snr, 8 December 1849, in *Pioneers of Canterbury*, p. 157.

11 Thomas Roberts to John Roberts, 22 November and 20 December 1877. Sir John Roberts Papers, ms625 20/1, Hocken Collections, University of Otago, Dunedin.

12 Ville, *Rural Entrepreneurs*, p. 19.

13 The records of the Bradford Chamber of Commerce are held in the West Yorkshire Regional Archives, Bradford repository. First annual meeting 26 January 1852; second annual meeting 31 January 1853, Bradford Chamber of Commerce Annual Reports. WYB 111/2/1 1851–69. The famous missionary, David Livingstone, had given a lecture in Bradford to some 4,000 people and the Chamber congratulated him for his 'exertions on behalf of Christianity, of Science, and of Commerce' which, 'as the natives of South Africa grow more civilised, and as the productions of their country become valuable' were seen as 'opening out to England a wide field for future commercial transactions, in which the Worsted District may fairly hope largely to participate'. Livingstone comments in seventh annual meeting 18 January 1858, Bradford Chamber of Commerce Annual Reports.

14 Titus Salt, sixth annual meeting 26 January 1857, Bradford Chamber of Commerce Annual Reports.

15 Report of delegation appointed to visit Paris Exhibtion 26 Nov. 1855; fourth annual meeting 29 January 1855, Bradford Chamber of Commerce Annual Reports.

16 Sixth annual meeting 26 January 1857, Bradford Chamber of Commerce Annual Reports.

17 Ninth annual meeting 16 January 1860, Bradford Chamber of Commerce Annual Reports.

18 Ninth annual meeting 16 January 1860, Bradford Chamber of Commerce Annual Reports.

19 An appendix to the letter to the trade, in ninth annual meeting 16 January 1860, Bradford Chamber of Commerce Annual Reports.

20 *Nelson Examiner*, 9 July 1859.

21 Peden, R., 'Sheep farming practice in colonial Canterbury 1843 to 1882: the origin and diffusion of ideas, skills, techniques and technology in the creation of the pastoral system', MA thesis, University of Canterbury, 2002, p. 145, has pointed out that South Island newspapers varied greatly in the space they devoted to pastoralism. The two main Christchurch newspapers, the *Lyttelton Times* and *The Press*, gave it relatively little space. The *Timaru Herald* gave the subject much more attention. Clearly, the *Otago Witness* was more attentive than the Christchurch newspapers.

22 *Otago Witness*, 22 October 1859.

23 *Otago Witness*, 10 December 1859.

24 Seventh annual meeting 18 January 1858, Bradford Chamber of Commerce Annual Reports. Eighth annual meeting 17 January 1859, Bradford Chamber of Commerce Annual Reports.

25 An appendix to the Letter to the Trade, in ninth annual meeting 16 January 1860, Bradford Chamber of Commerce Annual Reports.

26 Dalziel's letter quoted in an appendix to the Letter to the Trade, in ninth annual meeting 16 January 1860, Bradford Chamber of Commerce Annual Reports.

27 *Nelson Examiner*, 12 October 1861. See also General meeting 29 June 1860; tenth annual meeting 21 January 1861, Bradford Chamber of Commerce Annual Reports.

28 Eleventh annual meeting 20 January 1862, Bradford Chamber of Commerce Annual Reports.

29 *Nelson Examiner*, 12 October 1861.

30 *Nelson Examiner*, 12 October 1861.

31 *Nelson Examiner*, 12 October 1861.

32 *Otago Witness*, 16 May 1857. As so often, this material was printed in a number of New Zealand newspapers.

33 Mein Smith, P., Hempenstall, P. and Goldfinch, S., *Remaking the Tasman World* (Christchurch, 2009); Olssen, E., 'Lands of sheep and gold: the Australian dimension to the New Zealand past, 1840–1900', in K. Sinclair (ed.), *Tasman Relations: New Zealand and Australia, 1788–1988* (Auckland, 1987), pp. 52–70.

34 *Otago Witness*, 26 November 1859.

35 *Otago Witness*, 12 January 1866.

36 *Otago Witness*, 27 January 1866, and also 24 February 1866.

37 *Otago Witness*, 16 May 1857.

38 The letter is in *Nelson Examiner*, 19 December 1863. It was also printed in the *Lyttelton Times*, 22 December 1863, from where it was quoted in Peden, 'Sheep farming practice', p. 52; from that, Dr Peden drew my attention to the direct connections between Bradford manufacturers and New Zealand pastoralists.

39 Nineteenth annual meeting 24 January 1870, Bradford Chamber of Commerce Annual Reports. WYB 111/2/3 1870–84.

40 *North Otago Times*, 6 May 1870.

41 Wool Supply Committee, in report of twenty-first annual meeting 15 January 1872, Bradford Chamber of Commerce Annual Reports.

42 *Otago Witness*, 29 May 1869; *Otago Witness*, 24 July 1869; 25 September 1869.

43 Twenty-second annual meeting 20 January 1873, Bradford Chamber of Commerce Annual Reports.

44 Report by Henry Mitchell on Philadelphia Exhibition, twenty-sixth annual meeting 15 January 1877, Bradford Chamber of Commerce Annual Reports.

45 Thirty-sixth annual meeting 17 January 1887, Bradford Chamber of Commerce Annual Reports. WYB 111/2/4 1885–94. Ville, S., 'The relocation of the international market for Australian wool,' *Australian Economic History Review* 45/1 (2005), pp. 73–95. Peden, 'Sheep farming practice', pp. 51–60.

46 Belich, J., *Replenishing the Earth: The Settler Revolution and the Rise of the Anglo-World, 1783–1939* (Oxford, 2009), pp. 206–08 and 364–68 makes this point.

47 As Worster defines the term, it is 'an ecosystem reorganized for agricultural purposes – a domesticated ecosystem' which is 'always a truncated version of some original natural system … Commonly, it is a system for export.' Worster, D., 'Transformations of the earth: toward an agroecological perspective in history', *Journal of American History* 76/3 (1989), pp. 1093–94.

48 Boast, R., *Buying the Land, Selling the Land: Governments and Māori Land in the North Island 1865–1921* (Wellington, 2008).

49 *Hawera & Normanby Star*, 23 April 1881.

50 *Taranaki Herald*, 22 October 1864.

51 *Taranaki Herald*, 25 May 1867.

52 *Taranaki Herald*, 16 November 1867.

53 *Taranaki Herald*, 3 October 1874; 6 May 1882.

54 Wilkin, R., 'Grasses and forage plants best adapted to New Zealand', *New Zealand Country Journal* 1/1 (1877), pp. 3–12; Ford, J.T., 'System of farming best adapted for the Kirwee district,' *New Zealand Country Journal* 12/6 (1888), pp. 467–80.

55 *Tuapeka Times*, 12 June 1895.

56 *Taranaki Herald*, 2 February 1903.

57 Warr, E., *From Bush Burn to Butter: A Journey in Words and Pictures* (Wellington, 1988), pp. 58–61.

58 Long, J., *Reports on the Relation of Dairy Produce of New Zealand to the English Market* (Wellington, 1889) p. 83.

59 'Notes on the dairy industry by the Agent-General', *Appendices to the Journals of the House of Representatives (AJHR)*, H-23, 1888.

60 Ville, *Rural Entrepreneurs*, p. 150.

61 J.M. Ritchie to Capt Kitchener, 12 November 1877, Ritchie Private Letterbook 1877–9, National Mortgage and Agency Company (NMA) archives, Hocken Collections, University of Otago, Dunedin.

62 J.M. Ritchie to W.S. Davidson, 5 August 1882; Ritchie Private Letterbook no. 2, 1881–3, NMA Archives, Hocken Collections, University of Otago, Dunedin.

63 J.M. Ritchie to J. Ross, 1 June 1886, Ritchie Private Letterbook no. 3, 1883–6, NMA Archives.

64 J.M. Ritchie to London, 12 February 1901, 10 Dec 1904, London Letterbook no. 8, NMA Archives.

65 W. Henderson to London, 12 February 1901, London Letterbook no. 8, NMA Archives.

66 G. Ritchie to London, 10 March 1914, London Letterbook no. 10, NMA Archives.

67 Timaru branch, 31 October 1913, in NMA Prelim List 4 Branch Reports, NMA Archives.

68 J.M. Ritchie to London, 16 June 1909, in London Letterbook no. 9, NMA Papers, UN28, Hocken Collections, University of Otago, Dunedin.

69 Feilding to Head Office, 7 March 1916, Levin and Co MSY 766, Alexander Turnbull Library, Wellington.

70 W.H. Levin to J. Duncan, 4 July 1892 and 30 September 1892, in W.H. Levin correspondence 2/2/1, Levin papers MS 1347, Alexander Turnbull Library, Wellington.

71 A. Roberts to J. Roberts, 31 March 1909, 28 July 1909, 4 August 1909, 16 August 1909, Alexander Roberts Letterbook qMS 1703, Alexander Turnbull Library, Wellington.

72 Levin 2/6/13, Levin papers MS 1347, Alexander Turnbull Library, Wellington.

73 *Taranaki Herald*, 3 March 1909.

74 Hamilton, P., 'The history of Oropi', Honours essay in history, Victoria University of Wellington, 2009, pp. 41–42.

75 'Ovis', 'The supply of mutton for export purposes', *New Zealand Country Journal* 13/5 (1889), pp. 361–63.

76 'Ovis', 'The supply of mutton for export purposes'.

77 'Ovis', 'The frozen meat trade', *New Zealand Country Journal* 14/2 (1890), p. 95.

78 Belich, *Replenishing the Earth*, p. 491.

79 'Ovis', 'The aspect of the frozen mutton trade', *New Zealand Country Journal* 16/2 (1892), p. 99.

80 'Ovis', 'The pastoral industry', *New Zealand Country Journal* 18/3 (1894), p. 189.

81 Reeves to Seddon, 16 April 1896, Inward letters from W.P. Reeves, MS-Papers-1619-001, Seddon family: Papers (MS-Group-0170), Alexander Turnbull Library, Wellington.

82 Confidential memorandum on frozen meat, in Reeves to Seddon, 16 May 1896.

83 'The New Zealand produce trade in England: report by the Agent-General', *Appendices to the Journal of the House of Representatives*, 1898, H-17.

84 Reeves to Seddon, 23 January 1897, Inward letters from W.P. Reeves, MS-Papers-1619-001, Seddon family: Papers (MS-Group-0170), Alexander Turnbull Library, Wellington; The New Zealand Produce Trade in England: Report by the Agent-General, *Appendices to the Journal of the House of Representatives*, 1898, H-17.

85 Higgins, D.M., '"Mutton dressed as lamb?" The misrepresentation of Australian and New Zealand meat in the British market, c. 1890–1914', *Australian Economic History Review* 44/2 (2004), pp. 161–84.

86 Reeves to Seddon, 28 October 1896, Inward letters from W.P. Reeves, MS-Papers-1619-001, Seddon family: Papers (MS-Group-0170), Alexander Turnbull Library, Wellington.

87 W. Weddell and Co., *Annual Review of the Chilled and Frozen Meat Trade* (London, 1899).

88 Weddell, *Annual Review*, 1901.

89 Weddell, *Annual Review*, 1911.

90 Weddell, *Annual Review*, 1901.

91 Weddell, *Annual Review*, 1905.

92 Weddell, *Annual Review*, 1906.

93 Barnard, *Australian Wool Market*, p. 132.

94 A matter which I have discussed in McAloon, J., 'Gentlemanly capitalism and settler capitalists: imperialism, dependent development and colonial wealth in the South

Island of New Zealand', *Australian Economic History Review* 42/2 (2002), pp. 204–23; see also Hopkins, A.G., 'Gentlemanly capitalism in New Zealand', *Australian Economic History Review* 43/3 (2003), pp. 287–97.

95 Ville, *Rural Entrepreneurs*, p. 156.

96 Casson, M. *The Entrepreneur: An Economic Theory* (Oxford, 1982) emphasises 'the essence of entrepreneurship is superior judgement, and the reward to this judgement depends critically upon the entrepreneur enjoying monopoly power' (p. 117). He notes not only monopoly, but also first-mover advantage: 'if several people arrive at the same source [of information] simultaneously, then no-one can gain a monopoly. Competition will be present right at the outset' and it follows that the information must be kept secret (p. 117).

97 See generally, Higgins, '"Mutton dressed as lamb?"', p. 162.

98 For a slightly contrasting perspective see Ville, *Rural Entrepreneurs*, p. 151.

99 Brooking, T. and Pawson, E., 'Silences of grass: retrieving the role of pasture plants in the development of New Zealand and the British Empire', *Journal of Imperial and Commonwealth History* 35/3 (2007), p. 423.

CHAPTER 7

1 Cowan, J., *Official Record of the New Zealand International Exhibition, 1906–07* (Wellington, 1910), p. 124.

2 Cockayne, A.H., 'Impure seed: the source of our weed problem', Bulletin 21 NS, Department of Agriculture, Commerce and Tourists (Wellington, 1912).

3 Wood, V., 'Akaroa cocksfoot: examining the supply chain of a defunct New Zealand agricultural export', in C. Stringer and R. Le Heron (eds), *Agri-Food Commodity Chains and Globalising Networks* (Aldershot, 2008), p. 215.

4 Pawson. E., 'Plants, mobilities and landscapes: environmental histories of botanical exchange', *Geography Compass* 2/5 (2008), pp. 1464–77.

5 Wild, L.J., *The Life and Times of Sir James Wilson of Bulls* (Christchurch, 1953), p. 69.

6 Wood, 'Akaroa cocksfoot', p. 217.

7 Mackay, T., *A Manual of the Grasses and Forage Plants Useful to New Zealand* (Wellington, 1887), pp. 123 and 125.

8 Catalogues in the personal collection of Mr G. Westell, Reading, Berkshire.

9 Ivey, W., 'School of Agriculture, Lincoln, Canterbury', *New Zealand Country Journal* 7/1, p. 46.

10 *Reading Mercury*, 24 January 1885, cited in Pawson, E., 'Biotic exchange in an imperial world: developments in the grass seed trade', in Stringer and Le Heron, *Agri-Food Commodity Chains*, pp. 233–35.

11 Wynn, G., 'Remapping Tutira: contours in the environmental history of New Zealand', *Journal of Historical Geography* 23/4 (1997), p. 431.

12 Wild, *The Life and Times of Sir James Wilson*, p. 68; Buchanan, J., *Manual of the Indigenous Grasses* (Wellington, 1880): its preparation was 'ordered by the New Zealand Government in consequence of a resolution adopted by the House of representatives on 29 June 1876, on the motion of Sir George Grey KCB' (p. iii).

13 McIntyre, R., *Whose High Country? A History of the South Island High Country of New Zealand* (Rosedale, 2008), pp. 41, 47–48 and 53.

14 Star, P. and Brooking, T., 'Fescue to the rescue: Chewings fescue, paspalum, and the application of non-British experience to pastoral practice in New Zealand, 1880–1920', *Agricultural History* 80/3 (2006), p. 321.

15 Buchanan, *Manual of the Indigenous Grasses*, p. 81.

16 Star and Brooking, 'Fescue to the rescue', pp. 322–23.

17 Star and Brooking, 'Fescue to the rescue', pp. 316–17.

18 Star and Brooking, 'Fescue to the rescue', p. 318.

19 Star and Brooking, 'Fescue to the rescue', pp. 319–20.

20 Pawson, 'Biotic exchange'; Arthur Yates and Co., *Catalogue of Farm Seeds* (Auckland, 1893), p. 2; Arthur Yates and Co., *Catalogue of Farm Seeds* (Auckland 1898–9), p. 48; Arthur Yates and Company, MS 1706, Box 6, Ledger 1887–1891, Auckland Museum archives.

21 Wood, 'Akaroa cocksfoot', p. 218.

22 Elliot, R.H., *The Clifton Park System of Farming and Laying Down Land to Grass*, 5th edn (London, 1943) pp. 95–96, quoting *inter alia* Curtis, W., *Practical Observations on the British Grasses*, 4th edn (London, 1805).

23 Letter, 4 January 1825, in R. Davis, 'Letters and journals, 1824–63', MS-1211, Hocken Collections, University of Otago, Dunedin.

24 *Weekly Press*, 5 August 1865; Gray, E., 'The early history of ryegrass production in Scotland', *Seed Trade Review* 4 (1952), p. 109.

25 *Southern Cross*, 22 April 1843, 6 July 1844; *New Zealand Colonist and Port Advertiser*, 31 January 1843, 18 April 1843.

26 *New Zealand Spectator and Cook Strait Guardian*, 20 December 1845, 11 August 1849; *New Zealander*, 27 March 1847.

27 Wilson in the *Lyttelton Times*, 12 March 1886.

28 *Daily Southern Cross*, 22 March 1870; *Taranaki Herald*, 16 April 1870; *Otago Witness*, 13 January 1883.

29 Carruthers, W., 'Report of the Consulting Botanist on laying down land to permanent pasture', *Journal of the Royal Agricultural Society of England*, 2nd Series 18 (1882), pp. 366–68; De Laune, F., 'On laying down land to permanent pasture', *Journal of the Royal Agricultural Society of England*, 2nd Series 18 (1882), pp. 229–64.

30 'Pasture grasses', *Glasgow Herald*, 19 April 1889; Bear, W.E., 'Farm and field', *Manchester Times*, 12 July 1890.

31 *Agricultural Gazette*, cited in 'The farm and the field', *The Leeds Mercury*, 5 January 1889; Fream, W., 'Rye-grass in pastures', Letter to the Editor, *The Times*, 27 May 1890; Your Correspondent, 'Rye-grass in pastures', *The Times*, 2 June 1890.

32 Young on 'the exclusive attention that has been given to ryegrass', quoted in Elliot, *The Clifton Park System*, p. 95. The Hampshire farmer's experience, and the attributes of cocksfoot 'in consequence of its earliness …', as attributed to Young by Elliot, p. 95.

33 Hesketh and Aitken, *Descriptive and Priced Catalogue, General and Agricultural Seeds* (Auckland, 1893), A HORT 1892-4, Alexander Turnbull Library, Wellington.

34 McPherson, G.M., 'Seed production in New Zealand: cocksfoot', *New Zealand Journal of Agriculture*, pp. 33–41; Arthur Yates and Co. Ltd, *Yates' Farm Seeds* (Auckland, 1918), B HORT YATES 1910–1930s, Alexander Turnbull Library, Wellington.

35 Foy, N.R., 'The official seed-testing station: record of operations for 1926', *New Zealand Journal of Agriculture* 34/3 (1927), p. 187.

36   *Otago Witness*, 23 August 1879.

37   Wood, 'Akaroa cocksfoot', p. 219.

38   *Lyttelton Times*, 28 November 1888.

39   Stapledon, R.G., 'Seeds mixtures: controversies', in Hunter, H. (ed.), *Baillieres Encylopaedia of Scientific Agriculture*, Vol. 2 (London, 1931), pp. 1108–09.

40   Wood, 'Akaroa cocksfoot'.

41   Newton, F.C., *Recollections of the Cocksfoot Industry on Banks Peninsula* (Akaroa, 1979); Wood, V. and Pawson, E., 'The Banks Peninsula forests and Akaroa cocksfoot: explaining a New Zealand forest transition', *Environment and History* 14/4 (2008), pp. 449–68.

42   Thomson, Jane: Papers relating to 'Southern People'; Moritzson A: notes drawn from obituary in *New Zealand Traveller*, 26 June 1935, MS-1926/1271, Hocken Collections, University of Otago, Dunedin; Wood, 'Akaroa cocksfoot'.

43   Moritzson and Hopkin Scrapbook 1894–1906, MS-0659, Hocken Collections, University of Otago, Dunedin.

44   Stapledon, R.G., 'Herbage seed production in New Zealand: III – cocksfoot', *Journal of the Ministry of Agriculture* 34 (1927), p. 417; Wood and Pawson, 'The Banks Peninsula forests'.

45   *Western Mail*, 25 September 1890.

46   Townsend, R., 'Sub-enclosure. Mr R. Townsend to Mr C. Davie', in 'The present condition of the forests of New Zealand', *Appendices to the Journal of the House of Representatives*, D22 (1869), p. 10.

47   Jacobson, H.C., *Tales of Banks Peninsula*, 3rd edn (Akaroa, 1917), p. 296.

48   Henry, M., 'Mobile geographies of New Zealand botany: Leonard Cockayne and the imperatives of mobility', *Cultural Geographies*, in press.

49   Wilson, in *Lyttelton Times*, 12 March 1886.

50   Stapledon, 'Herbage seed production', p. 416.

51   Jacobson, *Tales of Banks Peninsula*, pp. 346–48; Coulson J., *Golden Harvest: Grass-seeding Days on Banks Peninsula* (Palmerston North, 1979), p. 21.

52   Wood, 'Akaroa cocksfoot', p. 223.

53   Wood, 'Akaroa cocksfoot', p. 224.

54   Montgomery, W.H., *Notes on My Life* (Christchurch, 1995), pp. 43–44.

55   Wallace, V.B., *Cocksfoot Seed Production – Ashburton County, 1935–36: A Comparison with Banks' Peninsula* (Lincoln, 1936).

56   *The Press*, 1 July 1926.

57   Stapledon, 'Herbage seed production', p. 417; Pawson, 'Biotic exchange'.

58   Russell, E.J., *A History of Agricultural Science* (London, 1966), p. 394.

59   Brooking, T. and Pawson, E., 'Silences of grass: retrieving the role of pasture plants in the development of New Zealand and the British Empire', *Journal of Imperial and Commonwealth History* 31/3 (2007), pp. 417–35; Remington, J.K., *Seed Testing* (London, 1928), p. 1; Robin, L., 'Ecology: a science of empire?', in T. Griffiths and L. Robin (eds), *Ecology and Empire: Environmental History of Settler Societies*, (Melbourne, 1997), pp. 67–75.

60   Elliot, R.H., *The Clifton Park System of Farming and Laying Down Land to Grass*, 5th edn (London, 1943), pp. 105–06; Stapledon, R.G., 'Introduction' to *The Clifton Park System*, pp. 5–6.

61   Advertisement in the *Otago Witness*, 20 February 1886.

62   Arthur Yates and Co., *Farm Seeds 1904* (Auckland, 1904), MS 1707, Box 30, item 95, Auckland War Memorial Museum.

63   'A bushman', 'Seeds and seedsmen', *The Southern Cross*, 17 December 1862; 'Agriculturalist', 'Seed matters – "seedy seed"', *The Southern Cross*, 20 December 1862.

64   *Lyttelton Times*, 8 October 1888; Pawson, 'Biotic exchange'.

65   Arthur Yates and Co., Catalogue of Farm Seeds (Auckland, 1893), pp. 2–3; Pawson, 'Biotic exchange'; F. Cooper Ltd, *Catalogue of Cooper's Seeds of Success, Season 1916–17*, inside back cover, A HORT 1916 Cooper, Alexander Turnbull Library, Wellington.

66   Pawson, 'Biotic exchange'; 'Seed adulteration', *The Times*, 26 November 1877, p. 7; James Carter and Co., 'Adulteration of seed', *The Times*, 7 December 1877, p. 7; *Report of the Departmental Committee appointed by the Board of Agriculture to Enquire into the Conditions Under Which Agricultural Seeds Are At Present Sold* (London, 1901), p. vii.

67   *Report of the Departmental Committee*, p. vii.

68   Wynn, G., 'Remapping Tutira', p. 431.

69   Coulson, J., *Golden Harvest*, pp. 35–49.

70   Wood, 'Akaroa cocksfoot'.

71   Circular, December 1894; Circular, January 1895, Moritzson and Hopkin Scrapbook 1894–1906, MS-0659, Hocken Collections, University of Otago, Dunedin.

72   'Grass seeds and weeds: a chat with Mr. C.A. Lees', *Weekly Press*, 6 September 1894, p. 10.

73   Cockayne, A.H., 'Impure seed', pp. 4 and 10.

74   Foy, N.R., 'Cocksfoot-seed', *New Zealand Journal of Agriculture* 25/3 (1922), pp. 165–67.

75   Foy, N.R., 'The official seed-testing station: record of operations for 1926', *New Zealand Journal of Agriculture* 34/3 (1927), pp. 186–94.

76   Nightingale, T., 'Cockayne, Alfred Hyde 1880–1966', *Dictionary of New Zealand Biography*, updated 22 June 2007, http://www.dnzb.govt.nz/.

77   Levy, E.B., 'The grasslands of New Zealand: principles of pasture establishment', *New Zealand Journal of Agriculture*, 23/3 (1921), p. 257.

78   Claridge, J.H., 'Seed production in New Zealand: grass and clover seed certification', *New Zealand Journal of Agriculture* 97/1 (1958), pp. 7–16.

79   Latour, B., *Science in Action: How to Follow Scientists and Engineers through Society* (Milton Keynes, 1987); Pawson, 'Biotic exchange'.

CHAPTER 8

1   Richards, S., '"Masters of Art and bachelors of barley": the struggle for agricultural education in mid-nineteenth century Britain', *History of Education* 12/3 (1983), pp. 162–63; Brassley, P., 'Agricultural science and education', in E.J.T. Collins (ed.), *The Agrarian History of England and Wales*, Vol. 7, Part 1 (1850–1914) (Cambridge, 2000), p. 645.

2   King, C., *The Handbook of New Zealand Mammals*, 2nd edn (Melbourne, 2005), p. 4; Grey, A.H., *Aotearoa and New Zealand: A Historical Geography* (Christchurch, 1994), p. 139.

3   Davidson, J., *The Prehistory of New Zealand*, 2nd edn (Auckland, 1987), pp. 115–19.

4   Leach, H., 'Food processing technology: its role in inhibiting or promoting change in staple foods', in C. Gosden and J. Hather (eds), *The Prehistory of Food: Appetites for Change* (London, 1999), pp. 129–32.

5   Lester, A. and Dussart, F., 'Trajectories of protection: protectorates of Aborigines in early 19th century Australia and Aotearoa New Zealand', *New Zealand Geographer* 64/3 (2008), pp. 205–20.

6   MacDonald, S., 'The diffusion of knowledge among Northumberland farmers, 1780–1815', *Agricultural History Review* 27/1 (1979), p. 33.

7   Goddard, N., 'Information and innovation in early-Victorian farming systems', in B.A. Holderness and M. Turner (eds), *Land, Labour and Agriculture, 1700–1920: Essays for Gordon Mingay* (London, 1991), pp. 166–68.

8   Beckett, J.V., *The Agricultural Revolution* (Oxford, 1990), pp. 29–30 and 32–33; Overton, M., *Agricultural Revolution in England: The Transformation of the Agrarian Economy 1500–1850* (Cambridge, 1996), pp. 142–43 and 184.

9   Wilmot, S., *'The Business of Improvement': Agriculture and Scientific Culture in Britain, c. 1700–c. 1870* (London, 1990), pp. 16–17; Marti, D.B., 'Agricultural journalism and the diffusion of knowledge: the first half century in America', *Agricultural History* 54/1 (1980), pp. 30–32.

10 Wilmot, *'The Business of Improvement'*, p. 9.

11 Goddard, N., 'Agricultural institutions: societies, associations and the press', in Collins, *The Agrarian History of England and Wales*, Vol. 7, Part 1, p. 668.

12 Boud, R.C., 'Scottish agricultural improvement societies 1723–1835', *Review of Scottish Culture* 1 (1984), pp. 80–81; Fox, H.S.A., 'Local farmers' associations and the circulation of agricultural information in nineteenth-century England', in H.S.A. Fox and R.A. Butlin (eds), *Changes in the Countryside: Essays on Rural England, 1500–1900* (London, 1979), p. 49.

13 Goddard, 'Agricultural institutions: societies, associations and the press', pp. 652–54.

14 Brigden, R., 'Equipment and motive power', in Collins, *The Agrarian History of England and Wales*, Vol. 7, Part 1, pp. 507–08.

15 For the change to racing crowds see Porter, J.H., 'The development of rural society', in G.E. Mingay (ed.), *The Agrarian History of England and Wales*, Vol. 6 (1750–1850) (Cambridge, 1989), pp. 922–23.

16 Goddard, N., 'Agricultural literature and societies', in Mingay, *The Agrarian History of England and Wales*, Vol. 6, pp. 361–63; Goddard, N., '"Not a reading class": the development of the Victorian agricultural textbook', *Paradigm* 23 (1997), pp. 12–13.

17 Goddard, N., 'The development and influence of agricultural periodicals and newspapers, 1780–1880', *Agricultural History Review* 31/2 (1983), pp. 129–30; Goddard, 'Agricultural literature and societies, pp. 366–67 and 370

18 Fox, 'Local farmers' associations', p. 54.

19 Vann, J.D. and Van Arsdel, R.T. (eds), *Victorian Periodicals and Victorian Society* (Toronto, 1994), p. 5.

20 Goddard, 'The development and influence of agricultural periodicals', pp. 129–30; Goddard, 'Information and innovation', pp. 166 and 168; Goddard, N., *Harvests of Change: The Royal Agricultural Society of England 1838–1988* (London, 1989), p. 78.

21 Amongst the firms which produced postal catalogues were agricultural implement manufacturers and seed merchants. See Brigden, R., 'Equipment and motive power',

pp. 507–08; Pawson, E.,'Biotic exchange in an imperial world: developments in the grass seed trade', in C. Stringer and R. Le Heron (eds), *Agri-food Commodity Chains and Globalising Networks* (Aldershot, 2008), pp. 233–34.

22 Richards, '"Masters of Art and bachelors of barley"', pp. 161–62.

23 Richards, '"Masters of Art and bachelors of barley"', p. 167; Brassley, 'Agricultural Science and Education', p. 625.

24 Brassley, 'Agricultural science and education', pp. 629–32.

25 Johnstone, P.H., 'Old ideals versus new ideas in farm life', in United States Department of Agriculture, *The Yearbook of Agriculture 1940: Farmers in a Changing World* (Washington, DC, 1940), pp. 114–15.

26 See, for example, *Bruce Herald*, 29 January 1868; *Otago Witness*, 18 April 1868; J. Vogel, 18 September 1872, *New Zealand Parliamentary Debates* 13, p. 244.

27 *New Zealand Country Journal* 5/3 (1881), p. 171.

28 Wood, G.V., 'Soil fertility management in nineteenth century New Zealand agriculture', PhD thesis, University of Otago, 2003, pp. 171–72 and 193.

29 See, for example, *New Zealand Journal*, 28 March 1846; Swainson, W., *Auckland, the Capital of New Zealand, and the Country Adjacent* (London, 1853), pp. 12–13 and 20–22.

30 See, for example, the essays on Wellington farming in *New Zealand Gazette and Wellington Spectator*, 23 March and 10 April 1844. Also see the account of institutional activities in Auckland in Kalaugher, J.P., *Historical Chronicles of the Auckland Agricultural and Pastoral Association* (Auckland, 1925), pp. 44–48 and 70–71.

31 Kalaugher, *Historical Chronicles of the Auckland Agricultural and Pastoral Association*, pp. 31–32; Belich, J., *Making Peoples: A History of the New Zealanders from Polynesian Settlement to the End of the Nineteenth Century* (Auckland, 1996), pp. 214–15; Watson, M.K. and Patterson, B.R., 'The growth and subordination of the Maori economy in the Wellington region of New Zealand 1840–1852', *Pacific Viewpoint* 26/3 (1985), pp. 532–35.

32 Hargreaves, R.P., 'The Maori agriculture of the Auckland Province in the mid-nineteenth century', *Journal of the Polynesian Society* 68/2 (1959), pp. 62 and 72; Hargreaves, R.P., 'Changing Maori agriculture in pre-Waitangi New Zealand', *Journal of the Polynesian Society* 72/2 (1963), pp. 114–15.

33 Wood, V., Brooking, T. and Perry, P., 'Pastoralism and politics: reinterpreting contests for territory in Auckland Province, New Zealand, 1853–1864', *Journal of Historical Geography* 34/1 (2008), pp. 231–32.

34 *New Zealand Spectator*, 8 January 1853.

35 *Nelson Examiner*, 14 December 1850 and 2 February 1853.

36 Peden, R., 'Sheep farming practice in colonial Canterbury, 1843 to 1882: the origin and diffusion of ideas, skills, techniques and technology in the creation of the pastoral system', MA thesis, University of Canterbury, 2002, pp. 138–40.

37 Wakefield, E.J., *The Handbook for New Zealand* (London, 1848), p. 441.

38 In 1842, for example, a Mr Mayers gave to the Wellington's Mechanics Institute copies of *Lowes' Agriculture* and the *Farmer's and Grazier's Practical Assistant*. *New Zealand Gazette and Wellington Spectator*, 23 November 1842.

39 Gillespie-Needham, D.M., 'The colonial and his books: a study of reading in nineteenth century New Zealand', PhD thesis, Victoria University of Wellington, 1971, p. 327.

40 *Auckland Weekly News*, 30 July 1864.

41 Wood, V. and Pawson, E., 'Information exchange and the making of the colonial farm', *Agricultural History* 82/3 (2008), pp. 41–42.

42 Schofield, G.H., *Newspapers in New Zealand* (Wellington, 1958), p. 8.

43 Harvey, R., 'Bringing the news to New Zealand: the supply and control of overseas news in the nineteenth century', *Media History* 8/1 (2002), pp. 24–26.

44 *Nelson Examiner*, 13 May, 8 July, 2 December 1843, 9 March 1844.

45 *Sydney Morning Herald*, 5, 20, 27 July 1850; *Otago News*, 14, 21, 28 September 1850.

46 Hursthouse, C., *An Account of the Settlement of New Plymouth* (London, 1849), pp. 92–93; *Otago Witness*, 11 December 1852.

47 *Wellington Independent*, 17 June 1857.

48 With reference to Canterbury, see Cant, R.G., 'The agricultural frontier in miniature: a microstudy on the Canterbury Plains, 1850–1875', *New Zealand Geographer* 24/2 (1968), pp. 163–66.

49 See, for example, Scotter, W.H., 'Canterbury, 1857–68', and 'Canterbury, 1868–76', in W.J. Gardner (ed.), *A History of Canterbury, Vol. 2* (Christchurch, 1971), pp. 185–87 and 305–06.

50 See Simkin, C.G.F., *The Instability of a Dependent Economy: Economic Fluctuations in New Zealand, 1840–1914* (Oxford, 1951), pp. 126–45.

51 Pawson, E. and Quigley, N.C., 'The circulation of information and frontier development: Canterbury 1850–1890', *New Zealand Geographer* 38/2 (1982), pp. 65–74; Garner, J., 'Rural society expands and adapts', in G. Cant and R. Kirkpatrick (eds), *Rural Canterbury: Celebrating its History* (Wellington, 2001), pp. 106–11. The provincial councils were abolished in 1876.

52 Wild, L.J., 'Agricultural and Pastoral Societies', in A.H. McClintock (ed.), *An Encyclopaedia of New Zealand* (Wellington, 1966), Vol. 1, pp. 16–17.

53 Carter, W., 'The opening furrow: a centennial history of the Canterbury Agricultural and Pastoral Association', unpublished typescript, Canterbury Agricultural and Pastoral Association, 1963, pp. 9–10; Garner, 'Rural society expands and adapts', p. 103.

54 *New Zealander*, 18 December 1861.

55 Vincent, G.T., 'Sports, and other forms of civilisation in colonial Canterbury, 1850–1890', PhD thesis, University of Canterbury, 2002, pp. 171–72; Scotter, 'Canterbury, 1868–76', p. 309.

56 *Taranaki Herald*, 25 June to 29 October 1859, *passim*. Hostilities, prompted by an ongoing dispute over a land sale, began in March 1860.

57 *New Zealander*, 8 December 1860 to 27 November 1861, *passim*.

58 Grey, *Aotearoa and New Zealand*, pp. 213 and 219; Wood *et al.*, 'Pastoralism and politics', pp. 221–22.

59 Schofield, *Newspapers in New Zealand*, pp. 86, 173, 216–17 and 220.

60 Wood and Pawson, 'Information exchange', p. 355.

61 For example, the Auckland firm, Gilfillan and Co., supplied an accompanying pamphlet to buyers of Peruvian guano. *New Zealander*, 6 October 1855.

62 See, for instance, the circular for Hood and Co.'s soluble sheep dip, and likewise that for J.N. Reynolds' agricultural seeds catalogue. *Lyttelton Times*, 24 November 1866; *Tuapeka Times*, 25 July 1868.

63 *Tuapeka Times*, 25 July 1868.

64 Peden, 'Sheep farming practice in colonial Canterbury', pp. 137 and 147; Acland, A., *A Devon Family: The Story of the Aclands* (Chichester, 1981), pp. 89–95.

65 Paul, R.B., *Letters from Canterbury* (London, 1857), pp. 88–104; Hursthouse, Charles, *New Zealand, or Zealandia, the Britain of the South* (London, 1857), pp. 329–416.

66 Wood and Pawson, 'Information exchange', p. 362.

67 Sinclair, K., *A History of New Zealand*, 4th edn (Auckland, 1988), p. 102.

68 Wood and Pawson, 'Information exchange', p. 338.

69 *New Zealand Country Journal* 1/2 (1877), p. 72.

70 Lloyd Prichard, M.F., *An Economic History of New Zealand to 1939* (Auckland, 1970), p. 155.

71 Wood and Pawson, 'Information exchange', pp. 346–48 and 359.

72 Cirencester was established in 1845 and Glasnevin model farm in Dublin, which became the Albert Institution in 1853, in 1838. There were two early agricultural schools in Quebec (Ste Anne de la Pocatierre, from 1859, and L'Assomption 1867–99). An agricultural school, now part of Tamil Nadu Agricultural University, was started near Chennai in 1868, and the Ontario Agricultural College at Guelph dates from 1874. The first Australian agricultural college is Roseworthy (1883), and in South Africa the oldest is Western Cape (1898), making Lincoln the oldest teaching institution in Australasia, and probably in the southern hemisphere.

73 *New Zealand Farmer* 15/5 (1895), p. 167; Blair, I.D., *The Seed They Sowed: Centennial Story of Lincoln College* (Lincoln, 1978), pp. 23–24 and 329.

74 *Lyttelton Times*, 11 January 1878. At the time of the 1878 census, Leeston had a settler population of 319. Other notable extension lecturers were Professor James Black (an agricultural chemist) based at Otago, and Professor A.P.W. Thomas (an animal physiologist) at Auckland. See *Southland Times*, 6 February 1880, and *Hawke's Bay Herald*, 29 July 1893, respectively.

75 Ewing, J.L., *Origins of the New Zealand Primary School Curriculum 1840–1878* (Wellington, 1960), pp. 87–89, 134–35 and 139.

76 *Otago Witness*, 11 June 1896, p. 4.

77 *New Zealand Farmer* 103/15 (1982), p. 23.

78 *Waikato Times*, 6 March 1879. Wilkin's essay had been published in the *New Zealand Country Journal* in 1877.

79 See advertisement in *Brett's Handy Guide to New Zealand* (Auckland, 1890), p. 290, and masthead of *New Zealand Farmer* 5/1 (1885), p. 1.

80 Gray, G., 'Agricultural education', in *Report of the Conference of Delegates of Agricultural Societies throughout New Zealand* (Christchurch, 1898), Appendix, pp. 6–7.

81 See Potter, S., *News and the British World: The Emergence of an Imperial Press System* (Oxford, 2003); Lester, A., 'Imperial circuits and networks: geographies of the British Empire', *History Compass* 4/1 (2006), pp. 124–41.

82 *New Zealand Country Journal* 1/1 (1877), p. 45, and 7/1 (1883), p. 81; *New Zealand Farmer* 5/6 (1885), p. 164.

83 *New Zealand Country Journal* 5/1 (1881), p. 48; Hunt, W.F. and Easton, H.S., 'Fifty years of ryegrass research in New Zealand', *Proceedings of the New Zealand Grassland Association* 50 (1989), pp. 16–17.

84 Wood and Pawson, 'Information exchange', pp. 356–57.

85 'Canterbury Agricultural and Pastoral Association', *New Zealand Country Journal* 10/3 (1886), p. 252.

86 Wood and Pawson, 'Information exchange', pp. 351, 353 and 357.

87 The Canterbury Agricultural and Pastoral Association published the first volume of the *New Zealand Herd Book* (excluding shorthorns) in 1886.

88 Wood and Pawson, 'Information exchange', pp. 353–54.

89 *New Zealand Country Journal* 11/3 (1887), p. 203.

90 Wood and Pawson, 'Information exchange', pp. 53 and 357.

91 Wood and Pawson, 'Information exchange', pp. 353–54 and 357–58.

92 *New Zealand Country Journal* 18/1 (1894), p. 92.

93 Wood and Pawson, 'Information exchange', p. 354.

94 Crops and Pastures (field crops, pastures, market gardening), Soils and Manures/ Agricultural Chemistry, General Survey (accounts of farms, farming regions), Livestock (husbandry of farm animals), Pests and Diseases (including weeds), Production and Machinery (including horse power), Shows and Exhibitions (plus Agriculture and Pastoral Society business), and Miscellaneous (irrigation, drainage, buildings, arboriculture, flower gardening, agricultural education, law, book reviews, natural history).

95 Goddard, 'Information and innovation', pp. 169–71.

96 Farrell, R.T., 'Advice to farmers: the content of agricultural newspapers, 1860–1910', *Agricultural History* 51/1 (1977), pp. 215–16.

97 Wood and Pawson, 'Information exchange', pp. 350–52.

98 Wood and Pawson, 'Information exchange', pp. 354.

99 *New Zealand Country Journal* 4/1 (1880), p. 1.

100 *New Zealand Farmer* 103/15 (1982), p. 42.

101 Holland, P.G. and Hargreaves, R.P., 'Rural society: people and services in the 1880s and 1890s', in M. McKinnon (ed.), *New Zealand Historical Atlas* (Auckland, 1997), Plate 54.

102 Wood and Pawson, 'Information exchange', pp. 354–55.

103 Wood and Pawson, 'Information exchange', pp. 355–56.

104 *The Press*, 27 November 1914, p. 10.

105 Wood and Pawson, 'Information exchange', p. 355.

106 *New Zealand Country Journal* 14/2 (1890), pp. 148–49; *Otago Witness*, 17 April and 8 May 1890. Koebele's mission is described in Debach, P. and Rosen, D., *Biological Control by Natural Enemies*, 2nd edn (Cambridge, 1991), pp. 140–48.

107 Carter, 'The opening furrow', p. 20.

108 *New Zealand Farmer* 14/8 (1894), p. 282.

109 See, for example, *New Zealand Country Journal* 14/4 (1890), pp. 321–40.

110 *Canterbury Agricultural and Pastoral Association Journal* 12/1 (1910), p. 20.

111 Arnold, R., *New Zealand's Burning: The Settlers' World in the Mid 1880s* (Wellington, 1994); *Settler Kaponga, 1881–1914: A Frontier Fragment of the Western World* (Wellington, 1997).

CHAPTER 9

1 Stephens, P.R., 'The early years: finding the best way ahead, 1892–1945', Part I of Journeaux, P. and Stephens, P., 'The development of agricultural advisory services in New Zealand', available on www.maf.govt.nz; Nightingale, T., *White Collars and*

Gumboots: A History of the Ministry of Agriculture and Fisheries, 1892–1992 (Palmerston North, 1992).

2 Fitzgerald, D., in 'Beyond tractors: the history of technology in American agriculture', *Technology and Culture* 32/1 (1991), pp. 114–26, notes that 'Studies in the history of ecology offer historians of agricultural technology a much-needed perspective, a sort of antidote to the long overreliance on political history as an explanatory model.'

3 For an introduction to Guthrie-Smith, see Wynn, G., 'Remapping Tutira: contours in the environmental history of New Zealand', *Journal of Historical Geography* 23/4 (1997), pp. 418–46.

4 Wiebe, R.H., *The Search for Order, 1877–1920* (London, 1967), pp. 11, 149 and 145.

5 Cronon, W., *Nature's Metropolis: Chicago and the Great West* (New York and London, 1991), p. xvi.

6 Arnold, R., *Settler Kaponga 1881–1914: A Frontier Fragment of the Western World* (Wellington, 1997), pp. 200 and 270–72. See also Arnold's less geographically localised study, *New Zealand's Burning: The Settlers' World in the Mid 1880s* (Wellington, 1994).

7 Scott, J.C., *Seeing Like a State: How Certain Schemes to Improve the Human Condition Have Failed* (New Haven and London, 1998), p. 286. See also Hodge, J.M., *Triumph of the Expert: Agrarian Doctrines of Development and Legacies of British Colonialism* (Athens, Ohio, 2007).

8 Fitzgerald, D., 'Farmers deskilled: hybrid corn and farmers' work', *Technology and Culture* 34/2 (1993), pp. 324–43, and *Every Farm a Factory: The Industrial Ideal in American Agriculture* (New Haven and London, 2003). See also Cooke, K.J., 'Expertise, book farming, and government agriculture: the origins of agricultural seed certification in the United States', *Agricultural History* 76/4 (2002), pp. 524–45.

9 Brooking, T. and Pawson, E., 'Silences of grass: retrieving the role of pasture plants in the development of New Zealand and the British Empire', *Journal of Imperial and Commonwealth History* 33/3 (2007), pp. 417–35, discuss the dearth of historical work on this topic.

10 Based on figures from the *New Zealand Official Yearbooks*, 1920–9.

11 Guthrie-Smith, H., *Tutira: The Story of a New Zealand Sheep Station* (Edinburgh, 1921); Belshaw, H. *et al.*, *Agricultural Organization in New Zealand: A Survey of Land Utilization, Farm Organization, Finance and Marketing* (Melbourne, 1936).

12 Nightingale, *White Collars and Gumboots*, pp. 62 and 41.

13 From 1890, the names were published each year in 'Nature of letters patent ... applied for in New Zealand, and total number of applications per year, under the act of 1883', *Appendices to the Journal of the House of Representatives*, H-1.

14 Evans, B.L., *A History of Farm Implements and Implement Firms in New Zealand* (Feilding, 1956).

15 Prof. Lowrie, *New Zealand Farmer* 24/10 (1904), p. 839. This was particularly the case, from about 1900, with basic slag: 'none has come to the front more quickly' enthused the editorial on 'Progress in agricultural methods', *New Zealand Farmer* 29/1 (1908), p. 49.

16 See Ville, S., *The Rural Entrepreneurs: A History of the Stock and Station Agent Industry in Australia and New Zealand* (Melbourne, 2000).

17 Sutton and Sons to Richardson (Wilson's agent), 24 December 1889, Richardson to Wilson, 28 December 1889, Carruthers to Wilson, 3 August 1897, New Zealand

Loan and Mercantile Agency Palmerston North to Wilson, 19 September 1898, MS-Papers-0137, Alexander Turnbull Library, Wellington.

18 Although a Member of Parliament (1881–96), Wilson achieved greater national prominence as president of annual conferences of the Agricultural and Pastoral Association, inaugural president of the New Zealand Farmers' Union, and inaugural president of the Board of Agriculture. See Wild, L.J., *The Life and Times of Sir James Wilson of Bulls* (Christchurch, 1953).

19 'North Auckland Peninsula: Original and present land values: from waste lands to pasturage: II: Kamo', *New Zealand Farmer* 37/1 (1916), p. 8; 'District reports: Whangarei', *New Zealand Farmer* 29/2 (1908), p. 154; 'Perennialised rye grass', *New Zealand Farmer* 33/4 (1912), p. 395.

20 Star, P. and Brooking, T., 'Fescue to the rescue: Chewings fescue, paspalum, and the application of non-British experience to pastoral practice in New Zealand, 1880–1920', *Agricultural History* 80/3 (2006), pp. 312–35.

21 'H.A.W.', 'Sowing surface fern land', *New Zealand Farmer* 12/3 (1892), p. 134; Wilkinson, J.R., 'The growth of pasture in winter', in *New Zealand Farmer* 11/12 (1891), p. 508.

22 See Brooking, T., 'Agrarian businessmen organise: a comparative study of the origins and early phase of development of the National Farmers' Union of England and Wales and the New Zealand Farmers' Union, ca. 1900–1929', PhD thesis, University of Otago, 1978.

23 Advertisement in *New Zealand Farmer* 17/8 (August, 1897), p. 330.

24 See Agricultural and Pastoral Show reports in *New Zealand Farmer* 29/3 (1908), pp. 254, 255, 260, 262, and 29/5 (1908), p. 423.

25 Wilson, J.G., 'Serviceable grass', *New Zealand Farmer* 17/5 (1897), p. 152; 'The improvement of grass lands', *New Zealand Farmer* 28/11 (1907), p. 982; Wilson, J.G. *et al.*, 'Improvement of grass lands', *New Zealand Farmer*, September supplement 28/9 (1909), pp. vii–viii.

26 *New Zealand Farmer* 29/5 (1908), p. 428; Anon, 'Putting down to grass', *New Zealand Farmer* 34/2 (1913), pp. 137–38; Levy, E.B., 'Grass-seed mixtures for various soils and conditions', *New Zealand Journal of Agriculture* 26/5 (1923), p. 265.

27 See Birket, F., *Sacred Ecology: Traditional Ecological Knowledge and Resource Management* (Philadelphia and London, 1999).

28 As expressed through the person of Bull McCabe in the 1964 play, *The Field*, collected in Keane, J.B., *The Field and Other Irish Plays* (Cork, 1994).

29 Anon, 'Nutritive pasture: value of rye grass and clovers', *New Zealand Farmer* 38/6 (1917), p. 608; 'Conservative', 'The introduction of new grasses: a word of caution', *New Zealand Farmer* 29/11 (1908), p. 883.

30 Guthrie-Smith, H., *Tutira: The Story of a New Zealand Sheep Station*, 3rd edn (Edinburgh and London, 1953), p. 231.

31 *New Zealand Farmer* 21/3 (1901), p. 111. Also Clayton, N., 'Weeds, people and contested places: selected themes from the history of New Zealanders and their weeds, 1770–1940', PhD thesis, University of Otago, 2007, pp. 297–389.

32 Star, P., 'Ecology: a science of nation? The utilisation of plant ecology in New Zealand, 1896–1930', *Historical Records of Australian Science* 17/2 (2006), pp. 197–207.

33 'The Waikato state farm', *New Zealand Farmer* 21/11 (1901) p. 475; 'Experience in topdressing grass', *New Zealand Farmer* 27/7 (1906); *New Zealand Farmer* 27/8 (1906), p. 596.

34 Mortimer, D., 'The Tokorahi Settlement: An Evaluation of the Liberal Government's Land Settlement Policy', BA Hons long essay, University of Otago, 1979; Beattie, J., 'Environmental anxiety in New Zealand, 1840–1941: climate change, soil erosion, sand drift, flooding and forest conservation', *Environment and History* 9/4 (2003), pp. 379–92, and 'Rethinking science, religion and nature in environmental history: drought and early twentieth century New Zealand', *Historical Social Research* 29 (2004), pp. 82–103. In drier areas such as the Amuri in North Canterbury farmers turned instead to demand more irrigation and finally got their wish in the 1960s and 1970s. See Gardner, W.J., *The Amuri: A County History* (Christchurch, 1983), pp. 435–36 and 448–58.

35 Wynn, G. and Cant, G., 'The bonanza wheat boom', and Wood, V. and Brooking, T., 'Canterbury farming intensifies', in G. Cant and R. Kirkpatrick (eds), *Rural Canterbury. Celebrating its History* (Wellington, 2001), pp. 61–99.

36 'A Canterbury Farmer', 'Rotation vs fertilisers: an important consideration', *New Zealand Farmer* 33/8 (1912), pp. 915–17.

37 'Land making in the North: from scrub to grass land – the application of modern methods', *New Zealand Farmer* 32/8 (1911), pp. 850–52 and 885; Editorial in *New Zealand Farmer* 33/7 (1912), p. 895.

38 The School was successively renamed as Canterbury Agricultural College at Lincoln in 1896, Lincoln College in 1961, and Lincoln University in 1990.

39 'Auckland district report', *New Zealand Farmer* 10/9 (1890), p. 344; *New Zealand Farmer* 15/3 (1895), p. 106.

40 Masterton correspondent, in *New Zealand Farmer* 13/12 (1893), p. 435; *New Zealand Farmer* 16/9 (1896), p. 287; Waikato correspondent, 'Cheap lime', *New Zealand Farmer* 18/9 (1898), p. 325.

41 Nightingale, *White Collars and Gumboots*, p. 102.

42 Advertisement in *New Zealand Farmer* 33/9 (1912), p. 1179.

43 Star, P. and Brooking, T., 'The Department of Agriculture and pasture improvement, 1892–1914', *New Zealand Geographer* 63/3 (2007), pp. 192–201.

44 Nightingale, *White Collars and Gumboots*, p. 76.

45 See Roche, M., '"Wilderness to orchard": the export apple industry in Nelson, New Zealand, 1908–1940', *Environment and History* 9/4 (2003), pp. 435–50.

46 *New Zealand Farmer* 36/7 (1915), p. 926; *New Zealand Farmer* 37/2 (1916), p. 286.

47 Anon, 'Plant breeding: Dr. Cockayne's proposed work', *Canterbury Agricultural and Pastoral Association's Journal* (1908), pp. 38–39.

48 J.G. Wilson at the Farmers' Union's seventh annual conference, *New Zealand Farmer* 29/9 (1908), p. 737; Baylis, G., 'Grass-variety trials', *New Zealand Journal of Agriculture* 6/2 (1913), p. 1058.

49 Wild, *The Life and Times of Sir James Wilson of Bulls*, pp. 155–78.

50 Pretty, J. and Uphoff, N., 'Human dimensions of agroecological development', in N. Uphoff (ed.) *Agroecological Innovations: Increasing Food Production with Participatory Development* (London and Stirling, 2002), pp. 243–50.

51 *Department of Agriculture Annual Report*, 1908, cited in McCaskill, L., 'Fertilisers in New Zealand 1867–1929', M Ag thesis, University of Otago, 1929, pp. 134–35.

52 'The Waikato State Farm', *New Zealand Farmer* 11/11 (1901), p. 475, 'Grass manuring experiments in the Waikato', *New Zealand Farmer* 22/2 (1902), p. 91; Clifton, E., 'Experiments of grass and oats', *New Zealand Farmer* 26/12 (1905), p. 1062; *New*

Zealand Farmer 28/5 (1907), p. 422; 'Field experiments: the trials at Timaru', *New Zealand Farmer* 30/6 (1909), p. 478.

53 Brown, J., 'Intensive and extensive methods in farming', *New Zealand Journal of Agriculture* 11/2 (1915), pp. 87–94.

54 Macpherson, A., 'Personal record of Alexander Macpherson, agriculturist, New Zealand, for a period of over 61 years from 1876 to 1937', Alexander Turnbull Library, Wellington.

55 'New Zealand Agricultural Conference: report of the ninth biennial conference of the A & P Associations of New Zealand', *New Zealand Farmer* 32/9 (1911), pp. 1057–59.

56 'Better seeds: what the Minister intends', *New Zealand Farmer* 31/7 (1910), p. 607; 'New Zealand Agricultural Conference: report of the ninth biennial conference of the A & P Associations of New Zealand', *New Zealand Farmer* 32/9 (1911), pp. 1057–77; *New Zealand Farmer* 35/2 (1914), p. 191.

57 Shannon, F., *The Farmers' Last Frontier: Agriculture, 1860–1897* (New York, 1968), pp. 272–80; Danbohm, D.B., *Born in the Country: A History of Rural America* (Baltimore, 1995), pp. 172–74.

58 Hill, W.S., 'Plant selection', *New Zealand Journal of Agriculture* 6/1 (1913), pp. 22–23; Green, A.W., 'Co-operation in plant-improvement', *New Zealand Journal of Agriculture* 8/4 (1914), pp. 275–76. See also *Waikato Argus*, 25 July 1912 (supplement).

59 Hilgendorf, F.W., 'Methods of plant-breeding', *New Zealand Journal of Agriculture* 19/5 (1919), pp. 354–58. The article on 'systematised plant-breeding' by R.H. Biffen, the Professor of Agricultural Botany at Cambridge University, in the volume of essays on *Science and the Nation: Essays by Cambridge Graduates*, ed. A.C. Seward (Cambridge, 1917), was also exclusively about wheat.

60 Brooking, T., 'Agrarian businessmen organise', pp. 364–72, and 'Economic transformation', in G. Rice (ed.), *The Oxford History of New Zealand*, 2nd edn (Auckland, 1993), pp. 231, 234, 236, 238 and 240; and Watson, J., 'Patriotism, profits and problems: New Zealand farming during the Great War', in J. Crawford and I. McGibbon (eds), *New Zealand's Great War: New Zealand, the Allies and the First World War* (Auckland, 2007), pp. 534–59.

61 Alderton, G.E., 'Land and the returned soldiers: a suggested scheme', *New Zealand Farmer* 37/8 (1916), p. 1175.

62 Levy, E.B., 'Memoirs of Bruce Levy, grasslander – an autobiography', n.d., MS-Papers-3410, Alexander Turnbull Library, Wellington, p. 25; Cunningham, G.H., 'Autobiography' [1936], MS-Papers-3950 Alexander Turnbull Library, Wellington, p. 123.

63 Livingstone, D.N., *Putting Science in its Place: Geographies of Scientific Knowledge* (Chicago and London, 2003), p. 21.

64 Cunningham, 'Autobiography', p. 143.

65 See Stenhouse, J., 'Darwinism in New Zealand, 1859–1900', in R. Numbers and J. Stenhouse (eds), *Disseminating Darwinism: The Role of Place, Race, Religion, and Gender* (Cambridge, 2001), pp. 61–90; and Livingstone, D.N., *Putting Science in its Place*.

66 Levy, 'Memoirs', p. 35.

67 Seward (ed.), *Science and the Nation*, pp. xi and xv.

68 Levy, E.B., *Grasslands of New Zealand*, 3rd edn (Wellington, 1970), pp. xxx and xxxii.

69   Williams, M. and Macdonald, B., *The Phosphateers: A History of the British Phosphate Commissioners and the Christmas Island Phosphate Commission* (Carlton, Melbourne, 1985), pp. 126–29; and Kay, R., 'In pursuit of victory: British–New Zealand relations during the First World War', PhD thesis, University of Otago, 2001, pp. 275–76.

70   Belich, J., *Paradise Reforged: A History of the New Zealanders from the 1880s to the Year 2000* (Auckland, 2001), pp. 29–30 and 53–86.

71   Stephens, P.R., 'Farming in New Zealand', in A.H. McLintock (ed.), *A Descriptive Atlas of New Zealand* (Wellington, 1960), p. 41.

CHAPTER 10

1   Sinclair, K., *A History of New Zealand* (London, 1969), p. 244; Brooking, T., *Milestones: Turning Points in New Zealand History*, 2nd edn (Palmerston North, 1999), pp. 146–47.

2   Williams, M. and Macdonald, B., *The Phosphateers: A History of the British Phosphate Commissioners and the Christmas Island Phosphate Commission* (Carlton, Vic, 1985), pp. 126–29; and Kay, R., 'In pursuit of victory: British–New Zealand relations during the First World War', PhD thesis, University of Otago, 2001, pp. 275–76.

3   Wood, V., 'Soil fertility management in nineteenth century New Zealand agriculture', PhD thesis, University of Otago, 2002, pp. 398–403; Roche, M., *Land and Water: Water and Soil Conservation and Central Government in New Zealand 1941–1988* (Wellington, 1994), pp. 25–26.

4   Brooking, T., Hodge, R. and Wood, V., 'The grasslands revolution reconsidered', in E. Pawson and T. Brooking (eds), *Environmental Histories of New Zealand* (Melbourne, 2002), pp. 172–73.

5   Slag was a by-product of the Thomas-Gilchrist steel-making process. See Aston in *New Zealand Journal of Agriculture* 9/5 (1914), pp. 353–56 and *New Zealand Journal of Agriculture* 11/2 (1915), pp. 111–14 and 11/4 (1915), p. 283. On early fertiliser production in New Zealand see Wood, 'Soil fertility management', pp. 398–403.

6   Brooking, T., 'Agrarian businessmen organise: a comparative study of the origins and early phase of development of the National Farmers' Union of England and Wales and the New Zealand Farmers' Union, ca. 1880–1929', PhD thesis, University of Otago, 1977, pp. 364–72; Brooking, T., 'Economic transformation', in G. Rice (ed.), *The Oxford History of New Zealand*, 2nd edn (Auckland, 1993), pp. 231, 234, 236, 238 and 240; Watson, J., 'Patriotism, profits and problems: New Zealand farming during the Great War', in J. Crawford and I. McGibbon (eds), *New Zealand's Great War: New Zealand, the Allies and the First World War* (Auckland, 2007), pp. 534–59.

7   Rice, G., *Black November: The 1918 Influenza Epidemic in New Zealand* (Wellington, 1988), p. 1.

8   Brooking, Hodge and Wood, 'The grasslands revolution reconsidered', pp. 169–82.

9   'Southern Pastoral Lands Commission', *Appendices of the Journal of the House of Representatives*, 1920, C-15; and Roche, *Land and Water*, pp. 26–27.

10   Cumberland, K.B., *Landmarks* (Surry Hills, NSW, 1981), pp. 162–63.

11   McCaw, J., 'Report for the Minister of Lands on Returned Soldiers Settlements and Farms in the Auckland Land District', 16 February 1924, MSC 4, Folder E, Hamilton City Archives.

12 Thom, D., *Heritage: The Parks and the People* (Auckland, 1987) p. 137.

13 George, D.J., 'The Depression of 1921–22 in New Zealand', MA thesis, University of Auckland, 1967; Dunne, B., 'The Ideal and the Real. Soldiers, Families and Farming: 1915–30', BA Hons long essay, University of Otago, 1993; Gould, A., 'Proof of gratitude? Soldier land settlement in New Zealand after World War One', PhD thesis, Massey University, 1994; Roche, M., 'Soldier settlement in New Zealand after World War 1: two case studies', *New Zealand Geographer* 58/1 (2002), pp. 23–32 and 'Failure deconstructed: histories and geographies of soldier settlement in New Zealand circa 1917–39', *New Zealand Geographer* 64/1 (2008), pp. 46–56; Parsons, G., '"The many derelicts of war"? Great War veterans and repatriation in Dunedin and Ashburton, 1918–28', PhD thesis, University of Otago, 2009, pp. 160–88.

14 Cumberland, *Landmarks*, pp. 162–63; Carver, J.M., 'Combating isolation: the women of the Mangapurua 1917–1942', MA thesis, Massey University, 1998.

15 Brooking, T., *Massey: Its Early Years – A History of the Development of Massey Agricultural College to 1943* (Palmerston North, 1977); Blair, I. *The Seed They Sowed: Centennial History of Lincoln College* (Lincoln, 1978); Cain, P. and Hopkins, A.G., *British Imperialism: Crisis and Deconstruction 1914–1990* (London, 1993); Galbreath, R., 'A grasslands utopia? Pastoral farming and grasslands research in New Zealand', in R. Galbreath, *DSIR: Making Science Work for the Nation – Themes from the History of the Department of Scientific and Industrial Research, 1926–1992* (Wellington, 1998), pp. 58–79; Brooking, Hodge and Wood, 'The grasslands revolution reconsidered', p. 177.

16 Constantine, S., *Buy and Build: The Advertising Posters of the Empire Marketing* Board (London, 1986).

17 There is a complicated and yet unwritten story on most of these subjects. For forestry in Canada, see Nelles, H.V., *Politics of Development: Forests, Mines and Hydro Electric Development in Ontario, 1849–1941* (Hamden, Conn., 1974) and Gillis, R.P. and Roach, T.R., *Lost Initiatives: Canada's Forest Industries, Forest Policy and Forest Conservation* (Westport, Conn., 1986). For mining, Zaslow, M., *Opening of the Canadian North, 1870–1914* (Toronto, 1971) and *Reading the Rocks: The Story of the Geological Survey of Canada, 1842–1972* (Toronto, 1975). On South Africa, see Dubow, S., *Commonwealth of Knowledge: Science, Sensibility, and White South Africa 1820–2000* (Oxford, 2006), and Brown, A.C. (ed.), *A History of Scientific Endeavour in South Africa* (Johannesburg, 1977).

18 Cain and Hopkins, *British Imperialism*; Robin, 'Ecology: a science of empire?'; Galbreath, *DSIR*, pp. 62–64; Anker, *Imperial Ecology*; Star, P., 'Ecology: a science of nation? The utilisation of plant ecology in New Zealand, 1896–1930', *Historical Records of Australian Science* 17/2 (2006), pp. 197–207.

19 Galbreath, R., 'Marsden, Ernest 1889-1970', *Dictionary of New Zealand Biography*, updated 22 June 2007, http://www.dnzb.govt.nz/.

20 Galbreath, *DSIR*, pp. 63–64; Nightingale, T., *White Collars and Gumboots: A History of the Ministry of Agriculture and Fisheries, 1892–1992* (Palmerston North, 1992), pp. 120–02; Cunningham, G.H., 'Autobiography' (1936), MS-Papers-3950 Alexander Turnbull Library, Wellington, p. 123. The changes of 1936 were made by the new Labour Government.

21 Stapledon, R.G., *The Way of the Land* (London, 1943), pp. 45 and 47.

22 *New Zealand Farmer* 36/8 (1915), p. 1051; McConnell, P., 'The improvement of pastures', *New Zealand Farmer* 39/1 (1918), p. 8; McConnell, P., 'The making of a pasture', *New Zealand Farmer* 38/2 (1917), p. 262.

23 *New Zealand Journal of Agriculture* 40/4 (1930), pp. 220–25.

24 *New Zealand Journal of Agriculture* 8/3 (1914), pp. 233–61.

25 Levy, E.B., 'The grasslands of New Zealand: principles of pasture establishment', *New Zealand Journal of Agriculture* 23/5 (1921), pp. 257–65.

26 *New Zealand Journal of Agriculture* 23/5 (1921), pp. 257–65; *New Zealand Journal of Agriculture* 30/5 (1925), pp. 357–74.

27 *New Zealand Journal of Agriculture* 4/5 (1912), pp. 454–60.

28 *New Zealand Journal of Agriculture* 12/5 (1916), p. 489.

29 See Williams and Macdonald, *The Phosphateers*, pp. 126–29. Ocean Island had been annexed in 1901 and access was further increased in 1920.

30 Williams and Macdonald, *The Phosphateers*, pp. 31–35 and 51.

31 *New Zealand Journal of Agriculture* 25/2 (1922), pp. 99–105.

32 Compare *New Zealand Journal of Agriculture* 25/6 (1922), pp. 321–23 with *New Zealand Journal of Agriculture* 35/4 (1927), pp. 239–42.

33 *New Zealand Journal of Agriculture* 25/2 (1922), pp. 99–105.

34 *New Zealand Journal of Agriculture* 27/3 (1923), p. 185; 35/4 (1927), p. 242; 37/1 (1928), pp. 28–30.

35 Salesa, D., 'New Zealand's Pacific', in G. Byrnes (ed.), *The New Oxford History of New Zealand* (Melbourne, 2009), pp. 162–63.

36 Smallfield, P., *The Grasslands Revolution in New Zealand* (Auckland, 1970), p. 9.

37 Levy, E.B., *Grasslands of New Zealand*, 2nd edn (Wellington, 1955), p. 204.

38 Cockayne, A.H., 'The grasslands of New Zealand: component species', *New Zealand Journal of Agriculture* 16/4 (1918), pp. 210–20.

39 Whitehouse, I.E., 'Erosion in the eastern South Island high country – a changing perspective', *Tussock Grasslands and Mountain Lands Review* 42 (1984), p. 17; McSaveney, M.J. and Whitehouse, I.E., 'Anthropic erosion of mountain land in Canterbury', *New Zealand Journal of Ecology* 12 (supplement 1989), p. 159; Whitehouse, I.E. and Pearce, A.J., 'Shaping the mountains of New Zealand', in J.M. Soons and M.J. Selby (eds), *Landforms of New Zealand*, 2nd edn (Auckland, 1992), p. 151.

40 *The Press*, 1 July 1926.

41 *Dominion*, 14 July 1926.

42 *New Zealand Herald*, 14 August 1926.

43 *New Zealand Herald*, 14 August 1926.

44 *The Press*, 1 July 1926.

45 Levy, E.B., 'Fundamental grassland research', *New Zealand Journal of Agriculture* 37/1 (1928), p. 2; Hilgendorf, F.W., *Pastures and Pasture Plants of New Zealand*, 3rd edn (Christchurch, 1932), p. 10. Alfred Cockayne sided strongly with Levy, arguing in his article summing up advances between 1920 and 1925 that the 'threat to pastoral farming created by the fad for the Clifton Park system has thankfully diminished'. Cockayne, A.H., 'Surface-sown grass mixtures: some recent changes', *New Zealand Journal of Agriculture* 14/3 (1917), p. 171.

46 Levy, E.B., 'Autobiographical memoir' [1975–76], MS Papers 3410, Alexander Turnbull Library Wellington, p. 43.

47 Galbreath, *DSIR*, p. 62

48 These figures come from Cockayne, A.H., 'The grasslands of New Zealand: component species'; Claridge, J.H., 'Seed production in New Zealand: the grass and clover seed industry', *New Zealand Journal of Agriculture* 76/2 (1948), pp. 231–35, and Claridge, J.H., 'Seed production in New Zealand: the grass and clover seed industry', *New Zealand Journal of Agriculture* 94/2 (1957), pp. 172–77.

49 *New Zealand Journal of Agriculture* 39/1 (1929), pp. 1–8.

50 Galbreath, *DSIR*, p. 66.

51 Based on Stapledon, *The Way of the Land*, pp. 204–05.

52 See Levy, 'Fundamental grassland research', p. 7, in which he concluded that 'The conditioning of all the better soil types towards the rye-grass and white-clover ideal may be regarded as the best immediate method of increasing production from the sown grasslands of New Zealand'. In this article he went further than Alfred Cockayne in 'New Zealand agriculture: its trends in the past quarter century', *New Zealand Journal of Agriculture* 22/2 (1926), pp. 88–92. Cockayne listed grasses which had 'been tried and found wanting' and suggested that future efforts would concentrate on 'pasture manipulation and pasture management' rather than on annual crops such as turnips. Stapledon in Stapledon, R. G., 'Seeds mixtures: controversies', in H. Hunter (ed.), *Baillieres Encylopaedia of Scientific Agriculture*, Vol. 2 (London, 1931), pp. 1108–09, privileged ryegrass over cocksfoot and in discussing the 'ryegrass controversy' argued for a rye-dominant mix of a few species rather than the older, broad-ranging seed mixes.

53 Three references to Levy's articles on ryegrass in the *New Zealand Journal of Agriculture* (each co-authored with William Davies – significantly Levy is lead author) are included in Stapledon's essay on 'Seed mixtures: controversies', p. 1107.

54 Nightingale, *Whitecollars and Gumboots*, pp. 118–20.

55 Brooking, Hodge and Wood, 'The grasslands revolution reconsidered', pp. 168–72.

56 Levy, 'Fundamental grassland research', pp. 1–7.

57 Massey, D., *For Space* (London, 2005), p. 119, quoted in A. Lester and F. Dussart, 'Trajectories of protection: protectorates of Aborigines in early 19th century Australia and Aotearoa New Zealand', *New Zealand Geographer* 64/3 (2008), p. 206.

58 Star, 'Ecology: a science of nation?'

59 Stapledon, R.G., *A Tour in Australia and New Zealand: Grassland and Other Studies* (London, 1928), pp. 63–64; Stapledon, *The Way of the Land*, p. 198.

60 William Davies should not be confused with his brother – another Stapledon student – who emigrated to Australia and became a leading agrostologist there. He increasingly emphasised the importance of developing new strains of Australia's indigenous grasses. See Davies, J.G., 'Contributions of agricultural research in pastures', *Journal of the Australian Institute of Agricultural Science* 17/1 (1951), pp. 54–66.

61 Hannaway, D. *et al.*, 'Perennial ryegrass (*Lolium Perennial L.*)', Pacific Northwest Extension Publication 502, University of Oregon (April, 1999), http://extension.oregonstate.edu/catalog/html/pnw/pnw503/.

62 Levy, 'Memoirs', p. 188. Later admirers took up the phrase, e.g., Brougham, R.W., 'Tribute: Sir Bruce Levy', *Proceedings of the New Zealand Grasslands Institute* 47 (1986), pp. 306–07.

63 Nightingale, *Whitecollars and Gumboots*, p. 116; Galbreath, *DSIR*, pp. 64 and 69.

64 Levy, E.B., *The Grasslands of New Zealand: Series I – Principles of Pasture Establishment* (Wellington, 1923).

65 Levy, *Grasslands of New Zealand*, 1st edn, pp. 10–47.

66 Salmon, J.T., *Heritage Destroyed: The Crisis in Scenery Preservation in New Zealand* (Wellington, 1960), was one contemporary protest against the kind of approach Levy espoused. Cunningham produced a similar critique in his 'Autobiography'.

67 Smallfield, *Grasslands Revolution*, pp. 11, 13 and 17; Nightingale, *Whitecollars and Gumboots*, p. 120.

68 Nightingale, *Whitecollars and Gumboots*, pp. 126–30; Galbreath, *DSIR*, pp. 29–31; Brooking, T., 'Applied science to the rescue', *Environmental History* 12/2 (2007), pp. 292–94.

69 Winder, G.M.,'Grassland revolutions in New Zealand: disaggregating a national story', *New Zealand Geographer* 65/3 (2009), pp. 187–200.

70 Galbreath, *DSIR*, pp. 77–78.

71 Claridge, 'Seed production in New Zealand: the grass and clover seed industry' (1948).

72 Hamilton, W.M., *The Dairy Industry in New Zealand* (Wellington, 1944); Brooking, *Massey*, p. 84.

73 McMeekan, C.P., *Grass to Milk: A New Zealand Philosophy* (Wellington, 1960); Nightingale, *Whitecollars and Gumboots*, pp. 50–52 and 155–56; Nightingale, T., 'McMeekan, Campbell Percy 1908–1972', *Dictionary of New Zealand Biography*, updated 22 June 2007, http://www.dnzb.govt.nz/.

74 Brooking, *Massey*, pp. 86–89 and 90–91.

75 Galbreath, *DSIR*, p. 75.

76 Galbreath, *DSIR*, pp. 75–77.

77 Nightingale, *Whitecollars and Gumboots*, pp. 144–50.

78 Cumberland, K.B., *Soil Erosion in New Zealand: A Geographic Reconnaissance* (Wellington, 1944).

79 Roche, *Land and Water*, pp. 66–96.

80 Roche, *Land and Water*, pp. 34–48, and Roche, M., 'The state as conservationist, 1920–60: "wise use" of forests, lands, and water', in Pawson and Brooking (eds), *Environmental Histories of New Zealand*, pp. 192–97; Winder, 'Grassland revolutions in New Zealand'.

81 Cumberland, *Landmarks*, p. 5.

82 Taylor, N.H., *Land Deterioration in the Heavier Rainfall Districts of New Zealand*, DSIR Bulletin, no. 62 (Wellington, 1938), p. 676.

83 Macpherson, A., 'Personal Record of Alexander Macpherson, Agriculturist, New Zealand, for a Period of Over 61 years from 1876 to 1937' [c. 1937], MS-Papers-1955, Alexander Turnbull Library, Wellington, pp. 10 and 15.

84 Fitzgerald, D., *Every Farm a Factory: The Industrial Ideal in American Agriculture* (New Haven and London, 2003).

85 *New Zealand Official Year Book* (Wellington, 1940), p. 371.

86 Brooking, 'Economic transformation', pp. 237–38.

87 Russell, J., 'Diary of a visit to New Zealand' (1928), unpublished MS, Rothamsted Research Station, Harpenden.

88 Levy, E.B., 'Memoirs of Bruce Levy, grasslander – an autobiography', n.d., MS-Papers-3410, Alexander Turnbull Library, Wellington; and Levy, E.B., 'Some impressions of British dairyfarming', *Massey Agricultural College: Dairyfarming Annual* 5 (1950), pp. 1–16.

89 Mein-Smith, P., *A Concise History of New Zealand* (Cambridge, 2005), pp. 138–45; Steel F., '"New Zealand is butterland": interpreting the historical significance of a daily spread', *New Zealand Journal of History* 39/2 (2005), pp. 179–94.

90 O'Connor, P.S., *Mr Massey and the Meat Trust* (Palmerston North, 1973); Gould, J.D., *The Grassroots of New Zealand History: Pasture Formation and Improvement, 1871–1911* (Palmerston North, 1974); Macdonald, B., *Massey's Imperialism and the Politics of Phosphate* (Palmerston North, 1982); Fairburn, M., 'The farmers take over (1912–1930)', in K. Sinclair (ed.), *The Illustrated Oxford History of New Zealand* (Auckland, 1990), pp. 185–210.

CHAPTER 11

1   Belich, J., *Replenishing the Earth: The Settler Revolution and the Rise of the Anglo-World, 1783–1939* (Oxford, 2009), pp. 367–68.

2   Levy, E.B., *Grasslands of New Zealand*, 3rd edn (Wellington, 1970), p. xlv.

3   Brooking, T., 'Economic transformation', in G. Rice (ed.), *The Oxford History of New Zealand*, 2nd edn (Auckland, 1992), pp. 236–38; Somerset, H.C.D., *Littledene: Patterns of Change* (Wellington, 1974).

4   Levy, B., 'Grasslands in retrospect', Episode 2, D831.1b, Radio New Zealand Sound Archives/Nga Taonga Korero (Christchurch, n.d.).

5   Matless, D., *Landscape and Englishness* (London, 1998), p. 47.

6   Levy, *Grasslands of New Zealand*, p. xlvi; Stapledon, R.G., *The Way of the Land* (London, 1942), p. 59.

7   Levy, *Grasslands of New Zealand*, p. xlvi.

8   Department of Agriculture, *Farming in New Zealand* (Wellington, 1950), pp. 11–12.

9   Butler, S., *A First Year in Canterbury Settlement, with Other Early Essays* (London, 1914), p. 66.

10 Levy, *Grasslands of New Zealand*, p. xxxiii.

11 Report of the Royal Commission on the Sheep Farming Industry in New Zealand, *Appendices to the Journals of the House of Representatives*, 1949, H-46A.

12 Report of the Royal Commission on the Sheep Farming Industry, pp. 63–64.

13 Report of the Royal Commission on the Sheep Farming Industry, p. 61.

14 Report of the Royal Commission on the Sheep Farming Industry, pp. 88–89.

15 Levy, *Grasslands of New Zealand*, p. l.

16 Gradwahl, M., University of Otago, personal communication, based on figures in *Statistics of New Zealand*, the *New Zealand Monthly Abstract of Statistics* and Food and Agriculture Organisation of the United Nations data (after 1961).

17 Wildblood-Crawford, B., 'Grassland utopia and *Silent Spring*: rereading the agrichemical revolution in New Zealand', *New Zealand Geographer* 62/1 (2006) pp. 65–72.

18 Warr, E., *From Bushburn to Butter: A Journey in Words and Pictures* (Wellington, 1988).

19 Britton, S., Le Heron, R. and Pawson, E. (eds), *Changing Places in New Zealand: A Geography of Restructuring* (Christchurch, 1992); Le Heron, R. and Pawson, E. (eds), *Changing Places: New Zealand in the Nineties* (Auckland, 1996).

20 *New Zealand Official Yearbook*, 2008, pp. 359–60.

21 Ministry for the Environment, *Environment New Zealand 2007* (Wellington, 2007), p. 46.

22 The Ministry of Agriculture and Fisheries is closely monitoring water use in Canterbury: MAF Bulletin on 'Ground water development. How much is too much?', http://www.maf.govt.nz/sff/about-projects/search/01-055/01055article. htm. Concerns about take-off from underground aquifers are also emerging in the drier parts of northern Southland: Sorrell, P. (ed.), *Murihiku: The Southland Story* (Invercargill, 2006), p. 156.

23 Ministry for the Environment, *The State of New Zealand's Environment, 1997* (Wellington, 1997), Section 5, especially p. 32.

24 McLeod, C.J. and Moller, H., 'Intensification and diversification of New Zealand agriculture since 1960: an evaluation of current indicators of land use change', *Agriculture, Ecosystems and Environment* 115 (2006), pp. 201–18; Gradwahl, M., University of Otago, personal communication.

25 Hagerty, J.H., '"I'm not a greenie but ...": environmentality, eco-populism and governance in New Zealand – experiences from the Southland whitebait fishery', *Journal of Rural Studies* 23/2 (2007), pp. 222–23.

26 Primdahl, J. and Swaffield, S., 'Segregation and multifunctionality in New Zealand Landscapes', in F. Brouwer (ed.), *Sustaining Agriculture and the Rural Environment: Governance, Policy and Multifunctionality* (Cheltenham, 2004), pp. 266–85; Wood, G. and Pawson E., 'The Banks Peninsula forests and Akaroa cocksfooting: explaining a New Zealand forest transition', *Environment and History* 14/4 (2008), pp. 449–68.

27 Levy, *Grasslands of New Zealand*, pp. 49–57.

28 Sorrell, P. (ed), *Murihiku: The Southland Story* (Invercargill, 2006), p. 156.

29 Little has been published on the reasons for New Zealand's neglected agricultural history but some are suggested in Brooking, T., 'Can't see the people for all the sheep: the strange case of New Zealand's neglected rural history', paper given to the Northern Great Plains History Conference, Fargo, North Dakota, October 1992.

30 Cumberland, K.B., *Soil Erosion in New Zealand: A Geographical Reconnaissance* (Wellington, 1944), p. 9 and p. 1.

31 Ministry for the Environment, *The State of New Zealand's Environment, 1997*; Parliamentary Commissioner for the Environment, *Growing for Good: Intensive Farming, Sustainability and New Zealand's Environment* (Wellington, 2004); Ministry for the Environment, *Environment New Zealand 2007*.

32 Winder, G.M., 'Grassland revolutions in New Zealand: disaggregating a national story', *New Zealand Geographer* 65/3 (2009), pp. 187–200.

33 Frye, N., *The Bush Garden: Essays on the Canadian Imagination* (Toronto, 1971), p. 224.

34 Holland, P.G., 'Plants and lowland Canterbury landscapes', in *Geography for the 1980s: Proceedings of the Twelfth New Zealand Geography Conference* (Christchurch, 1984), pp. 25–31.

35 Pound, F., 'Pastoral, the city and the land sexed', in *The Invention of New Zealand: Art and National Identity 1930–1970* (Auckland, 2009), pp. 165–223. This idea is also developed by Northrop Frye in *The Bush Garden*, p. 246, with respect to Canadian writers and especially poets.

36 Hempenstall, P., 'Getting inside the Tasman world: a case for remembering local histories in New Zealand, Australia and the Southwest Pacific', The Jim Gardner Lecture 2009, The Canterbury History Foundation (Christchurch, 2009), p. 4.

37 McAloon, J., 'Gentlemanly capitalism and settler capitalists: imperialism, dependent

development and colonial wealth in the South Island of New Zealand', *Australian Economic History Review* 42/2 (2002), pp. 204–23.

38 Stevens, P.G., *Sheep: Part 2 – Sheepfarming Development and Sheep Breeds in New Zealand* (Christchurch, 1961), p. 95.

39 Cardellino, R.C. and Mueller, J.P., 'Fibre production and sheep breeding in South America', *Proceedings of the 18th Conference of the Association for the Advancement of Animal Breeding and Genetics* (2009), p. 367.

40 Wood, V., 'Akaroa cocksfoot: examining the supply chain of a defunct New Zealand agricultural export', in C. Stringer and R. Le Heron (eds), *Agri-food Commodity Chains and Globalising Networks* (Aldershot, 2008), p. 215.

41 Stapledon, R.G., *The Way of the Land* (London, 1942) p. 47.

42 Elliott, W., 'Introduction', in R.G. Stapledon, *A Tour in Australia and New Zealand: Grassland and Other Studies* (London, 1928), p. xii.

43 *Evening Post*, 22 February 1922, p. 4.

44 Annual Report and Accounts, Primary Products Marketing Department, 1939, *Appendices to the Journals of the House of Representatives*, H30 (1940), opposite p. 28.

45 Marcus King, untitled town and country landscape, in oil, 1172 mm by 1837 mm: c. 1950–5. King was a New Zealand landscape painter and architect, born 1891, died 1983: Thompson, H., *Paste Up: A Century of New Zealand Poster Art* (Auckland, 2003).

46 Marx, L., *The Machine in the Garden: Technology and the Pastoral Ideal in America* (New York, 1964), p. 220. The reference is to George Inness's painting of the 'Lackawanna Valley'.

47 Durie, E.T.J., *New Approaches to Maori Land in the 1980's with Particular Reference to its Settlement and Resettlement in the Northern Half of the North Island* (Auckland, 1981).

48 Robin, L., *How a Continent Created a Nation* (Sydney, 2007), p. 63.

49 Cronon, W., 'A place for stories: nature, history and narrative', *Journal of American History* 78/4 (1992), pp. 1374–75.

Index